ISBN:- {9788170227687}

PERSPECTIVES ON PSYCHOLOGY AND SOCIAL DEVELOPMENT

"Advances in Psychological Research in India Series"

1. *Perspectives on Psychology and Social Development*
   U.N. Dash and **Uday Jain** (Eds)
2. *Psychology of Poverty & Disadvantage*
   Ajit K. Mohanty and **Girishwar Misra** (Eds.)
3. *Perspectives on Indigenous Psychology*
   Girishwar Misra and **Ajit K. Mohanty** (Eds.)

About the Institution

The centre of Advanced Study in Psychology, Utkal University, is the first such centre for psychology in India. The centre specializes in broad areas of Educational and Developmental Psychology, Social and Organizational Psychology as well as Comparative and Physiological Psychology. Members of its faculty, one of the largest among the university departments of Psychology in India, are highly qualified and internationally reputed for their contributions in various fields of research and applications, in social Psychology, cognitive development, information processing, early childhood education, psycholinguistics, testing and measurement, and exploratory behaviour. The centre which has a large number of acclaimed publications to its credit, has currently launched a publication serices "Advances in Psychological Research in India". Its teaching programme includes, Diploma in Early Childhood Education, besides Masters, M.Phil. and Doctoral work in psychology.

About the Editors

With a Masters degree from Utkal University and Ph.D. from the University of Alberta, Canada, **U.N. Dash,** is the Head of the centre of Advanced study in Psychology at Utkal University where he has been teaching for over 20 years. He has been a KILLAM Scholar and a visting Professor in Canada. He has published extensively in national and international Journals in the areas of Cognitive and Educational Psychology as well as Research Methodology. Schooling and cognition, and "Statistics" are the areas of his special interest. He is the principal author of "*Schooling and Cognition*" (with M.M. Mohanty) published by the centre of Advanced study in Psychology, Utkal University. **Uday Jain**, M.A. Sagar University, Ph.D., Rajasthan University, is currently the Professor and Head, Department of Psychology, Barkatullah University, Bhopal. Earlier he taught at the University of Rajasthan, Allahabad University, North Eastern Hills University and Sagar University. Professor Jain was a fulbright Fellow at the University of Chicago and Swartmore College in USA. He has published in reputed Journals in India and abroad, in the area of social, and environmental psychology. He is the author of "*Psychological Consequences of Crowding*" (Sage 1987) and has edited: "*Perspectines on Environment and Behaviour*" (Har-Anand, 1997). He has been the Principal-co-investigator of CIDA-Shastri Indo-Canadian Project on "Community and Regions Overcoming Ecological Crisis."

Advances in Psychological Research in India Series - 1

PERSPECTIVES on Psychology and Social Development

(Proceedings of the VII & VIII Congress of the National Academy of Psychology, India)

Edited by

U.N. Dash
Utkal University

Uday Jain
Barkatullah University

Foreward by

Prof. Ajit K. Mohanty

CONCEPT PUBLISHING COMPANY, NEW DELHI - 110059

ISBN 81-7022-768-2

First Published 1999

Published and Printed by
Ashok Kumar Mittal
Concept Publishing Company
A/15-16, Commercial Block, Mohan Garden,
NEW DELHI - 110059 (India)

Phones : 5649024, 5648039
Fax : 091-11-5648053

Foreword

The last decade of the present century is set to be a decade of a new turn for psychology in India. After years of mindless following and replication of western psychology, followed by fervent search for an indigenous identity, Indian psychologists are showing definite signs of self-consciousness; research problems, methodology and conceptual framework are beginning to look more natural, spontaneous and driven by the immediate socio-cultural concerns and contexts, and, hence, more relevant. Despite a large bulk of researchers who still remain embedded in the past, blissfully unaware of the new wave and unable to shake off the colonial shackles, there is a visible, *albeit* minority, group of psychologists who have responded more positively to the felt needs for giving psychology in India its own identity, a new sense of urgency and relevance. The optimism is not misplaced because those who ride the new wave have the power to change the shape of psychology in India and to project a positive image characterised by its distinctiveness. The Centre of Advanced Study in Psychology, Utkal University is happy contributing, at least in small measures, to this new wave and the optimism.

In its current phase of UGC special assistance, which extends upto the year 2002, the Centre is committed to play its desired role in facilitating a meaningful movement of Indian psychology into the next millennium. This comes at a time when the Indian society, as never before, is characterised by a feeling of restlessness in the face of many a challenge. Social scientists are rising to the challenge willing to outgrow the colonial hangover, to come out of the narrow limits of their own discipline and to contribute to national development. Thus, when the National Academy of Psychology (NAOP), India extended a belated invitation to the Centre to host its annual Congress in the Golden Jubilee Year of Independence with the theme

"Psychology for India" we readily accepted. The specific themes for the various sessions of the Congress with a clear emphasis on 'Psychology and National Development' suited our own priorities very well. The Department of Psychology at Utkal has a long tradition of research pertaining to the issues and problems of national development. Beginning with the studies on caste-tension and attitude toward socio-economic and political issues in the early sixties to the numerous studies on psychoeducational and social problems of the disadvantaged segments of the Indian society during the last three decades, the Department has been among the leading centres of research in this area. At present, faculty members as well as research scholars working in all the broad thrust areas of the Centre of Advanced Study in Psychology, Utkal University are engaged in various research and extension activities which are relevant and meaningful in the present national context. The NAOP theme was close to our heart and the Academy had a successful congress from December 18 to 20, 1998 at Bhubaneswar. Selected papers from the proceedings of the NAOP Congress find a place in this edited volume which is a joint venture of the CAS in Psychology at Utkal and the National Academy. Aptly, the volume is co-edited by Dr. U.N. Dash, the Head of the Department of Psychology, Utkal University and the Organizing Secretary of the Congress, and Professor Uday Jain of Barkatullah University, Bhopal, the present Convenor of the NAOP. *Perspectives on Psychology and National Development* seeks to present a cross-section of current psychological research in India showing trends towards a new wave of psychology much more spontaneous in its zeal to become a meaningful participant in the process of national development. To project a more complete picture, some papers from the earlier NAOP Congress at Bhopal, relevant to the present theme, have also been included.

I thank the editors for painstakingly putting the volume together and the National Academy of Psychology (NAOP), India for letting us publish the proceedings. I also wish to acknowledge, with much appreciation, the behind-the-scene support and help received from Professor Girishwar Misra of Delhi University in enhancing the quality of this volume. He was also the Convenor of NAOP Congress, Bhopal. In response to the papers in the volume, he has written, along with Professor Jain, an epilogue which points at some definite conceptual directions for future of psychology in India.

Through this volume, I pay my tribute to the memory of late lamented Professor Durganand Sinha who was a founder member and Fellow of the National Academy of Psychology and the guest of honour at the inaugural function of the NAOP Congress at Utkal. Professor Sinha's contribution to psychology in India has been phenomenal and, more than any one else, he was responsible for a respectable place for psychology in India in the international fora. His role in the development of his discipline in India, in general, and of the Centre of Advanced Study in Psychology at Utkal as well as the NAOP, in particular, will always be remembered with gratitude.

Professor G.K. Das, the Vice-Chancellor of Utkal University not only presided over the inauguration of the Bhubaneshwar Congress of NAOP but also provided a caring support which made it possible for the CAS to host the same. We are all very grateful to him. The honourable Minister of Rural Development, Government of Orissa, *janab Sk. Matlub Ali* inaugurated the Congress as the Chief Guest calling upon the psychologists to act as facilitators in the process of rural development. We thank him for his support and encouragement. All my colleagues at the Centre contributed to the efforts in organizing the Congress and in publication of this volume. Their help is gratefully acknowledged.

The Centre of Advanced Study (CAS) at Utkal has launched a new series of publications under the general series title *Advances in Psychological Research in India.* It is envisaged that the publications under the series would be able to capture the essence of developments in the discipline in India in its various facets. The present volume is the first in the series. The vital assistance of the

University Grants Commission in organizing the Congress and in bringing out this publication is gratefully acknowledged. I thank Shri Ashok Mittal of the Concept Publishing Company for his willingness to take up the publication programme of the Centre. I hope the publications will meet the expected standard to merit attention of researchers and scholars of psychology and other related disciplines.

As the Coordinator of the Centre of Advanced Study in Psychology as well as the President of the NAOP for its Bhubaneswar Congress, my role in publication of this volume has been doubly satisfying.

Ajit K. Mohanty
Coordinator,
Centre of Advanced Study in Psychology

Utkal University,
Bhubaneswar
March 26, 1998

CONTENTS

1

Introduction

U. N. Dash and **Uday Jain**

This volume presents a set of selected papers presented at the 7th and 8th Congresses organized by the National Academy of Psychology (NAOP) of India. They were held at Bhopal and Bhubaneshwar in 1996 and 1997, respectively. The papers document a cross-section of some of the trends in contemporary psychological research in India. One of the criticisms of psychological research in this country, has been about its emulative nature. It has often been expressed at various forums that psychologists have been engaged in the replication of Euro-American studies and ignoring the Indian context and its characteristic problems. The discipline has remained alien to its social utility. Blind imposition of alien models provided and promoted a false notion of universal psychological reality. The Indian psychological reality was treated as a variant of the universal psychology. In recent years some attempts have been made to come out with research relevant to the understanding of the Indian social problems and have shown certain directions to deal with them. In such efforts the applied orientation of psychology seems to be emerging. In order to make psychological research intelligible and applicable it has to be oriented towards the 'social reality' shared by the people constituting that very reality. One must not forget that Western psychological concepts and theories had emerged within a particular socio-historical context hence have high probability of application to that society. Research in cross-cultural and cultural psychology tends to show that the western psychological concepts have limited generalizability.

The NAOP from its very inception has been pursuing the goal of developing culturally appropriate psychology and has been extending support to the socially relevant research focus. Selection of research problems relevant to the Indian context not only helps in describing and understanding Indian social reality better but also towards solving these problems. Unfortunately, till now the policy makers have shown only limited interest in utilizing psychological research. This was not surprising as psychological research, in the strictly western frame, has limited potential to offer policy implications.

The readers of this volume will get a flavour of the changing concerns of the Indian psychologists. There is a definite move towards the study of Indian social issues and sincerely exploring the modalities to achieve solutions of social problems. The degree of such a concern may vary in the different contributions to this volume. A change from the traditional experimental research on theoretical issues to applications of theories for solving social problems can easily be discerned from the papers contained in this volume. Accepting the need for national development it is imperative that psychology must engage in the process of socially relevant understanding.

The idea of social development as an integrating theme of the present volume deserves some attention. The notion of social development is a controversial one and its conceptualisation depends on the theory one subscribes to. Modern development as conceived in the Western industrialized world heavily focuses on the accomplishments in the economic and material domains, as a result exploitation of natural resources, through technology and working for a global market have increasingly assumed greater significance. Psychology has been predominantly individual centred and the models of social development are usually loaded by a self serving bias. Following this model organizational development, social change, modernization, entrepreneurship development become of great concern for psychologists. With the changing scene from universal to culture-specific issues the concept of social development is slowly and gradually acquiring 'more social' and local meaning. Such a shift is relevant to the developing world. The contributions to this volume implicitly or explicitly have articulated this concern to different degrees.

Since the problems of social development vary from nation to nation their solutions have to be nothing but indigenous. Those who argue that science deals with universal phenomena usually forget that social behaviour is rooted in the local cultural traditions and practices. The observed universality in the scientific accounts is in part, a function of the scientific methods and *a priori* assumptions about the universal human nature. Understanding the culturally specific problems and characteristic ways of behaving may provide a foundation on which the edifice of universality may be erected. And even if one accepts the emergent nature of 'social reality' then again universality of behavioural phenomena becomes a further suspect. At present we emphasize the effort towards understanding the socially relevant issues and the possible strategies to overcome the problems. This is amply evident from what follows.

About the Chapters

D. Sinha in a lucid manner examines the problems in understanding and analyzing the psychological characteristics of the people of India. While search for a distinctive mark of Indianness has been undertaken by many scholars the attempts have not yielded any unambiguous picture. The modal view is that of the cherished and ideal goals and values rather than those which are functional or operative. Characterization of Indians in terms of the ways of living and the philosophical attitude has been emphasized by many authors. The view of Indians given by the Westerners has been stereotypical and impressionistic. Some of the characteristics of Indians reported by Sinha include attitude of resignation, acceptance of *status quo*, external locus of control, love of ease and comfort, flexible ego boundaries etc. He suggests the need of more systematic efforts to examine the Indian characteristics.

Abhilasha Srivastava provides an overview of major psychological works done in India pertinent to national development. She outlines the wide range of themes relating to national development encompassing endogenous development, rural development, poverty and deprivation, inter-group conflict, education, population and crowding. Starting with a brief analysis of the reasons for the limited role played by the Indian psychologists in the process of national development she goes on to show how the earlier trend is changing in the direction of indigenous approaches with emphasis on socially relevant research. The remaining papers in the volume add substance to the optimistic note by Srivastava in providing specific examples of application oriented psychological research in India.

Arvind K. Sinha and Sumita Rai proceed to "take a stock of what to expect" in the field of organizational behaviour while the next century is around the corner. They examine the national scene and the trends in the context of changing economic and political scenario and plead for a holistic, people focused management of organizations. Singh-Sengupta's study of managers and medical representatives in different pharmaceutical organizations shows a need to focus on the psychological well-being of employees to improve the quality of work life and enrich organizational health. Shailendra Singh demonstrates the relationship of managers' work values with job related behaviour in organizations such as organizational identification, organizational loyalty, job satisfaction, alienation, intent to leave, frustration, work aversiveness etc. In this study Protestant work ethic was found to be positively related to better job outcome. Tewari compares the nationalized and non-nationalized banks on several organizational variables.

Reflecting on the feminist theme in social sciences, Vindhya examines various issues in women's mental health and seeks to reconcile the feminist and psychological perspectives. Srivastava and Gupta report an interesting study of dual career families looking at the work and non-work related factors pertaining to job satisfaction and life satisfaction as working wives and their husbands. Jachuck reports a study examining the role of maternal employment in cognitive development and academic achievement of primary school children from high and low SES families. The next paper by Johri and Anand Prakash observes that the present developmental psychology does not offer space for cultural conceptions of mothering. In this context they report the interviews of mothers having daughters. The analysis revealed that Indian mothers and their daughters maintain separate indentities. Mother's voice as reported in this account is generally ignored and mothering continues as a life long process. Such a style of mothering is different from that of western style of mothering. Discussing the problems of community participation for rural development Dalal remarks that involving local people in development programmes has been a major challenge before government and non-government organizations. He argues that community participation should build on the traditional practices.

In the context of pluralistic Indian society, Sahoo looks at certain aspects of the problem of managing cultural diversity in the study of attitudes and perceptions of Hindu and Muslim adults in respect of cultural diversity, acceptance of adaptation, ideology and value preferences. The findings show a "picture of tolerance rather than active support for multiculturalism" and suggest a need for cultural education to strengthen plurality. Jyoti Verma pursues the thesis of collectivism in her study of Biharis (Residents of the Bihar state of India). It was observed that Biharis are relation oriented persons and consider casteism as an evil which has a practical value.

Drawing from the systems approach Krishnamurthy rejects the robot model of man. Viewing human beings as an active system the author has analyzed its implications for psychotherapy. It is concluded that the aim of psychotherapy should be creating a new relationship between individual and society and not only changing individual's attitude.

Krishna Mohan's opinion survey of the young psychologists in India regarding the state of their discipline reveals interesting findings of significance for planning of teaching and research in psychology in India. K. Suneetha analyses the phenomenon of delay in emotional experience resulting in emotional cudding. Based on this analysis, she seeks to explain the nature of performance of depressive individuals. In her study, Aminabhavi relates emotional adjustment of post-graduate students to their family and social adjustment. In their study of arousal and work adjustment of 9 and 10 year-old delinquent and normal children, Dutta Gupta and her colleagues show a lower arousal level amongst the delinquent children compared to the normal controls.

Continuing with the focus on applied orientation and social relevance the next four papers in the field of educational psychology dealt with practical problems in respect of reading development and the choice of medium of instruction in schools. A.K. Srivastava and Raina present an analysis of research papers published in the area of teaching-learning process. They also suggest that the real educational needs and problems of the society have not been addressed by the researchers in the field. The following two papers have addressed the reading skills following an information processing model. The paper by Mahapatra and Dash has compared skilled and less skilled grade 5 teachers in respect of planning, attention, simultaneous and successive (PASS) processes. The findings showed that the skilled teachers were superior to the less skilled ones in conceptual planning and in selectively attending to the conceptual features of the text. The skilled readers preferred simultaneous to successive processing in word decoding and comprehension activities. The authors point to the implications of findings for remediation of reading difficulties. Further exploration by Manaswini Dash and U.N. Dash provide evidence for the appropriateness of the PASS model in explaining reading processes.

Comparison between mother tongue medium and

English medium schools is a matter of great practical significance in Indian educational scene. Patra and Babu expose the myth of English medium superiority. Taking SES and IQ controlled samples of grade 6 and 8 children from English and Oriya (Mother tongue) medium schools, they show that the Oriya medium children performed better than the English medium ones on tasks in their respective languages of instruction. Further, medium of instruction did not seem to affect the mathematics and science achievement of children. The authors integrate the findings with the relationship between mother tongue proficiency and cognitive academic development.

School motivation is another crucial area. Tripathi and Singh analyze the achievement goals of higher secondary school students and the underlying mechanisms in setting these goals. The two contributions in the field of developmental psychology, one by Sahoo, Das and Mahapatra on environmental indicators of child development among the Santhal tribals, and the other by Babban Misra on motherese hypothesis, focus on the role of environmental and cultural inputs in child development. Sahoo, Das and Mahapatra show the differences between Santhal and non-tribal mothers in terms of their responses to a Child Development Inventory. The developmental indicators of sensory input, child and care taker interaction, care-taking behaviour, and intra-family factors emerged critical. The authors also report gender based differences in environmental input to child development across the two cultural groups. Babban Misra relates pragmatic dimensions of children's speech to those of their mothers in a test of motherese hypothesis which emphasizes the primary role of the maternal input in language development of children. He recorded the speech development of children and mothers in game playing and free speech conditions longitudinally. The findings lend partial support to the motherese hypothesis.

Finally, there are two contributions to the field of comparative psychology. The first one by Misra and Banamali Mohanty shows interaction between nutrition and environment on learning and Hebb-Williams maze performance of albino rats. The second study by Banamali Mohanty varies the nutritional status and the nature of rearing environment on emotionality, spontaneous motor activity, discrimination learning and memory performance of rats. These two animal studies have great practical significance. Together they imply that the negative effects of early malnutritional can be somewhat ameliorated by the enriched perceptual experience early in development.

The epilogue by Misra and Jain makes an effort to examine the problems in conceptualizing social development in the Indian context and the potential of psychology to contribute to this goal. In a reflective mode they have critically looked at the available psychological knowledge and know-how and have ventured to offer some suggestions for a more positive role of psychology in promoting social development.

Taken together the present collection of contributions to Indian psychology present a socially responsive move in the academic enterprise. The reorientation needed in this process is obviously not a very smooth or tension free venture. It is hoped that the questions asked and debates initiated in the present volume will stimulate and foster the growth of a relevant psychology in India.

2

Studying the Psychology of the Indian People

Durganand Sinha

The Quest to Locate 'Indianness'

India has the second largest human population in the world—the number is expected to cross the billion mark before the end of the century. Despite the vast numbers, the data base for building a psychology of the Indian people is meagre. There have been attempts to delve into the "personality" of people from various regions and communities (e.g., the Nagas, the people of Kumaon) and some sects and business communities (like the Vaisyas of Howrah). Though no indepth and comprehensive analysis of the Indian people as such is available, there are a few attempts in the direction in recent years. Whatever data are available are, however, sporadic and unsystematic, based on inadequate incidental sampling which cannot be said to be representative of the variegated complexity that characterizes the Indian people. One gets pictures that are often contradictory (Sinha, 1988, p. 46).

The 'deficiency' in this direction posed a challenge for me. Exactly a decade back, inspired by the suggestions of my distinguished scholar-friend from Hong Kong, Professor Michael Bond, and impressed by his edited book, *The Psychology of the Chinese People* (Bond, 1986), I decided to prepare a volume on similar lines as a first step towards understanding the Indian people — a volume that would present an authentic psychological picture derived from available studies which would serve as an antidote to the ethnocentricism and biases that are so typical of the efforts of foreign as well as Indian scholars in this sphere. I planned to cover not only the personality of the Indian people but also special features of cognition, perception, socialization and growth, emotionality, psychopathology, group behaviour, leadership, power and influence processes, nature of attributions and control, and also the characteristics of work values and organizations, including the nature of Indian management — if there is anything like it. I looked around for colleagues who were sensitive to our cultural characteristics and conscious of the peculiar features of our contemporary behaviour, our foibles and idiosyncracies. I did not want only the so-called "objective" observers nor that brand of historians and social scientists who by the dubious employment of their intellect made facts fit their preconceived theories and ignored and twisted the evidence if it was unpalatable to their pet notions.

I contacted more than fifteen such psychologists and scholars to join me in my endeavour. The initial response was enthusiastic. But the fervour was short-lived. By the time the stage for 'reminders' came, the enthusiasm in most cases had waned. A point was reached when I stopped getting even formal acknowledgements to my letters. The task ws so colossal that it could not be accomplished without the active collaboration of a team of scholars with interest in varied facets of our behaviour. Therefore, very reluctantly, I had to abandon my effort.

I speculated about the possible causes of my failure. I would briefly outline the factors that look to me to be salient. The first, and probably the foremost, reason is the question whether there is anything like the Indian behaviour and Indian character. In other words, how far are we justified in using the definite article before the word 'Indian'? The question has been bothering me for over five decades since the time I made my first inroads into the world of scholarship. The doubt has lingered and has been greatly accentuated after I watched the recent telecast of the confidence motion in the parliament moved by the shortlived BJP government. Looking and listening to the debate, one inevitably got the impression of segmentation and deep cleavages in almost all spheres of our social and national life so much so that one begun to have lurking doubts about over-arching Indianness of the people. If there was anything like a unifying bond, it had very little to do with common socio-cultural influences. It seems to rely largely on slender foundations of narrow self-interest and politics. Such a unity is usually transitory. History has demonstrated that oneness of India remained intact whenever there was a strong central political power based on brute military strength. Any weakening there or any of the regions gaining power resulted in unleashing of centrifugal forces that threatened the very unity of the country. What is also interesting is that different kingdoms, despite their cultural commonalities, were usually hostile to one another ever ready to go to war. Distinctness appeared to be more relevant and salient than the common or shared unifying bonds.

At various periods of my career, I have had opportunities to discuss the question with some topmost scholars and thinkers. We tried to identify those socio-cultural features, dispositions, outlook and behaviours that could be said to be the "mark of Indianness" or the 'modal' psycho-social features of the Indian people that constituted the outcome of centuries of collective experiences, and were widely shared due to cultural learning and cultural transmission — very much analogous to biological transmission. I was greatly enriched through these discussions. But we never could identify with certainty even half a dozen modal features. There was no agreement even about the typical physical features. A few basic values and world-view that were frequently mentioned belonged to religious and philosophical spheres largely confined to the domains of scholars, thinkers, intellectuals and the so-called elites, and not widely shared and practised by people at the grassroots. The cultural goals and values that were said to be constituents of Indianness appeared more as *cherished* and *ideal*, and not widely *operative* at least in the contemporary context.

One discerns some light in Nehru's *The Discovery of India* (Nehru, 1946/1981). He points to the enormous diversities in physical appearances as well as in certain mental habits and traits of people hailing from different regions, and divisions of Indian life based on castes, religions, languages and degrees of cultural development. Yet, despite their differences and distinctive features, he firmly asserts that "all of them have still more the distinctive mark of India". He added that through all these ages, they are "distinctively Indian, with the same national heritage and the same set of moral and mental qualities. There was something living and dynamic about this heritage which showed itself in ways of living and a philosophical attitude to life and its problems." Nehru refers to "the impress of India". Irrespective of all diversities, there seems to have developed a unity of outlook and values that is peculiarly Indian — something that in today's parlance may be designated as the *Indian psyche* or Indianness.

I should repeat here that though there appears to be a general feeling that there are distinctive marks of India, despite my endeavours over these years, except for a few religious and philosophical qualities it has not been possible to get a clear and commonly agreed image of "the impress of India" nor isolate those "marks" clearly. One tends to feel that if there is something like "the impress of India", it is not articulate nor unambiguous unlike what we know about the Japanese, Germans, British and many other peoples. If there is uniqueness, it is too defuse, elusive and difficult to lay your fingers on. Therefore, it is not surprising that confronted with such an elusive phenomenon about whose existence one cannot be certain, scholars have largely kept themselves away from seriously pursuing objective studies of Indian psyche which, as the available evidence shows, often presents a somewhat confusing and contradictory picture (Sinha, 1988, pp. 46-47).

The second reason is, as I have pointed out in my

recent paper published in the *Interamerican Journal of Psychology* (Sinha, 1996), that in spite of our philosophical adage of *atmanam prathamam vidhya* (know and analyse yourself first), there does not seem to exist at least in the present time a tradition of self-analysis and an urge to know our inner self and personality. We are generally averse to looking deeply and critically at our own behaviour in a detached manner. We are hyper-sensitive about ourselves, and unlike, for example, the British, we do not possess in any appreciable measure a capacity to look at our own behaviour and idiosyncrasies as an outside observer and laugh at our own foibles. There seems a widespread "resistance" for analysing our own traits, and behaviour characteristics. Professor J.B. Sinha's (1985) observation that Indian culture does not encourage evaluating others in objective and impersonal terms is pertinent. Thus, we have only sporadic attempts at analysing the Indian personality and character. Therefore, we have largely relied on the analyses and descriptions provided by foreign scholars, anthropologists, psychoanalysts, historians, writers and travellers who have looked at very limited sections of our behaviour and society. Since they have generally viewed us through tinted glasses using alien categories, subtle meanings and nuances of our behaviours, attitudes and dispositions have eluded them and have not been understood or appreciated. To give an example of the blatant bias in this context, Hartnack (1987) has shown how in colonial times the foreign psychoanalysts used their own concepts as labels to reinforce their feelings of self-satisfied superiority, justifying thereby the British rule "since Hindus (were) neither interested in responsible leadership nor (did) they have a psychological disposition for it."

Scholars — both British and American, and following their lead many Indian social scientists with their empirical orientation — have isolated basic Indian cultural values and behaviour dispositions, the details of which would be provided later. The picture that emerges is generally impressionistic, stereotypical and almost caricature-like that ignores the heterogeneity and complexity of what constitutes the Indian people and culture. In this context, it is also significant to observe that the clusters of values and the characteristics that are highlighted, following Weberian line, have been considered as not being congruent with the requirements of modern technology, work organizations, and economic development (see Sinha, 1988 for details). They have been regarded as "major barriers" and "the determining factors in India's slow rate of development" (Kapp, 1963, p. 64). Without getting into details, I would point out that this kind of sweeping assertion is another example of Western ethnocentric bias, and a subtle way of asserting the superiority of the West with the implication that in order to go ahead on the path of rapid economic development, non-Western cultures and peoples have to give up their cultural values and ape the West.

The third factor relates to the controversy surrounding attempts at determining 'national character' or the basic modal personality. The soundness of the whole concept has been seriously questioned, especially if the culture of the people in question happens to be highly complex, dynamic and is characterized by enormous diversities. In such cases, establishing the "modal" becomes a difficult, if not an impossible task. However, in spite of obvious difficulties, it is indisputable that however diverse and complex it may be, there exists in every society "learned cultural behaviour" (Mead, 1951, p. 81) and there is regularity with which certain values and behaviour sequences are manifested in every culture. Through socialization and social learning and collective experiences, the cultural system does leave an indelible mark on individual's outlook, attitudes and modes of behaviour. It is likely that due to diversity of cultural experiences such unified all-pervasive Indianness may not be generated or is clearly visible. However, if there is sharing of a set of cultural experiences on the national level, the likelihood of its generating common behaviour characteristics, values, attitudes and personality which would constitute what Nehru has termed as the "mark" or the "impress" of India cannot be ruled out. The topic is a challenging one and worth exploring systematically and in depth by psychologists and social scientists. One is encouraged to note that several writers, novelists, travellers, historians and social scientists who have visited the sub-continent and studied and recorded their observations about the Indian people have frequently given surprisingly similar impressions and characterizations of their outlook to life, dominant values, attitudes and dispositions, There are even stories and jokes highlighting how Indians *generally behave* as contrasted with the French, Germans, the British and the Americans. Some "typical" patterns of behaviour do seem to exist. They may be highly exaggerated and stereotypical, but it is not unlikely that they have a strong kernel of truth in them.

Sources of Information on Indian Behavioural Characteristics

Observations made so far would indicate that it is essential to enlarge the search and utilize varied sources of information not simply confined to the contemporary nor to the conventional methods that psychologists are used to. To get an authentic picture, apart from data derived from tests, interviews and usual empirical techniques, many kinds of secondary sources and a wider range of methodological repertoire have to be tapped. Thus, I delved into different sources of information, both ancient and contemporary. Expecting to find descriptions of character and traits of personality of the Indian people — at least as they were in ancient times — I went to the epics of the *Mahabharata* and the *Ramayana*, Kautilya's *Arthashastra*, Bhartihari's *Nitisatak* and *Vairagyasatak* and other similar texts. But I did not get much that threw light on the psychology of the Indian people. My search was by no means thorough. But I felt that though these sources constituted a gold mine of information on Hindu values and behaviour dispositions, what one gathered were more of the nature of *ideal* and *normative* and very little that was *operative*.

Another source that I explored constituted the

accounts of travellers and visitors to the sub-continent at various periods in our history — right from the account of Patliputra and Magadha left by Megasthenese, the Chinese traveller and a number of European visitors like Francois Bernier (1656-68) to the Mughal courts. Their accounts consisted mostly of descriptions of places and the country with not many observations of people's personality characteristics. We get a few relevant observations in the account left by the French missionary Abbe Dubois who was for thirty years (1792-1823) in South India. Dubois (1992, p. 48) observed religious dissensions which sometimes were very intense (e.g., between the Vaisnavites and the Shaivites). Looking at their intensity, he wondered why the country was not set ablaze. The underlying reason he considered was the "*naturally mild and timid character of the Hindus*" (emphasis added). He felt that there was *ritualization* of antagonism between sects. Obviously, he had not observed our communal conflicts, desecration of shrines, violence and carnage that are let loose among the people of the land where Buddha, Mahaveer and Gandhi had inculcated the doctrine of *ahimsa*. In any case, a closer scrutiny of the accounts left by different travellers is likely to yield some useful material, especially because it would enable us to get an idea of any major transformations that had come about in the character and dispositions of the Indians over the years.

We get much richer material — though not necessarily unbiased — in the accounts of travellers who visited India in recent years. They include novelists, writers and journalists who came to the country to understand its people and the socio-political dynamics. Further, some historians, psychologists, psychoanalysts and social scientists (both foreign and native) have studied and made interesting — sometimes insightful — observations about the basic character of the Indian people. Different techniques have been utilized for the purpose including conventional survey methods, general observation, content analysis of children's stories and folk tales, analysis of themes in films, and projective techniques. It may be noted that interest in understanding the psychological characteristics of the Indian people has not always emerged from the desire to understand the people as such. It has frequently been inspired by the Weberian line of thinking that has sought to interrelate cultural and psycho-social characteristics of people with economic growth. It has resulted in peculiar twists in these studies.

I would give only brief description that emerge from these sources (see Sinha, 1988). Scholars have attempted to relate aspects of Hindu culture and way of life to the kind of personality and behaviour dispositions that develop. The first cluster concerns certain central values that characterize the Indian society. They pertain to the world-view, general *weltansuuang* and outlook to life and existence. Scholars have highlighted the basic religious and philosophical values of Hinduism that pervade the Indian outlook, namely, *karma* (action), *maya* (illusion) and *sanyas* (renunciation), and the social institutions of the joint family and the caste system. It is contended that the deep-rooted belief in *karma* and the idea of endless cosmic causation that it inculcates in the individual, generate an attitude of resignation and acceptance of *status quo*. The law of *karma* lends a fatalistic colouring to the outlook of the individual and the responsibility of action is regarded as being outside the individual (i.e., external locus of control). Acceptance of one's lot and that of others became inevitable — the result of one's *karma* which is not easily modified by human effort or action. It tends to generate an attitude of acceptance of imperfect human conditions without a desire to modify, master or improve. A few scholars (e.g., Kapp, 1963, p. 15) regard it as "a perfect example of religious rationalization of existing incongruities of suffering." It is said to inculcate fatalism and gets reflected in people's acceptance of the *status quo* — however imperfect it may be. It is exemplified when one exclaims *kya pharak parta hai* (what difference does it make), an attitude enshrined in the great epic the *Ramayana : Kou nrip hohi hame kya hani* (what harm does come to me, whoever may be the king?). Sovani (1963, p. 274) has asserted that the cause of the present malaise in India lies deeper in Hindu culture and personality which has shown "deadening efficiency in maintaining the *status quo.*" I may add that today this widespread nonchalance has further deteriorated into what I would call attitude of *hum-ap kar kya sakte hain* (what you and I can do?) — a state of *de-powerment* of the individual and the people at large and a lack of a sense of personal efficacy which is so essential for effecting social change and healthy functioning of society.

There are other basic values shared by a vast majority of Indian people as embodied in *purushartha* — the four cardinal values. *Moksha* (salvation) or the fusion of individual self with the ultimate reality (*Brahman*) is regarded as the terminal or ultimate goal of life — a release from worldly involvement, which, as Sudhir Kakar (1978) points out, remains a vital goal of life even among the very modern Hindus.

The pursuit of wealth (*artha*) and sexual satisfaction (*kama*) are essential components of *purushartha* and are considered legitimate in some phases of one's life. But in the Hindu scheme of things, they are not given the same importance as *dharma* (duty) and *moksha* (salvation). They are subordinated to the overriding value orientation of Hindu religion which regards the world of comfort and pleasure as illusory, occupying a very inferior place to contemplation, renunciation and liberation. In today's context, however, the picture seems to have changed radically.

Two other value orientations operate widely in our life, viz., considering the world as *maya* (illusory and unreal) and the institution of *sanyas* (renunciation). Without elaborating them, it would suffice here to point out that they tend to get reflected in the attitude to separate and detach oneself from the world and lack of urge and involvement to alter the material conditions and indifference towards misery and extreme poverty. Ronald Segal (1966, p. 14), the famous writer of Indian origin from West Indies, has pointedly remarked that Indian poverty is unique not because there are millions of poor, but because of indifference to poverty and fatalistic submission to it. With pervasive attitude of acceptance and indifference "such a society generates no mass revolution of rising expectations" (Segal, 1966, p. 119). It is to be noted that depicting the squalid life and miseries of Calcutta in his famous book *The City of Joy*, Dominique Lapierre (1986, p. 75) marvelled at how "people could actually remain good humoured in the midst of so much abjection."

Basic Behaviour Dispositions

Closely related to the value cluster are the basic dispositions, and common modes of behaviour that directly relate to personality. These attributes, it is said, have their roots deep in religio-philosophical values and cultural and social characteristics of the Indian people. They are briefly described.

On the basis of analysis of themes in films and proverbs, Narain (1957) describes typical personality characteristics as "mild, passive, dependent, other-worldly, non-materialistic, conditioned by basic values of Hindu religion." Spratt (1966) characterizes Hindu personality as passive, inner-directed and narcissistic. Taylor (1948) has noted low aspiration, passivity and conformity as basic characteristics. Low aspiration, especially among villages, has often been commented upon. About the poor peasantry, Kusum Nair (1961, p. 193) has observed that their level of aspiration had a "limited, static ceiling, but bottomless floor." Irrespective of their economic status, Sinha (1969) observed the Indian villagers as having stagnant level of aspiration, low striving, absence of risk-taking and displaying extreme caution and risk avoidance. Added to this is McClelland's (1961, p. 357) contention that need for achievement is not encouraged by Hinduism which explicitly teaches "that concern with earthly achievements is a snare and a delusion."

Basham (1971, p. 3), the famous historian who displays extraordinary sensitivity and understanding of the Indian culture and people, in his famous book *The*

Wonder that was India, hints that the natural and geographical phenomena characterizing the Indian sub-continent have shaped the basic disposition of the people. The total dependence on monsoon, frequent natural calamities, epidemics and disease that appear beyond human control causing enormous damages on one hand, and bounteous nature that demands little of man in return for sustenance have generated a character that "has tended to fatalism and quietism, aceepting fortune and misfortune alike without complaint." Basham adds that "If climate had any effect on the Indian character it was. . . to develop a love of ease and comfort, an addiction to simple pleasures and luxuries so freely given by Nature — the tendency to which the impulse of self-denial and asceticism on the one hand, and occasional strenuous effort on the other, were natural reactions" (p. 4). This aspect of Indian's predisposition is sometimes referred to as "*aram* culture" or a tendency to seek comfort and ease and avoidance of sustained effort and hard work. It is to be noted that looking at outstanding achievements of ancient times in the shape of enormous temples and immense irrigation works, Basham doubts that Indian attitude to life suggests a devitalised people. Even in contemporary times when occasion demands, the Indian people are found to rise to meet the exigencies of the situation. Such occasions, however, seem to be rare. Further, effort to avoid work is so patent and widespread that the Indians are said to display a poor work culture.

Passivity and conformity have often been considered as basic features of Indian psyche (Taylor, 1948). It is suggested that the very nature of socialization and interactions in the family ensures that the Indian child learns to conform at the cost of personal initiative and capacity to make decisions. Koestler (1960) in his *The Lotus and the Robot* argues that the joint family and caste system have been responsible for ingraining reluctance to take decisions and evade responsibility. He considers the process of character formation as "de-boning" producing only shapeless, spineless non-individuals". As Koestler puts it, "out of the sacred womb of the Indian family only yes-men could emerge" (p. 155). It is relevant to note that dependency and its attendant characteristics have been emphasized by many scholars. According to Taylor (1948, p. 5), the vary nature of familial interactions develop an acute sense of dependence through extreme emphasis on parental authority and minimizing opportunities for personal initiative, and the inculcation of a clear sense of subordination to social and religious sanctions which transcend even the parental authority. Personal initiative is replaced by obedience and conformity, and security for the individual is associated with dependence upon superiors (Taylor, 1948; Asthana, 1956; Carstairs, 1957). The pattern typifies the relationship that political leaders and superiors in administration seem to maintain in their followers and subordinates. Loyalty and conformity are expected and demanded rather than conpetence, efficiency and initiative. On the basis of vast clinical experience, B.K. Ramanujam (1979) has reported that "unarticulated bond beween son and his father persists even after the son grows up." Even in adults there is almost a nostalgic desire for approval and sanction of father at every step. In child-rearing practices, Minturn and Hitchcock (1966) have observed that positive reinforcement is sparingly used, punishment to control child's behaviour is a common devise, and there is excessive use of 'don't' in guiding his/her behaviour. The content in mother's scolding seldom provided models of *desired* behaviour. Training in self-reliance was as negligible as training in responsibility. The mother reinforced dependency, and seldom provided oportunities to solve problems by themselves—a feature that has also been noted by L.B. Murphy (1953). Obviously there was "crystallization of dependency complex" (Kapp, 1863, p. 59). J.B.P. Sinha (1970) further contends that the religious tradition of *bhakti* (devotion) which demands "abandoning all commendable acts, seek shelter with me alone, I will liberate you from all sins; do not worry at all" (*Bhagvadgita*, Chapter 18, verse 66) further strengthens what he calls, "dependence proneness". In terms of superior subordinate relationship, it implies complete dependence on the powerful, maintaining total dependency and affective intimacy, and remaining loyal and faithful to him only. It is to be noted that this kind of relational pattern constitutes an integral facet of the *nurturant task leadership* model (J.B.P. Sinha, 1980) which has been observed to be widespread and effective in different spheres of organization and interpersonal functioning at the present transitional phase in our country.

A related aspect of interpersonal functioning and relationships in our society is the hierarchical structure (Kakar, 1978; Roland, 1980). Most relationships are cognitively arranged in an hierarchical order of status, importance and power. It is so typical of our society that it would not be inappropriate, followng Dumont (1970), to call the Indian people "homo hierarchicus". Hierarchical structuring is so ingrained in India that it is easier to work in a superior subordinate role than as equals (Kothari, 1970). Status differences and hierarchical culture constitute essential cultural elements and a "carry-over of preindustrial elements into modern work organizations" (p. 299).

Content analysis of school textbook stories reveals some characteristic features of our interpersonal relationships. The image of the superior is that of an autocrat — assertive or nurturant — who enforces higher authority primarily by providing emotional rewards and arousing guilt among the subordinates (Kakar, 1971). Acceptance of authority takes the form of "active submission" leading to the development of individuals with enduring need for dependence as a core characteristic of the personality (p. 100). The image of the superior was either nurturant or assertive, never impersonal or fraternal.

Collective as contrasted with individual orientation is said to be fostered by certain aspects of Indian culture and is considered a dominant feature of the Indian psyche. It is suggested that an Indian's behaviour is characterized by reciprocity, strong mutual caring where emotional connectedness is essential with constant flow of affect between persons. Any feelings disruptive of the relationship are contained and inhibited. As Roland (1980) observes, ego boundaries are more open to others and there is little psychological space around oneself. Further, J.B. Sinha (1982, p. 153) comments that "Hindu experienced self is more structured around *we, ours* and *us* than around *I, mine* or *me.* There is preference to belong to a collectivity and to undermine autonomy, initiative and individualism." Even a novelist (Lapierre, 1986, p. 56) points out that "Every individual in India is always linked to the rest of the social body by a network of incredibly diversified ties, with the result that no one in this gigantic country . . . could ever be completely abandoned".

A related aspect of the Indian psyche is that self in India, as Markus and Kitayama (1991) point out, is defined more in terms of social relationships. In a recent cross-cultural comparison of self-concepts among Indian and American college students, it was observed (Dhawan, Roseman, Naidu, Thapa & Rettek, 1995) that while defining themselves Indian students made more references to social indentities. While American students had a significantly larger proportion of responses for self-identity, their Indian counterparts described themselves more in terms of role, group, caste, class, and gender role identity. As Roland (1987) observes, social obligations and filial duties are emphasized and the Indian self can be characterized as "familial". Individualism is subordinated to "familism". In this sense, self in India is less individualistic than in the West. It is, as Triandis, McCusker & Hui (1990) would put it, "an appendage of the ingroup" (p. 1008). In the context of development and functioning in modern work organizations, it is felt that the attitude of "submergence of the individual in the group" that is carried over into all performances and personal relationships is not conducive (Kapp, 1963, p. 58).

However, the collective orientation and self in India being relational and with a strong tendency to submerge the individual in the group, it is indeed paradoxical that in day-to-day functioning an average Indian is selfish, displays extreme forms of egotism, and is said to lack consideration for others. One has just to observe the behaviour of an ordinary Indian (like a rail traveller who does not switch off the light and talks loudly even late at night while passengers are sleeping, or a housewife who throws the garbage in front of neighbour's house) to be convinced that he/she lacks sense of neighbourhood, seldom thinks himself/herself as a member of the community, and blatantly lacks concern for others. In view of social identity being such a dominant feature of self in India and the age-old dictum of *vasudhaib kutumbakam* (the entire universe is your relation), ego-centredness and lack of consideration for others and similar other features observed in daily behaviour, the Indian psyche appears very paradoxical.

This brings us to the feature of the Indian psyche, viz., co-existence of contrasting values and behaviour dispositions, which is so commonly reflected in various facets of our life, and has been frequently commented upon by social scientists, historians, and writers. Nirad Chaudhuri (1966) in his famous book *The Continent of Circe* has commented upon it, and the author has been constantly hinting at and emphasizing for over three decades (Sinha, 1962, 1979, 1988; Sinha & Tripathi, 1994). Nirad Chaudhuri has called it "Janus Multifrons" and asserts that Indians are "torn by their internal psychological tussles". He talks about "the creation of a double consciousness, each complete and coherent, but capable of shutting out the other when one is dominant." There is a "terrible dichotomy" in Hindu personality with a large number of antithetical though connected traits shaping his behaviour : "a sense of solidarity with uncontrollable tendency towards disunity; collective megalomania with self abasement; extreme xenophobia with abject xenolatry; authoritarianism with anarchiac individualism; violence with non-violence; militarism with pacifism; possessiveness with carelessness about property owned; courage with cowardice; cleverness with stupidity." An average Indian is generally meek and submissive but at the same time prone to sudden outbursts of violence.

In a recent article entitled "Genial Giant" in *India Today*, two journalists Swapan Dasgupta and N.K. Singh (1977) have very insightfully observed that "for everything that is true of India, the opposite is equally true."

In another sphere, Sinha and Mala Sinha (1990) have observed "dissonance" in our work life. The highest ideal of work (as embodied in our ancient scriptures) stands side by side with the lowest examples of depravity in work culture and behaviour. There is eulogization of the ideal along with tolerance of the profane.

Authur Koestler (1960) has also remarked about the basic predisposition of Indians towards "indifference to contradictions . . . the peaceful coexistence of logical opposites in the emotional sphere. Carl Jung (1978) comments that "It is true that the logical processes of India is funny, and it is bewildering to see how fragments of Western science live peacefully side by side with what we, short-sightedly, would call superstitions. Indians do not mind seemingly intolerable contradictions." A.K. Ramanujam's (1990) observation here is very pertinent. He remarks that "when Indians learn, quite expertly, modern science, business, or technology, they "compartmentalize" these interests (Singer, 1972, pp. 320ff); the new way of thought and behaviour do not replace, but live along with older `religious' ways."

My own observations are similar. Analysing the cultural factors in the emergence of anxiety, I considered an average Indian to be "caught in a chaos of conflicting patterns, none of them wholly condemned but no one of them clearly approved and free from confusion" (Sinha, 1962, p. 34). Such contradictions and juxtapositions are so patently evident at the present time in our policies, and social and political actions. In any case, tolerance of dissonance (Sinha, 1962) appears to be the characterisitc of Indian social thinking. On the action plane, it has resulted in a juxtaposition of opposites that neutralises one another and, as Nirad Chaudhuri (1966) puts it, "the indecisive tug-of-war stultifies all his actions."

There are contradictions galore in our mythological 'heroes' and 'models' portrayed in our epics. These characters are in a way prototypes of the Indian psyche. They indicate that in the Indian mind, conflicting and opposite tendencies coexist and are seldom resolved.

It has been suggested that historical circumstances in which incoming cultural elements that came to India from outside through invasions were not absorbed to form a unique and unified system, but were simply "engulfed" or "encompassed". As a consequence, in our culture, religion and values, disparate elements came to coexist without any synthesis leading to the creation of outlook and behaviour dispositions that often reflect contradictory tendencies.

Some Day-to-day Observations of Common Behaviour Patterns

Observation of our day-to-day behaviour reveals a few other features that deserve to be studied systematically. It is a matter of common observation that a wide gap between the ideals propounded and the action, between what is professed and what is practised not only typifies the double-talk of the politicians and our social and political processes, but are frequently seen in the actions and behaviour of people in general. For example, it is a matter of common experience that high sounding promises are made, schemes and projects are outlined, and grand resolutions are passed which are seldom translated into action. In many instances, certain amount of ritualism is also involved—be it *vanamahotsava* (tree-plantation ceremony), land distribution, or launching of a large project. After the ritual of inaugural ceremony often with religious trappings, and enthusiasm, the matter is allowed to lapse into oblivion. Neglect and lack of care of the trees planted during *vana-mahotsava* resulting in their withering away is a good example of this hiatus.

In these days of highly competitive games and sports, one reason for our 'failures' is said to be the absence of "killer instinct" in our personality. An English sports commentator is reported to have remarked that Indians were unique in the world in that they could always be counted on to snatch defeat from the jaws of victory. Putting this on a larger context, Rikhye (1988) has commented that there is something about being an Indian that enables us all to make the most heroic of sacrifices, and then, when our goal is just within actual reach, we collapse all over the place. Further, it has been observed that Indians tend to compromise even when there is no reason for doing so. Rikhye (1988) points out that even when he/she is 'right' and on solid grounds, he/she compromises, because otherwise "you are violating the tacit rules that we Indians live by". He adds that "this is why it is easy to talk us into compromising even when we have no reason to compromise, when doing so is against our interests. Indians cannot go that last extra mile, grit their teeth and say to hell with everyone, we will do what is right."

These are general observations but do point to some patterns of behaviour that are frequently observed. They need to be examined in a systematic and scientific manner to determine if they are over-generalisations and just transitory patterns of behaviour or constitute important features of the Indian psyche.

A Recent Study on Basic Indian Beliefs and Practices

I shall close by referring at some length to an elaborate empirical investigation conducted by J.B.P. Sinha and his associates (J.B.P. Sinha, Daftuar, Gupta, Mishra, Jayseetha, Jha, Verma and Vijaykumar, 1994) on regional similarities and differences in people's beliefs, practices and preferences that provides a model for conducting investigations into the constituents of Indian psyche. Seven hundred fifty-three students from seven cities in India reported (a) their perception of what people in general believed, practised and preferred; (b) their own allocentric and idiocentric orientations; and (c) the extent to which they attached importance to other's (over their own) opinions, desires and interests. Five values, as contrasted from those of the West, were identified, namely, *embeddedness* in one's ingroup, *harmony* and *tolerance*, *duty* in contrast to hedonism, preference for *personalised relationships*, and arranging persons, objects, ideas and relationship *hierarchically*. Analysis revealed three distinct clusters to emerge out of seven locations : (a) Patna and Varanasi, (b) Lucknow, Kharagpur and Baroda, and (c) Bangalore and Madras. Within-cluster differences were either non-existent or quite small when compared to between-cluster differences. The three clusters corresponded to three geographical zones, viz., the northern, the central and the southern. In spite of some overlap, the northern and southern clusters yielded distinct and contrasting profiles. The former manifesting strong orientations to meet unjustifiable and inconvenient social obligations and to cultivate personalised relationships. Results indicated that the respondents from the North, preferred to take time off from work and visit their ailing friends, friends dropped in during office hours and were entertained, guests visited at odd hours, corrupt but loyal subordinates were protected, juniors tended to maintain personalised relationships with their seniors, and elaborate marriage negotiations were indulged in. People did not avoid confrontation or refrained from voicing disagreements. On the other hand, the South constituting samples from Bangalore and Madras did not have high scores on any of the items related to the above tendencies. They took time off from work less often to visit their ailing friends. They were less likely to visit socially without prior information. Guests seldom dropped in at odd hours or people engaged in sycophancy. Corrupt officers were less likely to be protected, juniors did not necessarily strive to cultivate personalised relationships with their superiors, and action could indeed be taken against loyal subordinates. The central cluster showed a different pattern than these two.

In spite of distinct North *vs.* South differences, there were some significant commonalities between the clusters. People irrespective of grographical locations or regions did subscribe to certain common beliefs, practices and preferences which could be said to be common and shared characteristics of the Indian people as such. The three prominent themes that seemed to emerge were (a) *familism*, which reflected embeddedness in the most salient ingroups; (b) *preference for hierarchy*, particularly based on class and caste; and (c) *maintenance of personalised relationships*. As we can see, these constituted the major dimensions of collectivism and can be considered as the core-characteristics of the Indian psyche.

To conclude, psychological characteristics of the Indian people as they emerge from scientific investigations, perceptions of writers and travellers, accounts given by some historians, as well as observations of day-to-day behaviours of people have been presented. The Indian psyche is so varied and complex that no claim is made about the picture being complete nor free from error. Moreover, as hinted at right in the beginning of the paper, the picture at times appears impressionistic, stereotypical, and even caricature-like (Sinha, 1988). This exercise has been undertaken with the hope that it would arouse interest among psychologists and social scientists in the country, some of whom would feel so 'angry' that they would challenge these findings scientifically. In any case, it is hoped that at least a few scholars would take up the challenge of delving into the nature and characteristics of the Indian psyche systematically and scientifically.

REFERENCES

Asthana, H.S. (1956). Some aspects of personality structuring in Indian (Hindu) social organization. *Journal of Social Psychology*. 44, 155-163.

Basham, A.L. (1971). *The Wonder That Was India*. Calcutta ; Rupa & Co.

Bond, M.H. (Ed.) (1986). *The Psychology of the Chinese People*. New York, Oxford.

Carstairs, G.M. (1957). *The Twice-born : A Study of the Community of High Caste Hindu*. London : Hogarth Press.

Chaudhuri, N.C. (1966). *The Continent of Circe*. Bombay : Jaico Publishing House.

Dasgupta, S & Singh, N.K. (1977). Genial giant, *India Today*, May 15, 1977, 36-38.

Dhawan, N, Roseman, I.J., Naidu, R.K., Thapa, K., & Rettek, S.I. (1995). Self-concepts across two cultures : India and the United States. *Journal of Cross-Cultural Psychology, 26*, 606-621.

Dubois, A.J. (1992). *Hindu manners, customs and ceremonies* (ed., trans., H.K. Beauchamp, 1906). Calcutta : Rupa & Co.

Dumont, L. (1970). *Homo hierarchicus : The caste system and its implications*. Chicago : Chicago University Press.

Hartnack, C. (1987). British psychoanalyst in colonial India. In M.G. Ack & W.R. Woodward (Eds.), *Psychology in twentieth century thought and society* (pp. 233-253). Cambridge : Cambridge University Press.

Jung, C.G. (1978). *The psychology of the East*. Princeton, N.J. : Princeton University Press.

Kakar, S. (1971). The theme of authority in social relations in India. *Journal of Social Psychology, 84*, 93-101.

Kakar, S. (1978). *The inner experience*. Delhi : Oxford University Press.

Kapp, W.K. (1963). *Hindu culture, economic development and economic planning in India*, Bombay : Asia Publishing House.

Koestler, A. (1960). *The lotus and the robot*. New York : Harper & Row.

Kothari, R. (1970). *Politics in India*. New Delhi : Orient Longman.

Lapierre, D. (1986). *The city of joy*, London : Arrow Books Ltd.

Markus, H.R., & Kitayama, S. (1991). Culture and self : Implications for cognition, emotion and motivation. *Psychological Review. 28*, 224-253.

McClelland, D.C. (1961). *The achieving society*. Princeton : Van Nostrand.

Mead, M. (1951). The study of national character : In D. Lerner & H.D. Lasswell (Eds.), *The policy sciences*. Stanford : Stanford University Press.

Minturn, L., & Hitchcock, J.T. (1966). *The Rajputs of Khalapur, India*. Six Cultures Series, Vol III, New York : John Wiley.

Murphy, L.B. (1953). Roots of tolerance and tension in Indian child development. In G. Murphy, *In the minds of men*. New York : Basic Books.

Nair, K. (1961). *Blossoms in the dust*. London : Duckworth.

Narain, D. (1957). *Hindu character*. Bombay : University of Bombay.

Nehru, J. (1946/1981). *The Discovery of India* Bombay : Oxford University Press.

Ramanujan, A.K. (1990). Is there an Indian way of thinking ? An informal essay. In M. Marriot (Ed.) *India through Hindu categories.* (pp. 41-58). New Delhi: Sage.

Ramanujan, B.K. (1979). Towards maturity: Problem of identity seen in the Indian clinical setting. In S. Kakar (Ed.), *Identity and adulthood.* (pp. 37-55). Bombay: Oxford University Press.

Rikhye, R. (1988). *The war that never was.* Delhi: Chanakya Publications.

Roland, A. (1980). *Towards a psychoanalytic psychology of hierarchical relationships in Hindu India.* Paper presented to the Psychoanalytic Society, Bombay.

Roland, A. (1987). The familial self, the individualised self, and the transcendental self: Psychoanalytic reflections on India and America. *Psychoanalytic Review, 74,* 237-250.

Segal, R. (1966). *The crisis of India.* New York: New York Library Publisher.

Singer, M. (1972). *When great tradition modernizes.* New York: Praeger.

Sinha, D. (1962). Cultural factors in the emergence of anxiety. *Eastern Anthropologist, 15,* 21-37.

Sinha, D. (1969). *Indian villages in transition: A motivational analysis.* New Delhi: Associated Publishing House.

Sinha, D. (1979). The young and the old: Ambiguity of role models and values among Indian youth. In S. Kakar (Ed.) *Identity and adulthood.* (pp. 56-64). Delhi: Oxford University Press.

Sinha, D. (1988). Basic Indian values and behaviour dispositions in the context of national development. In D. Sinha & H.S.R. Kao (Eds.), *Social values and development Asian perspectives* (pp. 31-55). New Delhi: Sage.

Sinha, D (1996). Culturally rooted psychology in India: Dangers and velopment. *Interamerican Journal of Psychology, 30,* 99-).

Sinha, . & Sinha, M. (1990). Dissonance in work culture in india. In A.D. Moddie (Ed.), *The concept of work in Indian society.* Shimla : Indian Institute of Advanced Study.

Sinha, D., & Tripathi, R.C. (1994). Individualism in a collectivist culture : A case of coexistence of opposites. In U. Kim, H.C. Triandis, C. Kagitcibasi, S.C. Choi & G. Yoon (Eds.), *Individualism and collectivism : Theory method and applications.* (pp. 123-136). Thousand Oaks, CA : Sage.

Sinha, J.B.P. (1970), *Development through behaviour modification.* Bombay : Allied Publishers.

Sinha, J.B.P. (1980). *Nuturant task leader.* New Delhi : Concept.

Sinha, J.B.P. (1982). Hindu (Indian) identity. *Dynamic Psychiatry, 15,* 148-160.

Sinha, J.B.P., (1985). Cultural bias in appraisal system. Paper presented during the International Seminar on Selection and Appraisal System. New Delhi. January 28-30, 1985, pp. 127-132.

Sinha, J.B.P., Daftaur, C.N., Gupta, R.K., Mishra, R.C., Jayseetha, R., Jha, S.S., Verma, J and Vijaykumar, V.S.R. (1994). Regional similarities and differences in people's beliefs, practices and preferences. *Psychology and Developing Societies*, *6*, 131-150.

Sovani, N.V. (1963). Non-economic aspects of India's economic development. In R.J. Braibanti and J.J. Spengler (Eds.). *Administration and economic development in India*. Durham : Duke University Press.

Spratt, P. (1966). *Hindu culture and personality*, Bombay : Manaktala.

Taylor, W.S. (1948). Basic personality in orthodox Hindu cultural patterns. *Journal of Abnormal and Social Psychology*, *43*, 3-12.

Triandis, H.C., McCusker, C., and Hui, C.H. (1990). Multimethod probes of individualism and collectivism. *Journal of Personality and Social Psychology*, *59*, 1006-1020.

3

Role of Social Psychology in National Development

Abhilasha Srivastava

The modern notion of development began as an idea of economic growth, which the west had already realized and the newly developing countries needed badly. The extreme poverty on the one side and the glamour of material affluence on the other, left them with no option but to imitate the west. The scope of the concept, however, continually expanded to include other aspects of life. From being purely a matter of economic growth through industrial and agricultural development, it has come to encompass social and environmental aspects also. From economic growth, now we have moved to the concept of human development. As a consequence, it has gradually brought into its orbit sociologists, anthropologists, political scientists and other social scientists. Since development is a complex issue, an integrative interdisciplinary approach is warranted. So far psychology has played a limited role in the process of national development. Recently, however, the research interests and activities are being geared in such a manner that the results could be of help in policy formulation and its execution, pertaining to national development.

Before discussing the role and place of psychology in the context of development, it is essential to look into the reasons for the limited role it has so far played in this field. The first reason is that for long psychology in India remained largely an Euro-American product having very little concern with the social reality. The total acceptance of western orientation led to two consequences, both of which were harmful to the healthy growth of the discipline in the country. First the Indian psychologists remained recipients rather than exchange agents of knowledge. Secondly, the sense of priorities was distorted in the minds of Indian psychologists. Since 1960's, with the emphasis on indigenisation of the discipline, this trend has changed and more socially relevant studies within the context of rapid socio-economic change have been undertaken.

Another problem lies in the basic orientation of psychology, which is microcosmic, placing disproportionate emphasis on narrow aspects of large social problems. Though the subject deals both with the social system and individual processes, its orientation is basically microsocial. However, this orientation can be considered as its strength also, as ultimately it is the individual for whom the policies are made and who accepts or rejects them.

The isolation of the subject from the complexities of social problems also comes from the constraints of a methodology that has been modelled after the physical sciences. Methodological refinement seemed to have become an end in itself so that the problems which do not easily permit the use of sophisticated experimental designs and multivariate techniques were avoided. To overcome this tyranny of methodology which led to the fragmentation and trivialisation of the discipline, the adoption of the 'scientific-professional model' has been suggested (Sinha, 1977b). In this model, the scientist on the basis of systematic knowledge his subject — whether individual or a complex social phenomenon — obtained primarily in real life situation, integrates it with the psychological theory and then consistently regards it with the questioning attitude of a scientist. There is a combination of reality based psychological understanding with the attitude of constant enquiry.

There is a growing feeling amongst psychologists that with an undisciplinary perspective, it is not possible to obtain a meaningful view of human problems, especially of matters concerning development and social change. The unidisciplinary approach can at best provide a partial, lop-sided view of social reality. In recent years, psychologists have become conscious of the overlap of different social sciences in understanding complex social processes, and have begun to borrow freely the concepts, tools and techniques of analysis from other social sciences. Recent research orientation in psychology shows that the process of "indigenisation" is gaining ground. The phenomenon in question is viewed within the specific socio-cultural context and the tools for study are so designed that they are rooted in the specific culture.

The nature of change in India makes the role of psychology important in the area of national development. India is trying to reach that level of development in less than fifty years, which took centuries to come about in the west. This telescoping or "temporal compression" of change and development (D. Sinha, 1986) involves not only the building of certain economic infrastructure but also all-round modernisation in social structure, institutions, attitudes and value system.

The changes that are taking place are not only telescoped but also cacophonic (Myrdal, 1968). The two in conjunction produce a condition that is highly unsettling both for the individual and the society. Some of the commonly observed ill-effects of this condition are an increase in the incidence of suicide, riots, social violence, crime, delinquency and impersonality of modern life (Triandis, 1971). Other ill-effects have also been noted, such as, ambiguity of values and role models (Sinha, 1979b), alienation, changing level of aspiration and increasing discrepancy between aspiration and achievement leading to widespread dissatisfaction, higher incidence of psychosomatic ailments, marginality and identity diffusion making the individual more susceptible to social deviance, rebellion and violence (Sinha, 1977a). Despite the myriads of problems that socio-economic development generates and which are inevitable, change as such is valued. Therefore the research interest of the psychologist has twin objectives (Kelman, 1968) : understanding the factors that facilitate social change and to increase the likelihood that social change will proceed in a constructive direction—meeting human needs, expanding the participation of people, and evolving ways to minimise the coercive, destructive and disabling consequences of rapid transformation. In short the aims of psychologists dealing with national development can be grouped under three broad headings, namely, analysing the factors conducive to desirable changes ('facilitators'), factors that act as impediments to change and operate as 'resistances' in various forms ('inhibitors') and avoiding and cushioning the psychological costs of rapid development (Sinha, 1980c).

Psychology is especially competent to trace in detail the mediating processes that account for the relationship between social, structural and individual factors. It is only in terms of such mediating processes that one is able to understand the operations of facilitating and inhibiting factors, as well as such changes that take unexpected and at times undesirable directions. Other social sciences more directly concerned with development tend to ignore these mediating processes which have their roots mainly in the motivational and cognitive structures of individuals. Since these psychological variables constitute an integral aspect of any social system, psychology has an important complementary role in the process of social planning and development. It is contended that development is a highly complex phenomenon and is the product of a very complicated interaction of a number of variables—economic, social, structural and psychological. In this context, Segall (1980) while dealing with the implications of the findings from social psychology to localised development projects, has rightly emphasized the policy of restructuring social environment towards inducing modern behaviour and also the importance of mediating variables, such as, individual perceptions, attitudes, values and other personality factors.

In the context of national development, the psychologists can have a two fold role. First, accepting the proposed developmental goals and strategies, the psychologists can help in facilitating their achievement and preventing and cushioning their undesirable fall-out. Apart from facilitating the goals chosen by the policy makers, the psychologists can also participate in the choice of goals, since, there appears to be an urgent need for an alternative model of development to replace the western model which emphasises accumulation of material affluence. J.B.P. Sinha (1984) has asserted that massive evidence have accumulated to prove that material affluence beyond a point may not lead to better quality of life either for individuals or social aggregates. If affluence beyond a point desensitizes us to other, acute poverty dehumanises even to a more alarming extent. It seems that economic growth has a curvilinear relationship with human development.

It is felt that economic development based on the principle of control over the environment in order to exploit the natural resources has caused many of the ills of progress. An alternative that has been suggested is not that of controlling but being in tune with the environment. It implies development with the environment rather than at the cost of the environment. J.B.P. Sinha (1984) has pointed out that "the logical corollary of man is to grow with the social groups and collectives rather than strive for personal excellence which might alienate him from the persons around him". Such a model of development is more in consonance with the Indian tradition where the relation between man and nature and man and society is not one of opposition or dichotomy but a kind of symbiotic relationship (Sinha, 1981c).

Endogenous Development

The concept of endogenous development evolved by UNESCO in the UN decade of development, emphasizing the development based on felt needs and internal resources of the society, was accepted by India in the plans in 1950's. Still the development fell far below expectations due to following reasons (Naqvi, 1982).

1. It was wrong on the part of state to assume full

responsibility to plan, direct and implement policies particularly with the help of administrative structure which has been bureaucratic and not quite receptive to the development needs of people.

2. Public sector was allowed to be exploited by individuals, groups and certain classes of people causing recurring losses which exchequer kept meeting.
3. Faith that law passed by legislatures can transform the socio-economic realities proved wrong.
4. The endogenous features of the people values etc. were paid lip service but were not utilized either in formulating or in implementing the plans.

India is still struggling with the problems of poverty, rural development, population growth, crowding, intergroup conflicts, illiteracy, unemployment and so on which are serious obstacles on the path of national development. Applied social psychology is rapidly gaining salience in India by undertaking research keeping in view the above mentioned problems of development. In the following pages, the contribution of social psychology in these problem areas has been briefly covered.

Rural Development

One of the areas in which social psychology is being applied in a big way in India is in the rural setting (D. Sinha 1984). Since 70.6% of the population resides in villages, the road to the country's development inevitably passes through its villages. Indian society and culture have maintained their resilience over centuries by establishing self-sufficient local community. Till recently, village community managed its educational system (Jha, 1983), effectively arbitrated village disputes and carried out welfare, religious and cultural activities. When state assumed all the responsibilities for all walks of life, village institutions started crumbling. It failed either to revitalize village institutions or to alter the socio-economic structure in majority of the villages.

For rural development, adoption of agricultural innovation and technology is very important. Many studies involving factors related to the adoption of new agricultural practices and studies of psychological factors which impede or accelerate agricultural development have been undertaken. Some of the variables associated with adoption behaviour are moderate level of aspiration and low level of conservation (S. Chattopadhyay, 1963), educational level (Dhaliwal, 1971), social participation (Dhaliwal, 1971; Supe, 1969) and degree of innovation proneness and awareness of the innovation (Moulik, 1965), farm-size, use of interpersonal versus cosmopolite source of information, risk orientation, market perception (Nair, 1970), urban contact, contact with agency, and knowledge possessed by the farmer (Somasundaram & Singh, 1978).

Muthayya (1982) has emphasized family needs and taking elders into confidence for facilitating motivation for accepting new innovations. R. Lal, S.K. Singh and R, Sharma (1982) have reported that progressive villagers had high radical and scientific values and high economic motivation. Economic motivation was found to correlate positively with caste hierarchy, size of land holdings and negatively with risk-preference.

Village leadership has also been noted to be factor in adoption. M.S.K. Reddy (1965) has reported that villages which were progressive in adopting new methods had innovators as their leaders. Lokhands and Singh (1977) also observed that political, opinion making and decision making type of leadership was more in evidence in progressive villages than the traditional leadership style.

The success of any rural development programme depends basically on three psychological factors—awareness, perception and motivation.

Awareness implies the building up of knowledge and capacity for reasoning based on logical facts rather than affective factors. The capacity to reason depends on the extent and accuracy of the information flow from different sources associated with a certain amount of authenticity to improve the credibility of information. While communicating information to the target population, these factors have to be kept in mind. Chole and Radhukar (1978) found that big farmers perceived personal formal source of information more credible whereas small farmers preferred personal informal sources.

Personal contact has been found to be more relevant in Indian rural situation for discussing information on sensitive issues like family planning.

Perception is the way people interpret the programme to which they are exposed and this by and large determines its acceptance or rejection. The interpretation of the programme depends on their past experience, general attitude towards life, values of social system and in some cases personality make-up. People's attitude to some of the economic programmes wherever subsidy is given is not necessarily oriented to production and meaningful economic activity, but to avail of this subsidy or loan for non-productive consumption purpose. Therefore an attempt should be made to improve the perception and factors leading to that perception should be diagnosed and efforts should be made to minimize the influence of undesirable factors by counter experience.

Generally, it is believed that in backward economies, money is the important motivator. Therefore, in majority of the policies, either in agriculture or in welfare, money has been used as an incentive. But using money for motivating people has only an immediate impact and does not have long term subsistence value. The curent emphasis on basic needs approach seems to provide an answer to this problem. Once the basic needs prepotent among different groups of people are identified and linked to the economic or welfare programmes along with the incentives, there would be a base for generating and sustaining the motivation among people. The first task is, therefore, to identify the basic needs and then to link it up meaningfully to the oportunities and incentives.

D. Sinha (1984) has found that motivation of the villagers was largely centered around the immediate problems of subsistence and daily living. Majority of them lacked the urge for growth and were reported to be lethargic and indifferent to material progress.

As for the motivational base of the disadvantaged group (Muthayya, 1982) it was observed that the perceived basic needs were food, clothing and shelter and to some extent health, education, land and irrigation.

It seems that for successful policy formulation and implementation, dissemination of knowledge regarding the programme is important through a medium which is perceived as reliable by the villagers of the region under consideration. The help of village leaders, non-bureaucratic change agents could be of great value in this regard. A novel suggestion is made by Patil and Mukhopadhyay (1983) to use folk media, such as puppetry, shadow play, dance, story telling, songs, ballads, music and drama which are popular in certain cultural regions for transmitting the messages of development.

The investment orientation of the plans has created excessive dependency in the recipients. There is a need to enhance their motivation, aspiration and risk-taking behaviour. It has been found that people organise best around problems they consider important. Then they assess the risks and gains associated with change. If there is a voluntary commitment of resources, such as, labour, time, and money, it leads to breaking up of patterns of passivity and dependency in the development process. Rehman (1987) has reviewed several participatory rural development projects in different parts of the world. He argues that

a) When people are encouraged to take initiative, they are able to tackle some of their livelihood problems.
b) By increasing access to productive resources like land, water and fishing, they are able to control exploitation by middlemen etc. and enhance their income and improve productivity.
c) They are not only able to improve their skills but also to enhance the dignity and status of their labour.

Poverty and Deprivation

Despite four decades of planned development poverty remains a pressing problem in India where one-fourth of the population is living below the poverty line.

The concepts of poverty and deprivation are multidimensional. So far poverty has been defined in "absolute" or "relative" terms by economists. Anandalakshmy (1982) has added the criteria of time and energy spent in bread winning activities to define poverty. J. Pandey and A. Singh (1985) have found perceived poverty as a better predictor for coping behaviours of the poor than income. Perceived poverty is significantly predicted both by PCI and physical quality of living and they were negatively related to escape, helplessness, learned helplessness and denial.

Psychologists have paid greater attention to deprivation than to poverty. Deprivation has been conceptualized as a state of deficit in individual's environment. Poverty cannot be viewed merely as an objective phenomenon. The poor are not a homogeneous mass but manifest an extremely heterogeneous picture on the psychological dimension, which results in their not responding uniformly to anti-poverty programmes. IRDP was implemented in a uniform manner throughout the country ignoring the regional, individual and social variations (Harway, 1988). Individual's subjective perception of his economic aspect of life i.e. perceived poverty, should supplement the economic measures of poverty (J. Pandey & Singh, 1985).

The psychological concomitants of poverty like helplessness, low motivation, low aspiration level, dependence proneness etc. render the individual incapable to cope with his problems, accentuating the degree of poverty. Indian psychologists have analysed the effect of poverty and deprivation on cognitive and perceptual processes (Sinha, 1977; Sinha & Shukla, 1974, Sinha & Misra 1982; Misra, 1982; L.B. Tripathi & Misra, 1976, Das & Singh, 1975; Rath, Dash & Dash, 1979; Muthayya, 1982). In addition to this, the nutritional dimension as related to poverty and its impact on the individual's psychological functioning have also been investigated. The association of mental health problems and emotional instability has also been studied in relation to poverty condition.

The main thrust of these studies is that the psychological impact of poverty renders the individual less capable of coping with the problems created by it thereby creating a kind of vicious circle. Psychologists have taken poverty as a kind of deficit not only in economic sense but in physical and sociocultural planes as well. Sinha (1977c) has developed an ecological map of disadvantaged child to understand the various restrictions imposed on him by the physical and sociocultural setting.

Such studies have yielded findings with distinct policy and action implications. A few investigators utilized their results to develop intervention strategies such as providing special kinds of experiences by which the gap between advantaged and disadvantaged groups can be wiped out (Rath, Dash & Dash, 1979).

For policy formulation and implementation, understanding the psychological characteristics of poor is as important as the analysis of the system that led to the condition of poverty. The 'broomstick effect' showed that the difference in performance on certain perceptual cognitive tasks continued to increase in favour of the advantaged, in the so called better institutions but not in the ordinary institutions. Such a 'broomstick effect' has also been noticed on the motivational plane (Pande & Tripathi, 1982). These findings raise serious doubts on the policy of special scholarships and reservations for the poor and the disadvantaged in superior educational institutions. Children from the socially disadvantaged groups are victims of the social system twice. First, they lack resources and wherewithals to do well in the schools which are basically meant for educating middle class children (D. Sinha, 1980b). Second, when they enter the school they are the victims of the unfavourable teacher expectations (Panda & Dash, 1980) leading to low academic adjustments (Ushashree, 1980; Gunthey, 1981) and high drop-out rates (Rath 1976). Supportive climate of school on the other hand is found to be conducive for the development of positive academic selfconcept, low degree of fear of failure, realistic level of aspiration and high need for achievement (Pande & R.C. Tripathi, 1982). A number of studies have shown that parental support compensates for the effect of low intelligence, adverse effects of the SES and improves scholastic achievement. Singh (1983b) has suggested the school to function as substitute for parents and families. He advocates the establishment of "Ashram type" schools which may salvage the socially disadvantaged students from the unfavourable conditions of their families. R.C. Tripathi and Pande (1982) have suggested a strategy to enhance the supportive school climate through teacher and peer suport to minimize the negative motivational consequences for S.C. students.

Rath (1982) has suggested compensatory programmes to enrich the cognitive background of the disadvantaged children. Besides, programmes to enhance academic achievement of the deprived students, strategies have also been suggested to bring about changes in the levels of living of the people. Clinard (1970) has demonstrated that by developing a positive self-image among the slum dwellers, motivational basis for effecting change in the desired direction could be created. To avoid creating dependence, the governmental support should be of such quality that people could feel competent enough to take initiative and feel responsible for their actions and have the experience of personal causation and self-efficacy. According to J.P.B. Sinha (1984) there are three preconditions which can mobilize groups and generate social energy:

1. Experience of extreme social deficit.
2. Belief that it is remediable.
3. Disposition to take initiative.

Government can identify viable groups, and institutions and their leaders to entrust them to mobilize the people for developmental efforts.

Pareek's (1970) paradigm of culture of poverty conceptualizes it as a structural pattern characterized by low need for achievement, low n-extension and high dependency. He suggested a paradigm of development according to which increasing achievement motive (concern for excellence) and extension motive (concern for others) are important for socioeconomic development. Similarly it is important to reduce the dependence motive (concern for direction) in order to accelerate development.

Intergroup Conflict and National Integration

Though India has been committed to 'unity in diversity', to secularism, yet recurrent intergroup tensions and conflicts pose a serious problem in the path of national development by forcing useful resources and manpower into socially destructive activities. In general, it creates an unhealthy environment where the concept of "nationalism" is overshadowed by commitment to specific religious, caste and ethnic groups.

The intergroup relation in India illustrates how psychological phenomenon of prejudice and conflict are rooted in historical, social and economic factors.

After half a century of partition, Hindu-Muslim relation continues to be a major source of social tension in India. The minority status of Muslims strengthens their sense of identity which they try to protect from the perceived real or imaginary threat of its absorption by the majority group. The touch-me-not attitude of non-proselytizing Hindu religion hurts their pride also. The partition, role of Muslims in it, the ties and sympathies of Muslims with people in Pakistan, the jealous protection of Muslim indentity as reflected in the strong resistance to any change in their personal law and mutual unfavourable stereotypes of the two religious groups are some of the factors underlying the intergroup disharmony.

Saxena (1984) has proposed seven conditions which transform social conflict into violence and trigger off communal riots. These are:

1. Relative deprivation—high
2. Legitimacy of government—low
3. Channels of communication—blocked
4. Insecurity among a group—high

5. Dehumanization—widely practiced
6. Belief and traditions—sanctioning violence
7. Instruments of violence—readily available.

Engineer (1984) has suggested certain common characteristics of riots based on a number of case studies.

a) Middle-sized towns
b) Proportion of Muslims more than 30%
c) Section of Muslims is well to do and appears to be paternal economic competitors of Hindus
d) Riots are preplanned rather than spontaneous
e) Core issues are economic or politically ignited by some trivial incident.

The political problem of Hindu-Sikh disharmony, on the other hand, is not a religious problem rather it has economic and social roots.

Next to religion, caste and tribes are the two other important basis of social stratification in Indian society. M.P. Singh (1979) has listed the following main trends in the domain of caste conflict in India:

1. In most conflicts Harijans have been the sufferers.
2. Conflicts have a geographical scatter covering the entire country, largely rural India.
3. Though caste conflicts are still between the top and bottom strata, there have been increasingly greater number of conflicts between middle peasant caste and Harijans.
4. The earlier ambivalence of identity, reflected in Sanskritization, religious conversion and migration to cities has been replaced by aggressive assertion of Harijan identity.
5. The earlier horizontal pattern of political conflict between major religious groups and certain upper castes of some socio-economic, status has given way to vertical political confrontation between different castes within the hierarchical Hindu society.

The psychological researches on the development of

ethnic identity and prejudice in India have revealed the following main points:

1. Ethnic identity and prejudice develop early in childhood. Mostly ethnocentrism and prejudice develop in the absence of religious information.
2. The minority status strengthens ethnic identity.
3. Ethnic identiy and prejudice are importantly influenced by parental child rearing practices such as non-permissiveness, harsh punitive practices.

All ethnic groups are ethnocentric having favourable attitude and stereotypes of their own group. Some studies have found unfavourable ingroup attitudes among low castes reflecting their lack of confidence and demoralization. High social prestige of outgroup influences stereotypes. Muslims and Hindus showed more favourable stereotypes of high castes than low castes transcending their religious affiliations (Majeed & Ghosh, 1981). The tribal Christian identified more with Christianity than with his tribal ethnicity. Prejudice is found to be negatively related to "modern" attitudes. Psychologically, the prejudiced persons of all ethnic and religious groups are twins, showing similar attitude and personality traits.

These findings have indicated a clear social policy implication for intervention programmes to reduce social tension and development of a secular national identity. Intervention for the development of a national identity and secularism has to be done in the early childhood before the ethnic identity have hardened (A.K. Singh, 1985) with widespread illiteracy use of mass-media with audio-visual technique becomes the inevitable choice for any intervention programme on a mass scale.

The feeling of relative deprivation (R.D) increases prejudice (Naqvi, 1982; Tripathi & Srivastava, 1980). The growing political consciousness alongwith the rise in aspirations among the socially and economically deprived groups have increased their sense of R.D. These researches imply that a solution for intergroup hostilities and social tensions has to be sought within the context of economic equality, social justice and political sharing of power. The findings underlie the fact that psychological variables of prejudice and hostility are rooted in the socio-political milieu, therefore, a final solution has to be sought within the socio-economic and political context. The strategy of state to promote social justice and equity has been limited to providing job-quota, reservation in educational institutions stipends to SC/ST students. Such measures help only a section of socially disadvantaged and create discontent in Hindus who feel discriminated. Those employed through job quotas and those selected through competitions, have certain misgivings about each other. Such measures, thus, instead of decreasing intergroup tensions and conflict, tend to aggravate them.

The psychological researches have highlighted an interesting finding with important social policy implication. When a person is faced with a dilemma of choosing one of his several identities, he chooses the identity which has greater social respectability (Hassan, 1981), Indians have plural identities based on caste, tribe, language, religion, nationality. To make the 'Indian' identity the strongest of all identities, it is important that it is viewed as the most socially respectable identity by the Indians. Intervention should aim not to thwart the growth of religious identity but to create a framework in which religion identity can be integrated with national identity.

Researches have found that if two groups are able to identify superordinate goals, they can surmount differences and cooperation for the realization of common goals (Sherif & Sherif, 1953). So together with national identity certain superordinate goals have to be identified and pursued. To achieve the goal of "secularism" the state should actively encourage dissemination of religious information without which people are more likely to be prejudiced and ethnocentric. This should be done through primary school education as the development of stereotypes and prejudice take place in early childhood.

Education

For national development, a country has to develop the

skills and knowledge of its people for which rapid quantitative expansion of education opportunities was believed to be inevitable. Recently the emphasis on the quality of education is gaining ground. Two very important components of qualitative dimension of development are school climate and classroom climate. The school climate varies from extreme closed to open type. Closed climate schools resemble the classical bureaucratic model of impersonalized standardized procedures, distribution of authority and power (Gandhi, 1981) and role conflict (Bhogle, 1971). Open climate emerges to be conducive for pupil achievement and teacher satisfaction (Rao, 1976). Meaninglessness of work was greater among teachers from closed climate school. Teacher's morale was highest in an open climate (Sharma & Quraishi, 1973) and it is highly related to achievement and innovative ability of pupils. Openness of climate facilitates the capacity of schools to adopt newer educational practices in greater number and in a shorter time (Pillai, 1973).

Classroom climate has been explained in terms of interactive processes that occur in a classroom between teachers and pupils on one hand and among pupils on the other. An open climate in a school or a classroom tends to show better personal social adjustment on the part of pupils, value formation and attitude development.

Regarding behaviour of the heads of schools, high relationship and high task oriented style of leadership is found to be directly related to the motivation of students and innovativeness. Various sociopsychological factors are also related to academic performance of the students. Academic achievement has been found to be negatively affected by social disadvantage (G. Misra, 1983; Singh, 1976; Ushashree, 1980). D. Sinha's (1970) analysis of academic achievers and non-achievers is multidimensional and is ilustrative of certain specific psychosocial variables such as n-ach, level of aspiration, persistence, self-concept. Sometimes lower value orientation, social class membership, family atmosphere, and peer group influence, labelling and role expectancy of teachers account for great deal of variation in academic achievement (Kohli & Joshi,

1978). Subramanyam (1979) demonstrated a high positive relationship between home environment and reading achievement among primary school children at each class level. B.B. Chatterjee (1977) found that there was little difference in achievement and cognitive development of children varying in sex, rural-urban background and good school and poor school climate. But when they reach grade 5, there were significant differences in favour of boys, children from urban background and those studying in schools than their counterparts in regard to achievement and cognitive ability.

Educational problems of the SC/ST and socially disadvantaged groups appear to be academic, motivational and social. Safaya (1976) identified several causes of wastage i.e. dropout and stagnation—poverty, apathy, poor quality of teaching, poor school environment, family circumstances, irregular attendance, indifferent teaching,—curriculum and defective examination system. Nonformal educational strategies can be one of the alternatives to decrease wastage.

The educational reforms need to be in the direction of bringing about change in school and classroom climate by reinforcing the high relationship and high task oriented type of leadership. Because of the high opportunity costs and low aspirations socially disadvantaged are the first to dropout. This trend can be changed by making the curricula more need based and relevant for them. Training the teachers such that the problems of differential and biased expectation may not mar the performance of the students and providing the incentives to increase the morale of the teachers can go a long way to improve the performance and adjustment of the students.

Early years are most critical in human life. Due emphasis has to be placed on organizing primary school systems along scientific lines. Apart from syllabi, physical facilities, quality of teachers and integration of school system with government administration and community, the main focus needs to be placed on learning activities of students, their group formation, sharing of intra- and inter-group activities etc. Such a preparation will help them interact as equals partners in school, colleges and subsequently in jobs.

Population Explosion

A grave social problem in India is that of overpopulation. Fertility behaviour is complex and is determined by a host of biological, sociological and psychological factors. All India Family Planning study by the Operation Research Group (1980) established that out of the 117 million eligible couples, 21 million were not practicing any method of family planning despite not desiring any children (Khan & Prasad, 1983). Highly favourable attitude towards family planning followed by low practice, posed serious problems to both researcher and planners alike. To understand the KAP GAP, tridimensional approach incorporating cognitive, effective and behavioural components of the attitude-behaviour paradigm should be used. The measure of verbal intentions to act is a better predictor of contraceptive behaviour than verbal feelings or verbal belief measures (Kothandapani, 1971).

Dave and Sadashivaiah (1981) have reviewed literature on family size. Some of the main findings are:

1. Lower social class urban men preferred a larger family size than their wives.
2. Rural men and women desired a larger family size.
3. Higher the education level and status of the women, the lower was the desired family size.
4. Traditionalism was associated with a higher family size norm.

There have been studies which show that fertility is higher in the joint families as a result of economic security, patrilineal system, lower status of women in the ascribed hierarchy, lack of direct responsibility of rearing children, traditional values and reproductive models of the adult.

Katiyar (1976) investigated the relationship between value orientation and family norm. Besides higher level of income, education and young age which were dominant in preferring small family norm, values of free-will, activism, individualism, modernism, secularism were also positively related to it.

Various researches have indicated that psychological measures play different role in different population subgroups. developmental effects are neither uniformly spread nor uniformly perceived. Gulati and Mani (1975) have discussed motivational and communicational means which can be used in propagating family planning: They believe that motivational methods should be consistent with the subcultures in which they are used because each society has its own system of communication. Programmes directed at providing education to children and women, reduction in infant mortality rates, providing employment opportunities to women, expanding mass-media and motivational facilities and improving economic conditions of the poorest section of society can be expected to raise the status of women and decrease in the demand for children. Although sociological literature indicates that status of women in a family set-up is not always subordinate to men as commonly believed to be in both urban (Ross, 1961) and rural areas (Dube, 1955), social psychological research in this regard is important. The perception of one's own status in society in general and in family in particular and its relationship with that of fertility decision are likely to throw light on fertility behaviour.

The research findings can be meaningfully incorporated in two significant aspects of family planning, i) important sociopsychological dimension can be fed into the training programmes of family planning field workers and their day-to-day routine schedule; ii) findings can help in developing appropriate communication material and social programmes.

Sandell (1976) has highlighted the rate of sex education in family planning and argues that it should be made an integral part of national family planning programme. Studies of health education have shown that acceptance and practice of family planning is greater where such education is provided. Schools education can be mobilized to foster the necessary conducive psychological factors.

Crowding

India is accommodating 16% of the world population while its land area is only 2.4% of the world land area. Thus a significant proportion of world population is found jam-packed in a small geographical area. High population density with paucity of resources has forced millions to live under inhuman conditions. In order to manage the abundant human resource and to move towards the goals of social development, the scientific studies on the psychosocial consequences of crowding are important. In general, crowding has negative psychological consequences. Jain (1983) found that crowding has a negative affective consequence. Kamal & Jain (1984) found greater incidences of ill-health in high crowding than in low crowding setting. Its negative effect on quality of life, perceived control, health and personal space has also been reported (Anand, 1983). Tripathi (1986) has reported negative behavioural effects, poor adjustment and neuroticism due to high density. The consequences of crowding are manifested at individual, interpersonal and societal levels. At individual level, it results in poor task performance (Nagar & Pandey, 1987), goal blocking and frustration; competition and hoarding of resources, anxiety, stress ambiguity, meaninglessness. At interpersonal and societal level it leads to increased competitiveness, decreased interpersonal attraction and pro-social behaviour.

In order to meet the challenge of social welfare, development and equality of opportunity, planning efforts have to be synchronised with population growth and consequent crowding. The issues involved in this area are complex — dealing with designing of houses and workplace, organizational structure and its size, use of technology and socio-political system. Psychologists and social scientists need to communicate with planners, architects and economists for evolving a plan of action to deal with the undesirable effect of crowding.

Conclusion

The idea of national development is enormously complex and it is unrealistic to expect any one particular discipline to decide its course By enhancing the understanding of psychological principles and premises of human behaviour, social psychology can join other social sciences in formulation and successful implementation of plans. In the area of national development, role of social psychology ranges from conducting socially relevant research, studies of facilitators and inhibitors of development and change, programme evaluation at micro level, to policy evaluation having implications for the whole system.

Social psychologists' preoccupation with individuals and small groups and the resultant nature of variables and research designs have initially prevented them from developing any perspective on national development. Yet, this psychological knowledge of the functioning of individuals and small groups can be utilized in national planning. It is quite clear that without the requisite value structure and motivation, no developmental scheme has a chance to succeed. Most development schemes assume that the necessary base for their acceptance is already present. The failure of Community Development Programme and National Adult Education Programme are just few examples in this connection. Researches on the effects of social disadvantage have shown that the policy of protective discrimination instead of helping those for whom it is meant may actually harm them. Various problems which the country is facing are interrelated and appear to be the cause and consequence of each other.

McClelland's (1961) work on need for achievement has implications for development. He contended that independence and mastery training during early childhood led to the emergence of an achievement oriented personality which produces entrepreneurial character and economic growth. In the Indian context, instead of encouraging only the individual achievement orientation, there is a need to empower the people for social achievement to break the vicious circle of poverty and deprivation. Udai Pareek (1968) has given a general paradigm in which development (D) is a positive function of achievement motivation (AM) and extension motivation (EM) reduced by the degree of dependence motivation (DM). Thus,

$$D = (AM \times EM) - DM$$

Long periods of socio-economic and political deprivation inculcate a sense of inefficacy and helplessness in the poor and disadvantaged group. The process of empowering them involves overcoming their ignorance and arousing critical social awareness of the causes of exploitation and poor quality of life. The process of empowering is, therefore, new kind of social learning designed to weaken their learned helplessness. Psychology has an important role to play in this regard. Enlightened, trained and motivated field functionaries and organizers can help initiate the process of empowerment. Once the sense of efficacy and competence is aroused in the disadvantaged people, they begin to perceive various hardships and blocks created by their socioeconomic environment and learn to articulate them, thereby assuming an actor role.

In conclusion, it can be said that, state action is essential in making provisions for basic infrastructure and amenities like education, health care, employment generation etc. But more important is that the people should be aware and they should assert themselves to gain access to and to utilize such amenities. People are not just consumers and recipients of aid, subsidies and assistance of the state and other such agencies. They have to be empowered to act on the environment and to assume an actor role in their own development, in which, lies the growth and development of the nation.

REFERENCES

Anand, M (1983). *In dweling and out dwelling experiences of crowding and special cognitive and affective responses.* Unpublished Master's dissertation, Allahabad University, Allahabad.

Anandalakshmy, S. (1982). There is a method to the measurement. In D. Sinha, R.C. Tripathi, & G. Misra (Eds.), *Deprivation : Its social roots and psychological consequences.* New Delhi : Concept.

Bhogle, S. (1971). Role conflicts in teachers. *Indian Journal of Psychology, 46*, 399-404.

Chatterjee, B.B. (1977) Pattern of school achievement in primary grades. *Indian Educational Review, 12*, 29-67.

Chattopadhyay, S. (1963). *A study of some psychological correlates of adoption of innovation in farming.* Unpublished doctoral dissertation, Indian Agricultural Research Institute, New Delhi.

Chole, R.R. & Radhukar, W.B. (1978). Source of credibility pattern among small and big farmers. *Indian Journal of Extension Education. 14*, 50-53.

Clinard, M.B. (1970). The role of motivation and self-image in social change in slum areas, In V.L. Allen (Ed.) *Psychological Factors in Poverty.* New York: Academic Press.

Das, J.P. & Singh, P.S. (1975). Caste, class and cognitive competence. *Indian Educational Review, 10*, 1-18.

Dave, C. & Sadashivaiah, K. (1981). Family size and quality of life. *Social Change, 11*, 35-44.

Dhaliwal, A.J.S. (1971). *An analysis of correlates in predicting the adoption behaviour of cultivators in model village of Ludhiana block.* Doctoral dissertation, Punjab Agriculture University, Ludhiana.

Dube, S.C. (1955) *Indian village.* London: Routledge & Kegan Paul.

Engineer, A.A. (1984). An analytical study of Meerut riot (pp. 271-280). The causes of communal riots in the postpartition period in India (pp. 33-41). In A.A. Engineer (Ed.). *Communal riots in post-independence India.* Hyderabad: Sangam Books.

Gandhi K.A. (1981) Organizational climate of schools and work alienation: A comparative analysis. *Journal of Educational Research and Extension 18*, 22-30.

Gunthey, R.K. (1981). Socio-cultural deprivation and adaptive behaviour. *Child Psychiatry Quarterly, 14*, 35-37.

Jain, U. (1983). *Effects of population density on human social behaviour and coping in dense environment, Project Report.* New Delhi: Indian Council of Social Science Research.

Jha, H. (1983). *Colonial legacy and higher education in Bihar.*

Patna: Sulabh Institute of Applied Research.

Kamal, P. & Jain, U. (1984). Effects of population density on mental health. Paper presented at the Indian Psychiatric Conference, Udaipur, Rajasthan.

Katiyar, R. (1976) Determinants of values in the small family norm. *Journal of Family Welfare, 22,* 62-68.

Kanungo, R.N; & Mendonca, M. (Eds.) (1994). *Work motivation models for developing countries,* New Delhi: Sage Publications.

Khan, M.E. & Prasad, C.V.S. (1980). *Fertility control in India: A critical evaluation of the role of incentives in promoting sterilization among industrial workers.* New Delhi: Manohar Publications.

Lal, R.; Singh, S.K. & Sharma R. (1982). A psychological study of privileged and underprivileged farmers with respect to value orientation, economic motivation and risk preference. *Research in Psychology, 1,* 53-62.

Lokhande, M.R., & Singh, S.N. (1977). Leadership patterns and social change. *Social Change, 7,* 14-19.

Majeed, A., & Ghosh, E.S.K. (1981). Ingroup and outgroup evaluation in intergroup context. *Psychological Studies, 26,* 34-40.

McClelland, D.C. (1961). *The achieving society.* New Jersey: Van Nostrand.

Misra, G. (1982). Deprivation and cognitive competence. In D. Sinha, R.C. Tripathi & G. Misra (Eds.) *Deprivation : Its social roots and psychological consequences,* New Delhi: Concept.

Misra, G. (Ed.) (1990). *Applied social psychology in India.* New Delhi: Sage Publications.

Moulik, T.K. (1965). *A study of predictive values of some factors of adoption of nitrogenous fertilizers and the influence of sources of information on adoption behaviour.* Unpublished doctoral dissertation. Indian Agricultural Research Institute, New Delhi.

Muthayya, B.C. (1982). The rural disadvantaged: A psychological study in Punjab and Madhya Pradesh. *Journal of Rural development. 1,* 143-260.

Myrdal, G. (1968). *Asian drama: An enquiry into the poverty of Nations.* Vol. I New York: Penguin Books.

Nagar, D., & Pandey, J. (1987). Affect and performance on cognitive task as a function of crowding and noise. *Journal of Applied Social Psychology, 17,* 147-157.

Naqvi, K.A. (1982). *Problems, strategies and conditions for implementing endogenous development in the context of Asian countries and in particular in India.* Paris: Unesco,

55-82/WS/74.

Naqvi, N. (1982). Relative deprivation and attribution of blame in communal riots. Doctoral dissertation, Allahabad University, Allahabad.

Panda, K.C., & Dash, P.C. (1980). Effect of simulated information on assessment of cognitive competency: A test of expectancy hypothesis. *Indian Educational Review, 13,* 22-35.

Pandey, J. (Ed. 1988). *Psychology in India: The state-of-the-Art Vol. II,* New Delhi: Sage Publications.

Pande, N; & Tripathi, R.C. (1982). Secheduled caste children in high caste schools. In D. Sinha, R.C. Tripathi, & G. Misra (Eds) *Deprivation: Its Social Roots and Psychological Consequences.* New Delhi: Concept.

Pandey, J. & Singh, A:K. (1985). Social psychology responses to perceived and objective indicators of poverty in India. In R.I. Langunes, & Y.H. Poortings (Eds) *From a different perspective: Studies of behaviour across cultures,* Lisse: Swets and Zeitlinger, B.V.

Pareek, U. (1968). The motivational paradigm of development. *Journal of Social Issues, 24,* 115-124.

Pareek, U. (1970). Poverty motivation: Figure and ground. In V.L. Allen (Ed.), *Psychological factors in poverty,* New York: Academic Press.

Patil, B.R., & Mukhopadhyaya, R. (1983). Folk-media and development. *Social Change, 13,* 3-8.

Pillai, K. (1973). *Organizational climate, teacher morale and school quality.* Doctoral dissertation, M.S. University, Baroda.

Rao, I. (1976). Education of disadvantaged children. *Indian Educational Review, 11,* 8-12.

Rath, R. (1976). Problems of equalization of opportunities for tribal children. *Indian Educational Review, 11,* 56-63.

Rath, R. (1982). Problems of integration of disadvantaged to the mainstream. In D. Sinha R.C. Tripathi & G. Misra (Eds.), *Deprivation: Its social, roots and psychological consequences.* New Delhi: Concept.

Rath, R., Dash, A.S., Dash U.N. (1979). *Cognitive abilities and social achievement of the socially disadvantaged children in primary schools.* Bombay: Allied Publishers.

Reddy, M.S.K. (1965). *A study of leadership patterns and role in the adoption of improved farm practices.* Doctoral dissertation. Indian Agricultural Research Institute, New Delhi.

Rehman, A. (1987). Participatory rural development and its implications for rural employment generation. In *Programme on Participatory Organizations of Rural Poor.* Geneva: ILO.

Ross, A.D. (1961). *The Hindu family in its urban setting.* Toronto: University of Toronto Press.

Safaya, R.N. (1976). Stagnation and wastage. *Educational Review, 11*, 217-220.

Sandell, J. (1976). Sex education and the national family planning programme. *Journal of Family Welfare, 22*, 62-65.

Saxena, N.C. (1984). The nature and origin of communal riots in India. In A.A. Engineer (Ed.) *Communal riots in post-independence India.* Hyderabad: Sangam books.

Sharma, M., & Quraishi, Z.M. (1973). Teacher moral and organizational climate. An exploratory study. *Progress of Education, 67*, 263-266.

Sherif, M. & Sherif, C. (1953). *Groups in harmony and tension.* New York: Harper.

Singh, A.K. (1980b). Parental support and acadmic achievement. *Social Change, 13*, 9-14.

Sinha, D. (1969). *Indian villages in transition: A motivational analysis.* New Delhi: Allied.

Sinha D., & Shukla, P. (1974). Deprivation and development of skill for pictorial depth perception. *Journal of Cross-Cultural Psychology, 5*, 233-246.

Sinha, D. (1977). Some social disadvantages and development of certain perceptual skills. *Indian Journal of Psychology, 52*, 115-132.

Sinha, D. (1986) *Pshchology in a third world country : The Indian experience.* New Delhi : Sage Publications.

Sinha, J.B.P., (1984) Towards partnership for relevant research in the Third World. *International Journal of Psychology, 19*, 169-78.

Somasundaram, D., & Singh, S.N. (1978) Factors affecting the knowledge of adopter and nonadopter small farmers. *Indian Journal of Extension Education, 14*, 30-34.

Subramanyam, S. (1979) Home environment and reading achievement in primary school children. *Experiments in Education*, 7, 39-42.

Supe, S.V. (1969) *Factors related to different degree of rationality in decision making among farmers*, Doctoral dissertation, Indian Agricultural Research Institute, New Delhi.

Triandis, H.C. (1971) *Some Psychological Dimensions of Modernisation.* Proceedings of the 17th International Congress of Applied Psychology, Bruxelles, vol. 2 (12), 57-65.

Tripathi, R.C., & Srivastava, R. (1980) Relative deprivation and intergroup attitudes, *European Journal of Social Psychology*, 2, 313-318.

Tripathi, S.K. (1986) *Effect of crowding on human behaviour*, Unpublished doctoral dissertation, Kashi Vidyapeeth, Varanasi.

Ushasree, S. (1980), Social disadvantage, academic adjustment, and scholastic achievement. *Social changes, 10*, 23-30.

4

Y2K Around the Corner : The O and B of OB for Survival and Growth

Arvind K. Sinha and **Sumita Rai**

A lot of hope, a lot more possibilities, but relatively less of expectations. This is how the general prospect of organization's and behavioural aspects within them seem to be. At least to the behavioural scientist who has been watching the development with keen eyes. The Y2K (an abbreviated form of the year 2000) is around the corner and with the advent of it, it is only natural that we take a stock of what to expect.

The Workplace

An increasing number of role incumbents reportedly see themselves as overworked, underpaid, and being unfairly treated by their employers. Deceptive slogans such as "challenging work" and "simple form, lean staff" are being floated in the name of organizational redesign. However, in reality, quite often all that a challenging work means is sweating one's own blood out trying to achieve impossible targets, or selling something that nobody wants to buy, or working longer hours for less pay. Similarly, the "simple form, lean staff' (a slogan championed by Peters and Waterman Jr., 1982, p. 15, pp. 306-317) has simply come to mean that the job security that the role of incumbents enjoyed only about 10 to 15 years ago has become a distant dream. The organizations that used to take great pride in their big happy family of workers are manned by workers who exist under a constant threat of being laid off, which again would be given a fancy label of "golden hand shake". Even the much cited IBM has discarded its "no-layoff" policy that was so dear to them until late 1980's and has laid off hundreds of thousands of its employees. Most major corporations have been forced to institute such layoffs in the hope of cutting costs and improving productivity. Those who survive are asked to work longer hours with either less pay or with the same old pay which today would have much less actual purchasing power. This is done in the name of improving competitiveness. Besides, the laid off workers are increasingly replaced by part time employees because of the flexibility and cost effectiveness that it lends to the employers. Such practices have serious repercussions for employee loyalty or commitment. Just as the employers are sending a message meaning that employees are expendable, employees also seem to be responding with a rather high turnover, Large layoffs, increased pressures for high productivity, and frequent replacement of permanent workers with temporary ones has helped create a new workplace climate which is highly threatening to people. Survey research data (as reported in "American workers trying to survive in the '90s," *Nightline*, September 6, 1993) shows that the factors that employees feel most important to them are better work environment, flexible jobs, and understanding bosses. Similar concerns have been observed in India as well (e.g., Mohanty and Mangaraj, 1994). However, these are precisely the factors that most organizations undermine while trying to increase productivity. Perhaps this simply means that we have made little progress in terms of the relevant behaviour in organization since the good (or may be bad) old days of Frederick W. Taylor and Elton Mayo.

The National Scene

The permeability of international boundaries has been a major focus of attention during the past few years. This means that the global events have more impact now on the national events and issues. Closer we come to our national boundary, greater the probable impact. In other words, the events of Asian countries may have more impact on Indian scenario compared to that of European or American. That apart, the events that have taken place in India, either on its own or in response to the external events, themselves deserve attention.

During the past 10 years or so, the political world has changed beyond all recognition, and the changes on the economic and social front have been as great. India exerts a kind of magnetic attraction for investment by companies from around the world. The source of this magnetism lies in India's huge upwardly mobile population consisting of a proportionately big consumer market which has so far remained relatively non-open to the approach of foreign multi-national corporations (MNCs) due mainly to socio-political, and in past, also economic considerations. Although India's economy is not on par with the economies of the advanced countries, in macro economic terms it is gradually becoming more affluent. if the trend continues, the time may not be very far away in future when the mass consumption will take off in Indian society. Another motive with which MNCs approach India is to grab a profit from the short term advantages of low labour costs and cheap land. All the same, even if their aim is only to earn profit over the short term, they do create employment opportunities within India, so that income of people rise. However, history tells us that local economic development brings with it a gradual loss of these cost advantages; and the foreign MNCs of other countries may soon start looking for even more cost-effective soils. Besides, it may not be out of place to mention here that some American companies that once took their production to low-wage countries are now shifting it back to the US, primarily because cheap labour ultimately remains that; cheap! It is difficult to get the kind of professional attitude, commitment, and performance from a cheap labour as one would expect and actually get from an "expensive" labour of the western countries. There may be a danger that the economic development of India may not be sustained if it must depend on the production for export of secondary manufacturers. We also cannot afford concentrating all the business potential in a selected few "viable" states for ever, simply because some other states are not business conducive at the moment due to socio-political reasons. In other words, expansion of the production base is an important requirement. However, this alone may not be enough, in coming days, maintenance and growth of infrastructure would be an important requirement. Infrastructures could be conceived as of two types. The tangible infrastructure that has already received inputs from business based industrialised countries in terms of capital investments in factories, telecommunication networks etc. The second type of infrastructure is less visible and may consist in such elements as the financial networks and distribution systems.

Distribution systems are best designed and operated by the natives of a country and the MNCs of the other nation should refrain from meddling in the distribution affairs of India. Concentration of commodities only in certain areas ought to be guarded against. Systems need to be devised, made operational, and maintained through which people across the country have the freedom of choice of goods, purchase timing, and the quantum of purchase according to their needs at affordable prices. Social scientists concerned with development talk of investment-led development, export-led development, and also distribution-led development. In a distribution-led development system, they say, the economic dynamics are created in the domestic market; and unlike the other two, it not only develops business, it develops people.

Incidentally, this has been the thrust of non-economist behavioural scientist's concern as well. That is, to concentrate upon development of people. In other words, there are behavioural scientists particularly the psychologists who would like to make a claim that people, not money, develop the economy. A case in point is the role of the World Bank which was founded about fifty years ago on the investment-led theory of development. It has not been able to prove out the theory in past half century primarily because the investment of the World Bank did not produce the human resources. World Bank investments were mostly made in big manufacturing facilities such as steel plants. These plants produced steel and jobs but failed to produce human competence. Production and jobs do not necessarily impart human beings the ability to adapt their competence to newer settings. It is argued that a distribution-led development system creates thousands of small businesses, creates human resources, and competence (Drucker, 1997, pp. 22-23). Perhaps an ideal combination would be that of a distribution led development system, a reliable and predictable legal system, and a fairly effective financial system. It is generally believed to be true that production endeavours benefit maximally in a region where technology, resources, costs are favourable and a free-trade environment is available. However, apart from these mainly economic considerations, one would need to focus also upon the considerations that contribute directly to human competence, flexibility of adaptation to newer situations, and innovative capabilities.

The Role of Employers

The large employers have a particular responsibility with regard to contribution toward human potential. Employment stability is one of the foremost considerations that the employers need to address themselves to. Nobody would be interested in his or her competence development under the threat of a "hand shake" even if it is *golden*. The next responsibility of the employers should be to generate and maintain the essential identity of interests between organization and the employees. This would entail evolving a policy to attempt at retraining for specific new job opportunities including perhaps placing redundant employees in newer role position. There may be a lot of sense in the private sector taking an initiative.

In so far as development can be taken as related to human resource development in the main, and history would bear it out, the developing countries have mostly benefited by allowing its organizations to work in close co-operation with the organizations of developed countries. For example, German companies are now being run by those people who first worked for American companies investing in Germany. A large part of Japanese development also came out of the joint ventures with American companies which transferred technology to Japan. Indian organizations can now seek collaborations from Germany, Japan and other developed countries including America and of course Russia and China could also be worthy entries in the list. There is good reason to believe that much of "under development" of countries such as India is not so much a matter of scarcity of resources. It is largely a matter of mismanagement.

Management, particularly at the level of common people's interest, may not be created through a government-to-government aid or by ingesting huge sum of money by agencies such as World Bank or International Monetary Fund (IMF). Rather, it is created by individual organizations through setting up of examples and providing leadership. For the purpose, such organizations attempt to repeat in a developing country what they have successfully tested and done in their own developed countries.

Some of the privately owned organizations have shown the way for globalisation of top management. Example could be Nestle of Switzerland. About half a dozen different nationalities are represented in its top management. The Coca Cola and Citibank are the other examples who have successfully build a trans-national top management in which people of different nationalities with varying background and experiences work together as a team. Such a team is not easy to build. The European subsidiary of the Ford Motor Company of the US has a common top-management team where Americans, Britishers, Germans, Italians, and French do work together. However, it has taken the Ford Motor Company more than twenty years to build this team. It is no easy task. But given the results, it is time and effort well spent; and there is no reason why more and more Indian private organizations should not begin thinking and actually functioning on these lines.

The private enterprises may take the lead also in redesigning the business on the lines of the automobile manufactures such as Ford of US and Toyota, Nissan, and Honda of Japan. These companies have been able to show that success in manufacturing industry can be achieved through converting manual labourers in the factories into sources of knowledge and information; and this can be achieved without pumping in much financial resources.

Given that knowledge, information, and competence of even the lowest common denominator in a work force are the qualities that are likely to make lasting difference, the society at large would have to undertake the responsibility of fostering these in its citizens. Values such as individuality, initiative, creativity, and innovativeness are the ones that seem to hold the key if the outcomes of doing things the Japanese and the American way are any indication. Not that the advantage of innovations and initiatives has gone unnoticed in Indian context, e.g., Gupta (1994). This is not to say that the Indian organizations need to be modelled after those alien culture in totality, but there could not be much harm in imbibing certain functional values and using them with suitable modification and control.

Preparing for the Future

There appears to be at least two ways of visualising the future. There are people who prefer to observe the *status quo*. There are others who would rather reach out. The coming century would prefer the latter even if that means being labelled as extrovert in comparison to being a rationalist, pragmatist, or even humanist. Corporate priorities of today resemble the Victorian notion of progress. Those who subscribe to it seem to describe future in terms of "more and more" of additional and onerous requirements, greater demands from customers, inevitably demanding, in whatever form, ever harder and harder work. Pressure to perform over longish hours of work is regarded as challenging and virtuous and a visible demonstration of commitment. However, there are other scholars who contend that the future orientation needs to be qualitatively different from the present emphasis on "more and more" of this, that, and the other. The need for knowledge development is being emphasised and an agrument is made in favour of things like business intelligence (BI) and perpetual strategies (Tyson, 1997, p. 195). Tyson (1997) holds that BI is a process that involves gathering bits and pieces of information about competitors, customers, suppliers, potential acquisition candidates, joint venture candidates, strategic alliances — virtually every entity and event in the environment external to the organization. This information would also include economic, regulatory, and political happenings that might have an impact on the company. The BI process then takes these bits and pieces of information and transforms them into strategic knowledge — knowledge about historical activities, past performance, strengths and weaknesses, and specific future intentions of others in the relevant competitive environment. Tyson (1997, p. 198) further argues that strategic planning, or strategic management, cannot be a once-a-year activity. It needs to be an ongoing activity, one where senior managers make strategic and tactical decisions daily, weekly, and monthly. This requires continuous input, processing and output that only a systematic BI process can provide. As Tyson (1997, p. 218) puts it, the bottom line is simple; *people*, communications, co-operation, *knowledge* development, knowledge sharing, intelligence, and *perpetual strategy* (italics added).

To sum-up, one could not agree more with Coulson-Thomas (1997, p. 399) that a holistic and people-focused management is the key to survival and growth in the years that would greet us beyond Y2K. Whether those years come to us as greetings or as confrontation is likely to depend upon the management choices we make. More precisely, upon whether we emphasise upon "more and more" or "different and holistic". Perhaps we stand a better chance of being greeted by emphasising upon the latter.

REFERENCES

Coulson-Thomas, C. (1997). *The future of the organization : Achieving excellence through business transformation.* London : Kogan Page.

Drucker, P.F., & Nakauchi (1997). *Drucker on Aisa : A dialogue between Peter Drucker & Isao Nakauchi.* Oxford, Gt. Britain: Butterworth Heinemann.

Gupta, N.K. (1994). Innovations and initiatives : Route to marketing advantages. In N.K. Gupta & A. Ahmad (Eds.), *Managing transition* (pp. 43 - 54). New Delhi: Wiley Eastern Limited, New Age International Publishers.

Mohanty, P.K. & Mangaraj, S. (1994). Organizational culture and values : A study in NALCO. In N.K. Gupta & A. Ahmad (Eds.) *Managing transition* (pp. 29-42). New Delhi : Wiley Eastern Limited, New Age International Publishers.

Peters, T.J., & Waterman Jr., R. H. (1982). *In search of excellence : Lessons from America's best run companies.* New York : Harper and Row Publishers.

Tyson, K.W.M. (1997). *Competition in the 21st century.* Florida, USA : St. Lucie Press.

5

Psychological Well-being and Perceived Quality of Work Life

Sunita Singh-Sengupta

Understanding the nature of QWL has been the preoccupation of many social philosophers and scientists for the last two decades or more. Consequently, one finds a vast amount of theoretical and empirical literature on subject, resulting in a plethora of divergent definitions and dimensions of QWL. Interestingly, despite such theoretical richness, many conceptual ambiguities and measurement inadequacies exist. The QWL literature consists largely of descriptions of techniques and projects, with anecdotal and impressionistic treatment of the accomplishments and results. The popular literature has been largely a theoretical. Academic writings on QWL first appeared in the middle 1970's (Walton, 1974; Davis & Cherns, 1975; Hackman & Suttle, 1977). The literature was concerned with defining the field and with reviewing relevant theory and research. Noticeably absent was empirical research.

From the review of QWL studies it becomes clear that the concept of QWL challenged existing views on the nature of work and led to new questions:

(1) Work need not be viewed as technologically determined. Social systems have to be identified which will lead to optimum benefits for the organisations as well as the person.
(2) Work has far reaching consequences for the individual. It creates feeling of self-worth and identity, therefore, meaningless work can lead to alienation

and poor individual health causing workplace problems.

(3) The important theme of QWL is more control for working people over their work lives leading to fulfilment of psychological needs.

Although a number of QWL studies are reported, there is still lack of adequate theoretical formulations on QWL issues. It is observed that :

> "In many cases, theory is sketchy or nonexistent. Particularly necessary is good descriptive research on the various quality of work life approaches. Because of the lack of research, it is difficult to reach conclusions about what works, where things work and what needs to be changed. The lack of theory hinders the understanding of why things happen as they do. What is needed is field research and theory building which captures the realities of what is happening in the workplace. It is no longer a matter of theorizing about the possible effects of various new management practices..... The need is for research that evaluates them and guides their development" (Mohrman & Lawler, 1984, p. 232).

Relevance of QWL in the Indian Context

Quite often the relevance of concepts like QWL to solve problems in underdeveloped countries is questioned and debated. In this section, ideas and opinions expressed by different writers and experts, on this issue are presented.

> "To many a mind concern for improving Quality of Working Life (QWL) in Indian context can at best be marginal, if not irrelevant ....any attempt at improving QWL will touch a mere fringe of the population... Although job creation is a very important issue in our country, the issue of improving QWL for those already employed cannot be ignored.... Increasing dissatisfaction among workers against jobs that are

tedious, monotonous and with apparent lack of responsibility, the evident strains of fast changing technology on individuals and society, and a realization that providing for people's control over jobs is a part of social responsibility of the government: have made concern for improving QWL, a reality in India... Further, perhaps it is more relevant in our context, as is our present level of development, we are in a position to learn from the mistakes of those ahead of us and avoid some of the pitfalls which became inevitable in the process of industrialization in more advanced societies" (Singh, 1982; pp. 13-14).

"Focus on the quality of work life and the development of human resources as an end in itself, are some of the emerging concepts in the context of Indian business organizations" (Pandey, 1991; p. 450).

Bharadwaj (1983) reviewing developments in the field of QWL comes to the conclusion that it is a valid concept in the Indian context. He is eloquent in urging the adoption of QWL principles to the Indian situation : "The QWL movement offers India a value-frame and a social technology of organizational change leading to task-effectiveness of micro entities through utilization and unfolding of the human potential" (p. 26).

Trist (1975) made an eloquent plea for the importance of QWL in a developing country. He observed : "In a developing country the quality of working life can become both ends and means. It is an end in itself because it is highly significant component in the quality of life — the goal of all development. It is a means because the experiences of participation in decision making at the work place and of progressive learning help workers acquire the civic competencies and skills on which a country developing in the social democratic mode just rely" (Trist, 1975, p. 78).

"It would be tragic if in industrializing the less developed countries adopt the authoritarian management styles from which the advanced countries are beginning to break .... Their best strategy would be to "century skip" — to ignore nineteenth-century models of industrial organization and the dehumanizing values embodied in them — and experiment in ways suitable to the conditions of the Third World, with new forms of organization that gives first importance to the quality of life in the workplace" (Trist, 1975, p. 79).

He has outlined a strategy for Peru to make use of local traditional skills. While referring to the list of desirable components of QWL provided by Thorsrud (1972), Sinha (1977) observed that : "The list concerns with in fact what Cherns (1974) calls metavalues ...... Although we cannot reasonably argue against the components, they sound like a distant music — attractive yet a bit out of reach and a bit out of tune with the noises or realities which engulf the system right now. The realities ..... demand a different order of priority and .... cast some doubts on the authenticity of these meta-values" (pp. 238-239).

Sinha (1977) spells out some needs in the Indian context : (i) economic survival, and (ii) beyond survival the task of reducing enormous economic disparity between the highest and lowest paid workers. Rao (1986) observed that :

"The concept of QWL is of relevance and use in the Indian context. While some of the meanings derived from QWL may be culture specific, the basic technological determinism of job fragmentation and bureaucratic organisation pose similar problems to us as those facing the west. In a country where poverty stalls more than fifty per cent of the population, economic incentives play a very significant role in determining the QWL. However, Indian managers and workers have shown a need for social achievement and improving their QWL. There are individual social-psychological needs which must be taken into account. Finally, the public sector organisations appear to be the most fertile ground to study and experiment with" (p. 71) .....the concept of QWL is of importance to India" (Rao, 1986, p. 59).

In a recent national conference on QWL organised by

National Productivity Council, the significance and relevance of QWL in the Indian context was emphasised and highlighted by many participants. The conference papers and proceedings are documented (Suri *et al.*, 1991).

"There can be hardly any argument over the legitimacy of one's concern with the quality of working life" (Sinha: 1977, p. 235).

QWL Studies in India

Work in India under the heading of QWL has been initiated in many quarters, but a major movement is not discernible as yet. At the present stage, the work in the Indian organisations appears to be largely: (a) Theoretical - descriptive, concerned with what QWL is or how it should be measured, or (b) In the form of action research to bring about changes in the design of work system in an organisation. Moreover, the concept of QWL has been examined in parts with emphasis on one aspect or the other as seen in measures developed by Joseph (1978) and Sinha and Sayeed (1980). However, few empirical studies have been reported from India, which tried to relate QWL to different variables.

In India, many initiatives to reorganise work have been undertaken by researchers, spontaneous experimentation at work sites without outside help, and through the help of agencies like ILO. The first known study of a redesigned work system is A.K. Rice's effort at Ahmedabad (Rice, 1958). A follow-up study carried out in 1970 by Miller (1975), showed that change could not be sustained. Several QWL experiments have been conducted by Nitish De and his associates at National Labour Institute (NLI). The status and results of these action research programmes are described and documented (De, 1984). An important point to notice is that all the QWL experiments reported in India, except a few (e.g. Rice, 1958), have occurred in public sector organisations, be it in industry, banking, life insurance, or the post offices.

Against this backdrop this study examined how the perceived quality of work life affects the employees' sense of psychological wellbeing.

The globalisation of economy and the deregulation of industries seem to have far reaching implications for Indian industries and even for the multi-nationals who are getting business from India. The signs are already being noticed. The pharmaceutical organizations are facing hard times as the competition has become intense and difficult. In such a tough time it becomes essential that the field force should experience the quality of their work life to be good otherwise their sale is going to suffer. The present study is designed to examine the quality of work life as perceived by the first-line managers and the medical representatives in a wide range of pharmaceutical organizations in this changed economic environment.

METHOD

Measures

Two separate questionnaires were developed. One was used for the first-line managers and the other for the medical representatives. Before designing the research, in-depth interviews of unstructured nature were conducted to understand the variables and the way they are likely to manifest. As there has been very few studies on pharmaceutical organizations the author had to develop all the measures. The total range of factors examined under Perceived Quality of Work Life can be put into two categories for convenience: (a) Organization based factors, and (b) Person based factors. The present study examined two broad categories of variables : (a) Perceived quality of work life and (b) Psychological well-being.

Organization Based Factors

The perceived quality of work life seemed to be the product of organizational as well as personal factors related to work, work environment and one's commitment and involvement in work.

1. *Work Context* : The work context was operationalized through different sets of variables:

(a) *Organizational Climate Scale.* The scale used by Singh-Sengupta (1990) was adopted for the present study. There were four climatic factors :

(i) *Superior-Subordinate Relationship* was operationalised as a kind of positive relationship in which a superior expects that his subordinate will work hard and the subordinate willingly comply with their superior's directions.

(ii) *Work Pressure* described the pressure of work experienced by the first-line managers and the medical representatives.

(iii) *Work Norms* meant shared expectation of work in the organization. It referred to the employees' hard work.

(iv) *Reinforcement* pertained to the perception of the employees that hard and sincere work are rewarded in the organization.

(b) *Union Strength.* An attempt was made to study the strength of medical representatives' union. Therefore, an item was used for both the categories of respondents for the purpose:

How strong is the workers' union? The response was obtained on a 4-point scale ranging from

(a) very strong, (b) strong, (c) weak, (d) quite weak.

The scores ranged from 1-4.

(c) *Attitude Towards Management.* The medical representatives were asked to express their views on few items in order to examine their attitude towards management because it is the positive or negative attitude of the workers towards their company and its managerial practices which frame their perception about work and commitment to the organization. An eight item scale was used (Singh-Sengupta, 1996) for the purpose. The respondents were asked to rate the items on a 4-point scale depending on the nature of the item. Hence, the score for each item ranged from 1-4.

2. Work Relations

Work Morale Scale. A 15-item scale was developed by the

author (Singh-Sengupta, 1997a) to examine the level of morale of the medical representatives. The responses were obtained on a two-point scale of Yes/No. The numerical value for Yes was 2 and for No. 1.

3. Work Content

Measure of Working Conditions. The working conditions are more or less same for the medical representatives and the first-line managers except a few. The scale developed by Singh-Sengupta (1995) was used for the purpose. The items were asked related to salary and perks, opportunities for career development, housing facilities, house allowances, leave conditions, working hours and basis of promotion. The range of scores for each item was 1 to 4. The responses were obtained on a 4-point scale with anchor points Quite Often (4), Sometimes (3), Once a while (2), and Rarely (1).

Personal Factors

Measure of Perception of Work. The measure had three similar items for both the level of respondents. The items were:

1. How much you enjoy your work ?
2. How challenging you feel your work is ?
3. How often you feel the nature of work to be routined and monotonous ?

The respondents were provided a continuum against each item with very much (4) and Not at all (1) as two extremes. The range of scores for each item was 1 to 4.

Job Satisfaction Measure. An eight-item scale (Sinha & Singh-Sengupta, 1991) was used as a measure of job satisfaction amongst the employees for both the level of respondents. The parameters of job satisfaction were operationalized through different items. Broadly, the intention was to know, how satisfied the employees were with: (i) nature of work, (ii) conditions of work, (iii) pay and perks, (iv) promotional avenues, (v) recognition in the company, (vi) behaviour of co-workers and colleagues, (vii) rules and regulations, and (viii) styles of management. The responses were obtained on a 4-point scales. The range of the scores was 1-4.

2. Psychological Wellbeing

The experience of psychological wellbeing of the respondents were examined in terms of absence or presence of health related problems and amount of stress and strain experienced by the employees.

(a) *Measure of Health Problems.* A 15-item scale (Singh-Sengupta, 1997a) helped to examine the health related problems in the employees working in different pharmaceutical companies. The respondents were asked to rate the frequency of occurrence for each health problem on a 4-point scale where 4 meant *Absence of the symptom*, 3 meant *Rarely*, 2 meant *Sometimes*, and 1 meant *Frequently*. The scores ranged from 4-1. Higher the score lesser the frequency of occurring the indicated health problems.

(b) *Stress and Strain Scale.* The Job Anxiety Scale developed by A.K. Srivastava and M.M. Sinha (1988) was used to examine the stress and strain of the employees. The scale had seven dimensions: (i) Job security, (ii) Recognition and fair evaluation, (iii) Human relations at work, (iv) Rewards and punishment, (v) Self-esteem and the status of the job, (vi) Future prospects and (vii) Capacity and confidence to shoulder job responsibilities. Altogether there were 80 items. the respondents were asked to make a tick mark when the statement seemed to be applicable and cross when it does not.

The Research Site. The main survey was conducted mostly in the Eastern part of India for a period of two years (1993-1995). The investigator was interested in examining the perceived quality of worklife in pharmaceutical organizations, therefore, a heterogeneous group of pharmaceutical companies comprising of multinationals, Indian houses and public sectors were chosen according to convenience. A brief description of the chosen companies are given in Table 5.1.

TABLE 5.1 : **The Sampled Pharmaceutical Companies**

Name of the company	Nature of the company
Glaxo	Multi-National
Biddle Sawyer	Indian House
Cadila	Indian House
Pfizer	Multi-National
Himalaya	Indian House
Hoechst	Multi-National
Astra-IDL	Indian House
Abbott	Multi-National
East India	Indian House
Elder	Indian House
Parke Davis	Multi-National
Alembic	Indian House
Nicholas	Indian House
Dey's	Indian
Franco-India	Multi-National
Sarabhai	Indian House
German Remedies	Multi-National
Ablert David	Indian House
Aristo	Indian House
Emmerck	Multi-National
Plethico	Indian House
Sandoz	Multi-National
Cipla	Indian House
Leaderle	Multi-National
Raptakos	Indian House
Ciba Geigy	Multi-National
Ranbaxy	Indian House

TABLE 5.1 : *Contd.*

Name of the company	Nature of the company
Roussel	Multi-National
IDPL	Indian Public Sector
Hindustan Antibiotics	Indian Public Sector
Rhone Poulenc	Multi-National
Boots	Multi-National
Burroughs Welcome	Multi-National

Note: Multi-National = 15, Indian House = 16, Indian Public Sectors = 2.

The Focal Groups. The first-line managers and the medical representative served as the focal group for the present study. A total of 50 first-line managers and 111 medical representatives constituted the sample. Thirty-three pharmaceutical companies provided the respondents.

TABLE 5.2 : **Mean and SD Scores of Respondents' Background Information**

Variables	Managers (N = 50)		Workers (N = 111)	
	Mean Scores	SD Scores	Mean Scores	SD Scores
Age	35.18	5.17	31.52	7.28
Education	1.24	0.43	1.16	0.39
Length of Service	11.92	5.80	9.41	6.93
Number of companies worked	2.14	1.23	2.06	1.45
Number of Promotions Received	1.64	0.72	0.37	0.86
Previous Salary	887.90	616.57	913.83	783.39
Present Salary	4610.20	2054.75	2760.95	1316.80

Table 5.2 suggests that the managers were on average 35.18 years old with graduation as the basic qualification. The respondents seemed to have about 12 years of length of service. The managers in general reported to receive

more than one promotion and most of them had the experience of working in more than two companies with Rs. 887.90 p.m. as initial salary and Rs. 4610.20 p.m. as present salary.

Table 5.2 further shows that the medical representatives who constituted the sample were on average 31.52 years old with graduation as the minimum qualification and about nine years and six months of length of service. These group of respondents have not received any promotion, however, they had the experience of working in two or more companies. The respondents reported to start their career with Rs. 913.83 p.m. as initial salary and Rs. 2760.95 p.m. as present salary.

Procedure. Before starting the main study the Zonal/ Regional Managers were contacted on telephone to seek an appointment. The address and phone numbers of the different companies were obtained from Sales Executives Association (SEA).

RESULTS

Perceived Quality of Worklife

Organizational Climate. The scale had four dimensions : Superior - subordinate relationship, pressure of work, organizational norm and reinforcement.

TABLE 5.3 : **Employees' Perception of Organizational Climate**

	Managers		Workers	
Variables	Mean	SD	Mean	SD
Superior-Subordinate Relationship	12.76	1.80	11.89	1.65
Pressure of Work	9.72	1.87	10.23	1.73
Organizational Norms	12.94	1.60	12.02	1.87
Reinforcement	13.00	1.82	11.02	2.59

Table 5.3 shows that the managers perceived their company to have appropriate pattern of reinforcement,

organizational norm of hard work, and good superior-subordinate relationship. As compared to these three dimensions pressure of work scored low which suggested that the managers did not perceive pressure of work to be much.

Table 5.3 further indicates that the workers perceived organizational norm of hard work to be more dominant. To add the findings presented good superior-subordinate relationship and appropriate pattern of reinforcement with sufficient amount of pressure of work.

Attitude Towards Management. The findings are reported in Table 5.4.

TABLE 5.4 : **Workers' Attitude Towards Management**

Variables	Mean	SD
Company as an employer	3.08	0.56
Managerial styles	2.70	0.64
Grievances handled	2.17	0.94
Promotion prospects	2.81	0.69
Basis of promotion	2.37	0.78
Rivalry for promotion	2.66	0.94
Whom to complain at first instances	2.37	0.99
Seriousness of employees complaint taken by the management	2.61	0.89

Table 5.4 hints that the respondents considered their company to be a good employer and seemed to view the managerial style of their company as good. The opinions of the workers on the issue, i.e. *Complaint about some of the grievances to the management* differed. The obtained frequency of responses suggest that 27 percent of the respondents believed it to be worthwhile whereas 41.4 percent reported it to be a worth try. 20.7 percent of the respondents held the view that it would not make any difference and 10.8 percent reported it to be a futile attempt. The quoted mean score in Table 5.4 (X = 2.17), too, support the findings.

The results further disclose that the respondents felt

good promotional prospects in the companies which seemed to have some amount of rivalry. As far as basis of promotion is concerned the obtained frequency of responses suggests that 60.4 percent of the respondents held merit or ability to be the criteria for promotion. About 24 percent of the respondents believed that favouritism decided the promotion of the employees. The reported mean score (X = 2.37) goes with the same line of findings.

To add, when the workers wanted to complain about some aspect of their job then on average they went to managers (X = 2.34). The frequency of responses suggest that 57.7 percent of the respondents said it to be manager. The next choice came for the coworkers which was reported by 22.5 percent of the respondents. Only 15.3 percent of them said to report it to the union office bearer and 4.5 percent said to report it to the union activist.

The extent to which employees· complaints are taken up by management helps in shaping the attitude of the employees towards management. The obtained mean score (X = 2.61) do not indicate a positive trend. The frequency of responses indicated that 39.6 percent of the respondents report that the management took somewhat seriously and 33.3 percent reported that the management took employees' complaints not seriously.

Working Conditions. The quality of working conditions were examined at five points, namely, salary and perks, opportunities for career development, housing facilities, house allowances and leave conditions. It was found that the conditions under which the both, i.e., managers and workers, worked seemed to be very much different except the leave conditions in which the managers reported that the workers enjoyed better leave conditions (X = 3.04) as compared to managers (X = 2.98). The findings overall indicated that the working conditions of the managers were perceived to be better as compared to the workers by both the levels of respondents (as all the differential scores were positive).

Correlational Analysis of the Working Conditions and the Organizational Climate

TABLE 5.5 : **Coefficients of Correlations between the Working Conditions and Organizational Climate as perceived by the Employees**

Working Conditions	Organizational climate			
	SN	PN	NN	RN
Salary and perks				
a. Managers	-14	16	-01	10
b. Workers	02	17	13	24*
Career Development				
a. Managers	-04	12	12	12
b. Workers	16	25*	23*	39**
Housing facilities				
a. Managers	-01	15	18	09
b. Workers	01	23*	23*	16
House Allowances				
a. Managers	16	06	01	06
b. Workers	-04	23*	17	22
Leave Conditions				
a. Managers	-03	03	01	13
b. Workers	-03	-06	02	19
Promotions				
a. Managers	13	-17	-11	-30**
b. Workers	12	-10	-12	-33**

Note : * $p < .01$; ** $p < .001$ level. SN = Superior-Subordinate Relationship,

PN = Pressure of Work, RN = Reinforcement, NN = Organizational Norms. Correlation values are in decimals.

Table 5.5 suggests that when the workers perceive their salary and perks to be adequate then they reported the reinforcement pattern of their organization to be good. The results further says that when the workers perceive adequate opportunities for career development then they seemed to be positive about the organizational norm of hard work. The respondents perceived the reinforcement system to be favourable and held positive attitude towards the pressure of work. The table further highlights that the workers seemed to have positive attitude towards pressure of work when they reported their housing facilities and house allowance to be adequate. The perception of adequate housing facilities by the workers resulted in positive attitude towards the organizational norm of hard work. Table 5.3 further suggests the trend that when the workers availed inadequate leave conditions they reported strained superior-subordinate relationship and somewhat negative attitude towards the pressure of work (though the coefficient of correlations were not significant but the tendency was clear). When the basis of promotion seemed to be favouritism or personal connections both the managers and the workers reported to hold unfavourable attitude towards the reinforcement system. Similar attitude were noticed with respect to organizational norm and pressure of work. Superior-subordinate relationship seemed not to be affected by this.

Strength of Union

It was observed that the workers rated the strength of union to be high ($X = 3.23$) as compared to the managers ($X = 2.94$). To add, the reported frequency of responses indicated that 74 percent of the managers reported the union to be strong against 53.2 percent of the workers rating of union as strong. 16.2 percent of the workers were of opinion that the union is very strong against 12 percent of the responses obtained by the managers on the same alternative. Surprisingly, 10 percent of the managers accepted union to be weak whereas it was accepted by 27.9 percent of the workers.

Workers' Morale. The obtained responses were put to factor analysis. Five factors emerged out of the related factor matrix. The factors were : (a) Workers' affability, (b) Workers' mutability, (c) Expectation Realization,

(d) Cajole and (e) Cynicism. Out of these five factors, the first two factors had positive direction and the latter three negative. The obtained mean scores are entered in Table 5.6.

TABLE 5.6 : **Mean and SD Scores of Employees' Morale**

Factors	Mean Scores	SD Scores
Employees' Affability	9.22	1.98
Employees' Mutability	4.76	1.21
Expectation Realization	4.22	0.79
Cajole	4.62	0.89
Cynicism	4.42	0.83

Note : The factor names were suggested by the author.

Workers Affability (Eigen value = 3.73, Pct. of variance = 24.9) is related with team spirit and comprises items like, *The immediate superior realizes the problem regarding sale. The superior is a better leader. Workers mutability* (Eigen value = 1.95, Pct. of variance = 13.0) denotes the flexibility of the workers' mind to change the organization. *Expectation Realization* (Eigen value = 1.60, Pct. of variance = 10.7) is related with the workers' assessment of realization of what he expected from the job in terms of comforts, mental peace, satisfaction etc. The fourth factor is *Cajole* (Eigen value = 1.11, Pct. of variance = 7.4) which is related to the workers' gentle persuasion to other members to join the profession. It constitutes of items like, *Advice close friends and relatives to join the sales profession, Working hours are longer than what it should be. Cynicism* (Eigen value = 1.03, Pct. of variance = 6.9) is the last factor.

Table 5.6 suggests that since pharmaceutical organizations are target oriented, therefore, some amount of cooperation and support seem to exist (X = 9.22). On rest of the factors the reported mean scores were quite low.

Perception of work. How do the managers and workers perceive their work?

It was found that 62 percent of the respondents reported to *enjoy their work* very much. Only 36 percent were of opinion that they liked their work as so-so. Almost negligible (almost 2 percent) number of respondents were of opinion that they enjoyed their work little. 82 percent of the respondents considered their work to be very much *challenging.* Only 14 percent reported it to be as so-so and 4 percent of the managers rated their work to be little challenging. On responding to the item, *How often do you feel that the nature of task that you have to do is routined and monotonous,* 34 percent of the respondents were of opinion Quite Often. 30 percent reported it to be sometimes. Interestingly, 26 percent of the respondents rated it as rarely.

In case of workers 44.1 percent of the respondents reported to *enjoy their work* very much and 41.4 percent seemed to enjoy it moderately. The level of enjoyment with respect to their work as enjoyed by workers seemed to be different from those reported by the managers. A 3.6 percent of respondents frankly expressed their opinion of not at all enjoying their work. Responding to the item, *How challenging the work is,* 3.6 percent of the respondents rated it as not at all challenging. 4.5 percent of the respondents seemed to enjoy their work very little. 63.1 percent of the respondents were found to *enjoy their work* very much. A good number of respondents (28 percent) indicated their work to be moderately challenging.

Job Satisfaction. Table 5.7 contain the findings.

The reported mean score in Table 5.7 suggests that the managers seemed to be satisfied with the nature of the work most and with their pay and perks least. The workers reported to be satisfied with their co-workers and colleagues to a greater extent. They seemed not to be dissatisfied with the nature of work but with the conditions of work and pay and perks.

Psychological Wellbeing

Health. The findings indicated that the first-line managers in different pharmaceutical organizations seemed to

TABLE 5.7 : **Mean and SD Scores of the Employees' Job Satisfaction**

Dimensions	Managers		Workers	
	Mean Scores	SD	Mean Scores	SD
Nature of work	3.42(1)	0.61	2.79(2)	0.84
Conditions of work	2.76(5.5)	0.82	2.33(7)	0.81
Pay and perks	2.48(8)	0.79	2.27(8)	0.91
Promotional Avenues	2.56(7)	0.76	2.34(6)	0.91
Recognition	3.14(3)	0.61	2.76(3)	0.81
Co-operation in Company	3.18(2)	0.59	2.92(1)	0.71
Rules and Regulations	2.80(4)	0.86	2.56(4)	0.80
Styles of Management	2.76(5.5)	0.80	2.39(5)	83

experience exhaustion and fatigue, they reported not rising early. Further, the workers were found to get exhausted and fatigued leading to decreased level of energy. The pressure of work and meeting the target caused nervousness in them which kept them awake even during night and therefore they were found to have poor appetite but increased smoking habit.

Stress and Strain. The obtained findings suggested that the quality of human relations at work place made the managers stressful to a great extent (X = 23.76). The reward system, as compared to the punishment in the organization generated a good amount of stress (X = 8.46 and 5.82 respectively) amongst them (the managers). To add, a majority of the workers reported to have low self-esteem (X = 12.10) while working in the company. The feeling may be because of the perceived status of the job in the society (X = 10.13). The workers seemed to be much worried about the insecure nature of job (X = 19.65). As a result they were found to lack confidence to shoulder the job responsibilities (X = 10.04). The respondents (workers) showed their anxiety over recognition and fair evaluation in the company (X = 8.41). They hardly seemed to be anxious about the future prospects in the company (X = 5.49).

Conclusions

The present study is an humble effort to investigate how the employees' perception about the quality of worklife affect their sense of psychological wellbeing. The experience of psychological wellbeing is very important because it generates the feeling of togetherness which is likely to enhance group cohesiveness and spirit for high performance. As Singh-Sengupta (1997b) reports "... Indian executives attach greater importance for work, job security, happiness at work, success at work and good human relations at workplace, being independent in one's activities and comfortable working conditions" (p. 28).

The results suggested a marked difference in the perception of managers and workers. The relationship between the two influences the perceived quality of worklife. Evidences (Singh-Sengupta, 1990, 1993, 1994, 1995) have shown that the managers and workers perceive each other to be outgroup members and treat them as others. This perception is clearly manifested in their behaviour and seems to be one of the major reasons behind joining unions.

The world view of managers. The managers were found to enjoy their work when they perceived their work to be challenging. Good human relations at the workplace seemed to be created by organizational norm of hard work with sufficient pressure of work followed by appropriate reinforcement system. The quality of worklife was perceived by the managers to be favourable in terms of nature of work, conditions of work, pay and perks, promotional avenues, recognition, styles of management etc. The young managers seemed to be satisfied with their job but they showed dissatisfaction with respect to rules and regulations of their company. When there is a strong supportive culture in the organization the quality of work life is likely to be high. Its absence may make the managers feel insecure which can quickly lower their self-esteem and hence causing lots of stress and strain which is neither good for the individual nor for the organization. It gradually contributes to employee alienation and organizational ineffectiveness.

The world view of workers. The way the workers perceive their organizational climate and working conditions affect their perception of quality of work life. When the employees have the pleasure of working in a supportive environment they tended to make gentle persuasion to their friends and relatives to join the profession. On the contrary, if the perception is negative then it leads to increased dissatisfaction as the work fail to make the workers realize their expectations. Consequently, cynicism develops and the result is involvement in non-work activities.

The more employees feel committed to the organization and identify themselves with it the greater is the chances of the experience of psychological wellbeing which may cut down most of their non-work activities. It is obvious from our observations that when the employees fail to feel that this is their organization, they start feeling uncomfortable at the work place but start enjoying their leisure time which quite naturally increases their non-work activities. Thus, when the immediate environment helps in realization of psychological wellbeing it is likely to enrich organizational health.

The positive efforts for organizational well being demands that the employees should have lesser degree of stress and strain without much health related problems. To improve the quality of work life the "quality experts" are pushing companies to make basic changes in recruiting, training, performance appraisals and merit-pay systems.

REFERENCES

Bharadwaj, S.B.L. (1983). *Quality of Working Life : Perspectives, Dreams and Realities.* Hyderabad : National Symposium on Quality of Working Life, July 25-26, Mimeographed.

Cherns, A.B. (1974). *Traditional values and modern organizations in developing countries in the perspective of technology.* Paper presented at the symposium on Traditional Values and Modern Organizations, International Association of Applied Psychology, 1974, Montreal.

Davis, L.E. and Cherns, A.B. (1975). *Quality of working life* (eds.). New York : The Free Press.

De, N.R. (1984). *Alternative designs of human organizations.* New Delhi : Sage.

Hackman, J.R. and Suttle, J.L. (1977). *Improving life at work : Behavioural Science approaches to organizational change.* Santa Monica : Goodyear.

Mohram, S.A. and Lawler E.E. (1984). Quality of work life. In K.M. Rowland & G.R. Ferris (eds.), *Research in Personnel and Human Resource Management.* (pp. 219-260). Greenwich : JAI press.

Joseph, J.S. (1978). Quality of working life and job attitudes of industrial craftsman. *Bombay Psychologist, 1,* 28-34.

Miller, E.J. (1975). Socio-technical systems measuring, 1953-1970. A follow-up study. *Human Relations,* 28, 349-386.

Pandey, S. (1991). An introduction to HRM (guest editorial). *The Indian Journal of Social Work, 111,* 447-455.

Rao, V.R. (1986). *Study of the quality of working life, self concept, aspirations and family life of working women.* Unpublished doctoral dissertation, Dept. of Psychology, University of Delhi.

Rice, A. (1958). *Productivity and social organization : The Ahmedabad experience.* London : Tavistock institute.

Singh, J.P. (1982). Improving quality of working life in the Indian context. *Productivity,* 22, 10-15.

Singh-Sengupta, Sunita (1997a). *The senior managers : Challenges and coping strategies.* New Delhi : A.P.H. Publishing Company.

Singh-Sengupta, Sunita (1997b). The value profile of Indian executives. *Growth, 25,* 25-31.

Singh-Sengupta, Sunita (1996). *The senior managers : Challenges and coping strategies.* New Delhi : A.P.H. Publishing company.

Singh-Sengupta, Sunita (1995). *Work culture in police*

administration. New Delhi : Ashish Publishing House.

Singh-Sengupta, Sunita (1994). Realizing labour force for high work involvement. *Abhigyan*, Autumn issue, 23-26.

Singh-Sengupta, Sunita (1993). Managing power for quality of work life. *Indian Journal of Labour Economics, 36*, 777-781.

Singh-Sengupta, Sunita (1990). *Emerging patterns of power distribution.* New Delhi : Common Wealth Publishers.

Sinha, J.B.P. (1997). Quality of working life in the Indian setting. *Journal of Social and Economic Studies, 5*, 235-247.

Sinha, P. and Sayeed, O.B. (1980). Measuring quality of working life : Development of an inventory. *The Indian Journal of Social Work, 41*, 219-26.

Sinha, J.B.P. and Singh-Sengupta, Sunita (1991). Relationship between manager's power and the perception of their non-manager's behaviour. *Indian Journal of Industrial Relations, 26*, 341-351.

Srivastava, A.K. and Sinha, M.M. (1988). The job anxiety scale. In D.M. Pestonjee (ed.), *Handbook of psychological tests.*

Suri, G.K., Singh, A. and Akhter, S. (1991). *Quality of worklife and productivity : Conference papers, cases and proceedings* (eds.). New Delhi : National Productivity Council.

Thorsrud, E. (1972). Policy making as a learning process. In Cherns, Sinclair, Jenkins (eds.), *Social science and government.* London : Tavistock.

Trist, E. (1975). Planning the first step towards quality of working life in a developing country. In L.E. Davis & A.B. Cherns (eds.), *The quality of working life* (vol. 1), (pp. 78-85). New York : The Free Press.

Walton, R.E. (1974). Improving the quality of working life. *Harvard Business Review, 52*, 12-21.

6

Organizational Behaviour and Work Values

Shailendra Singh

People attach different meanings and values to their work. Some regard it as punishment, hardship, or an unpleasant obligation. Some treat it as a duty to fulfil one's predestined calling. Still others treat it as a central aspect of their lives. Why some people work harder than others? Partial explanation may be their work values. Such work values may also have consequences for their effectiveness and affective reactions. In the age when many people are not taking their work very seriously there is enough justification to explore the work value of people and its consequences. This chapter examines the structure of work values of managers and their relationship with certain job related outcomes.

One of the most explored work values is Protestant work value. Protestant work value is usually considered as a dispositional variable characterized by a belief in the importance of hard work, rationality and frugality and which acts as a defence against sloth, sensuality, and religious doubt (Mirels & Garret, 1971). Beit-Hallahmi (1979) define it as an orientation towards which emphasizes dedication to hard work, deferment of immediate reward, conservation of resources, the saving of surplus wealth and the avoidance of idleness and waste in any form.

McClelland (1961) introduced Weber's theory to the literature of organizational behaviour and management. He explained the socio-psychological dynamics of the association between Protestant values and Capitalism. The theory proposed that Protestant values determine the child rearing practices of independence, postponement of need gratification, rationality and mastery training which in turn lead to development of high-achievement motivation among children. These high achievement motivated children when grow adults, become successful entrepreneurs and create expansion of business becoming capitalist.

McClelland (1961) subsumed the concept of Protestant work values into the concept of need for achievement which he treated as a core dimension of personality. Because of the clear linkage between need for achievement and Protestant work values, many researches became interested in studying its antecedents incidence, and consequences (Greenberg, 1979; Furnham & Muhindeen, 1984; Furnham, 1982; Furnham, 1983; Furnham, 1984; Ray, 1982).

Blood (1969) developed a measure of Protestant work ethic (PWE). He describes that person who possesses Protestant work ethic ideals as one who feels that personal worth results from self sarificing or occupational achievement. The Protestant work ethic scale proposed by Blood was designed to measure the strength of this orientation alongwith extent to which individuals dissociate themselves from such values. This scale, therefore, consists of two subscales labelled pro-Protestant Ethic and Non-Protestant Ethic, each containing four items. Blood related the two dimension of Protestant work ethic with job satisfaction in two samples of trainee airmen and aircraft maintenance workers. Pro-Protestant work ethic was positively but weakly correlated with indices of specific job satisfaction while Non-Protestant work ethic scores were negatively correlated with the same.

The study of Blood (1969) was replicated by Aldag and Brief (1975) using different sample and different measures of affective responses. Significant relationship were found between work value indices and employee perception of task characteristics and leadership behaviour. The common suggestion that the pro-Protestant ethic ideals should be associated with strong higher order needs was supported. In this study Non-Protestant work ethic was found to be negatively related with job satisfaction whereas no significant relationship between Pro-protestant work ethic and job satisfaction. Merrens and Garret (1975) suggested that the protestant work ethic holds that hard and steady work is worthy and unwilling to work is seen as symptoms of absence of grace or sinful. They proposed that people with high Protestant work ethic would do better on task designed to provide low motivation and interest level. As predicted they found high PWE scores spent significantly more time participating in boring repetitive task than low PWE scores. Ganster (1981) however failed to replicate this result.

Stone (1975) examined the relationship between job scope and job satisfaction and PWE as measured by Wollack *et al.* (1971) Scale. He found a positive relationship between job scope and job satisfaction but neither the PWE nor any of its subscales appeared to moderate this relationship.

The review of literature suggests that Pro-Protestant work ethic is usually positively related with job satisfaction and Non-Protestant work ethic is negatively related with the same. Blood (1969) suggested that further replication are required to develop confidence in findings. He also suggested that the work ethic should be related to more job related variables. The present study has included more comprehensive dimensions of job behaviour including both desirable and undesirable work outcomes from organizational point of view. The dependent variable set included job satisfaction, organizational commitment, intent to leave alienation, and dimensions of job strain. Thus the specific aim of the study is to re-examine the stability of factors extracted by Blood (1969) and to relate the emerging dimensions of work ethic with job related behaviour.

Method

Sample: The participants in the study were equitably drawn: 250 junior and middle level managers from seven private and three public sector work organizations of north India. All were males and their age ranged from 28-57 years with an average of 35.38 years. The executives belonged to wide range of functional areas, including accounts, engineering, personnel, production, quality control, R.D. and sales. An attempt was made to represent most of the departments in the companies, as far as practicable. The average job experience of the respondents was 11.13 years and their average educational qualification was a university or college graduation or equivalent professional training.

Measures

Protestant Work Ethic Questionnaire: Blood's (1969) Protestant Work Ethic questionnaire was used. It consisted of 8 items. Through Principal Component Analysis of the eight items with varimax rotation, Blood reported existence of two dimensions: Pro-Protestant Work Ethic and Non-Protestant Work Ethic. This study has used response categories on 5-point scale.

Organizational Commitment Questionnaire: Cook and Wall's (1980) 9-item organizational commitment questionnaire was used. Principal component Analysis of the nine items with oblique rotation revealed two factors. On the basis of factor loadings the two factors were named as:

1. *Organizational identification:* Pride in organization, internalization of organizational goal.

2. *Organizational loyalty:* Affection for and attachment to the organization, a wish to remain member of the organization.

Job Satisfaction Questionnaire: A 20-item questionnaire containing 20 facets of job satisfaction was used. Principal component Analysis with oblique rotation yielded two factors but none of the item loaded higher on the second factor, thus single factor of job satisfaction was used in the analysis.

Alienation : This construct was measured through single item:

- In this organization feel alienated.

Intent to leave: This construct was also measured through single item:

- I intend to leave this organization as soon as possible.

Job Strain Questionnaire: A 35-item questionnaire having various facets of negative experience and emotion was used. A Principal component Analysis with oblique rotation revealed eight factors in job stain.* The eight factors are :

1. *Frustration:* Experience blocking his goal directed behaviour characterized by energized negative emotion.
2. *Lack of leisure time:* An experience in which the person feels that one has not got any time to devote to self and for fulfilling social obligations.
3. *Feeling of uneasiness:* Experience of discomfort and symptoms of uneasiness.
4. *Physical strain:* Maladjustive bodily symptoms like difficulty in keeping temper, feeling fidgety, feeling of tightness in chest etc.
5. *Work aversion:* Feeling like taking long time off from the job without any guilt.
6. *Unjust work and reward:* Sense of helplessness by watching that the performers are given large amount of work, but reward is given to some one else. i.e. sense of helplessness because of inequitable distribution of work and reward.
7. *Latent hostility:* Experience of negative emotional arousal which is suppressed from being public with effort. Examples of latent hostility could be: Reaction to stupid instructions of a fussy boss.
8. *Bearing of others incompetence:* Experience of putting up with others incompetence.

Means, standardization and Alpha Reliability of each variable used in this chapter is presented in Appendix-I.

---

* Results of Factor Analysis is available from the author on request.

Result and Discussion

The eight items data on Protestant Work Ethic Questionnaire were subjected to principal component analysis with oblique rotation (Table 6.1). The analysis revealed two factors. The first factor consisted of 4 items No. 2, 4, 6 and 7. This factor contained exactly same items which were found by Blood (1969).

TABLE 6.1 : **Factor Analysis Results of Work Ethic Responses**

Items	Factor pattern	
	Factor-I	Factor-II
When the work is finished a person should forget his job and enjoy himself.	01	71
Hard work makes a man better person	75	21
The main purpose of man's job is to provide him with the means for enjoying his free time.	04	63
Wasting time is as bad as wasting money.	81	15
Wherever possible a person should relax and accept life as it is, rather than always trying for unreachable goals.	04	43
A good indication of man's worth is how well he does his job.	40	14
If all other are equal it is better to have a job with lot of responsibility than with little responsibility.	41	14
People who do things the easy way are smart ones.	04	28
Eigen values with interactions	1.53	1.25
Percent of variance explained	55.00	45.00

Note : Decimal points omitted from Factor loadings.

Value of not wasting time had highest loading (0.81) followed by value of hard work (.75). Value of work done well (.40) and value of responsibility (.41) showed relatively lower loadings. This factor explained 55 per cent of variance in data. Following Blood, the factor was named Pro-Protestant work value.

The second factor also contained four items and they are exactly the same as found by Blood (1969). This factor explained 45 per cent of variance in data: Value of enjoying life after work loaded highest (.71) followed by value of treating work as earning means for enjoying free time (.66). The other two items had relatively lower loadings. The factor was named as Non-Protestant work Ethic. The two factors had an insignificant relationship ($r = .03$, $p > .01$). The factor analysis results have confirmed the factorial stability of the Protestant Work Ethic Questionnaire. This questionnaire can be used to examine the value of managers and other levels of employees to get the feel of work values of work force with quite ease.

Relationship with Job Related Behaviour

The two dimensions of work values were related to thirteen variables of job behaviour. Pearson's correlation technique was used to establish the relationship. Results are summarized in Table 6.2.

Perusal of Table 6.2 reveals that out of 13 correlations of Pro-Protestant work values with job related behaviour ten are significant. Organizational identification, organizational loyalty and job satisfaction are positively related with Pro-Protestant work values while other seven variables, namely, intention to leave, alienation, frustration, physical strain, latent hostility and bearing of others incompetence were negatively related.

Organizational identification refers to pride in organization and internalization of the organizational goals. Such persons also invest high amount of effort to salvage the problem of organization, the persons self worth is attached to the upswing and downtrend of the organizational fortune. If Pro-Protestant work values is

TABLE 6.2 : **Work Ethic as related to Job Outcome (N=250)**

Job outcome	Pro-Protestant work ethic	Non-Protestant work ethic
Organizational identification	.56**	-.19**
Organizational loyalty	.20**	-.24**
Job satisfaction	.50**	-.13*
Alienation	-.31**	.12
Intent to leave	-.34**	.10
Frustration	-.29**	.16*
Lack of leisure time	.09	22**
Feeling of uneasiness	- 20**	09
Physical strain	-.40**	.18**
Work aversion	-.01	-.07
Unjust work and reward	.10	.25**
Latent hostility	-.19**	.17**
Bearing of others incompetence	- 34**	11

* P< .05, ** P< .01

positively related with organizational identification, it obviously suggests that a manager who is having high Pro-Protestant work ethic will also display high level of organizational identification. Pro-Protestant work value is also related with persistence and delay of need gratification. The two elements may be contributing to remain involved in the organization and persistence in organization to achieve higher goals is characteristic of n-Ach people who are also supposed to high on Protestant work values.

Organizational loyalty is also positively with Pro-Protestant work values. The explanation of not willing to quit the organization is again associated with the component of persistence. One aspect of organizational loyalty is that the incumbent is not willing to change to another employer for slight raise also related to delay of need gratification aspect of Pro-Protestant work values. A manager tries to plan his career in one organization instead of hoping here and there for quick promotion. If the manager has such career planning most likely he will be high on Protestant work ethic.

Job satisfaction has also emerged as positively related with Protestant work values. The study in line with Blood (1969) and Aldag and Brief (1975). The relationship does not need any extra interpretation, as it was theoretically expected that person who attaches so much value and importance to his work will also report statisfaction to his work and his job.

The seven job related behaviour negatively related with Pro-Protestant work values represent negative cognition, attitude and behaviour from organization point of view. Alienation and intent to leave are feeling and cognition of managers which suggest that the person has experienced some cultural shock and there is high gap between his expectations and achievement in organizations. A person with high Protestant work values will through his sheer effort, mould the situation in such a way that question of alienation or intention to leave shall not arise. Frustration, feeling of uneasiness, physical strain, latent hostility and bearing of others incompetence are the dimensions of job strain. The kind of results suggest that a manager with high Protestant work values will not show symptom of strain.

Non-Protestant work ethic (NPWE) was found to be negatively related with organizational identification, organizational loyalty and job satisfaction and it was positively related with five dimensions of job strain namely frustration, lack of leisure time, physical strain, unjust work and reward and latent hostility.

Result regarding job satisfaction was in line with Blood (1969) but not similar to Adag and Brief (1975). Aldag and Brief did not find a significant relationship between NPWE and job satisfaction. The trend in the present study suggests that managers with high NPWE will be more concerned with enjoying life and not willing to persist for relatively difficult goal hence will not take any challenge and show negative relationship with job satisfaction. Organizational identification and loyalty also includes a common factor positive work attitude towards one's organizations hence high NPWE managers will report negative organizational identification and loyalty.

Positive relationship between NPWE and job strain dimensions show that apart from organizational stress and other adverse organizational condition one's own work values also accentuates the experience of job strain.

The present results by and large supported Blood's conceptualization of Protestant Work Ethic measure. The Protestant Ethic scale revealed two dimensions: (1) Pro-Protestant Work Ethic, (2) Non-Protestant Work Ethic. Generally Pro-Protestant work ethic were positively related with positive effective responses job satisfaction, organizational commitment and negatively related with negative effective responses and behaviour: alienation intent to leave and dimensions of job strain. Non-Protestant work ethic had just the opposite relationship of what Protestant work ethic had. The study suggests that employers should look for people with high Protestant work ethic. Socializing agents should provide conducive climate for development of high Protestant work ethic.

REFERENCES

Aldag, R.J. & Brief, A.P. (1975). Some correlates of work values. *Journal of Applied Psychology, 60.* 757-760

Beit-Hallahmi, B. (1979). Personal and social components of the Protestant ethic. *Journal of Social Psychology, 109,* 263-267.

Blood, M. (1969). Work values and job satisfaction. *Journal of Applied Psychology, 53,* 456-459.

Cook, J., & Wall, T. (1980). New work attitude measures of trust, organizational commitment and personal need nonfulfilment. *Journal of Occupational Psychology. 53,* 39-52.

Furnham, A. (1982). The protestant work ethic and attitude towards unemployment. *Journal of Occupational Psychology, 55,* 277-285.

Furnham, A. (1983). The protestant work ethic, human values and attitudes towards taxation *Journal of Economic Psychology, 3,* 113-128.

Furnham, A. & Muhiudeen, C. (1984). The protestant work ethic in Britain and Malaysia. *Journal of Social Psychology, 122,* 157-161.

Ganster, D. (1981). Protestant ethic and performance: A re-examination. *Psychological Report*, *48*, 335-338.

Greensberg, J. (1979). The protestant work ethic endorsement and the fairness of equity inputs. *Journal of Research in Personality*, *13*, 81-90.

McClelland, D.C. (1961). *The achieving society*. New York : Van-Nostrand Reinhold.

Merrens, M. & Garrett, J. (1975). The protestant ethic scale as predicter of repetitive work performance. *Journal of Applied Psychology 60*, 125-127.

Mirel, H. & Garrett, J. (1971). Protestant ethic as a personality variable. *Journal of Consulting and Clinical Psychology 36*, 40-44.

Ray, J.J. (1982). The protestant ethic in Australia. *Journal of Social Psychology*, *116*, 127-138.

Stone, E. (1975). Job scope, job satisfaction and the protestant ethic: A study of exhausted men in relationship. *Journal of Vocational Behaviour*, *7*, 215-224.

Wollack, S., Goodale, J., Wijting, & Smith, P. (1971). Development of the survey of work values. *Journal of Applied Psychology*, *55*, 331-338.

APPENDIX-I

Mean, Standard Deviation and Alpha Reliability of Variables

Sl.No.	Variable	M	SD	No.of items	Alpha Reli-ability
1.	Pro-protestant work ethic	15.08	2.26	4	.64
2.	Non-protestant work ethic	13.02	2.41	4	.57
3.	Organizational identification	19.05	3.20	5	.81
4.	Organizational loyalty	18.92	3.06	4	.77
5.	Job satisfaction	63.32	12.57	20	.96
6.	Alienation	2.67	0.89	1	—
7.	Intent to leave	2.73	0.90	1	—
8.	Frustration	20.56	5.29	9	.89
9.	Lack of leisure time	15.42	5.28	6	.87
10.	Feeling of uneasiness	12.50	3.08	5	.71
11.	Physical strain	16.69	4.57	8	.84
12.	Work aversion	2.37	1.19	1	—
13.	Unquest work and reward	2.03	1.61	2	.45
14.	Latent hostility	8.95	2.40	3	.79
15.	Bearing of others incompetence	3.17	0.90	1	—

7

Organizational Dynamics in Banks: A Comparative Study of Nationalized Scheduled Banks

A.K. Tewari

It is a general observation that the psychological profile of public sector or government organizations differs from that of the non-government organizations. This observation has been supported by the findings of several empirical studies (Tewari, 1995). However, these studies have failed to suggest any answer to the question: Where does such difference originate from? Perhaps this question is not so easy to be answered. The study reported in this chapter, is based on assumption that an insight into the solution of the problem can be obtained by systematically comparing the government and non-government organizations. Such comparisons should be made on relevant variables—carefully selected for the purpose. In this context this study planned to compare the nationalized banks with the non-nationalized scheduled banks on the variables related to power and distribution of organizational control, components of burnout and some outcome variables. It can be recalled that 14 major banks were nationalized in 1969. Now almost more than 28 years have passed after that event. Before nationalization, all of these banks were private non-government organizations. They became government organizations after nationalization. It provided an appropriate opportunity to explore the differences which might have been caused by governmental control for the last 28 years by comparing them with non-nationalized banks.

The selection of variables on which the two types of banks are compared in this study was based on following considerations. Bases of power and characteristics of distribution of control among the different hierarchical echelons are important aspects of organizational structure and process. Burnout is conceptualized as a form of job stress, which occurs in jobs pertaining some kind of public dealing. It has been extensively studied in a large number of empirical researches. It has been found to be very useful in explaining the organizational behaviour of employees. The variables, selected as outcome variables in this study include intention to change job, general satisfaction, work related anxiety and absenteeism.

METHOD

Sample

The sample consisted of 300 participants. Half of them were selected from different branches of nationalized banks and the other half from branches of non-nationalized scheduled banks. Thus, each of the two types of banks was represented by 150 respondents. All these banks were situated in Uttar Pradesh and had, more or less, similar hierarchical structures.

Measures

A self administering questionnaire was developed which included following measures:

The three characteristics of distribution of organizational control namely; total amount of control, slope of distribution of control, and discrepancy between actual and ideal control were measured by control curve technique as developed by Tannenbaum and associated (Tannenbaum, 1968). In this technique total amount of control is obtained by summing the amounts of actual control of all the hierarchical levels of organization. Slope of distribution of control is calculated by subtracting the control of lowest hierarchical echelon from that of highest hierarchical echelon. The differences between actual and ideal amounts of control obtained for different hierarchical positions, when summed, provide the score for discrepancy between actual and ideal control. Change in organization control overtime—the fourth variable related to organizational control was measured by a single item question. The question was : How much change has occurred in the influences of different groups working in the banks during last few years?

To measure the bases of power, the respondents were asked: 'Why do you do, what your immediate boss asks you to do on the job?' The question was followed by six possible reasons for the compliance. Each of these reasons represented a particular base of power. The subjects were asked to rate each of them on 5 points rating scales.

Burnout was assessed by Maslach Burnout Inventory, popularly known as M.B.I. (Maslach & Jackson, 1986). The MBI contains three subscales that assess the three components of burnout; namely emotional exhaustion, depersonalization and feelings of low personal accomplishment. The subscale for feelings of personal accomplishment is so framed that lower score on this scale means higher feelings of low personal accomplishment and vice-versa.

Among the outcome variables intention to change job was measured by single question. The measures of general satisfaction consisted 5 items. Absenteeism and job related anxiety were measured by 3 and 2 questionnaire items, respectively.

Results and Discussion

The major concern of present study was to explore the differences between the nationalized and non-nationalized scheduled banks in terms of their organizational and psychological characteristics. Tabel 7.1, presents the t-values regarding these differences.

Table 7.1 shows that among the four characteristics of organizational control, the means of nationalized and non-nationalized banks differed significantly on slope of distribution of organizational control and change in control only. In comparison to nationalized banks the non-nationalized banks were found to have higher score on slope of control distribution (t=2.45, p < .05). But the amount of change in control during last some years was higher in nationalized banks in comparison to non-nationalized scheduled banks (t=2.93, p < .01). The means obtained for two types of banks on total amount of control

TABLE 7.1 : **Differences between Nationalized and Non-nationalized Banks**

Variables	Nationalized Banks		Non-nationalized Banks	
	M	SD	M	SD
Organizational Control Characteristics				
Total amount of control	19.35	2.53	19.79	2.52
Slope of distribution of control	1.08	1.69	1.57	1.02
Discrep. between act. and ideal control	0.59	4.37	1.37	2.83
Change in control	2.94	1.08	2.60	.92
Base of Power				
Expert	3.47	1.23	3.83	1.43
Reward	1.70	.87	1.87	.73
Coercive	2.35	1.17	2.94	1.23
Referent	2.48	1.21	1.98	1.10
Legitimate	3.62	.94	4.22	.96
Functional	4.35	1.01	4.63	.90
Burnout				
Emotional exhaustion	14.87	8.63	21.26	8.74
Feelings of personal accomp	36.76	9.88	32.90	6.99
Depersonalization	3.50	3.73	4.78	3.92
Outcome variables				
Intention to change job	1.99	1.26	1.93	.93
General satisfaction	17.82	1.78	16.05	2.76
Absenteeism	8.30	2.18	8.58	1.78
Job related anxiety	3.38	2.31	2.84	2.46

O p < .10   ** p <.01
* p < .05   *** p < .001

and discrepancy between actual and ideal control did not differ significantly (t-values being 1.51 and 0.98, respectively).

These results revealed that the nationalized banks were characterized by greater amount of change in control during last some years and less steeped slope of distribution of control. It suggests that the process of nationalization has brought a change in control distribution by decreasing the gap between controls of higher and lower hierarchical echelons. However, perhaps it has not enhanced the total amount of control in these banks as the amount of total control was found to be more or less same. According to Singh-Sengupta (1995), power is not derived just from hierarchical positions in organizations. Other factors also determine it. Above stated results suggest that governmentalization may be one such factor which provides greater power or control to relatively lower hierarchical echelons but at the cost of power shortage of higher hierarchical level. Therefore, the control of the lower echelons increases but not the total amount of control. This contention gets a little support from the studies in which the upper hierarchical groups have been found to feel powerlessness.

As Table 7.1 further reveals, in comparison to nationalized banks the non-nationalized banks scored significantly higher for all the bases of power except the referent power. The t-values were found 2.34 for expert power ($p < .01$), 1.83 for reward power ($p < .10$) 4.24 for coercive power ($p < .001$) 5.45 for legitimate power ($p < .001$) and 2.52 for functional power ($p < .05$). The score for referent power was higher in nationalized banks in comparison to that for non-nationalized banks. The mean difference in this case was highly significant ($t = 3.76$, $p < .001$).

These results indicate that the base for compliance is relatively broader in non-nationalized banks. The employees of nationalized banks comply more in case if the boss is a nice guy (referent power).

As stated earlier, burnout is operationalized as a three component syndrome. The nationalized banks scored significantly lower in cases of emotional exhaustion ($t = 6.35$, $p < .001$) and depersonalization ($t = 2.91$, $p < .01$), but higher in case of feelings of personal accomplishment ($t = 3.90$, $p < .001$) in comparison to non-nationalized banks. It can be recalled that the higher score on feeling of personal accomplishment means lower 'feeling of low personal accomplishment' — which is a component of burnout. Therefore, all three mean differences between two types of banks indicate lower burnout in employees of nationalized banks, in comparison to their counterparts in non-nationalized banks. Relatively higher burnout among the employees of non-nationalized banks draws attention. After nationalization, the entire thrust of the banking policy in India had been to project the image of public sector banks. In this process the officials of non-nationalized banks felt discriminated and neglected (Gelli, 1993). It might have caused burnout among them.

The two types of banks did not differ on intention to change job ($t = 0.47$). General satisfaction was significantly higher in nationalized banks in comparison to non-nationalized banks ($t = 6.58$, $p < .001$). The mean scores on absenteeism also did not differ in the two types of banks ($t = 1.22$). However, there was more job related anxiety in nationalized banks ($t = 1.96$, $p < .05$). These results are more or less same to that obtained in earlier studies. There was higher job related anxiety in nationalized banks. One can hypothesize that higher job related anxiety was due to excessive state interventions. However, it needs further exploration.

Although the non-nationalized banks compared with the nationalized banks were private organizations, they also were controlled by rules and regulations as prescribed by Reserve Bank of India for all the banks. Therefore, the generalizability of the results needs some caution.

However, the results seem to suggest that the natonalized banks are characterized by relatively less centralization of control associated with less base for compliance. Also, the employees of these banks had lower burnout and higher general satisfaction. Compliance by subordinates to their boss is essential for smooth and effective functioning of organizations. Therefore, one will have to think how the bases of compliance can be enhanced without increasing the centralization. Any such way can be helpful in making organizations more effective, further characterized by lower burnout and higher overall satisfaction among its employees.

REFERENCES

Gelli, R. (1993). Facing upto the future: A view from a private sector bank. *IBA Bulletin, 15* (1), 42-44.

Maslach, C. & Jackson, S.E. (1986). *Maslach Burnout Inventory (II Ed.)*. Palo Alto CA: Consulting Psychologists Press Inc.

Singh-Sengupta, S. (1995). A contingency approach to social power. *Indian Journal of Industrial Relations, 30*, 408-426.

Tannenbaum, A.S. (1968). *Control in organizations*. New York: McGraw Hill.

Tewari, A.K. (1995). Burnout and total amount of control in two types of banks. *Indian Journal of Industrial Relations, 30*, 454-460.

8

Women's Mental Health : Psychological/Feminist Issues

U. Vindhya

It is only since the seventies, due to the influence of feminist theory and the women's movement that research studies began to document the complex ways in which sex bias, sex role stereotyping and devaluation of women affect the nature, diagnosis and treatment of mental health problems (Zuckerman, 1979). Recent years have seen increasing recognition of the pervasive and destructive effects of gender inequalities and the stresses that differentially affect women by virtue of their unequal social status especially in their family roles. Consideration of women's needs, therefore, requires recognition of the impact of the social context on mental health, a position that challenges traditional intrapsychic, biomedical approaches to mental health.

This chapter makes a modest attempt to elaborate on the contradictions and tensions between the feminist and the psychological points of views on women's mental health and concludes by discussing how the feminist critique of mainstream psychology need not lead to an irrevocable breach with psychology. Rather the critique can be utilised for a more sensitive understanding of women's mental health issues. Such an understanding from the gender perspective is crucial in view of the repeated calls for making our research more relevant to the needs and dynamics of our society (e.g., Sinha, 1997).

Epidemiological studies done during the seventies and the eighties have highlighted the magnitude of the problem of mental illness in India. It, is now accepted that the general prevalence of mental disorder in the community is around 11 per cent, of which 3 per cent require active rehabilitation and 1 per cent need hospitalisation (Davar, 1995). Studies on the mental health needs of women in our country are however meagre. Even those studies which provide information on the socio-demographic characteristics of the mentally ill in the community (e.g., Dube, 1970; Isaac & Kapur, 1986; Nandi *et al.*, 1975; Shah *et al.*, 1980) do not tell us much about gender differences in the expression, prevalence, causes or course of mental illness.

In fact, some of the early epidemiological surveys have recorded that men predominate in psychiatric disorders, a trend that is contrary to that observed worldwide of a female preponderance. The explanation that has been offered for such a trend is that "the obligation and responsibilities that a male must fulfil (in our society) are full of challenge and stress" (p. 204, Sethi, 1978, cited in Davar, 1995). Questioning both the methodology and the assumption behind such a conclusion, Davar (1995) points out that these studies have employed the data based on hospital samples and not community samples, with the data on utility serving as if it were prevalence data. This is highly misleading since men and women in our country greatly differ in their access to hospital care. Without, therefore, taking into consideration the gender based inequity of access, it is misleading to conclude about the comparative prevalence of mental illness in the two sexes based on utility data from hospital samples, argues Davar (1995). Also by assuming that the male overrepresentation in mental illness statistics is due to the "stressful male role" is to ignore the crucial issues the women's movement has been raising such as the unequal decision-making power, unequal work distribution, work overload, unpaid labour, rigid role functions and stereotyping, all of which are dehumanising and stressful for women. Reanalysing the data from surveys done between the 1970s and the 1990s from a gender perspective, Davar (1995) in fact found that mental illness is higher in women rather than in men, with the frequency of occurrence being as high as 15 per cent as compared to 11 per cent among men. She also found that there is no gender difference in the prevalence of *severe* mental disorders whereas women are at least twice as frequently ill as men in the case of *common* mental disorders or neurotic disorders such as depression, anxieties, phobias and so on. In other words, where mental illness has a biological basis as in the case of severe mental disorders, frequency of illness is the same across gender; where mental illness has a psychosocial basis women are far more frequently ill than men.

The socio-demographic profile of mentally ill women in the country therefore suggests (a) frequency of illness is highest in the reproductive years i.e., between sixteen and forty years while in men illness does not seem to show any particular pattern or frequency or prevalence with respect to age until fifty years or so, after which it increases sharply, (b) married women are more frequently ill than single men although divorced, separated or widowed women are most frequently ill, and (c) as an occupational category housewives exhibit very high frequency of mental illness comparable only to unemployed persons and unskilled labour. Marriage and the family, contrary to the accepted view that the home is a stress-free sanctuary while the workplace is stressful, have been identified as necessary stressors causing mental illness among women in our society. The painful process of initiation into the world view of the marital family, lack of intimacy with the husband and lack of privacy, dearth of confiding relationships, long term social and economic adversity, role strain or overload of role related functions and domestic and other kinds of violence against women have been identified as important psychosocial stressors affecting women's psychological well-being.

Studies in the area of mental health have not, however, been sensitive to the socio-cultural context of women's mental health problems. The women's movement too in our country has not paid much attention to these concerns. By and large, women's health has been viewed in terms of their reproductive health or in terms of the impact of the work they do on their health. Although the stresses and strains women undergo in the course of marriage, child-raising and other reproduction-related events have been highlighted by activists and researchers, issues like— do women have specific mental disorders, what are the conditions that foster mental illness, what kind of intervention and prevention approaches can be adopted, can mental health in fact be a part of the agenda of women's groups — have not received much attention. This 'marginalisation' of women's mental health issues by the women's movement is understandable for two reasons.

First, the women's movement in our country, over the past two decades or so has had to deal with an enormously wide range of issues and problems, that are largely consequences and effects of societal oppression of women. Issues of survival — for land, for work and wages, for protection of environment — have for the most part dominated the concerns of the women's movement in the past few years. In addition, issues like sexual and family violence, harassment and discrimination in places of work and working conditions, inequities in services like literacy and health care, and examining and challenging the various ways the state through its legal system operates either to promote the *status quo* or to oppose changes favourable to women — are a few examples of the interventions and initiatives of the women's movement. Mental illness does not figure on the agenda perhaps because it is viewed as a manifestation of an individual problem, not directly related to societal oppression, and not common to all women.

Even though the women's groups in the country are not unified by a single feminist perspective, the basic underlying thread is a forward-looking ideology, calling for action and change while the body of knowledge or disciplines central to mental health — psychology and psychiatry is a conservative ideology calling for adjustment and continuity. Thus while the women's movement, grounded in the feminist framework is committed to political activity and collective change, psychology, rooted in individual experience and behaviour looks for individual solutions and individual change, which is why perhaps feminism and psychology have been held to be incompatible.

Second, traditional notions of mental illness are based mostly on the medical model that looks for underlying pathology to cure by its specialised treatment. The psychological model too encourages the notion that mental illness, incomprehensible in lay terms, is a domain best left to the specialist, be it a psychologist or a psychiatrist, and beyond the purview of women's organisations.

Mental Illness as an Individual Problem

Essentially, psychology as a science of the individual, is rooted in individual experience and behaviour. At the turn of the last century, when western psychology declared itself to be independent (from philosophy) and to be a rigorous experimental science, it indicated that it was committed to the objective, positivist paradigm of the natural sciences. Modern psychology's insistence on objectivity has led psychologists to claim that theirs is a value-free, ethically neutral science. There is also a reluctance and resistance on the part of psychologists to elaborate on the role of values in their discipline. To be fair to psychologists, this belief in value-neutrality of their science is but a part of the widespread belief in the possibility of an objective social science free of ideology that has informed the undergirding rationale for the post-war modernisation perspective in social science (Alvin, 1990).

But the power of psychology's claim to value-neutrality lies in the ideological function that such a notion conveys. It predisposes the public to accept psychology's assertions uncritically and to regard them as a political truisms rather than as socio-historically conditioned statements. By promoting thus a depoliticised image of psychological findings, the image has in fact served to promulgate the reigning ideology of the *status quo*. Thus the 'objective' descriptions of behaviour, in effect become prescriptions of what is desirable. And our definition of 'desirable' is generally in conformity with that of the ideological apparatuses of society whose major function is to bring about a successful socialisation (Sarason, 1981). In the guise of value-neutral research, psychology has in fact propagated values like individualism (Spence, 1985), male supremacy (Nahem, 1981), political conformity (Jacoby, 1975) and the glorification of technology in solving human problems (Woolfolk & Richardson, 1984), reinforcing the ideology of liberal humanism.

However, in no other area than in mental health perhaps do we witness the ideological, value-laden assumptions that are built in into definitions of normality and abnormality. In the garb of value-free definitions of mental health, psychology has actively promoted dominant assumptions about what society is like and what it means to be normal. Traditional psychology has for the most part, presumed that the masculine male and the feminine female are the models of 'healthy' development (Bem, cited in Vaughter, 1976).

Psychology's construction of women's mental illness, is based on dominant stereotypes regarding what is appropriate or inappropriate for women's behaviour. Thus if women deviated from socially-prescribed notions of 'feminine' behaviour they were liable to be labelled as 'disturbed' and 'sick'. The influential work of Phyllis Chesler (1972) and the much-quoted study of Broverman *et al.*, (1970) showed that there is a different, in fact, a double standard of mental health for men and women. The pioneering study of Broverman *et al.* (1970), for example, found that mental health professionals themselves held biased definitions of normalcy. These professionals were found to define normalcy for women at a lower level of mental health functioning than what was considered normal for men; on the other hand, women who ranked high in mental health measures became by definition 'deviant'. Therefore if women had good mental health, something was wrong with their womanhood; if they were well-adjusted to their gender role, they had poor mental health. In what has been termed as the Catch 22 of women's mental health, both conformity and nonconformity to the feminine role are liable to generate definitions of psychological ill-health. As Chesler has argued in her book *Women and Madness*, women who conform totally to the feminine role, if and when they are hospitalised are likely to be treated for "predominantly female behaviours" such as depression, suicide attempts, anxiety neurosis or paranoia while those who reject or are ambivalent about their female role could be hospitalised for "less female behaviour" such as schizophrenia or lesbianism (Chesler, 1972, p. 56).

We do not know how far this holds good for our society, although we do have evidence that women in our society suffer more from neurotic disorders which have a psycho-social origin rather than severe disorders which have an organic or biogenetic origin (Davar, 1995). We also can be more cetain that ambivalence or rejection of feminine qualities associated with 'good wifely and good motherly' behaviour is problematic for women. Dissatisfaction with traditional expectations of feminity in our society is perhaps considered to be more 'deviant'. A common 'symptom' of women brought for psychiatric treatment, expressed by accompanying male escorts is that "she does not do any housework and just sits around".

Psychology in fact lends 'scientific' support to the dominant view of women being judged severely and even of being labelled as sick if they do not fulfil the obligations of a good wife and mother. As Caplan and Hall-McCorquodale (1985) showed, clinical studies of pathological behaviour involve extensive mother-blaming for a number of disorders and difficulties. Mothers have been and continue to be implicated in psychopathologies ranging from arson to incontinence, drug abuse and bad dreams. The label of the 'schizophrenogenic mother' was a common explanation of schizophrenia till the recent acceptance of a more interactive biochemical psychosocial cause of the disorder.

Victim-blaming and Violence against Women

A related variant of this framework is victim-blaming. A basic assumption on which many psychological explanations are constructed — the acontextual view of the individual — leads to attribution of unfavourable experiences in a person's life to faulty mechanisms within herself or himself. An extensive lexicon of person-blaming concepts abounds in psychological research. The universality of victim-blaming is not without its sexist and racist assumptions. In a context like violence against women, victims of violence must contend with a culture which would rather stress on women's responsibility for provocation of sexual and physical assault. The affirmation and validation necessary to recover from the trauma are unlikely to take place when victim-blaming becomes a tool to endorse and justify male dominance and power and induce guilt and anxiety in women. In addition, as Lenore Walker (1989) points out, women victims of violence cannot understand neutrality. Their heightened sense of danger and the realistic need for safety leads them to categorise those who wish to study or help them as either 'with' or 'against' them.

A peculiar situation arises however in the context of domestic violence where both victim-blaming and a search for psychopathology in the (male) offender absolve the perpetrator of responsibility and deny justice and rights to the woman victim. Although psychological research in our country is not burdened by descriptions of pathological personality characteristics of men who commit violence against their wives, western psychological research has sought to understand domestic violence through examination of characteristics of individual men and women. The focus of such research (e.g., Roy, 1977) has been on personality traits or the presence of some psychopathology as causing the violence. For instance, abusive men have been characterised as passive-dependent, infantile or as lacking in impulse control while women who have been at the receiving end of such violence have been labelled as masochistic, paranoid or depressed. Feminist critiques have highlighted how psychological explanations can be differentially applied to men and women (Bograd, 1988). In general, trait theories tend to excuse the abusive man through reference to alcohol abuse or poor childhood histories. In contrast, battered women are implicated for their abuse, since many psychological theories suggest they need or tolerate the abuse. Women are seen as creating their own victimisation. For instance, Lion (1977) speaks of the battered woman's 'provocation' and states that "the victim may evoke violence in a vulnerable person" (p. 127). Faulk (1977) refers to battered women as "querulous and demanding" (p. 121). It is also not uncommon to find violence against wives being treated as a phenomenon no worse than women's verbal aggressiveness. For example, Deschner (1984) draws a parallel between a man's physical violence and what she refers to as a "woman's verbal persecutions (nagging)" (p. 19). By thus equating nagging with violence, the intensity and consequences of physical assault are trivialised.

The bulk of psychological literature assumes that the abusive man loses control over his behaviour. This notion that the man loses control, that the violence lies outside of the realm of choice and that battering occurs during brief irrational episodes — constructs, as Ptacek (1988) points out "a contemporary profile of the batterer as one who is not necessarily *sick*, but who is rather just *temporarily insane*. Seen from this perspective, the batterer is not abnormal enough to be considered a psychopath and not responsible enough to be considered a criminal" (p. 152). But this notion of loss of control is in fact contradicted by the violent men's own testimony. As Ptacek (1988) reports from his work with batterers, the men claim that their violence is beyond rational control, but they also simultaneously acknowledge that the violence is deliberate and warranted. And most importantly, through an emphasis on psychopathology, most psychological explanations ignore the question of power. They are unable to explain why allegedly out of control and pathological husbands beat up their wives and not say, their bosses or why they contain their rage until they are in the privacy of their homes. While victim-blaming thus abounds in psychological research on domestic violence, the responsibility of the man as well as that of the patriarchal social context which sanctions the use of power and violence are glossed over.

The mental health impact of violence on victims has also not been adequately addressed in the practices of mental health professionals. In an overview of research priorities for women's mental health, Russo (1990) draws attention to the traditional bias toward focusing on the perpetrators of violence against women, rather than on the effects of violence on its victims. The task of assessing the mental health impact of violence becomes all the more arduous when one has to reckon with the finding that women's victimization is more likely to be committed by family and friends than by strangers (Koss, 1990). The contribution of violence histories to several disorders ranging from major depression to post-traumatic stress disorder in women is neglected although several community sample surveys have found a strong relationship between a history of violent victimization and certain mental disorders (cited in Koss, 1990). In our own country we cannot perhaps imagine the gravity of the problem since even estimates of the extent of violence are not extensive or comprehensive. Neither do we have systematic accounts of the role that violent histories play in the etiology of mental disorders in women.

Medicalization of Reproduction related Events

The medicalization and psychologising (which in turn is dependent on the medical model) of women's experiences like pregnancy, menstruation and menopause have had far-reaching consequences, creating a series of paradoxes. Reismann (1983) points out, "As women have tried to free themselves from the control that biological processes have had over their lives, they simultaneously have strengthened the control of a biomedical view of their experience. As women visit doctors and get symptom relief, the social causes of their problems get ignored. As doctors acknowlege women's experience and treat their problems medically, problems are stripped of their political content" (p. 16). The medicalization of menstruation, for instance, reinforces the idea that women are controlled by biology, in general and their reproductive systems, in particular. As Reismann (1983) argues, this has been used to legitimate the exclusion of women from positions of power because of supposed emotional instability and irrationality due to raging hormonal imbalances. The fact that pre-menstrual syndrome (PMS) or "late luteal phase dysphoric disorder" is a diagnostic category, to be treated and controlled, deflects attention from social etiology. Rather than looking at the circumstances of women's lives that may make them irritable, depressed or angry, their strong feelings can be dismissed. The contradiction, as Reismann (1983) points out lies in the fact that "the label of PMS allows women to be angry and say what's on their minds at a certain time each month, while at the same time it invalidates the content of their protest" (p. 11). Furthermore, feminists have maintained that the discovery/invention of PMS and the rush to establish it as a diagnostic entity were bankrolled by pharmaceutical firms that were eager to market new drugs to "cure" it (Parlee, 1989).

Like menstruation, women's weight and the psychiatric diagnostic categories of anorexia nervosa and bulimia too are present-day examples of the relationship between the social norms for feminity and medical social control. As Conrad and Schneider (1980) note the potential for medicalization in fact increases as science discovers the subtle physiological correlates of human behaviour. In particular, as we know more about women's physiology and the complex biochemical components that are related to experiences like menstruation, pregnancy, weight and so on, the issue will be how to acknowledge this knowledge without allowing these human experiences to be distorted by scientific understanding. To 'demedicalize' is not to deny the biological components of experience or to turn our backs to discoveries and treatments that may ease pain and suffering. Rather, as Reismann (1983) maintains, demedicalization is to "alter the ownership, production and use of scientific knowledge" (p. 16). The need therefore is to develop alternatives to the masculinist biomedical view and place women's health including psychological health problems in the larger context of their lives. In fact, the predominance of women diagnosed with effective disorders underscores the importance of investigating the relationship of depression to reproductive related events, social roles, and life circumstances of women (Russo, 1990). The psychosocial nature of women's mental health problems therefore emphasises the need to go beyond narrow biomedical approaches and build a more comprehensive knowledge base.

The Social Construction of Mental Illness

It follows from psychology's conception of mental illness as an individual problem that it would seek individual solutions as well. These solutions, evolved from the clinical, therapeutic tradition are considered scientific and objective. Questioning the politics of inequity and the social causes of psychological suffering and advocating collective change are held to be incompatible with scientific goals of individual change. Perhaps such a notion derives from the polarisation of science as objective and value-neutral and politics as subjective and partisan (Kitzinger, 1990). On the other hand, much of the critical literature on psychology's conception of mental illness of women has been motivated by feminist theory which treats illness as a consequence of women's position in society which is shaped by the sexual division of labour and patriarchal power. Psychology's commitment to the experimental method has in fact served to obscure the connections between individual experience and social institutions and structures. Feminists accuse psychology and psychiatry of pathologising women, of attributing problems to the woman herself rather than viewing her illness as a product of the social and political context which oppresses her (Ussher, 1990). As Nancy Henley (1985) remarks rather sardonically, the psychology of women has in fact to contend with a psychology against women.

Psychology relies on an individualistic interpretation

of the world. It assumes that the problems people experience are due to an intra-psychic process which mediates the world through individual experience. Although it does acknowledge the 'forces of society', psychology asserts that these are not within its control and thus are not open to enquiry by psychologists. These intervening processes, when dysfunctional, can be seen as distorting the experience of individuals and as a result people experience distress. The immediate and natural response then of psychology to distress is to try and correct this dysfunctional process. There is nothing wrong with this kind of logic if it is limited to areas where distress is seen as a direct result of misperception of the real world. However, as feminist psychologists have pointed out, ". . . It increasingly seemed to us that misperceptions of this nature were rarely as simple as this and although psychology could (sometimes) alter this, it could also clearly further cause distress by failing to see the forces by which such misperceptions were set up, experienced and interpreted. The result of this focus thus views the distressed individual as in some sense faulty, and thus culpable. This sense of fault is easily equated with blame and increases feelings of inadequacy and guilt in most of us. If we then acknowledge why it suits society (while avoiding a functionalist analysis) to perpetuate such feelings, we come nearer, we believe, to understand why psychology is structured as it is, and how . . . women get the worst possible deal from this" (Adcock & Newbigging, 1990, p. 173).

It is not as if the feminist perspective denies completely or dismisses the validity or importance of psychological explanations in understanding women's mental health. Instead, feminists seek to connect our psychological analyses with understanding of the patriarchal social context, of the unequal distribution of power, and of the socially structured and culturally maintained patterns of man/woman relations and in what manner they contribute to problems of psychological health for women.

Current research both in the West and in our country indicates that it is not just women who figure more prominently in neurotic disorders, but rather that it is married women who experience more emotional distress than single, widowed, or divorced women (Gove, 1972). In a further study, Gove and Tudor (1973) confirmed the argument that married, housebound women are more likely to experience mental illness than unmarried women. An explanation for this difference is that the married unemployed woman is often confined with the restricted domain of the household where her self-image and social prestige are perhaps not significant when compared to that of the working woman. In addition the Gove and Tudor (1973) study also found that married women are more likely to have a problem of mental illness than married men. However, the results were opposite in the case of unmarried persons. Within each of the unmarried status (single, divorced or widowed) more studies found men to have higher rates of mental illness (Gove & Tudor, 1973, p. 828). In short, this means that marriage is more advantageous for men in minimising stress than it is for women. Suicide in fact is reported to be more prevalent for single than for married men (Turner, 1989). While marriage seems to work better for men perhaps because their emotional worries are 'laundered and processed' by their wives, the same cannot be said for women. Busy taking care of the emotional needs of others, women seem to be left with their own dependency needs unfulfilled. The results of sociological research (Gove & Geerken, 1977) show that the most vulnerable, from the point of view of mental illness, is the unemployed housewife.

It would be foolish to assume that men do not suffer emotional distress. Men's misery too could stem from the way society is structured. But the point here is that the causes of women's distress are different and that understanding this requires looking at what is going on for all women psychologically within the present conditions of patriarchal societal relations.

Let us take depression for instance, which not only affects a majority of women but more women than men are reported to suffer from this condition. The feelings of powerlessness, frustration, inadquacy, guilt and loneliness that combine as depression cannot be understood if we look at it only in terms of the woman's psychological characteristics, as a deficiency or inability to cope. It certainly seems probable that women are more likely to undergo experiences which generate those feelings, which is why women still tend to occupy the subordinate position in relationships with men. It is again women who are more likely to be inhibited from forming strong social bonds outside marital relationships, developing other interests or pursuing occupational achievements outside the home. Self-esteem which often acts as a buffer for depression is also problematic for women. Self-esteem is said to derive from (a) positive experiences of mastery or engagement in an important activity and (b) from involvement in intimate and satisfying relationships (Sniderman, 1983). Women have limited opportunities for experiences of mastery and work is not central to their self-definition. Even if family relationships are crucial to their self-definition they may not bolster their self-esteem either because these relationships are not egalitarian or because the family roles of wife and mother are dubbed as natural and hence do not call for any special pride or distinctiveness.

When things go wrong in the home, women are more vulnerable because they have fewer options. The discrepancy between the average earnings of men and women and the economic and social insecurities suffered by women also lead to feelings of depression. The social origins of depression, the impact of stressful life events, and the complex relationships between gender, social roles and mental health are by now well documented in sociological literature (Brown & Harris, 1978). The presence of social support has been identified as a key variable in moderating the effects of threatening life events which push the individual towards mental distress. The range of social relations available to an individual provides a mechanism whereby the burden of emotional stress can be relieved and the objective sources of stress managed in a collective fashion. This pull of social relations has been referred to as the fund of sociability which is composed of intimacy, the network of common concerns, the ability to develop supportive social relations, the confirmation of one's own prestige and the feeling of alliance with others who provide a supportive base (Turner, 1989, p. 78).

Fortunately for us, community support in the form of kin, friends, acquaintances, co-workers and the neighbourhood can still be counted upon to act as a form of buffer against threatening life events. The extent of an individual's, and in particular, a woman's social network is consequently important in protecting her from both external threat and stress.

In this context, instead of leaving the woman to locate her distress in terms of her own psychopathology, women's groups, I feel, can provide a milieu which will make visible the connection between private suffering and social causes. Secondly, if we are able to demystify the 'specialised' treatment of mental illness, we will perhaps be able to see more clearly that the treatment method at its simplest involves trust, talk and understanding. The collective sharing of personal experiences of women's oppression is in any case an existing and valuable aspect of the functioning of women's groups. Why should this sharing be only with respect to direct and explicit instances of oppression like for instance rape or wife-beating? Cannot this sharing include understanding of each other's needs?

Furthermore, mental distress can be at various levels ranging from those connected to material deprivation and poverty to interpersonal relationships, and to existential issues or life choices. Calling for restructuring of social arrangements alone will not bring an end to women's distress. While emphasising on the necessity of psychological understanding the help for mental health problems, we also need to emphasise on making connections between our psychological state and the structural position of women and that psychological distress is not caused by 'internal deficiencies' alone.

Conclusion

Psychology can add to a feminist analysis in research and offer individual women in distress an alternative to the medical model. Indeed, the feminist account of the social construction of gender fits with the understanding of women's mental health problems that they are mostly caused by psychosocial factors. The feminist insistence on the importance of context, though at odds with mainstream psychology's focus on the individual, has in fact led to changing definitions of psychological knowledge produced by feminist practice. Psychology as a reflexive discipline, created by people about people, is founded on a bedrock of 'scientific explanation' that is laden with ideological assumptions, most of which are part of the taken for granted currency of dominant culture. Acknowledgement of psychology as a social practice need not however detract from its value in understanding and providing insight into the distress of individual women or men.

REFERENCES

Adcock, C., & Newbigging, K. (1990). Women in the shadows : Women, feminism and clinical psychology. In E. Burman (Ed.), *Feminists and psychological practice* (pp. 172-188). London : Sage.

Alvin, Y.S. (1990). *Social change and development : Modernization, dependency and world system-theories*. New Delhi : Sage.

Bograd, M. (1988). Feminist perspectives on wife abuse : An introduction. In K. Yllo & M. Bograd (Eds.) *Feminist perspectives on wife abuse* (pp. 11-27). Newbury Park : Sage.

Broverman, I.K., Broverman, D.M., Clarkson, F.E., Rosenkrantz, P., & Vogel, S.R. (1970). Sex-role stereotypes and clinical judgements of mental health. *Journal of Consulting Psychology, 34*, 1-7.

Brown, G.W., & Harris, T. (1978). *Social origins of depression*. London : Tavistock.

Caplan, P.J., & Hall-McCorquodale, I. (1985). Mother-blaming in major clinical journals. *American Journal of Orthopsychiatry, 55*, 345-353.

Chesler, P. (1973). *Women and madness*. New York: Avon.

Conrad, P., & Schneider, J.W. (1980). *Deviance and medicalization : From badness to sickness*. St. Louis, Mo. : C.V. Mosby.

Davar, B. (1995). Mental illness among Indian women. *Economic and Political Weekly, 30*, 2879-2886.

Deschner, J.P. (1984). *The hitting habit : Anger control for battering couples*. New York : Free Press.

Dube, K.C. (1970). A study of prevalence and bio-social variables in mental illness in a rural and an urban community in Uttar Pradesh, India. *Acta Psychiatrica Scandinavica*, 15.

Faulk, M. (1977). Men who assault their wives. In M. Roy (Ed.), *Battered women : Psychosociological study of domestic violence*. New York : Van Nostrand Reinhold.

Gove, W.R. (1972). The relationship between sex roles, marital status and mental illness. *Social Forces*, 51, 34-44.

Gove, W.R., & Geerken, M.D. (1977). The effects of children and employment on the mental health of married men and women. *Social Forces, 56*, 66-76.

Gove, W.R., & Tudor, J.F. (1973). Adult sex roles and mental illness. *American Journal of Sociology, 78*, 50-73.

Henley, N. (1985). Psychology and gender. *Signs, 11*, 101-119.

Issac, K.& Kapur, R.L. (1986). A cost-effectiveness analysis of three different methods of psychiatric case finding in the general population. *British Journal of Psychiatry, 137*.

Jacoby, R. (1975). *Social Amnesia*. Boston : Beacon.

Kitzinger, C. (1990). Resisting the discipline. In E. Burman (Ed.). *Feminists and psychological practice* (pp. 119-136). London: Sage.

Koss, M.P. (1990). The women's mental health research agenda: Violence against women. *American Psychologist, 45*, 374-380.

Lion, J.R. (1977). Clinical aspects of wife battering. in M. Roy (Ed.), *Battered Women : Psychosociological study of domestic violence*. New York : Van Nostrand Reinhold.

Nahem, J. (1981). *Psychology and psychiatry today*. New York : International Publishers.

Nandi, D.N. *et al.* (1975). Psychiatric disorders in a rural community in West Bengal : An epidemiological study. *Indian Journal of Psychiatry, 17*.

Parlee, M.B. (1979). Psychology and women. *Signs, 5*, 121-133.

Ptacek, J. (1988). Why do men batter their wives? In K. Yllo & M. Bograd (Eds.) *Feminist perspectives on wife abuse* (pp. 133-157). Newbury Park : Sage.

Reismann, C.K. (1983). Women and medicalization : A new

perspective. *Social Policy*, 3-18.

Roy, M. (Ed.), (1977). *Battered women : Psychosociological study of domestic violence.* New York : Van Nostrand Reinhold.

Russo, N.F. (1990). Overview : Forging research priorities for women's mental health. *American Psychologist*, *45*, 368-373.

Sarason, S.B. (1981). An asocial psychology and a misdirected clinical psychology. *American Psychologist*, *36*, 827-836.

Shah, A.V. *et al.* (1980). Prevalence of psychiatric disorders in Ahmedabad : An epidemiological study. *Indian Journal of Psychiatry, 22.*

Sinha, D. (1997). Evading the challenge : A commentary on the research-culture of psychologists in India. *Trends in Social Science Research, Vol. 4, no. 1, June.*

Sniderman, M.S. (1983). Self-esteem in psychotherapy. *Canadian Journal of Psychiatry, Vol. 28.*

Spence, J.T. (1985). Achievement American style. *American Psychologist*, *40*, 1285-1295.

Turner, R.P. (1989). *Medical power and social knowledge.* Newbury Park : Sage.

Ussher, J. (1990). Choosing psychology or not throwing the baby out with the bathwater. In E. Burman (Ed.), *Feminists and psychological practice* (pp. 47-61). London : Sage.

Vaughter, R.M. (1976). Review essay : Psychology. *Signs*, *2*, 120-146.

Woolfolk, R., & Richardson, F.C. (1984). Behaviour therapy and the ideology of modernity. *American Psychologist*, *39*, 777-786.

Zuckerman, E. (1979). *Changing directions in the treatment of women : A mental health bibliography.* Washington, D.C. : DHEW Publication.

9

Dual Career Families : A Psycho-Social Study

Abhilasha Srivastava and **Meenakshi Gupta**

Social and economic changes since the second world war have altered the nature of work and family relations and also led to the emergence of new family patterns in the western world, Dual Career Families (DCF) being one among them. In India, DCFs is a relatively recent phenomenon. Such families where both the husbands and wives pursue a career, reflect the rapid socio-economic changes occurring in the country and entail certain socio-psychological consequences for the individuals. The dynamics of family and work life activities in DCFs are different from those of the traditional families. Individuals in such families experience unique strains and satisfaction. There is a growing concern about the quality of life in dual career families.

Sekaran has done a series of studies to examine the work and non-work related factors that influence the Quality of Life (QOL) of the spouses in such families (Sekaran 1982, 1983, 1986). Understanding the dynamics of and part played by the factors that affect the QOL of dual career couples (DCC) will help them to manage the work and non-work spheres in a better way to attain an improved QOL. Martin and Schermerhorn (1983) have postulated that three sets of variables — individual differences, work and non-work factors — influence Job Satisfaction (JS) and Life Satisfaction (LS) which, in turn, affect the mental health of individuals. Sekaran (1985) developed and tested a model tracing the antecedents of mental health. In this model she studied the effect of two individual difference factors (Age, Children), three work related factors Income, Discretionary Time (DT), Career Salience (CS) and three non-work related factors Self Esteem (SE), Enabling Process (EP), Multiple Role Stress (MRS) on JS and LS leading to mental health.

The Preliminary Study

Like the West, DCFs in India present a special case of work and family interface; but unlike the West the structure and dynamics of Indian DCFs are unique in their own way. Therefore the factors operating in the West may not be equally relevant in the Indian context. To identify the relevant factors which influence JS and LS of the dual career couples, the investigators adopted a case study approach wherein 10 DCCs were interviewed using an in-depth interview schedule. These interviews were unstructured and open-ended. On an average 45 minutes were spent in interviewing one individual. Among the 10 couples, in four cases, the couples were from the same profession, namely—academics, banking, medicine and engineering. In the other 6 cases, they were pursuing different careers. The analysis of these 10 cases revealed that in DCF's certain variables interact in a particular manner to decide the JS and LS of the couples. In all the 10 cases, age was found to be positively related to JS and LS. However, gender did not appear to have straightforward relation with JS and LS. Apart from age and gender, the analysis was done on the various aspects such as content of the job, needs and motives of the individuals, utilization of potential, environment at the work place, career salience, commitment, family involvement, external support, sharing of household work and so on.

After analysis four work related factors — CS, Social Support at Workplace (SSW), Salary, Discretionary Time spent on job-related activities and three non-work related variables — Family Involvement (FI), Social Support (SS), Self Esteem (SE) were selected for the final empirical study. Education, years of service, years and type of marriage, number of children and age of the youngest child were also taken up to see their predictive value regarding JS and LS. On the basis of previous studies, the following hypotheses were proposed:

1. The work related variables will have greater impact on JS than on LS.
2. The non-work related variables will have a greater impact on LS than on JS.
3. As compared to females, work related factors will have a greater impact on JS of males.

METHOD

Sample

A sample of 47 DCCs (a total of 94 respondents) was drawn from various corporate and service organizations, universities and research institutes. In some of the organizations the HRD/Personnel department or a liaison person took the responsibility of distributing the sets of questionnaires to the individuals with professional spouse and also of collecting them back. In some organizations such individuals were personally contacted and one set of questionnaire was given to each of them. Since the response rate from the organizations was not very encouraging, later on (after three weeks of follow-up) the DCCs were identified in the residential areas and were included in the sample. All the participants were assured of confidentiality and were requested both varbally and in the questionnaire to respond to the questionnaires independently without consulting their spouse. Ten sets were discarded because they were actually dual earner couples and six more because of their being DINKs (Double-income-no-kids). Eighteen respondents failed to give the response sheet of their spouse, so they were also not included in the analysis. Four self employed respondents' sheets were also discarded because of incomplete information on one or more scales. The mean age of the husbands in the sample was 41.15 years and that of wives was 37.23 years. The mean job tenure of the two groups was 16.79 and 13.37 years, and their monthly income on an average was 18.49 and 16.32, respectively. Regarding education, the individuals were at least graduates. They were classified into graduates, post-graduates and professionals (Engineers, C.A., MBA, MBBS, Ph.D and so on). In occupational terms, they belonged to academics or service class, the latter included those working in the corporate sector, banks, hospitals etc. The mean length of time the respondents were married was about 12.95 years and there were on an average 1.5 child per family. The average age of the youngest child was 8.94 years.

Variables and Measures

The demographic variables of age, gender, education, profession, years of service, salary, years of marriage, type of marriage, type of family, number of children and age of the youngest child were elicited by single questions. They were also required to indicate if their organization provide the family supportive policies by encircling "Yes" or "No" to a list of nine variables. The description of other variables is as follows:

Discretionary Time (DT)—Personal time spent on job-related activities was tapped by asking for the average amount of time per week spend on job-related activities beyond normal working hours, at home and at the work place. Like Sekaran, DT at home (DTH) and DT at work place (DTW) were to be combined, but many individuals gave very erratic response to DTW e.g. total number of normal working hours at work place or some implausible figure due to which only DTH has been taken up for analysis. DT is the time which the individual willingly spends on job-related activities but in the Indian context it is the extra time spent on job related activities which could be either at the individual's discretion or due to work-load.

Career Salience — Seven items (Sekaran, 1982) on a Likert type 5-point scale were used to tap the extent to which career formed a vital part of individuals' lives. The reliability for this scale was 0.83.

Self-Esteem (SE) — Individuals' feelings of self-worth and competence were tapped by ten items (Rosenberg, 1965). The reliability of this scale was 0.81.

Social Support Scale — To measure the social support at the work place (SSW) as provided by boss and co-workers (8 items) and social support as provided by the spouse, friends, relatives and hired help 6 items were prepared. The alpha values for the two scales were 0.85 and 0.80, respectively.

Job Satisfaction — A twenty items scale (Weiss & Davis, 1967) tapping the satisfaction level of individuals to various aspects of job was used to measure the JS. The reliability coefficient of the scale was .92.

Family Involvement (FI) and Life Satisfaction (LS)— Two scales were developed consisting of eleven and twelve items respectively to measure these variables. The reliability of each of the two scales was 0.81.

In all the measures, 5-point Likert type scale was used to tap the responses.

RESULTS

The results show that the majority of the DCFs in the sample are nuclear with at least 1 and at the most 2 children. The wives' mean scores on CS, FI, JS, LS, SS, SE are in the middle of five-point scale whereas husbands have scored higher mean values on CS, FI but the mean

TABLE 9.1 : **Regression of Work Factors against JS & LS for Husbands and Wives**

	Males (N = 38)		Females (N = 39)	
DV	R^2	F (4,33)	R^2	F (4,34)
JS	0.596	12.19**	0.629	14.42**
LS	0.216	2.28 ns	0.302	3.68**

** $p < 0.01$

values of LS, JS, SS are comparable to those of females. Mean DTH in case of husbands is 4.3 hours whereas it is only 1.5 hours in case of the wives.

The results of the multiple regression analysis indicate that the work factors are predicting 60% and 63% of the variance in JS in case of husbands and wives respectively, both significant at 0.01 level (Table 9.1). Both CS and SSW are found to be significant predictors of JS in case of both husband and wife.

TABLE 9.2 : **Regression of Non-Work Factors against JS & LS for Husbands and Wives**

	Males (N = 47)		Females (N = 47)	
DV	R^2	F (3, 43)	R^2	F (3, 43)
JS	0.228	4.23**	0.227	4.22**
LS	0.350	7.74**	0.594	20.99**

** $p < 0.01$

Work related factors are found to be significantly predicting variance in LS in case of wife only, CS being a significant predictor.

The non-work factors are found to be significant predictors of both JS and LS in case of both husband and wife (Table 9.2). In case of the husband SE is explaining JS, and SE and SS are explaining LS. In case of the wife JS is being explained by SE and SS; LS by FI and SE.

Discussion

The results are supporting the hypothesis 1 as work related variables are indeed found to be explaining more variance in JS than in LS both for husbands and wives. In case of husbands they do not account for the variance in LS, but in case of wives they do. However, non-work factors are having more predictive value in the latter case also. Unlike husbands, since work related factors are influencing both JS and LS in case of wives, it appears that for wives work and family boundaries are more permeable. Therefore, the work factors have an impact on the LS also, although to a lesser extent than on the JS. In case of husbands there may be more compartmentalization of the two spheres. It is interesting to note that mean FI score is slightly higher in case of the husband than in the wife, but DTH is drastically more in case of the husband indicating that he spends more time on the job-related activities even when he is at home, unlike his wife. Husbands may be perceiving themselves to be highly involved in the family by spending what they see as adequate amount of time, energy and money on the members. On the other hand, wives as they are digressing from their traditional role, may be experiencing guilt that their involvement in the family is not adequate.

The second hypothesis that non-work factors will have a greater impact on the LS than on JS, is also supported. Gender appears to be mediating the relationship as in case of wives 60% of the variance in LS is being explained, compared to only 35% in case of husbands. LS of the wife is found to be influenced by FI and SE, whereas for the husband SE and SS have more predictive value. Thus, it can be said that although women did not score as high on FI as men did, their level of life satisfaction is more influenced by it. In this study, it has been found that non-work factors are significantly accounting for both JS and LS in case of both husband and wife. The non-work sphere of life has a significant impact on the work sphere of an individual's life. The third hypothesis has not been supported in the study, as it has been found that work related factors have an almost equal impact on JS of males and females. These factors are accounting for a comparable amount of variance in the JS scores of males and females (60% and 63% respectively). In fact contrary to the hypothesis, females' JS level is explained more by the work factors than males. However, the same two factors — CS and SSW — are found to be significantly explaining the JS level of men and women, indicating that with the increase in the number of DCFs the women are now more at ease at their job front and are now being influenced by the similar set of factors in the work-life as men.

In sum, this study shows that work factors have equally greater impact on the JS of husband and wife. They also explain LS in females but not in case of males. On the other hand, non-work related factors significantly influence JS & LS of both males and females in DCFs.

REFERENCES

Caplan R.D., Cobb, S., French, JRP, Harrison, R.V., & Pin Neaus S.R. Jr. (1978). *Job demands and worker health.* Washington DC: HEW Publication No. NIOSH 75-160.

Martin, T.N., & Schermerhorn, J.R. (1983). Work and non-work influence on health : A research agenda using inability to leave as a critical variable. *Acedemy of Management Review, 8*, 650-659.

Rosenberg, M. (1965). *Society and the adolescent self-image.* Princeton : Princeton University Press.

Sekaran U. (1982). An investigation of the career salience of men and women in dual career families. *Journal of Vocational Behaviour, 20*, 161-174.

Sekaran, U. (1983). Factors influencing the quality of life in dual-career families. *Journal lof Occupational Psychology, 56*, 161-174.

Sekaran, U. (1985). The paths to mental health : An exploratory study of husbands and wives in dual-career families. *Journal of Occupational Psychology, 58*, 129-137.

Sekaran, U. (1986). *Dual career families : contemporary organisational and counselling issues.* San Francisco: Jossey-Bass.

Weiss, J; Davis, R. V.; England, J. W. and Lofquist, L.H. (1967) *Manual for the Minnesota satisfaction questionnaire, Minnesota Studies* in *Vocational Rehabilitation, Vol. 22.* University of Minnesota Industrial Relations Centre, Minneapolis.

10

Maternal Employment and Development of Cognitive Abilities and Academic Achievement

Kasturi Jachuck

More recently, mothers have been accepting employment outside the home to a great extent due to economic necessity, educational opportunities and upward mobility. There is every reason to believe that this increasing trend of maternal employment will continue. This phenomenon is an outcome of a variety of changes including technological developments that have affected the nature of jobs, the streamlining of household operations, the increased economic efficiency of outside the home production, small family size due to more effective contraceptive methods, increased life expectancy, increased health status of the female population, increased number of female headed households, and economic circumstances that make it necessary for wives to be employed in order to maintain an acceptable standard of living.

Further, there is reason to believe that the traditional female role of full-time housewife and mother is no longer psychologically satisfying for women. While the new feminist ideology may augment this discontent, much of it may be a response to the changing nature of the role itself. Household appliances and modern food processing techniques have diminished much of the necessary part of house work. Time use studies have shown (Pleck & Rustad, 1978) that the amount of house work done by the non-working mother has diminished, but much of the work cannot be justified as an essential contribution to the household or an adequate use of the woman's ability, particularly when she knows that she could use her time to earn for the family. In addition, women's educational levels have taken a considerable upswing since the sixties and this education provides both a motivation for and an ability to obtain more satisfying employment (Hoffman & Nye, 1974).

There are economic and psychological reasons for an increasing number of women taking up employment outside home and entering a dual role of house wife-mother and working woman. However, maternal employment may lead to some problem particularly as the child grows older and the mother fears that her major role is diminishing; she may feel a need to hang on when child's maturation requires letting go. But, studies have indicated that the working mother is more satisfied with her life than the non-working mother and so is her husband (Dizard, 1968; Gold & Andres, 1978 a, b; Hoffman, 1974).

Employment of mothers may present a number of problems for family life and child rearing. The nature of community and government services and institutions, the occupational structure and the family itself with its traditional sex-role based division of labour have not changed adequately to accommodate to the prevalence of maternal employment. In households, the husbands may help more when the mother is employed but not enough to equalise the task. For single working mothers, the economic and psychological need for employment is greater, but so is the task. An employed mother cannot provide after school care to her children. Thus, maternal employment under adverse circumstances can put the mother under heavy stress. Instead of the positive effects of maternal employment that can be mediated by mother's higher morale, we may find negative effects that are mediated by the strain of filling very demanding roles (Hoffman, 1974, Woods, 1972).

There is a dearth of studies investigating the relationship between maternal employment and the child's cognitive abilities and academic achievements. Studies, which have examined the statistical differences between working and non-working mother's children with respect to certain academic indices, paid little attention to why differences are or are not found. The effect of maternal employment on the cognitive abilities and academic achievements of young children is a frequently debated issue, yet infrequently studied. Etaugh (1974) pointed out that although more concern is expressed as to the effect of maternal employment on young children, more research has been directed at the older children. The present study aimed at examining the extent to which maternal employment status, SES and age affect the development of cognitive abilities and academic achievement of young Primary School children.

Hoffman (1974) observed a negative effect of maternal employment on academic achievement and scholastic performance of primary school children. On the other hand, some studies suggest that mother-child interaction pattern is not affected by maternal employment. In view of the conflicting findings, it seems worthwhile to conduct more systematic studies to examine the impact of maternal employment on cognitive abilities and academic achievement of children.

Maternal employment seems to be a complex combination of many different factors. The relationship between maternal employment and cognitive indices may be different for different SES groups. Hence the results may be confounded by the SES of the family if we take the maternal employment variable only. Goldberg (1978) found that maternal employment was associated with more problems for lower class than middle class parents.

In Indian context there are very few studies regarding the relationship between maternal employment status and SES so far as children's cognitive development and academic achievement are concerned. In western cultures, a number of studies have been conducted in this respect, giving much importance to maternal employment status rather than to the SES (Hoffman, 1974; God & Birns, 1976; Bradley, Caldwell & Elardo, 1977). In addition to maternal employment status, a number of studies also revealed that SES is an influential determinant of cognitive ability and academic achievement of children in Indian social set-up. As discussed earlier, the employed mothers are more satisfied with their life than unemployed mothers (Gold & Andres, 1978a; 1978b; Hoffman, 1980; Hoffman & Nye, 1974).

In the present study children from two age levels were taken to study the developmental differences in cognitive ability and academic achievements. There were for each of two age levels four subgroups generated by combination of high and low SES from employed and unemployed mothers' group.

The following two hypotheses were investigated:

1. Maternal employment status would significantly influence children's cognitive abilities and academic achievements. That is, children of Employed and Unemployed mothers would differ significantly in their cognitive abilities and academic achievements.
2. The socio-economic status (SES) of children would significantly influence their cognitive abilities and academic achievements. In other words, children of high SES and low SES groups would differ significantly in their abilities.

METHOD

Sample

Two hundred primary school children participated in the study. They were drawn following a 3 (2 × 2 × 2) Factorial Group Design. The first factor (A), maternal employment status had two levels : employed and unemployed. The second factor (B), Socio-economic status (SES), also two levels : High SES and low SES. The third factor (C), Age also had two levels : Younger (6-8 years) and Older (9-11 years). Thus, the Design (2 × 2 × 2) yielded 8 cells, each representing a subgroup of the total sample. There were 25 children in each subgroup.

All the children were taken from the regional language (Oriya) medium Primary Schools under Bhubaneswar

Municipality, the Capital City of the State, Puri Municipality, an international tourist centre and Cuttack Municipality, commercial capital of the State of Orissa.

At the initial stage 600 children both boys and girls belonging to Grade-II and Grade-IV of Oriya medium Primary Schools under the municipalities in the three cities were contacted in their schools to obtain information regarding their age, caste, parental income, educational qualification of parents, occupational status of father, maternal employment status, total number of family members and their present postal address. The investigator also interviewed their parents to confirm the informations collected from the schools.

The children above 75th percentile and those below 25th percentile of the income distribution were selected as belonging to high and low SES, respectively. As such, those having parental monthly income above Rs. 3000 belonged to the high SES group. Children belonging to families with monthly parental income below Rs. 1000 belonged to the low SES group.

The high and low SES children were further classified on the basis of their maternal employment status. The mothers were classified as employed when they were working at full time jobs, for at least four consecutive years and none of the unemployed mothers did ever hold a paid job. The four subgroups of maternal employment and SES were closely matched for age and grade. In grade II, the range of the age was between 6 to 8 years and in grade-IV, it was between 9 to 11 years. The mean age level for grade-II and grade-IV children independent of maternal employment and SES were 6.45 and 9.47 years, respectively.

The educational qualification of mothers of the sample belonging to low SES group and high SES group were below matriculation and above graduation, respectively. The minimum educational qualification of fathers of sample belonging to high SES group was post-graduation level and above. But the educational qualification for fathers of sample belonging to low SES group was below matriculation. The mean age of the fathers and the mothers were 38.54 and 31.55 years, respectively. All the children in the samples were taken from two-parent families.

Measures

Cognitive Abilities

The cognitive tasks suitable for both age levels in order to evaluate developmental difference in level of performance were used. Three tasks of the test battery namely Digit Span (forward) Test (Weschler, 1974), Free Recall Test (Jachuck & Mohanty, 1974), and Serial Recall Test (Das, 1973) were measures of associative memory and three other tasks namely Raven's Coloured Progressive Matrices, Digit Span (backward) Test, Figure Copying Test and Clustering Test (Jachuck & Mohanty, 1974) were used to measure conceptual ability of the children. All the tests have also been used widely in various studies in Orissa.

Academic Achievement Measures

The previous annual examination marks of the children in four compulsory subjects were taken as indicators of academic achievement. Five scores were obtained in all, four for each of the compulsory subjects and one total score combining all of them.

Procedure

All the tests were administered individually except the Figure Copying Test which was administered in groups of five children. The achievement scores of the children were obtained from the school examination records.

RESULTS AND DISCUSSION

The means and Standard deviations of cognitive abilities tests and academic achievement measures appear in Tables 10.1, 10.2 and 10.3 present the results of ANOVA.

TABLE 10.1 : **Mean and Standard Deviations for Cognitive Ability Tests and Academic Achievement Variables**

Variables		Employed Mothers				Unemployed Mothers			
		High SES		Low SES		High SES		Low SES	
		Younger	Older	Younger	Older	Younger	Older	Younger	Older
Digit-Span (Forward)	M	4.44	5.84	4.56	4.76	4.56	5.52	4.36	5.24
	SD	0.85	0.83	0.57	0.59	0.75	0.70	0.79	0.71
Free Recall	M	12.88	16.48	11.32	12.56	11.88	16.72	12.04	14.36
	SD	2.83	2.08	3.08	2.97	3.06	1.97	2.85	2.36
Serial Recall	M	36.00	47.00	31.52	40.28	35.80	48.72	30.04	39.80
	SD	6.59	7.86	6.68	7.34	7.33	4.83	6.02	9.64
Raven's Coloured	M	17.88	22.20	15.68	17.04	18.04	23.96	17.44	19.52
Progressive Matrices	SD	4.55	5.61	3.94	5.30	4.42	4.98	3.93	5.95
Digit-Span	M	2.88	3.64	2.64	2.80	2.72	3.60	2.76	3.16
(Backward)	SD	0.77	0.69	0.63	0.49	0.60	0.85	0.65	0.88
Figure Copying	M	17.32	20.44	15.84	16.72	16.68	20.36	15.60	18.00
	SD	3.42	2.37	2.75	2.38	3.72	2.71	2.56	3.05
Clustering	M	0.42	0.47	0.39	0.42	0.44	0.49	0.40	0.39
	SD	0.11	0.11	0.11	0.09	0.12	0.09	0.14	0.11
Language Subject	M	57.80	61.80	44.68	42.24	50.04	57.56	31.04	38.04
Achievement	SD	15.92	14.65	26.05	21.61	28.69	19.50	17.18	17.44

TABLE 10.1 : *Contd* . . . .

Variables		Employed Mothers				Unemployed Mothers			
		High SES		Low SES		High SES		Low SES	
		Younger	Older	Younger	Older	Younger	Older	Younger	Older
Mathematics	M	70.12	78.64	40.52	42.56	50.56	61.24	36.20	42.60
Achievement	SD	24.55	17.32	24.23	22.52	28.69	23.49	19.94	26.39
Science	M	64.48	63.92	32.16	42.24	43.88	61.92	34.16	42.20
Achievement	SD	16.67	17.32	10.83	19.56	21.19	18.88	11.80	23.99
Social Studies	M	57.40	61.80	25.00	40.00	42.56	57.56	31.16	42.29
Achievement	SD	17.67	19.73	11.37	22.70	18.36	16.22	11.20	23.30
Total Marks	M	249.80	266.12	142.32	167.04	187.04	238.60	127.36	165.12
of all subjects	SD	53.01	53.17	60.08	66.23	73.50	67.18	49.45	81.22

TABLE 10.2 : **Summary of Analysis of Variance for Cognitive Test Performance**

Variable	F Ratio						
	A	B	C	AB	AC	BC	ABC
Digit-Span (Forward)	< 1	11.57**	66.03**	1.29	<1	9.14**	7.00**
Free Recall	1.39	26.56**	64.84**	4.84*	2.42	10.72**	<1
Serial Recall	2.78	6.68**	82.72**	1.07	7.36**	9.70**	5.71*
Progressive Matrices	3.62	16.02**	19.62**	<1	<1	4.56*	<1
Digit-Span (Backward)	32.52**	70.89**	93.84**	32.54**	8.93**	1.85	19.67**
Figure Copying	<1	26.85**	36.49**	1.05	1.60	4.52*	<1
Clustering	<1	13.52**	4.16*	<1	<1	1.68	<1

* p < .05

** p < .01

A = Maternal Employment, B = SES, C = Age

TABLE 10.3 : **Summary of Analysis of Variance for Achievement Tests**

Achievement Tests	F Ratio						
	A	B	C	AB	AC	BC	ABC
Language	6.54*	37.24**	1.90	<1	1.23	<1	<1
Mathematics	90.78**	519.79**	40.78**	57.01**	2.27	6.18*	<1
Science	4.02*	64.35**	11.87**	5.38*	2.61	<1	3.78
Social Studies	1.04	60.05**	19.02**	6.95**	<1	<1	1.92
Total	8.06**	86.05**	12.01**	4.80*	1.41	<1	<1

* $p < .05$
** $p < .01$
A = Maternal Employment, B = SES, C = Age

Maternal Employment

Tables 10.2 and 10.3 show that the maternal employment main effect was significant in case of only one cognitive task namely Digit-Span (backward) and in 4 out of 5 (except social studies achievement) academic achievement scores. The mean scores presented in Table 10.1 show that in the Digit-Span (Backward) Test the children of unemployed mothers scored significantly higher than those of employed mothers. In the academic achievement scores, the children of employed mothers scored significantly higher than the children of unemployed mothers in all five measures.

Interaction of maternal employment and SES. It was found that only in case of two cognitive tasks i.e., Free Recall and Digit-Span (Backward), this effect was significant. In case of academic achievement, the interaction was significant in four out of the five (except language subject achievement) tasks. In case of free recall, the children of unemployed high SES mothers had lower mean scores compared to children of employed high SES mothers. But the children of employed low SES mothers had lower mean scores compared to those of unemployed low SES mothers. In case of free Recall test the children of employed low SES mothers scored the lowest. In case of Digit-Span (Backward) significant interaction was found. The pattern of the mean scores was similar to that of the mean scores of free recall.

Of the four academic achievement scores in which the maternal employment and SES interaction was found to be significant, two scores (Science and Social Studies achievement) showed similar mean score pattern as Free Recall and Digit-Span (Backward). In the other two (Mathematics and total marks of all subjects) significant differences in mean scores were noticed in the high SES groups of children of employed and unemployed mothers. In case of low SES groups maternal employment did not produce much difference in the mean scores of children in mathematics achievement and total marks of all subjects.

It was also confirmed from the application of Scheffe test that the simple effect of employment was not significant for the children belonging to high SES group in case of Free Recall and Digit-Span test (Backward) score, but significant in case of school achievement scores in Mathematics, Science, Social Studies and aggregate marks in all subjects. The simple effect of employment was also found to be non-significant for the subjects belonging to low SES group in case of these four academic achievement scores, whereas, it was found significant only for Free Recall scores.

With regard to the interaction between maternal employment and age it was observed that only in case of two cognitive test scores, Serial Recall and Digit-Span (Backward), maternal employment and age had significant effects.

In case of Serial Recall the maternal employment main effect was not found to be significant. The older children performed significantly better in Serial Recall than the younger children, irrrespective of maternal employment.

The Digit-Span (Backward) scores showed significant maternal employment × age interaction. The pattern of mean scores was almost similar to that of the Serial Recall test. That is, older children scored significantly higher than the younger children. Maternal employment produced minor differences. The Scheffe test confirmed that the simple effect of employment was non-significant for the children belonging to younger group and older group in case of Serial Recall and Digit-Span (Backward) Scores.

Maternal Employment Status, Cognitive Abilities and Academic Achievement

It was observed from the findings of present study that maternal employment status contributed positively to the academic achievement scores of children but not to their cognitive abilities scores. It means that when mothers are employed, their children do well academically. However, mother's employment status did not seem to contribute to children's cognitive abilities.

It was expected that maternal employment would contribute positively towards children's academic progress. This can be attributed to several direct and indirect influences of maternal employment. First, it improves the economic condition of the family, thereby, improving children's overall need satisfaction for optimal development as well as providing necessary expenses, for educational activities.

These findings support the earlier findings of a number of studies. Hoffman (1979) and Woods (1972) observed that maternal employment contributed positively to the various economic, social and psychological conditions of the family which led to qualitatively better child rearing practices. Gold and Andres (1978a; b); Dizard (1968) and Hoffman (1973) also observed that the working mothers were more satisfied with their life than non-working mothers. Similarly, Etaugh (1974), Nye and Hoffman (1963) and Hoffman and Nye (1974) found that maternal employment correlated with income, maternal educational status, presence of husband, number of children, ordinal position of the child and parental attitude, all of which also relate to academic abilities.

Some Indian studies have also corroborated these findings. Bala and Upadhyaya (1992) observed that employed mothers are very much protective, whereas unemployed mothers are more disciplinarian in case of child rearing practices. Similarly, Das and Mathur (1992) also found that working women have a significantly higher level of need achievement.

Further, maternal employment produces greater awareness and concern for children's education due to social exposure and interactions. Cassidy (1988) observed that full-time maternal employment was associated with better schooling and social adjustment. Studies of lower socio-economic status populations and one parent families observed that employed mothers are more likely to have structured rules for their children and consistency between theory and practice. Almquist and Angrist (1971) observed that working mother's families increased academic and occupational competence of daughters and contributed to positive adjustment in general.

On the contrary, studies by Gold and Andres (1978a; 1978b; Gold, Andres & Glorieux, 1979) indicated that employed mother's children showed better social adjustment but they did not show significant differences on any academic variables. Banducei (1967) also obtained similar findings.

The findings of the present study corroborate some earlier findings. Piotrkowski and Katz (1982) observed that relatively specific relationships may exist between the employment conditions of parents and aspects of children's school behaviour. Similarly Kriesberg (1970) found that employed mothers' children obtained higher grades in school when no husband was present, but the results were opposite in case of general family condition with husband. Delgrade *et al.* (1993) observed that mothers' demands were positively related to their beliefs about their children's ability and to the children's level of achievement.

Why maternal employment did not contribute to children's cognitive abilities needs some discussion. Firstly, the cognitive tests used in the present study might not be measuring the types of cognitive abilities fostered at home in the Indian context. Not only children but their parents are also ignorant about importance of such skills. Therefore, while employed mothers may be contributing positively to their children's cognitive developments in general or diffuse ways, they did not seem to be contributing to the specific cognitive skills assessed here. Similar findings have been reported in earlier studies (Polona, 1972).

The significant SES effect found in case of cognitive test scores indicated that the general impact of SES can be more easily detected than the specific effects of SES related variables like maternal employment status. Together with SES, maternal employment seems to have significant effects, but mother's employment status as such did not significantly affect children's cognitive development.

Role of Socio-economic Status

It was hypothesized that SES would significantly influence children's cognitive abilities and academic achievement.

The Summary of ANOVA presented in Tables 10.2 and 10.3 showed that SES main effect was significant in case of all the cognitive tasks and academic achievement measures. Children belonging to high SES group have scored significantly higher than their low SES counterparts.

As regards the effects interaction between SES and age, it was observed that such effects were significant for all the cognitive test scores except Digit-Span (Backward) and clustering test. In case of academic achievement the SES × age interaction was also found to be significant only for Mathematics achievement (Table 10.2).

The simple effect of SES was found to be significant for the children belonging to younger group, in case of Serial Recall test, Figure Copying test and Mathematics achievement scores, whereas in case of Digit-Span test (Forward), Free Recall and Raven's Coloured Progressive Matrices (RCPM) test scores there was no difference. The simple effect of SES was found to be significant for children belonging to older group in case of Digit-Span (Forward), Free Recall, Serial Recall, RCPM, Figure Copying and Mathematics achievement scores.

It was also observed that the interaction between maternal employment, SES and age was found significant for only three cognitive test scores — Digit-Span (Forward and Backward) and Serial Recall test.

It seems, the interaction between SES and employment is not consistent with age. But the application of Scheffe test revealed that there was not a significant difference between the performance of employed and unemployed mother's children, but a significant difference was obtained for children belonging to high and low SES group and younger and older group in case of Digit-Span test (Forward and Backward) and Serial Recall test scores. Similarly, the difference between the performance of high SES employed mother's children and low SES unemployed mothers' children was found to be significant and also the same result was obtained in case of high SES younger and low SES older group for the Digit-Span (Forward & Backward) and Serial Recall test scores, respectively.

It was observed that the SES of children's families was found to have significant effects in case of all cognitive test scores and school achievement scores. These findings suggest that SES, comprising of indices of parental education, occupation, family size, income, social caste, and material possessions of the home contributed positively to cognitive development and academic achievement of children.

Some Indian studies have corroborated these findings. Pathak (1974) and Chatterjee (1971) found that family background variables such as parental education, parental income, religion and caste were most important predictors of educational, cognitive and perceptual functioning of children. Similarly, Das (1973), observed that poverty and socio-cultural deprivations have adverse influences on cognitive and academic abilities of children.

The age main effect was found to be significant in case of all the seven cognitive test scores and in four out of five (except language subject achievement scores (Tables 10.2 and 10.3). The mean scores for all cognitive test (Table 10.1) showed that the children belonging to higher age group scored significantly higher than those of lower age group. In case, of academic achievement scores the similar pattern of mean scores were observed except the language subject achievement score.

Thus, in general, the findings of the present study indicated that maternal employment status contributed positively and significantly towards children's academic progress. It seems, in Indian context the maternal employment factor directly improves the SES of the family and satisfies the overall needs of children indirectly. In addition to that, compared to unemployed mothers, the employed mothers are more aware of and concerned about their children's academic progress due to greater social exposure. Apart from this, employed mothers are more likely to have structured rules for their children and greater consistency between theory and practice in child rearing.

A typical concern with maternal employment has been with the care that the child of a working mother receives during the mother's absence. The nature of the substitute care is of paramount importance. Evidently it is important to examine the nature of the maternal care itself, interchanges that occur between working mothers and their young children and the nature of input into the child's social and cognitive development when the mother is employed. The children of working mothers are not necessarily adversely affected.

Hoffman (1980) indicated that maternal employment may involve less supervision or more independence training and greater autonomy for the child. Hill and Stafford (1981) reported that less educated women reduced the amount of child-care as they increased their time in the labour force, but more educated women maintained closer to the same levels of child-care with increased labour force participation.

The findings of present study revealed that maternal employment did not contribute to children's cognitive abilities assessed by the tests used in the present study. This may be due to the fact that abilities fostered at home are different and low SES parents may not be focusing on these skills. But SES significantly influenced cognitive abilities and academic achievements. So it is evident that together with SES, maternal employment has significant effects, but perhaps not by itself. In other words, maternal employment may be a significant contributor to the SES of the family, but by itself it did not seem to contribute directly to children's cognitive development. although it has positive influence on their academic performance.

REFERENCES

Almquist, E. & Angrist, S.S. (1971). Role model influences on college women's career aspirations. *Merrill-Palmer Quarterly, 17*, 263-279.

Bala, P., & Upadhyaya, K. (1992). Child rearing attitudes of employed and unemployed mothers. *Journal of Personality*

& Clinical Studies, 8, 157-160.

Banducei, R. (1967). The effect of mother's employment on achievement, aspirations and expectations of the child. *Personnel and Guidance Journal, 46,* 263-267.

Bradley, R., Caldwell, B., & Elardo, R. (1977). Home-environment, social status and mental test performance. *Journal of Educational Psychology, 69,* 697-701.

Cassidy, J. (1988). Child mother attachment and the self in six year-olds. *Child Development, 59,* 123-134.

Chatterjee, B.B. (1971). Patterns of schools achievement in primary grades : A Critical review of the developmental norms of children. *Indian Educational Review,* April.

Das, J.P. (1973). Structure of cognitive abilities : Evidence for simultaneous and successive processing. *Journal of Educational Psychology, 65,* 103-108.

Das, I. & Mathur, R. (1992). Need achievement as related to Type A/B Behaviour patterns among working and nonworking women. *Indian Journal of Clinical Psychology, 19,* 18-22.

Delgrade, H; Maria & Miller, & Scott, A. (1993). Mother's accuracy in predicting their children's I.Qs. : Its relationship to antecedent variables, mother's academic achievement demands and children's achievement. *Journal of Experimental Education, 62,* 43-59.

Dizard, J. (1968). *Social change in the family.* Chicago : Community and Family Study Centre, University of Chicago.

Etaugh, C. (1974). Effect of maternal employment on children : A review of recent research. *Merrill Palmer Quarterly, 20,* 71-98.

Gold, D. & Andres, D. (1978a). Developmental comparisons between ten year old children with employed and unemployed mothers. *Child Development, 49,* 75-79.

Gold, D., & Andres, D. (1978b). Development comparisons between adolescent children with employed and unemployed mothers. *Merrill-Palmer Quarterly, 24,* 243-254.

Gold, D., Andres, D., & Glorieux, J. (1979). The development of Francophone nursery school children with employed and unemployed mothers. *Canadian Journal of Behavioural Science, 11,* 169-173.

Gold, M. & Birns, B. (1976). Social class and infant intelligence. In M. Lewis (Ed.), *Origins of Intelligence,* New York : Plenum.

Goldberg, R.J. (1978). Development in the family and School Context : Who is responsible for the education of young children in America? *Paper Presented at the National Association for the Education of Young Childen Annual*

Conference, New York.

Hill, C.R., & Stafford, F.P. (1981). Parental care of Children : Time diary estimates of quantity predicability and variety. *The working paper series, Institute of Social Research*, University of Michigan.

Hoffman, L.W. (1973). *The professional woman as mother*. In R.B. Kundsin (Ed.), *A conference on successful women in the sciences*. New York : New York Academy of Science.

Hoffman, L.W. (1974). Effect of maternal employment on the child - a review of the research. *Developmental Psychology*, *10*, 204-208.

Hoffman, L.W. (1979). Maternal employment : 1979. *American Psychologists, Special Issue*, *34*, 859-865.

Hoffman, L.W. (1980). The effect of maternal employment on the academic attitudes and performance of school-aged children. *School Psychological Review*, *9*, 319-335.

Hoffman, L.W. & Nye, F.I. (1974). *Working mothers*. Jossey Bass: San Francisco.

Jachuck, K., & Mohanty, A.K. (1974). Low-socio-economic status and progressive retardation of cognitive skills : A test of cumulative deficit hypothesis. *Indian Journal of Mental Retardation*, *7*.

Kriesberg, L. (1970). *Mothers in poverty : A study of fatherless families*. Chicago : Aldine.

Nye, F.I., & Hoffman, L.W. (Eds.) (1963). *The employed mothers in America*. Chicago : Rand-McNally.

Pathak, P. (1974). Mental development patterns during infancy and some related factors, *Pscyhological Studies*, *19*, 1-7.

Piotrokowski, C.; & Katz, M.H. (1982). Indirect socialisation of children : The effects of mothers' jobs on academic behaviours. *Child Development*, *53*, 1520-1529.

Pleck, J.H. & Rustad, M. (1978). Husbands' and wives' time in family work and paid work in the 1975-76 study of time use. *Unpublished manuscript*. Wellesley College, Centre for Research on Women.

Polona, M.M. (1972). Role conflict and the married Professional Woman. In C. Safilios-Rothschild (Ed.), *Toward a Sociology of Women*. Lexington, Mass : Xerox College Publishing.

Wechsler, D. (1974). *Wechsler intelligence scale for children*. New York : Psychological Corporation.

Woods, M.B. (1972). The unsupervised child of the working mother. *Developmental Psychology*, *6*, 14-25.

11

Cultural Differences In Mothering Daughters

Rachana Johri and **Anand Prakash**

Mothering constitutes a crucial part of the agenda of the discipline of developmental psychology. Despite differences on major issues, developmental psychologists of diverse theoretical predilections tend to emphasize the role of mothering in the emotional and cognitive development of the child (Burman, 1994). While mothers have been researched exclusively with the aim to study their impact on children, their own experiences have rarely been explored. The central assumption of the child centered discourse (within which the mother-daughter narrative is framed) is of the dependent child and the caretaker mother. It is assumed that the child is a repository of unmet needs which the mother must first 'understand' and then meet. In such a conceptualization there is little room for the mothers' agency.

Phoenix, Woolett and Llyod (1991) point out that most accounts of developmental psychology refer to the 'mother' and the 'child' as decontextualized entities. This is of significance to the present analysis in two respects. First, the child referred to in psychology is without gender. Secondly, cutural and contextual issues in the mothering of children are largely ignored.

This chapter makes an attempt at critiquing one aspect of this universalization, namely in the domain of mother-daughter relations. The past two decades have seen a resurgence of interest in the understanding of mother-daughter relations, sometimes referred to as the 'maternal turn' (Flax, 1993) in the feminist theory. Psychologists and feminists grappling with the problematic aspects of feminine identity have sought to understand it within the matrix of this relationship. The first part of this chapter begins with a brief overview of the dominant understanding of mother-daughter relationships. The second section examines the problems in such a conceptualization, highlighting in particular the differing cultural conceptualizations of the issue of separation — autonomy as described in literature and as it appears in the traditional Indian context.

Overview of Mother-Daughter Relationship

To contextualize the present analysis it is important to point to the origins of interest in this enquiry. Briefly, feminists working within consciousness raising groups initially conceptualized relationships between women within the metaphor of 'sisterhood'. Sisterhood implied a non-hierarchical relationship of equality between women. In working within these groups, however, it soon became apparent that relationships between women were fraught with their own difficulties and marked by the unconscious feelings of hostility and envy as well as the desire to nurture and be nurtured. Feminists troubled by issues such as these turned to psychoanalysis and to the mother-daughter relationship for a better understanding of the formation of female subjectivity.

Briefly, what is today referred to as the mother-daughter issue involves understanding the formation of the daughters' subjectivity in terms of her relationship with mother. As feminists, most writers engaged in the field view mother within a patriarchal society and to various degrees oppressed by it. The continuity between mother and daughter results in similarity between the mother and the daughter, creating the internalization of feminity within the daughter.

While continuity may be less traumatic in certain respects than the separation necessary for healthy development in a son. It may also means an internalization of the oppressed aspects of feminity. Eichenbaum and

Orbach (1983) particularly point to the projection of negative aspects of identity from the mother to the daughter. The daughter then picks up the neediness of the mother and is unable to turn to her for the meeting of her own needs. This burden of unmet needs remains a dominant aspect of a woman's subjectivity.

Both Chodorow (1976) and Eichenbaum and Orbach (1983) emphasize the continuity of gender identity in girls. They also share a common concern with mother-daughter relationships and hence, pre-Oedipal as opposed to Oedipal development. The mother occupies central position in the formation of the daughter's gender identity. Chodorow believes that for daughters the problem is not in the core gender identity which is in fact built on a sense of continuity but on the later developments as the girl child begins to understand the culture's devaluation of this feminity. As Chodorow puts it the greater identification with the mother accounts for the desire in girls to be mothers when they grow up. However, living in patriarchal societies, women in general and mothers in particular do not necessarily experience themselves as powerful. Thus, daughters internalize the powerlessness of being women in this process.

Relying on differing versions of post-Freudian theory it is argued that the mothering of daughters in patriarchal cultures results in a vicious cycle of dependency. Because society has not met her needs, the mother unconsciously transmits to the daughter the ideal of the desirability of suppression of needs. The adult daughter is therefore left with an unmet craving for nurturance along with feelings of guilt for seeking this, as well as aggression towards a mother who has failed to provide it to her. Adult relationships between women, and particularly that between the mother and the daughter are characterized by ambivalence and conflict. This is heightened by the foregrounding of sexuality in the culture, such that women in general (sometimes including mothers and daughters) experience competitiveness and jealousy towards each other.

This picture of mother-daughter relationships has not

met with unequivocal support from western psychology. Relational theorists and feminists argue that the expectation of autonomous development in daughters amounts to the imposition of a male norm. From the Indian context, it may also be pointed out that the ideal of separation and autonomy are derived from specific cultural contexts and may not apply to others. Nevertheless, where autonomy is the desired ideal, the 'unseparated daughter' is clearly constructed as immature and weaker than her male counterpart.

The Indian Context of Womanhood

Much has been written about Indian womanhood. Although the symbolic and social existence of women in India is certainly of relevance to an understanding of mothering daughters. This chapter will limit to a few significant points. As several commentators have pointed out, there are three positions usually available to the woman, those of the daughter, wife and mother, it is the latter through which she gains maximum power and prestige (Kakar, 1981). However, motherhood is legitimate and empowering only within the context of marriage. It is defined as an aspect of being a *pativrata* (dutiful wife) and is an extremely contingent power, resting on the ability to produce sons. Both classical texts and contemporary practices attest to the marked preference for male children in Hindu India.

Interestingly, despite the dominance of the motherhood idiom, representation of mother-child relations always refer to the mother-son relationship. Recent research has shown the relative absence of mothers and daughters in Indian myths. Even in modern times, there are few if any representations the mothering of daughters although recent exceptions can be found both in literature and in the visual media. This is in marked contrast to the pervasive image of Yashoda and Krishna to which divinity is ascribed. While the daughter is obviously missing in the popular narratives, it also points to the absence of the mother of daughters.

There is some evidence that a desire for sons need not imply a lack in the affectional relationship with the daughter. While sons are desired for the status, power and symbolic value they bestow on the mother, daughters too have an autonomous space (Kakar, 1981 : Mandelbaum, 1988). Anthropological research also suggests that daughters are not necessarily rejected, although the welcome to them can be contingent on a number of factors. Practices such as female foeticide and active as well as passive infanticide are far from being the norm, although there is a growing incidence of these particularly in the northern belt of India. Amongst the upper and upper middle classes there is some evidence of voluntary participation in these by mothers. Yet my own interviews as well as much anthropological evidence suggests that there is a separate space reserved for daughters and they can be treated with great affection particularly because it is well accepted that they will ultimately have to leave their homes. Nevertheless the dominant issue in parents' mind is the marriageability of the daughter. In Hindu North India particularly, parents of daughters are generally lower on the hierarchy of power than those of sons. The nature of the emotional relationship with the daughter is usually strongly mediated by her impending marriage.

In the Hindu cultural context a daughter is placed within the *apni/parayi* classificatory scheme. She is widely described as a guest within the home of her parents. The ritual of *kanyadaan* (the gift of the virgin) in marriage by the parents marks her transition from the natal home to the home of her husband. Once given away the daughter is classified as 'other'. Although this context is changing and being redefined, it nevertheless forms a significant aspect of both the representations of womanhood and the experienced existences of most women.

From the point of view of the mother embedded within such a context, the daughter's birth evokes thoughts of her immanent separation. Folk songs sung at the daughter's birth often make reference to the limited duration of this relationship. It is the central argument of this chapter that in a context where the mother-daughter relationship gets its basic definition within the notion of separation, this relationship is likely to be characterized by strong emotional ties with little guilt in the expression of the need for each other. However, the cultural sanctions may reduce its possibility.

Separation in the Indian Context

Western theorizing focuses on continuity in the identities of mother and daughter and the ensuing difficulties in separation and the formation of an individuated self. In the Indian context, it may be argued that the separation between the mother and daughter is assumed to be a central feature of the relationship. The widely reported mourning at the daughter's birth in many parts of India, is evoked not only because she is not the desired son — the access to power for the mother—but also because the daughter is constructed as someone who will go away. Unlike the West, where the daughter's task seems to be to maintain autonomy from the mother, the Indian context poses the opposite conflict for the mother and the daughter, that of retaining connectedness in a culture where daughterhood is virtually equated with separation.

In her early writing, Chodorow (1978) points out that mothering may not be accompanied by a sense of powerlessness in all cultures. She cites examples of relatively matrifocal societies where this dependency is accompanied by a sense of maturity and relative autonomy from the male sphere. These societies are characterized by extended kin networks amongst women as well as a greater participation in the economic sphere. Thus despite a very poor social status women display higher self esteem as far as gender identity is concerned. The greater demand for absolute separation from the mother in Western culture creates the pathological conditions of dependency that are sometimes seen in women patients. In such a system a vicious cycle of mother-daughter blame gets set up. In a context of mothering in which the mother is unable to help the daughter establish ego differentiation, the daughter establishes boundaries artificially by projecting those parts of herself that she defines as bad onto the mother thereby establishing a distance from the mother.

Recently, Chodorow (1995) has suggested that the feelings of shame and guilt are often a significant part of the daughter's emotions towards the mother. One form of guilt manifests itself as 'weeping for the mother'. Characterized by a tremendous sense of sadness for the mother, this is more likely to be seen in 'classic patriarchies' such as India.

This is characterized by a sense of extreme sadness at the memory of the oppression in the mother's life and a sense of guilt for one's own relatively trouble free life. Yet the specific patterns of gender identity may vary from repeating the pattern in an equally oppressive relationship with men, continuing the relationship by crying with one's own mother, to opting out of heterosexual relationships altogether. In such cultures there may be a greater empathic concern shared between mothers and daughters marking them out from the more ambivalent mother-daughter relationships that characterize the average middle class American women. This is one major difference between Chodorow and many of the other psychoanalytically oriented feminists.

The insights of Chodorow and others are simultaneously explanatory and problematic for the understanding of mother-daughter relationships in contemporary Indian society. While there is little doubt about the patriarchal construction of Indian womanhood and the connectedness between the identity of mother and daughter, important points of difference also seem to arise. It is with these that this chapter is concerned.

METHOD

The Participants

The data for this chapter is based on long interviews with 30 women who have at least three daughters. There were 10 women each from three categories. The first group consisted of lower class women living in the slums of

Delhi. A second group of women came from the upper middle to upper class. The third group was made up of professional women including doctors, teachers, administrators and social workers.

The main criteria for selecting the participants was the fact that they had three or more daughters. A few of them also had one son. Although the initial plan of the study was to work with only those mothers who had daughters, it was difficult to find such women, particularly in the lower class group. The other basis for selection was the age range of the daughters. The women who were interviewed had at least one adult daughter. This was significant to get a perspective on mothering experiences across the life span but including the years of adolescence and adulthood but also to highlight the role of the ideology of *kanyadaan* in the issue of mothering daughters.

Procedure

The interviews were largely unstructured. The flow was determined at least in part by the participants. The interviews were conducted in the homes of the women. Each interview took about two hours. This was apart from the time spent in making the initial contact. The researcher also spent considerable time in the slum colony in which some of the interviews were conducted. All the interviews were transcribed. The analysis presented here is entirely qualitative.

Results and Discussion

Listening to mother's accounts of mothering daughters suggested that mother's acknowledge the construction of the daughter as located within the *apni/parayi* classificatory scheme. Although the extent of their acquiescence to this varies, it seems that the ideal of *kanyadaan* within which this is constructed places limits on the extent of this challenge.

In response to questions regarding their feeling for their daughters, most mothers emphasized the closeness and the caring quality of the relationship. Mothers seemed to experience the quality of continuity mentioned by Chodorow and others.

Given the rapid changes in our society, it was not surprising to hear several voices on the description of the daughter as 'the one who has to be given away'. That the separation from the daughter figures as a significant aspect of the relationship is evident in the following excerpts from a few of the interviews.

The first quote is from Kanta. Kanta has four daughters and one son. She has lived in the *basti* since her marriage. Kanta herself is not educated but all her children are receiving the best education that she and her husband, a skilled worker, currently unemployed can give them. Both the eldest daughters have completed their schooling and have technical qualifications. Speaking of her love for her duaghters, Kanta said,

"I love her and the elder one the most."

"Not the sons", I asked

"Yes, I do but the daughter belongs to another home. Who knows if she will be loved in the next home. What kind of people she will be with? A son always remains close to one (*seene ke pas rehta hai*). We love them also but not as much as the daughter. My elder daughter has gone back yesterday. Since she left, I just can't feel at home (*man nahin lag raha hai*)."

Similarly, the extremely articulate, Swarn, responding to my question about the difference between having sons and daughters,

"When a daughter is born, there is no such anxiety (regarding the meeting of expectations). She belongs to another home. I have to separate from her some day. I believe you should give her as much love as you can because ultimately she is not going to stay on with us. Then there is no expectation from her that she should earn for us. There is no give and take which is the greatest source of enmity between people. We love her, give her everything possible, educate her and generate all sorts of capabilities in her."

It is apparent that the love for the daughter arises from an impending sense of loss and the time bound nature of the relationship. Embedded within a culture which prioritizes the daughter's marriage, and knowing from personal experience the possibility of oppression within it, their love for the daughter involves a quality of care and compassion. The note of compassion often arises early in the daughter's life and is involved in her construction of womanhood.

Listening to women speaking about their experience of motherhood suggests that the relationship with daughter is constructed by most women as one who must ultimately belong to another and hence separated. While western descriptions focus on continuity and the ambivalence this generates towards individuation, the traditional pattern here seems to involve an attitude of indulgence and compassion towards the daughter who must finally leave the mother.

The interviews also suggest that mothers and daughters wish for greater continuity but are often unable to gain this. Clearly, there is some space in the culture for this, for visits to the maternal home are sanctioned to the girl. In some cases she is also allowed to bring her own parents to her home and look after them. For most women, however, these spaces are not easily available.

Two poignant descriptions from the narratives speak of the participants speaking on the daughters sorrow in being unable to care for her mother. The element of mutual mourning is visible in Bharati speaking of her mother's loneliness.

Take my case, my mother was ill. From within, I wanted to stay with her. So I told him, you go back home, I'll stay on. He started fighting with me red with anger (*mujhe laal peeli ankhen dikhani suru kar di*). My mother said, "Beta, you go". So I came home protesting but I knew I would not see her again. He took me when she died, he did care for her but I keep wishing I could have stayed on, cared for her. I could have made food for her, whatever she wanted, and fed it to her, with my own hands. I wanted to bathe her, look after her with my own hands. Her soul would have rested, my children are looking after me . . . . I feel she ruined her life for us, we could have done something for her.

The cultural notion of detachment and the finitude of all relationships is often used to negotiate the pain felt on the daughter's departure. For a mother of daughters, 'it is simply not possible to keep a daughter at home'. There are fantasies of 'keeping one with me' but these are generally seen as a shameful aspect of the self. The marriage of the daughter and her departure from the home becomes symbolic of the impermanence of life.

Since separation between the mother and the daughter is accepted, there is little expression of aggression in it. In contrast, sons who are increasingly leaving home are viewed as excessively autonomous and therefore evoke either a sense of anger or a depression on the part of parents.

In the context of urban India, however, at least some of the narratives included a critique of this construction as well as some attempts to resist it. At the present historical juncture this construction is being modified through the changes in the position of the son. While increasing numbers of sons are moving away from the mother's home, daughters seem to be filling up the space by reasserting their relationships with their parents even after their marriage. Rather than protest over continuity and lack of individuation, the daughter is resisting her self description as 'other' and attempting access to powerful position of the son by reasserting her continuity with the natal home.

These resistances, which allow daughters to access more space to move away from categories where they would fit traditionally, may emerge as a result of modernizing forces operating in a society. The mother, too, is resisting herself description as 'separate' from the daughter by offering her possibilities to re-establish the relationship particularly in the case of marital breakdown. This has important implications as even today, marriage remains the dominant theme in their lives, and aspects such as education occupy a secondary position (Chanana, 1996).

This is not to suggest that such forces are necessarily liberating for women in all respects. On the contrary, certain aspects of modernization such as the availability of sex determination technologies seem to have disturbed the precarious balance in the ambivalent relationship towards the daughter characteristic of traditional India. The spaces for progressive development of women may similarly arise either from the continuity of these with traditional spaces or at times, from contradictions. The analysis of women's folk music reflects their resistance to the classification as *parayi* and is an attempt at reclaiming the position of the daughter in the natal home and is indicative of resistance within the traditional. On the other hand, contemporary mothers seem to refer to the discourse of gender equality in times of crisis for their daughters.

To return to the central argument of this chapter, the characteristic conflict and ambivalence that daughters feel towards the mother in the western context does not appear to be the dominant pattern in North India (Trawick, 1990 suggests otherwise in her study of love in Tamil Nadu). Mothers and daughters recognize the mutual constraints on their lives, daughters often long to return to the maternal home, the *maika* and any anger towards the mother is likely to be felt not at her inability to give autonomy but to her inability to nurture. A pattern of 'weeping for the mother' (Chodorow, 1995) may be prevalent in India but is often mutual and does not seem to include the sense of guilt Chodorow speaks of. This difference could arise from the differing voices of mothers and daughters although I would suggest that mutual mourning for their collective fate as women and a longing to return to the unseparated state may be more prevalent. Only where marked differences in cultural opportunity distinguish the position of the daughter from the mother is the daughter likely to experience guilt or its opposite—a rejection and sense of shame towards the mother.

The study points to the need for rethinking the issue of motherhood with an orientation to listening to the voices of mothers themselves particularly from differing cultural contexts.

REFERENCES

Burman, E. (1994). *Deconstructing developmental psychology.* London and New York : Routledge.

Chanana, K. (1996). Educational attainment, status production and women's autonomy : A study of two generations of Punjabi Women in New Delhi. In R. Jeffery and A.M. Basu (ed.). *Girls' schooling, women's autonomy and fertility change in South Asia.* Sage Publications. New Delhi.

Chodorow, N. (1995). Gender as a personal and cultural construction. *Signs: Journal of Women in Culture and Society, 20,* 516-544.

Chodorow, N. (1978). *The reproduction of mothering : Psychoanalysis and the sociology of gender.* Berkeley: University of California Press.

Chodorow, N. & Contratto, S. (1989). 'The fantasy of the perfect mother'. In N. Chodorow (Ed.) *Feminism and psychoanalytic theory.* New Haven; Yale University Press.

Eichenbaum, L and Orbach, S. (1983). *Understanding women.* Penguin Books.

Ernst, S. and Maguire, M. (Eds.) (1987). *Living with the Sphinx.* The Women's Press.

Flax, J. (1993) Mothers and daughters revisited. In van Mens Verhulst *et al.* (Ed.) *Daughtering and mothering : Female subjectivity reanalyzed.* Routledge : London.

Kakar, S. (1981). *The Inner World : A psychoanalytic study of childhood and society in India.* Delhi. Oxford University Press.

Mandelbaum, D.G. (1988). *Women's seclusion and men's honor. Sex roles in North India, Bangladesh, and Pakistan.* The University of Arizona Press.

Phoenix, A.; Woollett, A. and Lloyd, E. (1991). *Motherhood : Meanings, practices and ideologies.* Thousand Oaks : Sage.

Trawick, M. (1990) *Notes on love in a Tamil family.* Berkeley: University of California Press.

Weedon, C. (1987). *Feminist practice and poststructuralist theory.* London : Basil Blackwell.

12

Community Participation for Rural Development

Ajit K. Dalal

In the five decades of Independence, Central and State governments have initiated an impressive array of rural development programmes. Charged with the spirit of Nehruvian socialism, the government took upon itself the task of elevating living conditions of the underprivileged in society. People showed a great deal of enthusiasm in joining government efforts towards planned rural development. There was an air of expectation that economic development will become people's programme and that development will reach to all those who, for centuries, were having a servile existence. The government indeed put in enormous men and material resources to steer India on the path of speedy development. These dreams of the planners still far from being realized. On the contrary, poverty, unemployment and inequality are on increase and the goals of health and education for all by the year 2000 seem to be unachievable. In essence, all those ambitious programmes did not succeed in triggering a developmental process, i.e., failed to motivate rural communities to mobilize local resources for development activities. People did not get involved in the governance of even those development plans which intimately affected their lives. Community participation has failed to materialize in spite of all planning and preparations. The apathy and alienation of people are held as the major factors in the failure of rural development programmes. This article examines the rural scenario from a social-psychological perspective and deliberates on the ways to augment community participation for development.

As early as in 1952, Government of India started a massive community development programme under the Indo-US agreement. In all 55 Community Development Projects were launched, each covering 300 villages and a population of 3 lakhs. These projects were intended to be planned and implemented by the local people themselves, government just offering technical and financial assistance (Jain, 1985). The goal was to inculcate a spirit of self-reliance and cooperative action through local bodies. These projects endeavoured to increase rural employment and production through the active participation of all families in the project area. Giving a very high priority to these projects, the apex administrative organ of this venture was the Central Committee, headed by the then Prime Minister. An Advisory Board was established consisting of the secretaries of various ministries. There were committees from State level down to the village level to supervise all aspects of these development projects. A cadre to village level workers was also created at the lowest, but at the most vital ladder of the administrative hierarchy.

One of the remarkable features of these projects was the concept of 'aided self-help'. The Central Committee conceived these projects as truly participatory with active involvement of local bodies. The government put up a condition of selecting only those villages where people were prepared to contribute to the project activities. People were expected to give 50% of their idle time and the government provided matching technical and financial contribution for the schemes, such as irrigation, drinking water, health, education, roads, etc. Despite being very well thought out, these programmes of aided self-help did not work. These programmes lacked vitality due to unrealistic expectations, lack of coordination and low motivational level of the participants.

To effectively implement these projects, the government created a new Ministry of Community Development in 1956. The projects were constantly monitored and evaluated. The Fourth Evaluation Report in 1956 stressed that the projects should have greater flexibility to adapt local conditions and aspirations, and should be compatible with social and cultural milieu. The Report lay greater emphasis on training people to take up the responsibility of planning and implementation of various development activities (see Jain, 1985). The government subsequently appointed the Balavantrai Mehta Committee to comprehensively review these projects. The study based on empirical data found that inspite of lofty ideal and professed policy, in real practice, communities were not involved in both the principles and method of determining priorities of these projects. The projects activities were dominated by the government bureaucracy with too many hierarchies, resulting in lack of coordination and accountability. In fact, the Seventh Evaluation Report in 1960 conclusively showed that with few exceptions community development programmes failed to attain their stated goals. They primarily remained as government programmes with rare instances of local communities mobilizing resources and running the programmes. This failure was conspicuous given the fact that the government machinery was still motivated, charged with the idealism of the post-Independence era. The failure of these projects was a serious setback to the community development movement in India, so much so that the Ministry of Community Development was reduced to the status of a Department in 1966-67. There was definite decline in fund allocation for community development programmes in 3rd and 4th Five Year Plans. The revival of these schemes in 5th and 6th Plans was only marginal and that too without any follow-up strengthening of local bodies (panchayati raj institution).

The Changing Scenario in 1980s

Two major developments in 1980s and later period qualitatively changed the development scenario in India. First was the entry of international funding agencies and the second was rapid expansion of NGO sector. Not that these two did not exist earlier, but there was never such a heavy inflow of foreign funding for community development in India. Apart from the United Nations' agencies (WHO, UNICEF, UNDP, etc.), many other agencies like World Bank, USAID, NORAD, CIDA started pouring in a large sum of money for development projects. It is estimated that more than Rs. 2000 crores comes in every year from foreign donors for rural development, and about 10,000 registered voluntary organizations receive this amount. The hold of foreign funders can be gauged from the fact that 90% of the voluntary organizations working in rural sector are dependent on this assistance for their survival. The policies and priorities of these NGOs are much guided by those of their funders. A World Bank Report (1994) revealed that (rather than grassroot planning) project implementation is the most common form of NGO involvement. More than 86% of the NGOs receive funding on project basis and their organization structure revolves round implementation activities.

The international funding agencies generally prefer to work with NGOs than with government departments. Starved of funds these NGOs are more amenable to donor influence than the government bureaucracy. Besides, there was a marked shift in the government policies by 1980s. As a policy change there was greater dependence on NGO sector for implementing all kinds of development projects. The inherent limitations of target-centred, top-down, paternalistic development models brought into sharp focus the significant role and contribution of NGOs. The NGOs are seen as ideal substitute for monolithic, rigid and corrupt government bureaucracy.

Flush with foreign funds and government patronage, the NGOs no longer remained marginal players in community development programmes as they were before 1980s. They are substituting the government in all spheres: literacy health employment, education, vocational training, etc. The assumption is that these NGOs have better appreciation of rural social realities, can work at the grassroot level to involve people in their development projects and have operational flexibility. These organizations are often idealized as people-centred, bottom-up, democratic and participatory in their functioning. Indeed, there are NGOs, as in the past, who are doing excellent work to improve the quality of life in Indian villages. The accumulating evidences do not convince that this 'article of faith' is an accurate characterization of the reality of NGOs' working in India.

No matter how much they differ in their goals and practices, there is almost a consensus among the government, NGOs and funding agencies that without active community participation the rurual development programmes are unlikely to succeed. All models of 'development from outside' were found to have a short life; they last as long as outside support lasts. Review reports indicate that top-down development projects designed and implemented by the State and NGOs have proved to be counterproductive, further marginalizing the poor (Dash, 1995). The long track record of failure has led to many questions about the present approach to development. That the government is not laying greater stress on community participation is evident from the fact that many schemes are now going through a major policy change. Many schemes are rechristened. For example, the nomenclature of reproductive health care scheme was recently changed from target-free approach to 'community need assessment', whatever that term signify. Participatory approach has now become an important consideration in funding development projects. With all development agencies outdoing each other to pay allegiance to community participation and holding it as a final solution to eradicate poverty and inequality, community participation has come to acquire the status of a demi-god.

In reality, with all experiments and experience, discussion and debate in last five decades, involving local communities in development activities has remained a formidable challenge. The fact remains that the demand and pressure for community participation has emanated from external agencies (funding agencies mostly) rather than as an outcome of felt need from the 'within'. NGOs have recognized the instrumental value of community participation both for seeking funds and for successful implementation of their project plans. Community participation is also employed as a strategy to generate additional resources at the local level. Incentives are provided to the key players in the community to mobilize local people for the project activities. Such efforts are often shortlived and participation dissipates when funding depletes.

Community participation, in essence, ought to be viewed as an internal mechanism by which a development programme becomes people's programme. It is not only economic but social process whereby disadvantaged groups get integrated in the social mainstream. It accords decision making powers to the so called 'target groups'. Rather than doling out material rewards, an important function of any development programme is to create opportunities for people to participate and derive satisfaction in their collective ventures. Community participation can be a vehicle to move towards a more egalitarian society, where human dignity, group cohesion and personal happiness are as important as economic development.

Social-Psychological Barriers

Community participation is contingent on a wide range of considerations : social, political, economic, historical, etc. All these are valid contenders for a serious discussion on augmenting community participation. The present article primarily focuses on cultural, social and psychological factors that shape the participatory behaviour of community members and their families. The challenge before social scientists to understand the barriers in community participation and bring about change in perception and interactional patterns in a community. Social scientists have to think about the factors facilitating community participation.

In fact, the same hierarchical interactional pattern seen in social life manifests in community development programmes also. People bring the same attitudes, values and relationships to community participation which structure their community life. The groups which wield social power in the community also take over the charge of development programmes. Local panchayats are the best examples of such social relationships in action. The prevailing mistrust and tension also constrains participation, and often development programmes are caught in the quagmire of intricate social dynamics. Any social psychological study of community participation must take into cognizance the social realities of Indian villages. Furthermore, what is happening in rural sector is not unrelated to the changing scenario at the national and international level. Here an effort will be made to critically examine some social and psychological barriers in participation and the possibilities of overcoming them.

Culture of Dependence

It is widely believed that Indians in general, and poor and underprivileged in particular, look outward for solutions of their problems. That when life conditions are oppressive, people endure suffering in hope that one day a saviour will appear on the scene and will set the things right. They see the problem a formidable and see no possibility of their efforts succeeding. Such a saviour syndrome leads to a passive wait for some influential person to arrive from outside, take charge of the situation, and as if with some magic wand would transform the situation and redeem their lives. This wishful thinking, indeed, turns into conviction when life conditions get worse and all their efforts fail to produce positive results. People lose faith in their personal and collective efforts. All local initiatives are seen with scepticism and are ridiculed. On the contrary, an outside agency or individual when perceived as resourceful easily becomes a rallying point for the masses. The legends of *avatars* which have deep impressions on Indian psyche only tend to reinforce people's faith in saviours.

This propensity to believe in saviours has, in fact, been exploited by both government and non-governmental agencies over the decades. The welfare officers and workers as new *avatars* make tall promises, do things to show off their influence and indulge in obtaining personal favours. They resort to free distribution of food, medicine, books, clothes and other commodities. Camps are organized and all allurements are given to people to attend them. The charitable societies and social welfare schemes of the government have reinforced this culture of dependence in last five decades. The poor and underprivileged often get carried away by these gimmicks. This situation is ideal for rich and powerful who, by default, get free hand in planning and spending funds. They patronize and favour those who accept their authority. The exploiters feign the saviours. Ramchandran (October 1, 1997) wrote in *Times of India*, "If the poor rise in revolt, there will be million mutinies. It is the faith that their status is predetermined, which makes them mute witness to rapacity perpetrated in their name. Because they never participate in programmes shaping their future, they never ask for accounts of hundreds of billions of rupees spent to elevate living standards of the poor." This culture of dependence is cultivated and sustained by engaging in ritual and rhetoric of participation which masks the real intentions.

Dube (1990) has, however, contested that people really manifest saviour syndrome. He argued that much depends on the structure of opportunities. When the community people exhaust all possibilities and meet repeated failure, they learn to accept the consequences in a spirit of resignation. When non-traditional opportunities surface, or when new technical choices were available, the same people do not lack in trying out. These were often the poor and disadvantaged who learn to accept the fate and feel helpless. Again, when it comes to religious and social activities, people show initiative, independence and collective action in planning and implementation. The question is how this spirit of collective action can be harnessed for development programme.

Changing Concept of Voluntarism

The concept and practice of voluntarism have gone

through metamorphosis in last two decades. Voluntarism is traditionally viewed as a spirit of sacrifice and sharing what one had for the general good of the society. It was considered selfless service; where a person works without any expectation of salary, or any other material reward. These were the activities which one does, besides what one does for livelihood. Such voluntarism has a long and cherished tradition in India. Rajani Kothari (1987) observed that Indian society is fundamentally voluntarist society. For ages, communtiy services primarily relied on generosity of the local people. There are instances of excellent work being done by such people in improving the quality of the underprivileged.

With the change in government policies and increasing availability of funding, a large number of NGOs have started working on development projects. They, in a way, started supplementing the work of government departments to meet official targets. These service organizations started hiring people for specific jobs for specified pay and perks. A new breed of advisors and consultants was emerging to provide professional services to service organizations. If poverty was a big business in the 1980s, Voluntarism became a big business in the 1990s, with every non-gazetted officer (ngo) starting an NGO (Bankar Roy, 1996).

With massive influx of foreign funding for various development projects, social service, indeed became a lucrative career. The foreign funding agencies lay greater emphasis on professionalism, training, documentation, programme evaluation and scientific management. The projects staff could be hired by offering high salaries, so much so that many programme managers get salary on par with senior executives of multinational companies. They live in style and conduct their business of development in the five star luxury. Community participation for them is a matter of strategy to achieve goals of their programmes.

On the contrary, the village level workers sweating in the project have a hand-to-mouth existence. They are unpaid volunteers who are expected to work hard to meet the targets. The WHO Manual (1994) for community based development clearly states that these village workers should generate local resources and that they should be self-supporting. They mostly come from the poor strata of the society and the major incentive is the social prestige they acquire due to their affliation with some reputed (aptly, an international) agency. They faithfully obey the commands of their masters to mobilize people for participation in project work. The contrast becomes glaring and baffling to a common villager when high-flying programme managers and advisors descend on their village centres. Suspicion, servility, jealousy, mistrust are the hallmarks of such lopsided relationship between project managers and village workers. Participation of the larger community in this set-up is bound to remain a goal unrealized.

Oppressive Village Environment

Many community development programmes view villages as cohesive functional units. Village community, for example, in WHO Charter (1986), is presumed to be an integrated, peaceful, mutually caring society, which lack resources and technology for development. Such a glossy picture does not project realities of Indian villages which are fragmented along the lines of caste, religion, lineage, etc. There is often mutual mistrust among various groups who are competing for scarce resources. In the villages 10% of the rich and influential control about 90% of the village resources. They control most of the development funds in villages. Any serious effort towards involving the underprivileged is considered as a threat to their hegemony and privileged status. In large number of places a long history of exploitation and oppression has numbed the spirit of downtrodden. They do not raise questions, nor do they demand participation in the programmes which affect their lives. Paternalistic and humiliating relationships are embedded in the social structure, in which the wealthy patronize the servile poor, who in exchange of charity have to show proper gratitude to those who paid them low wages and perpetrated exploitation (Petras, 1997).

Indian villages are plagued by criminalization and power politics. The criminalization is so rampant in the eastern UP that an estimate suggests that 70% of the elected block heads have criminal cases pending against them. These people have clout at all levels and it is difficult to keep them out of the community services (Dalal, 1997). They would grab all opportunities to hog the limelight and run community programmes as their personal ventures. The pretence of community participation provides a cover to their self-serving vested interests.

However, with greater media exposure (TV particularly), political awareness and with rising expectations of a better quality life, Indian villages are ushering into a new era. There is now greater resistance to injustice everywhere. The disadvantaged people are realigning to claim their share in the development-pie. They are not prepared to accept the hegemony of feudal masters, resulting in frequent clashes within the community. The widening gap between the rich and poor is unleashing the forces of realignment and fragmentation, which are operating simultaneously. People are demanding accountability and transparency. This awakening is providing a new meaning to community participation.

Building on the Strength

With all community development projects emphasizing active participation of local people, the field is buzzing with large scale grassroot activities. Often tall claims are made and glossy reports are produced by big NGOs highlighting community support which their programmes received. On the other hand there are many grassroot organizations which are doing commendable work but have generated little in terms of documentation. Again, there are very few failure stories reported and analyzed. Much of this reporting by the development organizations are dictated by the requirements of the funding agencies.

Despite all these constraints, a substantial body of knowledge is now available to deliberate on social and psychological factors which contribute to effective community participation. There are few lessons to be learned.

Community participation which build on local knowledge and resources are more likely to succeed than those which are dependent on the outside experts and specialists. Each community has its own strengths and it is important that this strength is acknowledged and incorporated in the village-sponsored development programmes. There is substantial time tested organic knowledge rooted in practical experience of the community. There are instances in which tribal people provided better skills and knowledge for reforestation than outside experts. The local knew about the climate, soil, water and could predict more accurately what will grow in that land. Given support and free-hand, often communities have shown their skills in pooling local resources and in taking a collective action.

The problem lies somewhere in the misplaced notion of development which we have borrowed from West. In the industrialized western societies development signifies economic and scientific rationality. It is equated with modernization and technological progress of a society. Tradition has no place in this view of development; in fact, it is seen as the opposite pole of development (Tripathi, 1987). Traditional beliefs and attitudes are held as impediments in speedy development. Many western writers have considered tradition as the root cause of India's low economic development (e.g., Max Weber, 1958). McClelland and Winter (1969) alleged that Hinduism does not encourage need for achievement and is responsible for low level aspirations, which characterizes Indian personality. This view is not only myopic but restricts the definition of development only in terms of economic progress. A holistic view of development should take into consideration the network of relationships which define the well-being of an individual in the Indian context.

It is often seen that when it comes to festivals and

social events there is a spontaneous response from the whole community. People organize themselves to share responsibilities and work as a cohesive-motivated group. There is a long tradition of community participation in religious functions, which need to be harnessed for development activities. The strong spiritual faith of the community which binds them altogether can also be a guiding spirit for socio-economic development. The social reformist movement of Anna Hazare in Maharashtra and Swadhyaya Movement of Shastri Athawale are the examples of using spirituality for development. The programmes build around religious centres in the community are very likely to be accepted by people as their own programmes. The danger is that one successful project cannot become a prototype, as all communities work in different social, political, economic, and cultural environment. As spirituality manifests in different ways in different communities, these communities must work out their own plans of sustainable development.

One aspect which is relatively ignored in the host of development activities is the revival of existing government infrastructure and schemes. If all the schemes for the eradication of poverty launched in last 45 years had worked, India would have been a developed country by now. Billions of rupees are spent every year on various schemes for the poor and disadvantaged. Rather than replacing the government, a major task for local NGOs could be to revive these government schemes. People should mobilize as pressure group and watchdogs, making government more responsive and accountable. Success of such initiatives are likely to bolster community's faith in collective action. Our own experiences of working with a group on a social action programme in Sirathu block of Allahabad district was very educative. We found that people tend to engage in collective action when such action are seen as yielding quick return. When they realize the power of participation it becomes self-reinforcing (Dalal, 1997).

With increasing exposure to the outside world and global influences reaching countryside on electronic waves,

Indian villages are going through a metamorphosis. They are as if waking up from a long slumber. There are indications that people are no longer prepared to be passive partners in the development process. The success of many cooperative movements and global shift with an emphasis on people-oriented development, the local communities are gearing to play a more active role. This changing scenario makes one hopeful that the time is ripe for development programmes going community way.

REFERENCES

Dalal, A.K. (1998). CBR in action : Some reflections from the Sirathu Project. *Asia-Pacific Disability Rehabilitation Journal, 9,* 29-31.

Dash, A.K. (1995). NGOs and development : Learning from failures. *The Fourth World, 4,* 74-90.

Dube, S.C. (1990). *Tradition and development.* New Delhi : Vikas Publishing House.

Jain, L.C. (1985). *Grass without roots : Rural development under government auspices.* Sage : New Delhi.

McClelland, D.C., & Winter, D.G. (1969). *Motivating economic achievement.* New York : Free Press.

Petras, J. (1997). Volunteerism : The great deception. *Economic and Political Weekly, 32,* 1587-1589.

Radley, A. (1994). *Making sense of illness.* London : Sage.

Ramachandran, S. (1996, September 5). Prospecting in poverty: Crucible of the sacred and profane. *Times of India,* New Delhi, p. 7.

Roy, B. (1996). Open letter to Home Minister : Foreign funds and threat to voluntary sector. *Economic and Political Weekly, 31,* 3161-3162.

Tripathi, R.C. (1997). Culture as a factor in community interventions. Unpublished manuscript. Psychology Department, University of Allahabad, Allahabad.

Weber, M. (1858). *The religion of India : The sociology of Hinduism and Buddhism.* Glencoe, CT : Free Press.

WHO Charter (1986). Ottawa Charter for health promotion. *Canadian Journal of Public Health, 77,* 425-430.

13

The Hindu-Muslim Relationship in Indian Plural Society

Fakir M. Sahoo

The cultural pluralism is fast becoming an important aspect of our social reality in many parts of the world. Cultural pluralism or multiculturalism is also one of the most important psychological constructs in this decade (Hall, 1997). Recently, Fowers and Richardson (1996) have argued that multiculturalism agenda is to stop imposing any one group's cultural value on all other groups. However, the promotion of multiculturalism requires several considerations at an applied level. The effective management of our personal and social life depends on the quality of our interactions with other members of the society. Participation in community life requires us to develop harmonious relationships, not only with members of our own group but also with members of other groups that are embedded in our society. This is both a necessity and a challenge. However, the challenges are tremendous when a society is plural. In such societies, groups characterized by a multiplicity of languages, ethnicity and religions place several, sometimes conflicting, demands on the adaptive processes of individuals. The management of this problem requires research-based knowledge in a number of domains including political, economic, socio-cultural, and psychological sciences. In many societies, the first-three domains have been rather well-studied; while psychological aspect has lagged behind.

In recent years, studies of ethnic relations have proliferated. Berry, Kalin and Taylor (1977) initiated programmatic research on ethnic relations in Canada;

since then a number of studies have examined group relations in the context of Canada's multicultural ideology (Fletcher, 1989). While the pluralism of Indian society has also stimulated studies of intergroup relations in India, most of these studies have been carried out within the confines of two or three groups (see Singh, 1988, for a detailed review). It seems appropriate to design a study in India to examine some of the basic ideas that emerged from studies in plural societies. With a comparative perspective, both the transcultural as well as culture-specific aspects of group relations can be delineated.

An Overview of Empirical Studies

Canadian society is composed of various ethnic groups that have migrated to Canada for permanent settlement. At the level of national policy, the country has also adopted a policy of multiculturalism. The ideology of multiculturalism posits maintenance of ethnic diversity both for the psychological well-being of individuals as well as for the cultural enrichment of Canadian society. The notion of cultural pluralism has engaged the attention of social scientists. The first study to examine attitudes towards multiculturalism was the non-official language study (O'Bryan, Reitz & Kuplowska, 1976).

The first survey on a representative sample of Canadians was conducted in 1974; it is commonly known as the Majority Attitude Study (MAS) (Berry, Kalin & Taylor, 1977). It assessed attitudes towards specific ethnic groups and towards the maintenance and sharing of cultures. Apart from these two major goals the study dealt with attitudes towards immigration and psychological characteristics of prejudiced individuals. The findings indicated that the respondents appeared to be at least tolerant of other ethnic groups and there was no evidence of extreme ethnic prejudice. They appeared to distinguish groups on the basis of two dimensions. One dimension distinguished groups by race and/or culture and the other dimension distinguished groups on the basis of their length of settlement in Canada. The general attitude towards multiculturalism was more positive than negative.

The role of psychological factors such as ethnocentrism was identified. The study generated a number of implications for promoting intergroup tolerance.

Many of the questions asked in MAS on a representative sample of the Canadians have been re-examined. Fletcher's (1989) study dealt with racial and ethnic prejudice and attitude towards human rights. Bibby (1987) used mail survey method to investigate ethnic and race relations. While some themes show convergence, there are also substantial contradictions. Berry and Kalin (1991) have recently repeated their earlier national study in order to identify general propositions and to deduce some policy implications.

The Indian Setting

The ethnic, cultural, linguistic and religious pluralism of India has posed a basic challenge. Indian history is replete with communal conflicts, Hindus (82.64%), Muslims (11.35%), Christians (2.43%) and Sikhs (1.97%) constitute the main religious groups in India. Although Hindus constitute the majority in the total population, they are outnumbered by Muslims in Jammu and Kashmir, by Sikhs in Punjab, and by Christians in Nagaland and Mizoram. Furthermore, the Muslim population in India makes the country one of the four largest Muslim countries of the world along with Indonesia, Bangladesh and Pakistan. The proportion of Muslims in the population is much higher in several towns, and in 37 cities Muslims constitute more than 20% of the local population.

The social demography with respect to caste is also complex. The Scheduled Castes (16%) and the Scheduled Tribes (8%) constitute about one quarter of the total Indian population. However, Scheduled Tribes constitute approximately two-fifths of the population of some States (e.g., Orissa) and four-fifths in others (e.g., Meghalaya and Nagaland). The second Backward Classes Mandal Commission (1982) has identified 3,743 backward classes covering 52% of the total population. Although the Constitution of India has provided certain protective measures for the welfare of Scheduled Castes and Scheduled Tribes, issue of protective measures for other backward classes has emerged as an explosive social problem complicating intergroup relations in India. At the political level, the demand for a separate Jharkhand State by tribal communities adds further complexity to the problem.

Although various States of the Indian Union have been created on the basis of languages, the question of official language(s) both at the State and Union levels brings conflicting demands. The Constitution of India so far has recognized 18 languages as national languages under the VIII Schedule. Yet, a number of linguistic groups vie for constitutional recognition.

In such a complex Indian mosaic, a number of assumptions relating to cultural pluralism need to be examined. While a large number of studies have been carried out in India in the area of attitudes towards other groups, no specific propositions have been advanced or examined.

In India, a matrix of inter-group attitudes needs to be delineated for promoting national integration and reducing social tension. In general, the study seems to examine whether basic concepts used to studying group relation in other plural societies are also valid in Indian society. The study is conceived of as a multi-phasic one with specific goals attached to each phase.

The basic objective of Phase 1 was to examine the pattern of intergroup relationship while Phase 2 was intended to investigate specific hypothesis of intergroup harmony/conflict. The present report is based on Phase 1. More specifically attitude of the majority group (i.e., Hindus) towards Muslim is examined in the context of plural India. The study is geared to investigate several aspects of pluralism. The aspects include the evaluation of the consequences of pluralism and level and domains of support for multiculturalism programmes. Hindus and Muslims are also compared on their awareness of cultural diversity, acceptance of adaptation ideology and endorsement of national policy. In addition, ethnocentrism, authoritarianism and value preferences are also assessed to determine the extent of group difference.

METHOD

Sample

Eighty-five adult Hindus and 46 adult Muslims participated in the study. The sample was drawn from both urban and rural areas. The sampling frame was extended by drawing participants not only from large cities of Orissa but also from small city and towns of the State. People with higher education and people with less education participated in the study. Males and females were also represented.

The Survey Instruments

The survey instrument is developed in accordance with the prevailing pattern of multiculturalism research. Care is taken to render if comparable with survey instruments used in other multiculturalism studies (i.e., Majority Attitude Study in Canada). In addition, culture-specific items are also included to make it relevant and meaningful in Indian socio-cultural system.

Part 1 presents 12 items to denote possible consequences of cultural pluralism such as increased unemployment, heightening chaos and loss of identity. Respondents are asked to indicate their approval/ disapproval of the statement on a seven-point scale. In the next part, 14 items are presented to scale an individual's authoritarianism and ethnocentrism. Eight items are indicative of authoritarianism and six are indicative of ethnocentrism. This portion is followed by nine statements indicative of cultural pluralism ideology separately. There are six integration-related statements, two are related to assimilation, one pertains to segregation. The response format used for authoritarianism-ethnocentrism portion and ideology portion is same as used for evaluating consequences.

Part 2 of the survey instrument seeks information with

respect to people's endorsement of level and support for various culture-maintenance programmes such as multiplicity in school dress, medium of instruction and other cultural activities. Part 3 attempts to find out the relative frequency of people's preference in establishing social relation within their own religious community vis-a-vis other community. This part further seeks to examine whether the choice is different for business relation. The role of status of the target of relationship is also examined.

Part 4 presents 12 personal values, such as comfortable life, a world of peace, a world of beauty, equality, family security, freedom, happiness, national security, liberation, self-respect, social recognition and true friendship. Respondents are asked to rank-order these values in terms of their preference. Part 5 requires respondents to answer a number of questions relating to the number and specification of religion, languages, tribes and castes in India. This part is useful in determining people's awareness about caltural pluralism in India.

Finally the survey instrument presents three statements to indicate national policies of assimilation, integration and multiculturalism. Respondents are asked to choose one of the policies. In addition to these goals, personal information is sought.

Procedure

Participants were contacted at their natural habitat. They were individually administered the survey instrument. Responses were quantitatively tabulated. The descriptive statistics obtained from data suggested a number of salient features.

RESULTS

Perceived Consequences of Pluralism

The total score on the perceived consequences of pluralism scale is slightly above the neutral point of 4 (see Table 13.1).

TABLE 13.1 : **Perceived Consequences of Cultural Pluralism**

Items	Mean		% Disagree		% Neutral		% Agree	
	H	M	H	M	H	M	H	M
1. There would be more unemployment	4.2	4.7	40.0	33.0	7.0	4.0	53.0	63.0
2. This country would be better off	4.8	5.6	29.0	20.0	5.0	2.0	66.0	78.0
3. The relationships between Hindus and Muslims would become worse	4.6	5.0	30.6	32.6	10.6	6.5	58.8	60.9
4. Hindus (the majority group) would lose their identity	5.1	6.3	28.2	6.5	3.5	2.2	68.3	91.3
5. The minority religious groups would lose their identity	5.6	5.8	32.9	13.0	11.8	8.7	55.3	78.3
6. There would be more chaos	3.2	4.6	67.1	41.3	4.7	4.4	28.2	54.3
7. The purity of Indians would be affected	5.0	5.6	32.9	13.0	1.2	2.2	65.9	84.8
8. Cheap labour would lower the standard of living	3.6	3.7	50.6	50.0	7.1	6.5	42.3	43.5
9. There would be conflict between tribals and non-tribals	4.7	4.8	31.8	30.4	8.2	8.7	60.0	60.9
10 There would be more anti-social elements in our society	3.9	4.0	52.9	47.8	2.4	15.2	44.7	37.0
11. There would be more political problems	2.8	2.5	72.9	84.8	5.9	2.2	21.2	13.0
12. There would be hostility against different language groups	3.8	4.6	52.9	41.3	7.1	2.2	40.0	56.5
Total Mean	4.2	4.5						

Note : H = Hindus, M = Muslims.

It seems safe to say, therefore, that respondents do not perceive the consequences of pluralism to be negative. It is equally clear that they do not perceive these consequences to be overwhelmingly positive.

Overall scores close to the neutral point could indicate that respondents are uncertain or neutral concerning several aspects of pluralism. An examination of the percentage distribution in Table 13.1 indicates that such is not the case. Rather, people seem to be considerably divided on various issues. The two highest item means are associated with statements that "Hindus would lose their identity" and "the minority religious groups would lose their identity". It is also interesting to note that Hindus and Muslims show similar pattern of approval/ disapproval so far as external consequences of pluralism are concerned. However, Muslims outnumber Hindus is expressing concern for the possible loss of identity as a negative consequences of pluralism.

Authoritarianism and Ethnocentrism

Authoritarianism and ethnocentrism have been included because of their significance as psychological characteristics of prejudiced persons. As depicted by Table 13.2, the mean endorsement ratings given by Hindus and Muslims is higher than neutral point. Both Hindus and Muslims appear to be authoritarian in their approach. It is also shown that Muslims demonstrate greater authoritarianism than do Hindus (M=5.8 and 5.4, respectively).

Similar pattern is shown with respect to ethnocentrism. As shown in Table 13.3, both Hindus and Muslims exhibit high degree of ethnocentrism. As with authoritarianism, Muslims show greater ethnocentrism than Hindus (M=4.8 and 4.7, respectively). Muslims with exception to the fourth item, Muslims indicate higher endorsement of ethnocentric statements compared with Hindus.

TABLE 13.2 : **Authoritarianism in Hindus and Muslims**

Items	Mean		% Disagree		% Neutral		% Agree	
	H	M	H	M	H	M	H	M
1. People can be divided into two distinct classes : the weak and strong	4.1	4.2	47.1	41.3	3.5	4.4	49.5	54.3
2. An insult to our honour should always be punished	5.6	5.8	16.5	13.0	2.4	0.0	81.1	87.0
3. What the youth needs most is strict discipline, rugged determination, and the will to work and fight for the country and family	6.9	6.6	6.0	2.2	2.0	0.0	92.0	97.8
4. A person who has bad manners, habits and breeding can hardly expect to get along with the descent people	4.1	4.8	41.2	26.1	3.5	6.4	55.3	67.5
5. There is hardly anything lower than a person who does not feel a great love, gratitude and respect to his parents	5.8	6.4	17.6	0.0	0.0	4.4	82.4	95.6
6. Sex crimes such as rape and attack on children deserve more than mere imprisonment : such criminal ought to be publicly whipped	5.9	6.4	15.3	4.4	0.0	0.0	84.7	95.6

TABLE 13.2 : *Contd . . . .*

Items	Mean		% Disagree		% Neutral		% Agree	
	H	M	H	M	H	M	H	M
7. Obedience and respect to authority are more important virtues children should learn	5.3	6.1	8.2	8.7	2.4	0.0	89.4	91.3
8. Young people sometimes get rebellious ideas, but as they grow up they ought to get over them and settle down	5.1	5.8	23.5	13.0	1.2	6.5	75.3	80.5
Total Mean	5.4	5.8						

Note : H = Hindus, M = Muslims.

TABLE 13.3 : **Ethnocentrism in Hindus and Muslims**

Items	Mean		% Disagree		% Neutral		% Agree	
	H	M	H	M	H	M	H	M
1. People belonging to other religion-cultural groups are all right in their place, but they carry it too far when they get too familiar with us	5.4	5.4	17.6	19.6	4.7	0.0	77.7	80.4
2. India may not be perfect, but the Indian way has brought us about as close as human beings can get to a perfect society	5.0	6.0	22.4	4.3	3.5	0.0	74.1	95.7
3. The worst danger to a real Indianism during 50 years has come from external ideas and agitators	4.7	5.0	29.4	24.0	4.7	4.0	65.9	72.0
4. It would be mistake ever to have minority people for foremen and leaders over majority people	4.1	2.3	42.4	76.0	7.1	2.0	50.5	22.0
5. People who do not believe that we have best kind of culture in the world should be made to leave the country	4.5	4.7	38.8	28.3	4.7	4.3	56.5	67.4
6. It is only natural and right for each person to think that his family is better than any other	4.5	5.0	36.5	22.0	3.5	9.0	60.0	69.0
Total Mean	4.7	4.8						

Note : H = Hindus, M = Muslims.

Ideology of Cultural Pluralism

It is shown that respondents, in general, are uncertain about positive effects of cultural pluralism. Their mean ratings of endorsement hovers around the neutral point of 4 (see Table 13.4).

However, it is interesting to note that respondents generally endorse certain possible outcomes such as multiplicity of language as cultural resources (for example, Item 1). But they are apprehensive of the effect of diversity on problem-solving (for example, Item 6). Yet, overall pattern of result suggests Muslims have an edge over Hindus in endorsing cultural pluralism (M=4.6 and 4.0, respectively). This difference is in expected direction.

Domains of Support

The distribution of responses to various pluralism programmes is shown in Table 13.5. In general, the level of endorsement is slightly above the neutral point of 4. However, there are wide variation across items. Both Hindus and Muslims advocate uniformity, in certain domains such school dress. On the contrary, plurality is endorsed in domains such as food, dress in public places, language in communication media and variety in art, music and literature. It is interesting to note that 72% of Hindus emphasize uniformity in legal system whereas 59% of Muslims stress plurality in legal system.

Analysis of Relationship

Respondents idicate their chosen social/business relationship in terms of own group versus other group preferences. As depicted by Table 13.6, it is indicated that both Hindus and Muslims have greater preference for their own group members than for other group members. Both Hindus and Muslims also indicate greater preference for high status person in their own group as well as in other group compared with their choice for low status person.

TABLE 13.4 : **Cultural Pluralism Ideology**

Ideology of Pluralism	Mean		% Disagree		% Neutral		% Agree	
	H	M	H	M	H	M	H	M
1. India would be a better place if members of different groups (across-religion, language and tribe) would keep their own way of life alive	5.4	6.4	19.0	4.0	4.0	0.0	77.0	96.0
2. There is a lot, that Indians can gain from friendly relations amongst different groups	5.3	6.1	9.0	0.0	5.0	2.0	86.0	98.0
3. Having different groups in India makes it difficult to solve problems.	5.9	6.4	79.0	65.0	6.0	5.0	15.0	65.0
4. It would be good to see all the groups in India retain their own identity	2.6	3.5	38.0	9.0	9.0	6.0	53.0	85.0
5. The unity of this country will be weakened if groups stick to their old ways	4.3	5.7	76.0	78.0	4.0	2.0	20.0	20.0
6. A society which has a variety of groups is more able to tackle new problems as they occur	3.6	3.2	34.0	48.0	9.0	9.0	57.0	43.0

TABLE 13.4 : *Contd . . . .*

Ideology of Pluralism	Mean		% Disagree		% Neutral		% Agree	
	H	M	H	M	H	M	H	M
7. It is best for India all cultures forget their religious/cultural background as soon as possible	3.4	3.2	53.0	57.0	4.0	4.0	43.0	39.0
8. People who live in India should change their behaviour to be more like persons in the main stream	2.5	2.6	69.9	54.0	9.0	17.0	32.0	29.0
9. If members of same groups want to maintain their own way of life, they should keep it to themselves and not bother other people in this country	3.5	4.1	21.0	11.0	5.0	2.0	74.0	87.0
Total Mean	4.0	4.6						

Note : H = Hindus, M = Muslims.

TABLE 13.5 : **Domains of Support for Pluralism**

Domains	Mean		% Disagree		% Neutral		% Agree	
	H	M	H	M	H	M	H	M
1. Dress pattern of school children (e.g., children of different religious and cultural groups wearing different kinds of dress)	2.6	2.6	74.1	73.9	1.2	2.2	24.7	23.9
2. Medium of instruction in school (e.g., teaching Telgu children in Telgu and Bengali children in Bengali)	3.8	2.9	48.2	67.4	8.2	2.2	43.6	30.4
3. Medium of instruction in college/ Universities	3.8	4.0	46.0	39.1	16.0	10.9	38.0	50.0
4. Food (e.g., different communities displaying different food habits and preferences)	4.9	5.7	28.3	17.4	3.5	2.2	68.2	80.4
5. Dress in public places	4.9	5.0	28.2	28.3	5.9	6.5	65.9	65.2
6. Observing of holidays (e.g., permitting job holders to take leave on days specific to their religion and community)	4.8	6.4	28.2	6.5	4.7	0.0	67.1	93.5

TABLE 13.5 : *Contd . . . .*

Domains	Mean		% Disagree		% Neutral		% Agree	
	H	M	H	M	H	M	H	M
7. Legal system (e.g., permitting different types of laws for different communities such as Hindus laws and Muslim laws)	2.6	4.4	71.8	39.1	4.7	2.2	23.5	58.7
8. Communication media (e.g., encouraging the use of language other than the main stream language)	4.9	5.6	28.2	13.1	2.4	6.5	69.4	80.4
9. Art and music	5.1	6.0	21.2	6.5	7.1	4.4	71.7	89.1
10 Literature	5.6	6.2	17.6	4.4	3.5	2.2	78.9	93.4
Total Mean	4.3	4.9						

Note : H = Hindus, M = Muslims.

TABLE 13.6 : **Frequency of Chosen Relationship**

Target	Hindus		Muslims	
	Own group	Other group	Own group	Other group
1. Low status social relationship	85.9	14.1	71.7	28.3
2. High status business relationship	87.1	12.9	89.1	10.9
3. High status social relationship	74.1	25.9	71.7	28.3
4. Low status business relationship	88.2	11.8	84.8	15.2
5. High status business relationship	71.8	28.2	93.5	6.5
6. Low status social relationship	52.9	47.1	73.9	26.1
7. Low status business relationship	61.2	38.8	82.6	17.4
8. High status social relationship	45.9	54.1	73.9	26.1

Personal Values

On the basis of priority ratings given to 12 personal values, salient and non-salient values are identified for Hindus and Muslims. Both Hindus and Muslims identify a world of peace, freedom, and equality as their salient values. There is also similarity in the choice of non-salient values. Both groups mentioned social recognition, a comfortable life, and happiness.

Level of Support for Multicultural Programmes

Responses in terms of the level of support for various multiculturalism programmes show that people in general endorse such programme, though the level of support is not very high. Muslims indicate greater support for such programmes compared with Hindus (M=2.2 and 1.9, respectively).

An interesting feature is shown with respect to the pattern of support indicated by Hindus vis-a-vis Muslims. The pattern of support shown by Hindus depicts an inverted U-type picture; it shows that maximum number of people extend moderate support (with very low percentage for both no-support and high-support). On the contrary, frequency of Muslim respondents increase with rise in level of support. This exhibits a straight line function with an increase in the level of support.

National Policy Preference

Respondents are asked to choose one of the possible policies for the country. The preferences include integration, assimilation and multiculturalism. It was found that about half of the respondents of each group (Hindus 45.9%, Muslims 41.3%) select integration as their preferred national policy. Out of other half, majority of Hindus prefer assimilation (43.5%) whereas majority of Muslims prefer multiculturalism (37%).

Taken together, the examination of pattern of data suggests a picture of tolerance, rather than active support for multiculturalism and its furtherances.

Discussion

The present study is a part of the programmatic research on intergroup relation in India. A special focus of this study concerns Hindu-Muslim relation in plural India. The intergroup relation between the majority group (Hindus) and the visible minority group (Muslims) seems to underlie the dynamic interaction of multiple social forces. As pointed out by Ghosh, Kumar and Tripathi (1992), the Hindu-Muslim relation plays a crucial role in management of several ugly incidents such as communal riot in India. The findings of the present study provides both optimism for integration-building measures as well as cautions against oversimplifying the issue.

The picture of tolerance is depicted by the analysis of responses of perceiving the consequences of cultural pluralism. It is interesting to note that the possible loss of identity is perceived to be a matter of concern. Although this concern is shared both by Hindus and Muslims, anticipation is higher amongst Muslims. Ghosh and Huq (1986) have shown in an earlier study the importance of social identity in the context of group relations in India and Bangladesh.

The moderate level of support is also indicated in the context of specific domains and programmes. In general, uniformity is stressed in the context of children's school dress. It implies that parents want the school to function as a leveller and play down differences. On the contrary, respondents favour plurality in food habits and preferences dresses in public places, variety in art, music and literature. Furthermore, Hindus predominantly favour uniformity in legal system whereas Muslims advocate plural forms of legal system. The study goes one step forward to assess their level of support for various programmes. Voting a candidate favouring a programme is indicative of mild support whereas personal activity favouring the programme is indicative of moderate support. Moreover, paying taxes for such programme is indicative of strong support. With this format of measuring support-level, it is shown that people do not demonstrate support that could be considered "higher". Thus, a moderate level of endorsement of programme is evinced.

Adorno Frenkel-Brunswik, Levinson, and Stanford (1950), in their classic study of racial prejudice, have stressed authoritarianism and ethnocentrism as psychological factors of group dynamics. The present study draws items from their measures and assesses these psychological characteristics in Hindus and Muslims. Both Hindus and Muslims indicate high levels of authoritarianism and ethnocentrism. It posits the implication that people need cultural education to free themselves from their ethnocentric bias.

As expected, both Hindus and Muslims indicate their preferences for greater relationship within their own group. When they go beyond, their own group, the high status of the person belonging to the other community functions as an attraction. Finally, the comparison basic personal values shows similarity across groups. Both Hindus and

Muslims view a world of peace, freedom and equality as the most important values. Even the non-salient values are also found to be similar across groups. It is important to recognize certain policy implications. India, as a nation, has pursued the ideals of cultural pluralism. However, it is felt that a planned programme of cultural education is needed to strengthen our commitment to plurality.

REFERENCES

Berry, J.W., Kalin, R., & Taylor, D.M. (1977). *Multiculturalism and ethnic attitudes in Canada.* Ottawa : Minister of Supply and Services, Canada.

Berry, J.W. & Kalin, R. (1991). *Design Specifications for Major Attitude and Opinion Reader Survey Research on Multiculturalism.* Unpublished report. Department of Psychology, Queen's University Kingston, Canada.

Bibby, R.W. (1987). Bilingualism and multiculturalism : A national reading. Int. Driedger (Ed.), *Ethnic Canada : Identities and Inequalities.* Tornoto : Copp Clark Pitman.

Flectcher, J. (1989). *Results of the survey on racial prejudice.* Toronto : University of Toronto.

Fowers, B.J., & Richardson, F.C. (1996). Why is multiculturalism good? *American Psychologist, 51,* 609-621.

Ghosh, E.S.K. & Huq, M.M. (1985). A study of the social identity of two ethnic groups in India and Bangladesh. *Journal of Multilingual and Multicultural Development, 6,* 239-254.

Ghosh, E.S.K., Kumar, R., & Tripathi, R.C. (1992). The communal cauldron : relations between Hindus and Muslims in India and their relations to norm violations. In R. de Ridder and R.C. Tripathi (Eds.) *Norm violation and intergroup relations.* Oxford : Clarendon Press.

Hall, G.C.N. (1997). Misunderstandings of multiculturalism. *American Psychologist, 52,* 654-655.

O'Bryan, K.G., Reitz, J.G., & Kuplowska, O.M. (1976). *Non-official languages : A study in Canadian multiculturalism.* Toronto: Minister of Supply and Services, Canada.

Sahoo, F.M. (1993). Canadian cultural pluralism : Implications for study of group relation in India. *Proceedings of the National Seminar on Indo-Canadian Relation : Future Perspective.* (pp. 1-10). Berhampur : Berhempur University, Orissa, India.

Singh, A.K. (1988). Intergroup relation and social tension in J. Pandey, (Ed.) *Psychology in India* : The state of the art (Vol. 2). New Delhi : Sage.

14

Collectivism in The Cultural Perspective

Jyoti Verma

There are four defining attributes of collectivism. First, collectivists view the self as interdependent with others, which is accompanied by sharing resources. Second, the goals of collectivists are compatible with the in-group goals. Third, their social behaviour is determined primarily by social norms, duties and obligations. Finally, collectivists give priority to relationships taking the needs of the relevant others into account.

India has been termed collectivist in its cultural orientation (Bond, 1985; Hofstede, 1980; J.B.P. Sinha *et al.*, 1994; J.B.P. Sinha & Verma, 1987; Triandis *et al.*, 1986; Verma, 1989, 1992). However, in most of these studies it was pointed out that Indians were located either somewhat towards the higher side of the individualism-collectivism (I/C) continuum or somewhere close to the mid point. Recently, Hofstede (1994) while talking about "the unique cultural inheritance of countries with regard to individualism and collectivism in spite of poverty or affluence" (p. xii) pointed out that though India scored half way on the I/C index scale in his 1970 data, according to the average poverty it could have been expected to score even more collectivist.

Lately, Indians have been found fit to be assigned the category of "vertical collectivists" (Triandis, 1995) where the characteristics of embeddedness and power distance appear prominently in their personal and social disposition. Indian researchers (e.g., Mishra, 1994; D. Sinha & Tripathi; 1994) find India as a case of "individualism in a collectivist culture" and a case of "co-existence of opposites", while some up-to-date empirical studies (J.B.P. Sinha *et al.*, 1994) have not been able to present any clear cut pattern of Indian collectivism.

It seems that Indians self appraise themselves as collectivists; however, there is definite streak of individualistic tendencies in their apparent life style. Similarly, literature supports preference for individualist and collectivist both kinds of values by Indians. The harsh social reality of India, the upsurge of consumerism values, and the deeply ingrained spiritual values of duty, right action and self growth knit a very complex context for the "context sensitive" Indians to decide 'what to do' and 'who to be'. The important question that the Indian sages put to themselves to know their true identity asking "who am I"? remains the question for the Indian psychologists too.

Indian Collectivism : Unravelling the Construct

J.B.P. Sinha and Verma (1987) tried to empirically examine the structure of Indian collectivism on an adult sample. The aim was to develop measures of collectivism at cultural and individual levels (referred as collectivism and allocentrism respectively) and check their validity by relating them to variables of (a) relative salience of the various in-groups, (b) the extent of individual's embeddedness in the group, (c) the perception of collectivism in the Indian people and (d) the nature of relationship orientations of three kinds. The study provided some useful information and the scale was found to possess criterion and construct validities. Factor analysis (Verma, 1992) revealed the following five factors as themes of Indian collectivism. These were: Harmony and tolerance; Inquisitiveness about others; Support; Concern for others' evaluation; and Utilisation of social contacts. On the other hand, Networking for mutual gain, and other orientation were marked as important dimensions of allocentrism.

In a recent study (J.B.P. Sinha *et al.*, 1994) Indian

collectivism appeared with regional differences and a few common themes, namely, relationship orientation, familialism and belief in hierarchy also emerged. The themes of "belief in hierarchy" and "power distance" have encouraged experts to examine India as a case of "vertical collectivism" where despite embeddedness with the collective, the self desires to "stick out." On the other hand, relationships that are likely to last and remain beneficial for both the parties are preferred (J.B.P. Sinha & Verma 1987; Verma, 1992), while for very close in-group members, love and affection may be offered unconditionally. Furthermore, family is the most important in-group. However, there are indications that the desire to enjoy individual freedom may take toll of the spirit of familialism.

Indian social psychologists have tried to examine the construct of Indian collectivism and have made the following observations. Indian collectivists make demarcation between in-group and out-group members, and their social behaviour and morality is likely to be decided by contextual parameters. It appears, that Indians define norms as accommodative rules for meeting the demands of the situation and function in a context sensitive manner.

Lately, interest has been shown in studying the "self" as a cultural product. In one of the studies, the college students', responses on the "Who am I" test suggested that their self referents mirrored their immediate context and concerns and expressed their private preoccupations (Verma & J.B.P. Sinha, 1993). On the other hand, there is evidence that the young students' self referents fall into the categories of social identity and self evaluation (Dhawan, Roseman, Naidu, Thapa & Rettek, 1995). The concept of a happy life for the young students meant a good small family, good social and physical environment, peace and contentment plus health, wealth and education (Verma & J.B.P. Sinha, 1993). Finally, psychological well-being was found to be positively related with allocentrism but only in a highly supportive environment (J.B.P. Sinha & Verma, 1994).

In the present study, the researcher attempted to understand how collectivism is socially represented (Moscovici, 1984, 1988) in the thinking and talk of Bihari Indians (people belonging to an Eastern State of India called Bihar). 36 people (young students and middle aged adults) were interviewed in small groups with the help of eight directive questions. The questions were developed with the purpose to reach the core and the dynamic content and features of Indian collectivism as represented in the shared beliefs, thinking and conversation of the Bihari respondents.

Accordingly, attempts were made to tap the respondents' aspirations for their children and their own guiding principles of life. Furthermore, the respondents were required to tell, something about the special characteristics of Biharis. A relevant question in this context was casteism. Efforts were made to understand people's attitude towards casteism and whether they practiced the same. Another directive question led the group to discuss relationship orientation in Indians. Finally, the proposition that the "cultural co-construction of the field of human feelings" was possible (Valsiner, 1994, p. 4) and personal feeling fields are canalized in ways that fit into the collective — culturally prescribed forms, inspired the investigator to have an impression of the feeling fields of the respondents.

The scope of the present study did not allow very serious concentration of this particular issue, however, we wished to know about such events that were likely to move the respondents emotionally and also that whether people of a particular society shared emotions of compatible nature against such affective situations.

The interviews aimed at initiating a mental exercise which was centered around the interviewee as a social being, born and brought up in an eastern state of India generally known to be traditional and less developed. The interview situation was an invitation for sharing one's aspirations, values and preferences on the one hand, and reflecting upon one's special characteristics as Biharis on the other. The qualitative data from the interviews was likely to be viewed as complementary or incongruent whatever, with the observations of the Indian researchers who tried to empirically study the structure and construct of Indian collectivism.

Furthermore, the qualitative data were to be looked upon with hope for providing a glimpse of the co-constructive role of persons that "guarantees maintenance of their common cultural-historical heritage in all of its heterogeneity, by way of constructing their personally unique life course" (Valsiner, 1994; p. 3). Generally speaking, the present study was a modest venture in the direction of elaborating systemic relationship between the person and the social world and in the process arriving at an understanding of the individuals' cultural and personal social representations.

METHOD

Sample

The sample of the study comprised of 36 middle class urban adults, who could be divided into two broad groups. One group comprised of 15 male adults, between the age group of 30 years to 60 years and above. The other group comprised of 21 students belonging to Post Graduate departments of social sciences of Patna University, Patna. This group had both male and female students in almost equal numbers.

The adults in the 30 to 60 years age group were both working and retired persons. Furthermore, they belonged to another city close to Patna but smaller in size namely, Begusarai. The interviews were conducted in Begusarai with the help of a local trained student research assistant. The students were interviewed by the present researcher in small groups.

Procedure

The respondents were approached in their free time for the interviews. We took notes of the group discussions. The interviewer initiated the discussion by putting one of the questions. No predecided plan guided the order of the questions. The interviewers allowed free group discussion and intervened for seeking clarifications. The following directive questions were asked.

1. What are your aspirations for your children? Mention at least four to five such aspirations that you have for them.
2. What kind of events affect you very much or move you?
3. Which are some values (3 to 5) that you think are important for you as "guiding principles of life"?
4. Give at least four to five such characteristics / attributes that are typical for us as Biharis.
5. What are some worst things about us as Biharis?
6. What are some good things about us as Biharis?
7. How much importance do you give to casteism in your life?
   a) Fully. b) Somewhat, according to the situation or need. c) Not at all.
8. While making a relationship, what kind of relationship would you prefer to have?
   a) Reciprocal (when the other party is available in time of need). b) Selfless. c) Contractual.

Analysis

It was decided to examine the data separately for the group of Patna University students and the relatively older group of adults from the city of Begusarai. This was to be so, because initially we did not want to miss any information which might have presented a contrast between the shared ideas of the two groups on the research questions. However, where the data did not suggest any contrast, the observations were to be presented together for both the age groups. Furthermore, we thought of drawing general conclusions out of the major observations made against the different research questions.

Observations

The Profiles

1. Aspirations for Children (Adults of 30 to 60 years of age group) : It was interesting to watch how the parents' aspirations for their children were divided into two clear streams of concerns. According to one stream, the parents wanted their children to be moral persons, but according to the other, a materially successful person enjoying high social status in the society.

The most frequently used terms for a moral individual was *charitravan* and almost all the parents wanted their children to be adults having good character (*charitra*) and habits. The term *charitravan* was explained as being honest, truthful and having good nature and conduct (once their was mention of "keeping away from drugs" in this category). *Charitravan* also referred to being chaste and fidel in interpersonal relationships, and not being troublesome for others. A moral person was seen as a good human being (*accha adami*) and an ideal citizen (*adarsh nagrik*). An ideal citizen was visualized as a person who knew his/her responsibilities and used his/her rights in a proper manner.

Thereafter, one could see a distinct trend in the parental aspirations which suggested that they wanted to see their wards as obedient, duty conscious, sons and daughters who would maintain the good name of their family and never bring shame to it. This was a shared idea which has support in literature and has been also noted in the concerns of the young people (Garg & Parikh, 1993). This social representation captures one of the prominent shades of Indian collectivism which is reflected in values of embeddedness, familialism, and belief in hierarchy, etc. (J.B.P. Sinha *et al.*, 1994). It may be added, that perhaps with the aspirations of seeing one's offsprings as "good human beings" and "moral persons" the parents hope for good sons and daughters who will not cease to be dutiful, and caring towards them.

As an Indian observer, one would like to caution that

in practice generally parents do not seem to be taking serious pains to make their wards internalize the moral values that they talk about so much. On the other hand, much more is invested in sources that guarantee social status and materially successful life for their offsprings.

It appears that a successful life means having a good job, and if possible the prestigious Government service. The parents desired to see their children as doctors, engineers, Judges, teachers and always on top in their respective fields. All the parents wanted to see their wards in a high social status job which was better than their own.

All the talk about the "good character" of the children and their being "good human beings", are for sure the dormant cherished wishes of the Indian parents, nevertheless, they are not the ideals that the children are genuinely taught or witness in their families or in the society. The aspirations of both the parents and the children, are inducted and influenced by social comparison, the consumeristic messages of the mass media and the life styles of the successful persons.

Furthermore, the parents', aspirations are also grounded in the information that only education and professional skills can offer opportunities and make their children the consumers and the beneficiaries of the modern day technological advancements and hence, to become successful professionals and technocrats one has to have money, ambition and fighting spirit to begin with.

The Students' Aspirations for their Children

It was interesting to see that the young students, envisaged having children who were polite, disciplined, selfless, civil and practitioners of moral values. Like their senior counterparts they too desired to see their children better than themselves in all respects. One student summarised his aspirations by saying that "his child should be a hero in the real sense of the term."

However, we did mark a dash of aspirations that represented the thinking of today's youth and mirrored some of their own unfulfilled aspirations as sons and daughters. Accordingly, we were told that they looked upon their children as healthy, liberal (*pragativadi*), and non-complaining individuals, who would feel satisfied with whatever assets they have. It was also suggested that as future parents, they wanted their children to have their own values and enjoy their achievements and status as the result of pursuing their own core values. The students said that they did not wish to impose their desires and wishes on their children but would certainly provide them love, affection and guidance.

2. *The Values* : The directive question, that invited a list of values considered to be important as the "guiding principles of life", elicited the following. Good character, truthfulness, dutifulness, honesty towards one's duties and responsibilities, being careful towards others and not hurting them, etc.

On the other hand, we heard about values that referred to having strong will power, being outspoken and clear-cut in expressing one's views, being courageous, and being ambitious. At least a couple of values namely, being of good character (*charitravan*) and being *karmath* (willing to take responsibilities, being a fighter and doer of things), was mentioned frequently. There was once mention of a value namely *purushartha* which has a philosophical connotation. It refers to the efforts of a man (*purusha*) which makes possible for him to realise the worldly and spiritual goals of life. In simple terms it would mean perseverance, or concentrated effort towards completing one's worldly and humanly duties.

However, with a value list as above, and quite a different scene in practice, one is about to say that (a) these values are still the cherished values and (b) some of these values are still in practice but only in reference to some appropriate context.

It appears, that undertaking one's duties and responsibilities seriously was the dominantly shared idea of the respondents however, when they refer to "duty and responsibility", it often has reference to their social role as family members, and does not have so much to do with their professional or civic roles. Carrying on one's duties and responsibilities is still a normative requirement in traditional society and people conform to these norms with much cost and pain. On the other hand, duties and responsibilities may be contexualized (Ramanujan, 1990; Ronald, 1984; D. Sinha & Tripathi, 1994; J.B.P. Sinha, 1990; Triandis, 1995; Tripathi, 1988).

The value list of the young students comprised of success, achievement and being fair. It also included being truthful and honest (in one's work), and being cooperative and respectful towards the elders. The list represented a mixture of familial values, moral values and values that represented the concerns of young aspirants of happy and successful future. This appears to be the value state of today's middle class Indian youth who often find themselves in a situation where they have few choices and to get hold of one desirable state, they might have to give up the other desired one. This is perhaps, the irony and the misfortune of Indian scene where the traditional and the non-traditional values seem to coexist, but they still have to strike at the right combination.

3. *Casteism* : There was clear message from all the respondents that although casteism was bad, "one learns it". It was suggested that people have a "soft corner" for their own caste and if one has suffered due to casteist discrimination, he/she was likely to become vindictive. In general, the respondents agreed, that they do not approve of casteism but they practiced it sometimes depending upon the situation. If Indian collectivism has theme of "embeddedness" with one's collective (J.B.P. Sinha & D. Sinha, 1990), and also support for in-group out-group distinction in social behaviour, the present data supports the same. In sum, casteism is alive in the social representation of Biharis.

4. *Relationship Orientation* : According to the respondents, relationships were made with the hope that people will support and help each other in time of need. This social representation has support in literature (Roland, 1984; J.B.P. Sinha & Verma, 1987; Verma, 1994).

It may be marked that "Biharis oblige people if they

know them or feel close to them". Relatives and friends are bailed out of trouble and people feel emotional affinity with one's caste persons and fellow Biharis outside the state. However, they do expect others to reciprocate favours in time of need. Expectations and demands in interpersonal relationships are seen as `rightful claims'. But one gains this `right' by the virtue of the emotional affinity that one feels towards the concerned relevant others. A fully selfless relationship is possible but only exceptionally and most likely between very close in-group members. It may be seen once in a while, between the individual and some helpless stranger in serious trouble.

The young students pointed out that the hope for reciprocation of favours is perhaps always there but it does not mean that all relationships are initiated with such intentions. It was suggested that the young people are becoming opportunist, nevertheless, a contractual relationship was still quite unacceptable. The dominantly shared idea was that people preferred to have relationships that were not contractual and promised long lasting reciprocal associations.

5. *The Bihari Profile* : Bihar is a State whose masses (almost 80% of the total population of Bihar) belong to villages. Even those who have become educated or have come to towns for job and business purposes, seem to somewhat portray the village bumpkin image which is taken with a pinch of salt. Moreover, Bihar is a very politically active State and majority of the politicians have their roots in villages. Bihar's political activities affect the national political scene in a big way (Bihar being the second most populous State of India), and around the year Bihar remains the stage for enactment of all kinds of political maneuverings.

With upcoming of a whole generation of politicians who believe in making money and enjoying power during their political tenure, there has been an upsurge of malpractices at higher levels involving politicians and Government officials. This has tarnished the image of Biharis in and outside Bihar, and has lowered their self-esteem everywhere in the country. However, the present state of affairs stands in total contrast to the glorious past of Bihar. Historically, Bihar has been the proud birth place and work place of saintly politicians and conscientious citizens. This background may be helpful for looking at the qualitative data of the study in the right spirit.

We ended up with an exhaustive list of attributes and characteristics describing a typical Bihari. We scanned the list for such attributes and characteristics that supported the presence of collectivist orientation and allocentric tendencies in Biharis. Allocentrism refers to collectivism at individual or personal level (Triandis, Leung, Villareal & Clack, 1985). At the same time, we were open to all the relevant information that came across and helped us understand how Indian collectivism was socially represented in the thinking and talk of the respondents.

We realised that a few dominant themes were evident. First, Biharis, were frequently mentioned as social and "hospitable" people. Secondly, they were seen as persons willing to show "in-group affinity" and were likely to treat their caste and state fellow members with warmth. It was suggested that Biharis were" loyal to their Bihari community" and showed solidarity with other Biharis outside the State. They also preferred to speak their regional languages and many liked their own simple food.

It was pointed out that in comparison to people of Delhi or other metropolis, Biharis were warm, benevolent, cooperative, generous and sacrificing by all respects. A prominent theme emerged suggesting Biharis as family persons. It was suggested that Biharis were "sentimental" about their parents, children, friends and relatives. They were "transparent" for close family members and friends and respected old and elderly. Once it was mentioned that Biharis respect the women folk. Women were seen as persons who engaged themselves in religious rituals. It is true that Indian women often observe fasts and practice rituals for the welfare of the family members (Verma, 1995).

Biharis, for sure, were seen as relationship oriented

individuals who cared for maintaining relationships and were generally "caring" and "concerned" partners in interpersonal relations. The respondents mentioned that when "we opted for a relationship we would not care for the consequences". Otherwise, it was common to expect reciprocation in relations. Biharis were "home sick" people, cared for "belongingness" and were willing to share their feelings. They were also seen as "non-posers", "adjustable" and "tolerant" people who would usually follow the social norms and would not like to go against the tradition.

These observations yield a neat profile congruent with the description of people who believe in collectivist orientation. Similarly, the themes of familialism, embeddedness and relationship orientation are evident. The remaining data refer to the idiosyncratic features and negative things about Biharis. We would like to look at these as part of the social representation of the Bihari profile.

To begin with, Biharis were seen as bright and intelligent persons with some kind of innocence around them but people, with a "low self-esteem". We were told that Biharis do not get adequate support and opportunities in the State for becoming achievers. Perhaps, linked to the concern of low self-esteem is their tendency to "show-off" and socially compare themselves with others on the one hand, and succumb to the powerful influences on the other.

A substantial amount of emphasis was given on Bihari life style and outlook. Biharis were seen as easygoing, clumsy and unsophisticated. They were hard workers but perhaps, only under compulsion. Moreover, they were not punctual, were talkative, critical and bad listeners. A few respondents believed that Biharis gave free advice and could be envious and jealous of their more prosperous counterparts. However, it was added that this could be due to the scarcity of resources and lack of opportunities for all.

The worst part of Bihari characteristics featured casteism, dishonesty and indiscipline. A few respondents perceived Biharis as inefficient, complaining kind and rough tongued.

It may be concluded that, the social representation of Biharis had some prominent themes of Indian collectivism. At the same time they were portrayed as somewhat clumsy, easy going and unsophisticated individuals (which may be attributed to their rural background and lack of proper grooming in this direction). More or less, consistent with the latter image of Biharis, one may find their uneasiness in complying with some Protestant Ethic values (i.e., not being habitual hard workers and not being punctual, etc.). Finally, their casteist attitude make them appear somewhat orthodox to an extent. The above social representations seem to carry some reflections from the beliefs and thinking of the people of a developing society who have experienced deprivation and scarcity of resources on the one hand and belong to a cultural space which is not fully modernized on the other.

The students added that Biharis were attracted towards 'glamour' and "western consumerism". They marked that every one is desirous of affluence but may not be vocal about this. The malpractices at all the levels in public life in Bihar is a strong evidence that the trend is gaining ground.

6. *Moving Events* : It was widely shared that unforeseen' catastrophes (i.e. natural disasters or accidents) causing loss of innocent lives and human suffering moved Biharis. Similarly, human suffering and pain caused by unfortunate situations like poverty, acute deprivation and personal loss due to death, moved people.

The other emotionally disturbing events were violence and aggression. Accordingly, brutal killing, child abuse, rape, communal riots, etc. were unacceptable experiences. On the other hand, human misery caused by exploitation of the powerless, and the disparity between the 'haves' and the 'have nots' were viewed as upsetting events.

It was mentioned that people's indifference towards chaos, someone going astray due to unfortunate circumstances, personal humiliation, and unexpected happiness or sorrow, were the 'stirring' events but such views were expressed individually.

It seems that 'sympathy' and perhaps 'pity' were the most dominant emotions for the Bihari people. However, apparently one does not find much in their action to match their emotions at a given point of time. Nevertheless, feeling in a special way towards others, was an indication that the feeling field was shared and extended towards those in trouble and pain.

The data suggested that the respondents' emotional experiences were quite comparable against events having similar content. Since, sympathy and pity for the sufferer (or the victim) emerge as the dominant feeling fields, one wonders as to why the social reality has not changed much and still remains exploitative and violent.

It may be said that there are some serious barriers on the route to desirable change and a common Indian cannot do much in this context. Nevertheless, the urgency for change is felt quite strongly. Consequently, there is willingness to use the culturally prescribed forms for canalization of the feeling fields in response to the emotionally disturbing events. It seems, that 'sympathy' and 'feeling sorry' for the victims are the suitable emotional expressions for such occasions. We are tempted (but open to correction) to say, that extension of the feeling fields towards others, generally in a sympathetic mood is the collectivist way of going through unfortunate powerful events in life.

SUMMING UP

The data presented a descriptive account of the respondents' shared beliefs, feeling and thinking against certain issues of relevance for them. Some prominent themes of Indian collectivism namely, familialism, belief in hierarchy and embeddedness were intact in the social representation of the respondents.

It was marked that the parents' aspirations for their children with two clear streams of concern. One in the direction of seeing their children as moral beings, while the other as socially, individually and economically successful persons. This social representation is quite typical of the "Indian scene". The future parents' (students') aspirations for their offsprings were not very different. However, there was some indication that the children should be self sufficient, liberal and capable of pursuing the ideals they chose for themselves.

The respondents' own "guiding principles of life" comprised of values of 'duty and responsibility' quite prominently. However, it is important to know the 'context' when these values are examined as "guiding principles of life". For the young students, success and achievement constituted the conception of the desirable besides familial and moral values. The value issue provided a fair idea of the values that are still cherished and those that are viable and part of the social representation of Biharis.

In general, casteism was seen as a social evil but nevertheless practiced. Relationships were welcome, maintained and seen as obligatory. Biharis in particular were seen as relationship oriented people who were also suggested to be home loving and hospitable. The data appeared to be consistent with the concept of Indian collectivism in the literature and the Bihari profile was not an exception to this. The moving events for Biharis were those causing human suffering and pain due to natural calamities, deprivation and violence. The most commonly shared feeling field was "sympathy" for the victims.

Biharis had some negative characteristics and the worst among these were casteism, indiscipline and dishonesty. The students pointed out that lately the consumeristic values were affecting Biharis in a significant manner.

It may be concluded, that the present social representation of the "Indian scene" has colours of Indian collectivism as suggested in the literature. At the same time it is also a picture representing the beliefs, preferences and practices of the people who have experienced deprivation, and lack of opportunities and scarcity of resources. Lately, this scene has been showing deep shades of self-centric individualism, violence and malpractices which may be attributed in a major way to the manipulative and power craving political agility of the State of Bihar promoted by its politicians and people in higher public places. However, we find that some healthy aspirations and values are still cherished and desired and represented in the thinking and talk of common Biharis.

REFERENCES

Bond, M. (1985). *Teasing etics out of emics: The case of Chinese values.* Shatin, N.T., Hong Kong : The Chinese University of Hong Kong.

Dhawan, N., Roseman, I.J., Naidu, R.K., Thapa, K. & Rettek, S.I. (1995) Self concepts across two cultures: India and the United States. *Journal of Cross Cultural Psychology, 26*, 606-621.

Garg, P. & Parikh, (1993). *Young managers at the cross roads : The Trishanku complex.* New Delhi : Sage.

Hofstede, G. (1980). *Cultures' consequences.* Beverly Hills, CA : Sage.

Hofstede, G. (1994). Forward. In U. Kim, H.C. Triandis, C. Kagitcibasi, S.C. Choi, & G. Yoon, (Eds.), *Individualism and collectivism : Theory, method and application.* Thousand Oak: Sage.

Mishra, R.C. (1994). Individualist and collectivist orientations across generations. In U. Kim, H.D. Triandis, C. Kagitcibasi, S.C. Choi, & G. Yoon, G. (Eds.), *Individualism and collectivism : Theory, method and application* (pp. 225-238). Thousand Oak : Sage.

Moscovici, S. (1984). The phenomenon of social representations. In R. M. Farr & S. Moscovici (Eds.), *Social representations,* (pp. 3-69). Cambridge : Cambridge University Press.

Moscovici, S. (1988). Notes towards a description of social representations. *European Journal of Social Psychology. 18,* 211-250.

Ramanujan, A.K. (1990). Is there an Indian way of thinking? An informal essay. In M. Marriot (Ed.), *Indian thought through Hindu categories* (pp. 41-58). New Delhi : Sage.

Roland, A. (1984). The self in India and America. In V. Kavolis, (Ed.), *In designs of selfhood* (pp. 170-191). New Jersey : Associated University Press.

Sinha, D., & Tripathi, R.C. (1994). Individualism in a collectivist culture : A case of coexistence of opposites. In U. Kim, H.C. Triandis, C. Kagitcibasi, S.C. Choi, & G. Yoon, (Eds.), *Individualism and collectivism : Theory, method and application* (pp. 123-136). Thousand Oak : Sage.

Sinha, J.B.P. (1990). The salient Indian values and their socio-ecological roots. *Indian Journal of Social Sciences, 3*, 477-488.

Sinha, J.B.P. *et al.* (1994). Regional similarities and differences in peoples' beliefs, practices and preferences. *Psychology and Developing Societies, 6*, 131-150.

Sinha, J.B.P. & Sinha, D. (1990). Role of social values in Indian organizations. *International Journal of Psychology, 25*, 705-714.

Sinha, J.B.P., & Verma, (1987). Structure of collectivism. In Kagitcibasi, C. (Ed.), *Growth and progress in cross cultural psychology*. (pp. 123-129). Amsterdam and Lisse : Swets & Zetlinger.

Sinha, J.B.P. & Verma, Jyoti (1994). Social support as a moderator of the relationship between allocentrism and psychological wellbeing. In U. Kim, H.D. Triandis, C. Kagitcibasi, S.C. Choi & G. Yoon (Eds.), *Individualism and collectivism : Theory, method and application* (pp. 267-275). Thousand Oak : Sage.

Triandis, H.D. (1995). *Individualism and collectivism*. Westview Press.

Triandis, H.C. *et al.*, (1986). The measurement of the etic aspect of individualism and collectivism across cultures. *Australian Journal of Psychology, 38*, 257-267.

Triandis, H.C. Leung, K., Villareal, M. & Clack, F.L. (1985). Allocentrism vs idiocentric tendencies : Convergent and discriminate validation. *Journal of Research in Personality, 19*, 395-415.

Tripathi, R.C. (1988). Aligning development to values in India, In D. Sinha, & H.S.R. Kao (Eds.), *Social values and development : Asian perspectives* (pp. 315-333). New Delhi: Sage.

Valsiner, J. (1994). *Devdasi temple dancers and cultural construction of persons in society*. Manuscript available from Developmental Psychology Program University of North Carolina, at Chapel Hill, Chapel Hill, N.C. 27599-3270, USA.

Verma, (1989). Marriage opinion survey and collectivism. *Psychological Studies, 34*, 141-150.

Verma, (1992). *Collectivism as a correlate of endogenous development. New Delhi : Indian Council of Social Sciences Research.*

Verma, Jyoti (1994). Allocentrism and relationship orientation. In Iwawaki, S., Kashima, Y. & Leung, K. (Eds.), *Innovations in cross-cultural psychology*. (pp. 152-163). Amsterdam and

Lisse : Swets & Zeitlinger.

Verma, J. (1995). Transformation of women's social role in India. In Valsiner, J. (Ed.), *Child development within culturally structured environments*, (Vol. 3, pp. 138-163). New Jersey: Ablex.

Verma, Jyoti, & Sinha, J.B.P. (1993). Self referents and the concept of a happy life. *Psychological Studies, 38*, 45-54.

15

The Systems Approach to Socio-Psychological Problems

B. Krishnamurthy

To go straight to the nature of influence that systems thinking may have on the conceptualization of socio-psychological processes : Man is not an island but a part of the systems at various levels beginning with small groups and ending with civilization (Bertalanffy, 1968). The emergence of selfhood, the most basic system in the psychological processes of the individual relating to the individual to general social processes to the other individuals, and with the world outside, especially as conceptualized by Herbert Mead (1934), leaves no doubt about the integral connectedness of social behaviour at various levels.

The most basic shifting of views brought about by the systems approach consisted in the replacement of robot model of Man by the concept of Man as an active personality system. It is important to emphasize that this system is regarded as inherently active. The robot model is succinctly expressed and ridiculed by Murray (1962, pp. 36-54).

> Man is a computer, an animal or an infant. His destiny is completely determined by genes, instincts, accidents, early conditioning and reinforcements, cultural and social forces. Love is secondary drive based on hunger and oral sensations or a reaction formation to an innate underlying hate. In the majority of our personalogical formulations there are no provisions

> for creativity, no admitted margins of freedom for voluntary decisions, no fitting recognition of the power of ideals, no bases for selfless actions, no ground at all for any hope that the human race can save itself from the fatality that now confronts it. If we psychologists were all the time, consciously or unconsciously, intending out of malice to reduce the concept of human nature to its lowest common denominator, and were gloating over our success in so doing, then we might have to admit that to this extent that the satanic spirit was alive within us.

It may be noted in the passing that the industrialized mass society required the manipulation of Man into a robot. Bertalanffy (1968) says that the concept of Man as a robot was both an expression and a powerful motive force in industrialized mass society. Again : "it was the basis for behavioural engineering in commercial, economic, political, and other advertising and propaganda; the expanding economy of the "affluent society" could not subsist without such manipulation. Only by manipulating humans ever more into Skinnerian rats, robots, buying automata, homeostatically adjusted conformers and opportunists, (or bluntly speaking, into morons and zombies) can this great society follow its progress toward ever increasing gross national product" (Bertalanffy, 1968, p. 206)". Henry (1963) made this very clear when he said that the principles of academic psychology were identical with those of the "pecuniary conception of man".

The systems formulation reverses this trend and depicts Man as an inherently dynamic system. Part of this shift is the emergence of a critique of the homeostatic model of behaviour. The homeostatic model with its "tension-reducing", "equilibrium-seeking" frameworks is part of the package of robot model. It may be noted that many developments were responsible for the dominance of homeostatic model, besides behaviourism. Psychoanalysis and physiological reductionism may be cited as important examples.

Here again psychoanalysis itself may be thought of as an expression of the need of the mass industrialised society with not many openings for structural changes. The enormous influence of the through-going analysis of neurotic patients by the psychoanalysis on evolving the model of Man resulted in understanding him exclusively in the framework of homeostasis, ignoring the vital, non-homeostatic processes, the processes termed as the "priceless unessentials" by Cannon (Bertalanffy, 1968). Looked at purely from the academic point of view, essentially there are two or three inadequate, non-systems frameworks which are responsible for the dominance of homeostatic, robot-like models (1) The physiologising of human nature (physiological reductionism) i.e., the homophysiologicus which is dialectically the biological counterpart of the commodity-market's conceptualization of human nature as homo-economicus which attempts to sociologise human nature into marketable commodity; both these conceptualizations negate the systems conceptualization; (2) the attempt to project the neurotic tension as the dominant aspect of the model i.e., the crippled, the inadequate psychological make-up ever striving to strike some balance or equilibrium but hardly succeeding realistically because of the inadequate psychological equipment. This forces a picture of human nature in which the individual is ever trying but always in vain to reach the "satisfactory" balance.

The first trend, the homo-physiologicus, tends to deprive man of his most distinctive characteristic element i.e., the symbolic processes and reduces him to a bundle of instinctive processes and thus is forced to present him as ever striving to reduce some tension. It cannot explain the ongoing human activity caused by the vital non-physiological processes. Its sociological counterpart, the homo-economicus, paints Man again as a simple tension-reducing system because it deprives Man of all sociality except the economic motivation. The ignoring of the enormous motivation of the non-economic factors results in the simple homeostatic models.

The second framework deprives man of his very

creative activity—the self-enhancing, the self-actualizing—for, by stripping him of all positive life-building tensions and value frameworks, it reduces him to a level of a degenerate trying to come to grips with reality making use of his "perverted", "compensating" psychological equipment. While this characterization is entirely in keeping with the zeitigeist of our times for it is through and through structurally imbued with the properties for creating insecurity in the minds of the people, it is certainly not true of human nature. However, the above characterisation of human nature leaves no choice but to accept the homeostatic, tension-reducing models.

In any case, the striving for balance in the sense of adjusting with the existing social reality and not adjusting the existing reality to the needs of Man, emerges as the essential element of the model of Man. Both the conceptualizations ignore that the symbolic (e.g., value framework) which though emerges in the context of satisfying the physiological needs (Piaget, 1968) has its own independent claims for satisfaction. An extreme example would be aesthetic need. If the specificity and independence of the symbolic is not assumed, then, as said earlier, the creative activity of Man is inexplainable.

In general, from the standpoint of understanding the influence of systems thinking on the formulation of socio-psychological problems, the following shifts of emphasis may be noted: the model of an active organism as against the reactive; the socially sensitive, responsive as against the isolated; the self-actualising as against the self-confining; the meaning-seeking as against the homo-economicus; the self-enhancing as against the exclusively tension-reducing; the continuously-growing as against the exclusively homeostatic; the goal-oriented as against the blind, the instinctive; the integrative as against the non-integrative; and also basically the inernally activated as against the exclusively externally activated models (Allport, 1955; 1960; Bertalanffy, 1968; Blauberg *et.al.*, 1977; Murray, 1962).

Within this framework here as an example is considered the Systems formulation of the problem of attitude change and the implications of this formulation in the area of psychotherapy; i.e., the implications of Systems formulation of social psychological phenomena for bringing about attitude change on the part of the clients in the psychotherapeutic context.

First to the Systems formulation of attitude: that attitudes are systems of interrelationships is amply borne out by the mutual interaction among its three components: the cognitive (symbolic, linguistic, value etc) and the affective (emotional, endocrinal, etc.,) and the behavioural (Triandis, 1971).

These three components interact to produce change in each other. Further the three components normally form a unity. That is, given the object towards which the attitude is directed, all the three components of this attitude are either positive or negative. Now any disharmony or dissonance of adequate intensity among them creates the conditions for attitude change. If the change warranted by the nature of disharmony is not effected it is otherwise "resolved" through repression and other methods, thus paving the ground for the emergence of a pathological condition: for example, the dissociation of affect and thought or affect and behaviour, or thought and behaviour, which is a symptom in many psychological complaints.

However, the attitude change conceived either as contradiction on the cognitive plane or on the affective-cognitive plane (Osgood *et al.*, 1957) or on the behavioural plane (Festinger, 1957; Osgood *et al.*, 1957) assumes attitudes as a subsystem of bigger open system called personality: Personality needs to be conceived as open in exchange, in interactions with an outside world (Allport, 1955; 1960). This is because all forms of dissonance or disharmony which is the source of attitude change must ultimately stem from the individual's interaction with the environment.

If this property of open system, succinctly formulated in the Piagetian concepts 'Assimilation' and 'Accommodation', or in the Vygotsky's 'intereorization' and 'extereorization' (Blauberg, 1977), is negated, then a pathological condition arises: The individual retains even those attitudes and elements of attitudes that are in disharmony with the aspects of his environment, but this retention compels him to withdraw from the social reality because his attitude no more works but on the contrary aggravates the conditions for "unresolvable" tension.

Thus the attitude withdrawn but kept intact and active further accentuates the isolation of the individual because of lack of feedback from the social environment; since the attitude is intact, the individual turns in on himself for feedback, thus does he indulge in wishful and delusional thinking. That is, in the longer perspective, instead of the social reality determining the behaviour, the wishful, delusional fantasy projects itself as the more important and therefore the causal, the determinative aspect in the behaviour of the individual.

The problems of attitude change in the psychotherapeutic context warrants measures amounting to restoring the properties of open system to human personality. In Systems terminology, it is enabling the organism to have realistic feedback from the external social enviornment and to evolving the psychological equipment to effect changes in the social environment so that the needs of individual are met. In the general terminology, it is to enable the individual to realise effectively the process of self-actualisation. In Fromm's (1955) system there is a clear recognition of this System's position: According to him the sense of alienation is a by-product of the existing social structure and therefore theoretically one must recognise the causal relationship between the existing "sick" social system and the self-alienation. This formulation would have psychotherapy create in, or restore to the individual the properties of open system.

However, many of the present practices such as the sociotherapy, the mental hygiene programme of community psychology, the various rehabilitation approaches (Coleman, 1970) may only serve as cushions i.e., make the different existing practices a little more effective but they do not constitute a full authentic recognition of the system's nature of pathology and psychotherapy. For as practised and taught, they shortcircuit the life-link between the individual and the social system, i.e., they are founded on the denial of the individual as open system; in general, the treatment only forces the individual to fall back on his own "personal" resources to effect the "cure". Here the cure simply amounts to changing one's attitude towards reality in such a way as to "adjust" even if this "adjustment" means "living with" disharmony or chaos. It is to be however noted that though the emphasis on personal resources of the individual is very vital in the psychotherapeutic situation, it is extremely dangerous when taken without its complement i.e., recognition of the need to change the social reality for such a stand would blindly brush aside the necessity of "curing" another very important element, the social environment, of its pathogenic properties.

Many of the existing "modern" social systems structurally or programmatically exclude the individual from determining or conditioning or influencing the social reality. The individual's failure to influence the social system as also his failure to adjust with disharmony of the social environment results in his becoming a self-contained system or "closed" system leading in extreme to withdrawal, isolation, etc. The failure to influence the social environment results in the "closing" of the developmental process — the stopping, the arresting of the movement of change; the closing in of attitude and hence withdrawal. To put it in a general framework: the pathological emerges as the negation of his creative relation between the individual being and the social system. Fromm (1955) argued with the disappearance of the individual's experience of himself as an active being in pathological phenomenon. It has to be compensated for by substituted experience such as the individual considering himself successful, pleasant, useful etc., from the standpoint of others so that the damage that the inauthenticity would otherwise cause is avoided. Fromm (1955) regarded direct participation in decision-making, and in directing processes which influence Man's life as an essential, and not compensatory, way of recovering from the state of inauthenticity. Psychological balance is reached only by adapting the society to the basic, existential needs of Man: needs for love, creativity, brotherhood, freedom, objectivity, reason and identity with himself. Thus the psychological balance is defined in terms of society's adaptation to Man's needs and not in terms of Man's adaptation to society.

In other words, the above is a plea to restore to the individual the authentic right to change the elements in the social system, which are in disharmony with his own needs. However, in perspective it means initiating a process of relationship between Man and society in which there is a coincidence of development of Man's human qualities and the reshaping of society (Janousek, 1972). In this relationship Man is to be determined by that social reality which he himself is creating in accordance with his objective, human qualities.

Placed in the above context, the problem of attitude change in therapeutic situation amounts to necessarily creating, recreating and redesigning the social realities while resorting to the individual the "right" type of attitudes towards the social environment. No sustained attitude change can be effected without creating the real context in which it is to be reinforced. Moreover, attempts to change attitudes independently of the social reality are bound to prove futile and ultimately will only complicate the adjustment process.

To conclude: The systems nature of psychopathology warrants Systems nature of psychotherapy: to restore to the individual the ability to function as an open system, that is, in the present context the atttitudes that are sought to be changed are so changed or created as to enable the individual to change the social realities while changing himself. The usual one-sidedness of psychotherapy seeking the cure within the attitudes of individuals fails to take note of the integral connectedness of the attitude with the social reality. Also such an approach expresses the failure to appreciate the need to re-establish the creative relationship between the individual and the social reality. In other words, it fails to cope with the creative tasks of psychotherapy.

REFERENCES

Allport,G. (1955). *Becoming: Basic consideration for a psychology of personality.* New Haven: Yale University Press.

Allport, G. (1960). The open system in personality theory. *Journal of Abnormal and Social Psychology, 61*, 301-310.

Bertalanffy, L., Von (1968). *General systems theory*, New York: George Braziller.

Blauberg, I.V., *et.al.*, (1977). *System theory : Philosophical and methodological problems.* Moscow: Progress Publishers.

Coleman, J.C. (1970). *Abnormal psychology and modern life*, Bombay: Taraporevala Sons Company.

Dobrentov, V.I. (1976). *Neo-Freudians in search of truth*, Moscow: Progress Publishers, 1976.

Festniger, L. (1957). *A theory of cognitive dissonance* Evanstion: Ro Peterson.

Fromm. E. (1955). *The sane society.* New York: Rinehart.

Henry, J. (1963). *Culture against man.* New York: Random House.

Janousek J. (1972). On the Marxian concept of praxis. In J. Israel and H. Tajfel (Eds.) *The context of social psychology : A critical assessment (pp. 279-294).* New York: Academic Press.

Mead, G.H. (1934). *Mind, self and society.* Chicago : University of Chicago Press.

Murray, H. (1962). The personality and career of satan. *Journal of Social Issue, 18*, 36-54.

Osgood, C.E.; Suci, G. Tannenbaum, (1957). *The measurement of meaning.* Illinois, University of Illinois Press.

Piaget, J. (1977). *The structuralism*, Paris, 1968. quoted in: Blauberg I.V., *et al.*, *Systems Theory Philosophical and Methodical problems.* Moscow, Progress Publishers.

Triandis, H.C. (1971). *Attitude and attitude change.* New York: John Wiley and Sons, Inc.

16

Psychology In India : Perception of Young Psychologists

K. Krishna Mohan

Psychology as an academic discipline and as a profession made a beginning in India in the year 1915. In the initial years, the development was slow but after 1950 there was rapid development in establishment of psychology departments in Indian universities. At present 67 universities and few institutes are offering advanced courses in psychology in India. Simultaneously students enrolment for Masters and Doctorol courses also increased. The result of this expansion is seen quite evident in the bulk research output.

Inspite of these developments, psychology in India has been criticised for the present state of affairs. Sinha (1996) has rightly pointed out that psychology in India is facing crisis. Several Indian psychologists felt that the present crisis is mainly because of over dependence on alien psychology (Mohanty, 1988; Sinha, 1986), very little emphasis on application for solving socioeconomic problems and nation development (Sinha, 1993), lack of professional commitment and less concern for the development of profession by psychologists and national bodies in India (Dalal, 1997). In fact Dalal (1997), Mohan (1995), J.B.P. Sinha (1993) and D. Sinha (1996) have identified the impediments and drawbacks of psychology in India and suggested ways and means for its development, progress and lastly to achieve high status for psychology profession.

The progress and development of psychology in the West is reaching new heights and it is projected as highly demanding profession for the coming century (Wiggigns, 1994). The scene in India is different from the West inspite of growing importance of psychologists' services in the changing socioeconomic scenario in the developing countries. In India psychology has yet to develop its distinct identity to bring an impact in the society. The consequences of the crisis are lack of proper identity for psychologists and less awareness about the profession among the public, unemployment and underemployment for graduates of psychology, and decreasing demand for psychology education in India.

In the recent past few Indian psychologists have identified the reasons for the present crisis. Sadly, no concrete plan has been drawn to overcome the crisis and facilitate a smooth progress into twenty-first century. Before any development can take place, the discipline and the profession has to undergo a process of assessment of the present situation, identification of the problems, framing the solutions, and implementation of the plan effectively. Keeping this in view and also the fact that the future depends very much on younger generation, a national survey was conducted on young psychologists and students. It was felt that knowing their perceptions, opinions on the state-of-the-art of psychology in the country, how they perceive the status of profession in future, problems and needs, what measures to be taken for the development and progress and lastly their suggestions and views would help in planning the development of psychology in India. This survey is first of its kind in India and holds great significance as the study can elicit useful information on various issues and problems perceived by young psychologists.

Method

A questionnaire was developed keeping in mind and aims and objectives of the study and used for the survey. All precautions were taken to rectify the problems and difficulties in answering the questionnaire before it was finally mailed to the respondents. In the beginning, brief introduction was given about the national opinion survey and instructions were provided to complete the questionnaire. The questionnaire consists of thirty items which are both open and close ended in nature. The first few items are related to personal information and annual income of the parents. These are followed by the items related to educational details of the respondents. The items next in the order are about academic and professional details, interest to pursue higher studies, career interests, reasons for studying psychology, career goals, membership in professional bodies, and perception of useful specializations in psychology, problems likely to be faced in taking up a career in psychology, measures to be taken for betterment. At the end, respondents are requested to provide their valuable suggestions and views for development of psychology in India.

The respondents for the survey were Masters, Doctoral and P.G. Diploma students of psychology studying in universities and institutes in India. 182 scholars responded to the survey. All of them have responded to a questionnaire mailed to the Heads of psychology departments of 67 universities and few institutes offering advanced courses in psychology in India. A formal request was made in this regard to all the Heads to extend their help and cooperation for the national opinion survey on young psychologists and students. Five questionnaires each were mailed to the Heads requesting them to ask masters and doctoral students to take part in the survey. Three to four weeks' time was given to complete and return the questionnaire.

Data Analysis[1]

For planned data analysis, all items were numerically coded. For the items in which the respondents has to mark a yes/no the responses were coded as I for "yes" and O for "no". For the open ended items, all possible responses were taken into account and categorised. Code numbers were assigned to these categories.

Results

Completed questionnaires were received from 182 respondents by the cut off date. As there are no figures available for the total number of Masters and Doctoral students studying psychology in Indian universities, it is difficult to estimate the percentage of response to the survey. Definitely the number of respondents is small considering the actual enrollment of students in India. However, inspite of the low response rate, it is encouraging that the respondents belong to 29 (43%) out of 67 Universities. In terms of geographical representation the respondents covered all the four zones in the country. Nearly half of the respondents are from north zone, followed by south, east and west zones.

Personal Information of the Respondents: The personal information asked were sex, age, income and marital status. Female students representation is twice than the male students in the survey. This is not surprising as women students in psychology courses in India outnumber the male students. The same pattern is also seen in the United States and Canada (Jone, Jennifer & Raymond, 1996) and possibly, even in the other parts of the world. Majority of the respondents are between 20-25 years. Except a few, all of them are from higher and middle income groups. Among the respondents only small percentage was married.

Educational Information and Perceptions of Psychology: Coming to educational information of the respondents, half of them are doing Masters course and remaining were pursuing Doctoral and post-masters diploma courses. Except few, all have majored in psychology at undergraduation. Only few have diploma or certificate in professional psychology. When asked in which area of psychology they are specializing in their courses, nearly half said Clinical psychology and related areas, one-third in Industrial/Organizational psychology, one-tenth in Counselling psychology, remaining in Social psychology, Developmental psychology and Educational psychology.

When asked which are the important applied fields of

pscyhology as student should get trained in turn to be useful in their profession, majority named Clinical, Industrial/Organisational and Counselling psychology in respective order. In response to the question regarding the strong reasons for studying psychology more than half (61%) said that interest in the subject is the main reason, 22% cited career, (54% both interest and career) as the reason. Only 8% said they were studying to help the family and to lead a happy life with the knowledge gained in psychology.

Career Options and Aspirations : The survey aimed at knowing younger generation psychologists' career interests, their professional aspirations, interest to pursue further studies and why they are opting for other careers inspite of studying advanced courses in psychology. 48% said they want to pursue an academic career where the job involves teaching and doing research. 26% said they want to take up a career as clinical or counselling psychologist career. Less than one-fourth opted to take up a career in industrial/organisational setups. Only ten percent showed willingness to start independent clinical/counselling and consultancy services. Of those who gave two and more options, one-third said academic and clinical/counselling and less than one-fourth for academic and industrial/organisational psychologists' career. Less than one-tenth of the respondents do not want to take up a career in psychology due to personal reasons and because of the present state of the porofession in India.

Long term goals act as strong motivating factors in one's life. Keeping this in view respondents were asked to write what they want to become in their life. Interestingly more than half said they want to become a professor of psychology, one-fourth said a good clinical psychologist, less than that said industrial/organisational psychologists and counselling psychologists respectively. Only one-tenth aspired for professions other than psychology.

Keeping in view the importance of updating one's professional skills, as learning is a never ending process, respondents were asked whether they want to enroll for further studies. Majority of them (69%) said they want to go for further studies. Half of the respondents are doing Masters course and it is not surprising that they want to pursue research degrees of short-term professional courses. Majority said they want to pursue a diploma or certificate courses in psychology as it will help them to acquire professional skills. Counselling, clinical and industrial/organisational psychology respectively order are the preferred specialisations by the respondents.

Academic and Professional Information: Another objective of the survey was to know some of the academic and professional achievements of the respondents. Only 10% of the respondents have presented a research paper in national seminar/conference etc. Only seven percent have publications to their credit. 36% have worked/involved themselves in a project/research activity. 23% reported that they have some training experience in clinical, counselling and industrial/organisation psychology areas. Only one-tenth of the respondents are receiving financial support for their studies through fellowships/merit sholarships. Ten percent of the respondents are members of a national associations of psychology. 88% want a separate body for young psychologists and showed willingness to join if such body is started.

Problems, Measures and Suggestions: 49% of the respondents reported that they lack adequate practical training and exposure in their course work to perform effectively as psychologists' in practicing set up. 36% said that lack of awareness and misconceptions among the people in the country regarding applications of psychology might be a big problem. 11% of the respondents felt that lack of government recognition and support to the profession along with neglect of national associations for the development and progress as the main problem. Only four percent mentioned other problems. Almost all the respondents have named more than one problem and some named all these as major problems.

When asked about the present problems they are facing to take up psychology as a career, 54% of the young psychologists said lack of job opportunities in India as major problem for entering into the profession. 34% said that lack of government encouragement and professional status are the major problems. Seven percent felt that lack of proper awareness among the people about the importance of psychology is a real problem. By and large majority have felt that problems like, lack of job opportunities, lack of encouragement by the government for psychology profession and public are unaware of the usefulness of applied psychology to daily living.

The next important item of the survey is to know what measures the respondents think to be important to be seriously considered and implemented by the U.G.C., national associations and Indian psychologists, government and policy makers for the development and progress of psychology. Among the eight suggested measures given, half of them marked the first measure, the common guidelines for practising psychologists to be seriously considered for implementation. One-fourth felt the need for proper training to be imparted in applied psychology and compulsory internship at masters to all the students. Some of them also felt the need for licensing procedure to be adopted for the practicing psychologists.

Lastly the respondents were asked to give their suggestions and views for the development and progress of psychology for twenty-first century. The intention was to know how they perceive the present state of crisis in psychology and their concern for future psychology in India.

For convenience and clarity many sugestions and views are clubbed into groups. The majority of the suggestions were related to the curriculum at the Masters and Doctoral courses. Among such suggestions the major ones include practical training and exposure to professional skills in applied psychology, the training of the students in Psychology in India to suit the needs of the people, internship at masters level to be made compulsory like other professional courses such as medicine, engineering, management and so on.

The next important set of suggestions is about bringing awareness in the people about the importance of applications of psychology to daily life. Major suggestions in this respect are that people should be educated on mental health and illness and made to think in terms of seeking help of psychologists. To achieve this goal, the respondents suggested use of mass media like T.V., newspapers, magazines, to bring an attitude change. Distribution of reading materials and other methods in educating the public are some of the important suggestions in this regard. It is also suggested that organising public talks, seminars, conducting exhibitions will also aid in bringing awareness, special awareness camps for different professionals, administrators, executives, youth, parents, aged, students can also be an effective method for popularising psychology.

Yet another set of suggestions includes formulating guidelines and qualifications for practicing psychologists which will give a professional status to psychologists. It was suggested that national and regional associations should conduct special camps for mentally retarded childern, drug addicts, disaster victims, and relatives and parents of mentally disturbed people to bring credibility to the profession.

The suggestions also related to pressing the government to employ psychology professionals in hospitals, educational institutes, public and private sector industries and organisations, government welfare programmes, guidance and counselling bureaus meant for unemployed youth, family and marriage problems and womens' cells, prisons, juvenile delinquency homes, orphan homes and so on. It was also suggested that government should establish a body like psychological survey as in other disciplines in India. Few have suggested that psychology as subject should be introduced in schools at least from high school level as a compulsory subject.

Doctoral students have suggested that national associations in psychology should organise regular seminars, conferences, workshops, training programmes to mould the younger generation psychologists to face the challenges and demands of twenty-first century. They also felt the need for a newsletter which gives information on career opportunities in psychology, dates of conferences, workshops, training programmes, and latest developments in psychology. In the West the importance and need for career information for psychology students was greatly felt and provided regularly (Poe, 1990). Regular seminars for master's and doctoral students in psychology were held on professional issues, problems, status, achievements and trends in the field in U.S. (Ross, 1992). Kovacs (1991) argued for transformation of patterns of education and training to prepare future psychologists for career innovation outside of traditional applications in psychology.

Conclusions

The survey results indicate that clinical psychology and industrial/organisational psychology are the most popular areas of specialisations among the students. Besides these, counselling psychology is projected as useful applied area for the future. This trend is also seen in the United States as highest number of students opting for these specialisations in master's and doctoral programmes (John *et al.*, 1996).

That majority of the young scholars are pursuing psychology only for the sake of interest but not for a career is another major concern for the development of the profession in the country. This attitude among the younger generation psychologists is not encouraging since psychological services are yet to be available to the common man in India. The position remains the same even after more than a decade after Rosenzwig's (1984) estimate that only five psychologists per million are working in India. The situation might even become worse if attention is not paid in terms of developing professional outlook among the tomorrow's psychologists.

Results show that majority of the young scholars want to pursue a career in academics and very few are willing to work on independent basis as practicing psychologists. This reveals that the traditional priority of Indian psychologists for teaching and research jobs and also the curricular emphasis in training psychology students more for academic career rather than professional practices. However that a majority of the students are inclined towards clinical and counselling psychology and want to pursue higher studies basically to acquire professional skills, is another positive finding in this study. Similar findings have also been reported in respect of the students of psychology in United States (Finney, Snell & Sebby, 1989). The need for professional skills and demand for professional training in this age of professionalism calls for more emphasis on these line in master's and doctoral courses.

The major focus of the survey was to identify the problems and needs of the students of psychology in India. The study succeeded in bringing into light the inadequacies in training in psychology in India. Majority of the respondents felt the need for more practical training and exposure in professional skills in their course work. They also expressed the problems like lack of proper awareness among the public about the applications of psychology to daily living.

The respondents to the survey expressed their discontentment with the policy makers and the government for not encouraging and recognizing the services of psychologists to the society. They also expressed disappointment over the national associations and Indian psychologists, in general, for not showing interest in development to the profession. Adair (1995) rightly pointed out that until their is reshaping in the existing scene in developing countries, specifically India, and the national associations' active involvement in improving the standards of the discipline, the present state of affairs is likely to continue.

The results indicated that their is an urgent need for redesigning the curriculum by the psychology departments. This point was further emphasised by Sinha (1996). He stated that if steps are not taken for redesigning the courses in line with the societal needs and application orientation, there is a danger of psychology departments becoming "wastepaper basket departments" in India.

Future seems to be very bright for the students of psychology in the West but keeping in mind the future demands even in U.S. the Universities are thinking of reshaping psychology cirriculum so that students not only learn content, theory, and methodology, but also how to directly apply that knowledge to social problems. Unfortunately neither any guidelines nor registration policy for the practicing psychologists in India exists till today. This seems to be a major hindrance for growth and development of the profession (Prasad, 1997).

The study has given an opportunity to the younger generation psychologists to express their views and their suggestions. The significance of the study lies in the sugestions the respondents have provided for the development of psychology in India. Understandably there is discontentment with the state of the discipline (Mohan 1995). Sinha's (1996) statement that psychology is facing a second crisis certainly holds good. This study has thrown some light on many new issues. Taking this lead, it is time for the Indian psychologists to act upon and work for a healthy, respectable and relevant twenty-first century psychology in India.

NOTES

1. Details of the data obtained in the survey are available with the author.

REFERENCES

Adair, J. (1995). The Research environment in developing countries: Contribution to the National development of the discipline. *International Journal of Psychology, 30,* 643-662.

Dalal, A.K. (1996). A science in search of its identity: Twentieth century psychology in India. *Indian Psychological Abstracts and Reviews* 3, 201-244.

Finney, P., Snell, W & Sebby, R. (1989). Assessment of academic, personal and career development of Alumni from South East Missouri State University, *Teaching of Psychology.* 16, 173-177.

John, C.N., Jennifer, M.H., & Raymond, D.T. (1996). Graduate study in Psychology. *American Psychologist* 51, 631-643.

Mohan, K.K. (1995). Identity crisis of Young Psychologists in changing World order in India. Paper presented at XI National Academy of Psychology. Gulbarga University, India.

Mohanty, A.K. (1988). Beyond the Horizon of Indian Psychology: The Yankee Doodler. In F.M. Sahoo (Ed.), *Psychology in Indian context.* Agra : National Psychological Corporation.

Poe, R.E. (1990). Psychology careers material : Selected Resources. *Teaching of Psychology,* 17, 175-178.

Prasad, M. (1997). Registration of clinical psychologists : A long pending Issue. *Indian Journal of Clinical Psychology, 24,* 3-6.

Rosenz Wing, M.R. (1984). U.S. Psychology and world psychology. *American Psychologist, 39,* 877-884.

Ross, S. (1992). A graduate seminar on problems in professional psychology. *Psychology Reports, 70,* 1216-1218.

Sinha. D. (1986) *Psychology in third world countries: Indian experience.* Sage, New Delhi.

Sinha. D. (1996). Second crisis in psychology. *NAOP Bulletin.*

Sinha, J.B.P. (1993). The bulk and front of psychology in India. *Psychology and Developing Societies, 5,* 135-150.

Wiggigns. (1994). Would you want your child to be a Psychologist? *American Psychologist, 49,* 485-492.

17

Emotional Cudding : Towards Understanding of Emotional Experience

K. Suneetha

Emotional experience is one of the most debated topics in the area of emotions. Numerous theories were postulated, rejected and some reconsidered in the face of new evidence. Some of the theories are peripheral (e.g., James, 1890), some central (e.g., Bard, 1928; Cannon, 1927), and still others cognitive (e.g., Lazarus, 1981) in nature. In recent years, psychologists have begun to consider emotions as information processing (e.g., Bower, 1981; Lang, 1979; Mandler, 1984). The present article also postulates an Information Processing Model of emotions.

Emotions are usually defined as affective states (or feelings) that are accompanied by physiological changes (Izard, 1977; Strongman, 1973). Almost all psychologists divide them into those that are pleasant and those that are unpleasant (Hilgard, Atkinson, & Atkinson, 1971). However, the degree of pleasantness and unpleasantness varies among individuals and depends on the nature of the stimulus.

Commonsense tells us that we show different emotions to pleasant and to unpleasant stimuli. Even the degree of pleasantness or unpleasantness affects our responses. Usually for a very pleasant or a very unpleasant stimulus, our response could be in one of the following three ways: (a) We immediately react to the stimulus; (b) We repress the stimulus; or (c) We suppress the stimulus. This article deals with the third kind of response.

When we suppress the stimulus, we do not "act out"

our emotions completely at a given time. We carry over the undecoded aspects of the stimulus, think leisurely, and feel it. The way this happens is shown by the Information Processing Model of emotions (see Figure 17.1).

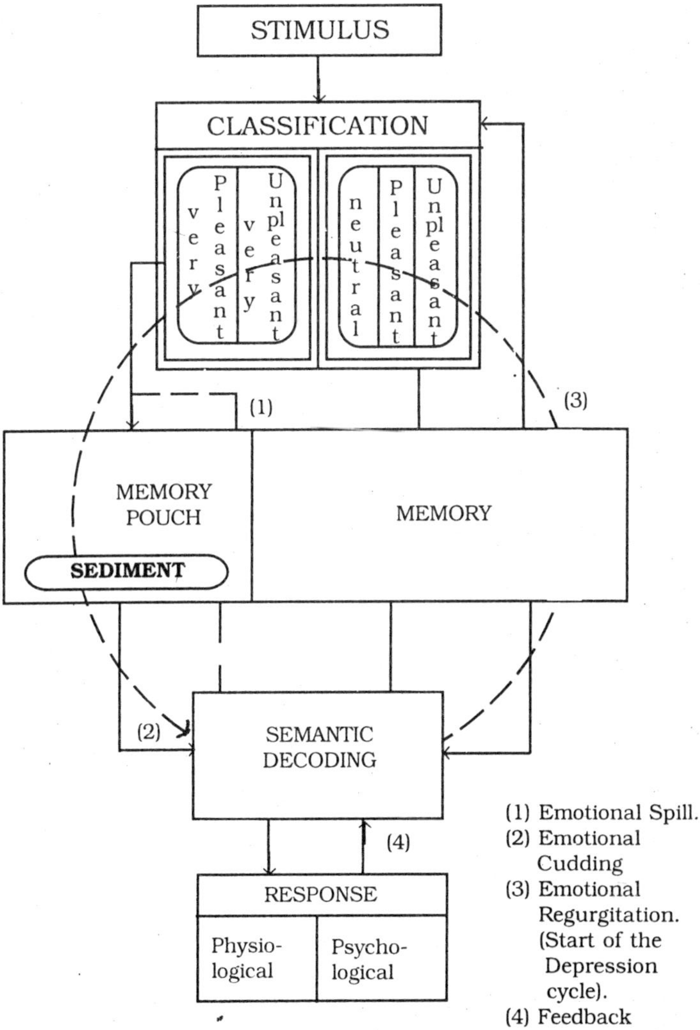

FIG. 17.1.: **The Information Processing Model of Emotions**

Memory Pouch

After the neural decoding of the stimulus, it is first classified into either neutral, pleasant, unpleasant, very pleasant, or very unpleasant stimulus. According to Zajonc (1980), we sense whether we like the stimulus or not before we know anything else about it. The classification is similar to the appraisal stage suggested by Arnold (1960) and Lazarus (1981).

After classification, while semantic decoding of the neutral, pleasant, and unpleasant stimuli is done, reaction to very pleasant and very unpleasant stimuli varies. Since such stimuli are exciting or threatening they are sent into a Memory Pouch to be dealt with gradually and at a time the individual is better prepared to face them.

A memory pouch is a hypothetical pouch wherein partly decoded very pleasant or very unpleasant deposits are stored. It is the ideas that are stored and not the affect as such (Oatley, 1988). However during this process there is an emotional spill [see (1) in Figure 17.1], since some stimuli are so strong that parts of them need immediate expression and are hard to be suppressed. According to Ellisworth (1994), there is no need that the interpretation of the situation must be completed before the body can begin to respond. Many of the physiological aspects of emotional expression like muscular tension or blushing, are not under voluntary control. Voluntary suppression may not completely suppress, much less always succeed in eliminating, the emotional state (Hilgard *et al.*, 1971). So such reactions appear on the face very quickly after an emotion-provoking event, before we can get our "masks" in place (Ekman & Friesen, 1975), or before we can deposit the material into our memory pouches. What happens to the suppressed, emotion-laden thoughts (Baron & Byrne, 1993) has puzzled psychologists.

Emotional Cudding

The deposit that has been successfully sent into our

memory pouch is brought out at a more appropriate time when we are ready to face and semantically decode it. This suppressed material has the capacity of arousing our emotions again (Baron *et al.*, 1993). It is then that Emotional Cudding [see (2) in Figure 17.1] takes place. Emotional cudding is the process of decoding the deposit which is in the memory pouch at a later time and usually in a different place. The emotions experienced during this process are very much similar to the immediate emotions. For instance, heart rate accelerates when subjects "recall" and "think" about unpleasant emotional material (Lacey, 1959; more recently Lang, Bradley, & Cuthbert, 1990; Vrana & Lang, 1990).

After we have decoded all of the deposits which are in the memory pouch, it will no longer evoke an emotion even when thought about. It is like chewing gum. For a while, the sweetness lingers, and afterwards, it slowly wanes away. Thus time heals. Carr (1925) states the well known fact that emotions disappear with action. Otherwise, one pleasant event in our life is enough to make us euphoric, and one unpleasant event is enough to send us into the depths of depression. We are no longer thrilled by some success in school for which we were thrilled then, if because there is no deposit of it any more in the memory pouch. We have decoded all of it emotionally and just the thought of it remains, bereft of emotion. But this is not the case for all past incidents. Emotional memories are to some extent indelible (Le Doux, 1990). Some successes when thought of still thrill us and some incidents still terrorize us. These have been sedimented at the bottom of the memory pouch (see Figure 17.1). The deposit that forms the sediment arouses our emotions whenever thought of, for a longer time.

Emotional Regurgitation

In a normal human being the sediment layer is a thin one and consists of both very pleasant and very unpleasant deposits. But in individuals who show symptoms of delayed stress reactions, depression and other anxiety disorders, the sediment layer is thick and is mostly made up of very unpleasant deposits. The personal histories of such patients consist more of failures than success experiences (Goldfried & Robins, 1983). They take a long time to decode the thick sediment.

Depressed individuals experience Emotional Regurgitation [see (3) in Figure 17.1]. It is the unconscious process of bringing up the already decoded, very unpleasant deposits, back to the memory pouch to be re-decoded. This process is initiated when they have many guilt feelings. Depression prone individuals indulge in increased negative thinking about the self (for review see Haaga, Dyck, & Ernst, 1991) and are bombarded by negative ideas about the future (Beck, 1967). The decoded messages these individuals receive reflect their negative view of themselves, such as, "I am bad !". Such thoughts (cognitions) arise as though by reflex and are no longer peripheral but occupy a dominant position in the consciousness (Beck, 1991). The individuals cannot face these threatening thoughts. So they re-decode the deposit with the hope of receiving a better message but again they get the same message. Thus they experience intense anxiety and feel depressed. Anxiety-ridden persons repeat the same phrases again and again (Munn, Fernald, & Fernald, 1967) and hence they are caught in a Depression Cycle (see Figure 17.1). In such a situation, these individuals have little conscious control (Beck, 1991) and cannot cope with the flooding of material due to emotional regurgitation and recudding. When very pleasant material is regurgitated individuals experience a manic episode.

Emotional regurgitation occasionally occurs even in emotionally stable individuals. When this happens, they experience the mood, depending on the nature of the deposit that has been regurgitated. Then they are at a loss to understand what has caused their particular mood. Only after deep analysis will they be able to understand what the stimulus is. This process is usually initiated in response to a cue that is mostly unconscious.

Liquidization of the Sediment

Some of the intense stimuli form a sediment at the bottom of the memory pouch. One way of liquidizing the sediment is by using cathartic techniques. If that is the case, the individual needs to be taught to face the strong positive or negative emotional experience that comes out during this process.

Cognitive therapies can aim at changing the classification system of the individual. People who feel emotions intensely have typical ways of thinking (Beck, 1976). For instance, when we fail an exam why is it that all of us are not depressed? Obviously for some of us it is just an unpleasant experience and we have learnt to cope with it, while for others it is a very unpleasant experience and thus have deposits of it in their memory pouches. If the individual learns to classify prior intense stimuli as less intense, then the sediment layer shall be very thin. The therapists task is to replace the misguised "cognitions" with a more realistic stimulus assessment (Beck, Emery, & Greenberg, 1985).

Factors Influencing the Memory Pouch

The memory pouch becomes bigger as age increases and is different from individual to individual. It is almost non-existent in infants and toddlers. The time taken by 6-year olds to make up with friends they have recently fought with, is lesser than that taken by adults. Since children's cognitive capacities are quite different from those of adults (Forgas, Burnham, & Trimboli, 1988).

The frequency of using the pouch is subject to individual differences (for instance, a moody person might use it often), as well as situational factors. When our boss shouts at us, obviously we cannot allow unpleasant feelings to show on our face. We probably have to smile a "goodbye" while leaving the boss's room. Then we might come straight to our room, carefully avoiding others' glances, and shut our door. We start reviewing all that has happened and feel bad about it. It is some time before we open our door again.

What has happened here? We have sent the unpleasant remarks made by our boss into the memory pouch. After going to our room we have emotionally decoded the material, since our room is a safe and a non-threatening place. Once the deposit has been decoded we are fresh again! Now contrast this with our behaviour at home. If we are angry with our children we can chide them then and there without depositing anything into the memory pouch.

The need to seek an appropriate place to cud the deposit is learnt. It has long been found that when people are in good mood they are more willing to do favours (Isen, 1987) and many people are more irritable when feeling low, than when feeling mellow (Anderson, 1989). This is because when a neutral stimulus is presented it is coloured according to the state of our functioning at the given time. During emotional cudding, psychologically and physiologically too, we react to the nature of the deposit being decoded. So when a very pleasant deposit is being decoded, otherwise neutral stimulus is also perceived as pleasant. Similarly when a very unpleasant deposit is being decoded, a neutral stimulus is perceived as unpleasant. Thus we find a safe place to decode, where we are not disturbed, avoiding inappropriate responses and embarrassing ourselves and others. In this manner the memory pouch helps us in our face-saving effort. However the colouring effect fades if the stimulus is stronger than the deposit being decoded.

Nature of the Memory Pouch

The memory pouch is used for storing emotionally loaded stimuli temporarily, and not neutral ideas. Its capacity is akin to that of the Long Term Memory. It can store large amounts of deposits and for a long time. Once a particular deposit fails to arouse an emotion, it is sent into the Memory to be stored there.

The process of suppression and later retrieval of the deposit from the memory pouch is a conscious process.

We can bring the deposit to our awareness whenever we wish. It is thus under our control.

There are deposits both in the memory pouch and in the unconscious which surface later. But the memory pouch is different from the unconscious in many ways. The deposit in the memory pouch is suppressed, while that in the unconscious, is repressed. Suppression is a conscious process (Worchel & Wayne, 1986) whereas repression is an unconscious process. Further, unlike in the unconscious where the material is largely unpleasant, both pleasant and unpleasant deposits are present here. Finally, while lying dormant the deposit in the memory pouch does not hamper normal functioning as opposed to the material in the unconscious.

Regarding the sediment, it usually comes to our awareness as a response to cues. These cues can be either internal or external in nature. Hence, it is in the preconscious and thus not totally under our control. However, preconscious mental contents can usually become conscious (Gillett, 1987a; b).

Emotional Response

We respond to the stimuli once they are semantically decoded and the relevant material is sent into the memory which aids in the future classification and semantic decoding.

Our response is of two types; psychological response (cognitive aspects of emotion) and physiological response (voluntary and involuntary). Varying degrees of psychological and involuntary physiological responses are elicited by all emotions. Depending on the situation we decide whether our response should be voluntary physiological too. For instance, if we are angry with our boss, we cannot slam the door of our boss's room. We wait till we come to our door and slam it with force. Until we have reached our room, our response is largely psychological and involuntary physiological. Later it becomes voluntary physiological too. Rappaport (1961) has long ago recognised that sometimes the physiological and sometimes the psychological manifestations of emotions become the more obvious. This channeling is possible because we receive feedback (Lazarus, 1991) [see (4) in Figure 17.1] about our behaviour and decide the best response in a given situation. Thus feedback serves as a reappraisal of our response.

Concluding Remarks

According to Chaplin and Kraewic (1979), a model must stimulate research and provide better understanding. The Information Processing Model of emotions, besides throwing light on the mechanisms of emotional experience, poses a variety of questions. For instance, what cues enable individuals to emotionally ruminate, for how long and how often.

This model can explain research findings which suggest that depressives experience cognitive problems: especially memory deficits (Hertel & Milan, 1994: for reviews, see Dalgleish & Watts, 1990; Hartlage, Alloy, Vazquez & Dykman, 1993; MacLeod, 1990; Williams, Watts, MacLeod, & Mathews, 1988) since depressives are engrossed in emotional cudding, and emotional regurgitation, they cannot pay enough attention and are in an "amotivational" state (Mogg, Bradley, Williams, & Mathews, 1993). Thus their cognitive resources are insufficient to work effectively on resource-demanding tasks (Ellis & Ashbrook, 1988). Sometimes when presented with a task, normals too might be engrossed in emotional cudding but it is of a controllable nature since they rarely experience emotional regurgitation. usually in such a situation they stop emotional cudding, allowing the deposit to lie in the memory pouch, and concentrate on the task. If emotional regurgitation can be made to be controlled in depressed patients, who make up 10% of the population (Alloy, Abramson, & Dykman, 1990). This theory shall be of great value to Clinical Psychology apart from contributing to General Psychology.

REFERENCES

Alloy, L.B., Abramson, L.Y., & Dykman, B.M. (1990). Depressive realism and nondepressive optimistic illusions: The role of the self. In R.E. Ingram (Ed.), *Contemporary psychological approaches to depression : Treatment, research, and theory.* New York : Plenum.

Anderson, C.A. (1989). Temperature and aggression: The ubiquitous effects of heat on the occurrence of human violence. *Psychological Bulletin, 106,* 74-96.

Arnold, M.R. (1960). *Emotion and personality.* (2 Vols.). New York : Columbia University Press.

Bard, P. (1928). A diencephalic mechanism for the expression of rage with special reference to the sympathetic nervous system. *American Journal of Physiology, 84,* 490-515.

Baron, R.A., & Byrne, D. (1993). *Social psychology : Understanding human interaction* (6th ed.) New Delhi, India: Prentice-Hall.

Beck, A.T. (1967). *Depression.* Pennsylvania: University of Pennsylvania Press.

Beck, A.T. (1976). *Cognitive therapy and the emotional disorders.* New York : International University Press.

Beck. A.T., (1991). Cognitive therapy : A 30 year retrospective, *American Psychologist, 46,* 368-375.

Beck, A.T., Emery, G., & Greenberg, R.L. (1985). *Anxiety disorders and phobias.* New York: Basic Books.

Bower, G.H. (1981). Mood and memory. *American Psychologist, 36,* 129-148.

Cannon, W.B. (1927). The James-Lange theory of emotions: A critical examination and an alternative theory. *American journal of Psycholgy, 39,* 106-124.

Carr, H.A. (1925). *Psychology: A study of mental activity.* New York: McKay.

Chaplin, J.P., & Kraewic, T.S. (1979). *Systems and theories in psychology.* New York: Holt, Rinehart & Winston.

Dagleish, T., & Watts, F.N. (1990). Biases of attention and memory in disorders of anxiety and depression. *Clinical Psychological Review,* 10, 589-604.

Ekman, P., & Friesen, W.V. (1975). *Unmasking the face.* Englewood Cliffs, NJ: Prentice-Hall.

Ellis, H.C., & Ashbrook, P.N. (1988). Resource allocation model of the effects of depressed mood states on memory. In K. Fiedler & Forgas (Eds.), *Affect, cognition, and social behavior* (pp. 25-43). Toronto : Hogrefe.

Ellisworth, P.C. (1994). William James and emotion: Is a century of fame worth a century of misunderstanding? *Psychological Review, 101*, 222-229.

Forgas, J.P., Burnham, D.K., & Trimboli, C. (1988). Mood, memory and social judgements in children. *Journal of Personality and Social Psychology. 54*, 697-703.

Gillett, E. (1987a). Defence mechanisms versus defence contents. *International Journal of Psychoanalysis, 68*, 261-269.

Gillett, E. (1987b). The relationship of repression to the unconscious. *International Journal of Psychoanalysis, 68*, 535-546.

Goldfried, M.R., & Robins, C. (1983). Self-schema, cognitive bias and the processing of therapeutic experiences. In P.C. Kendall (Ed.), *Advances of cognitive-behavioural research and therapy*. (pp. 35-73). New York: Academic Press.

Haaga, D.A.F., Dyck, M.J., & Ernst, D. (1991). Empirical status of cognitive theory of depression. *Psychological Bulletin, 110*, 215-236.

Hartlage, S., Alloy, L.B., Vazquez, C., & Dykman, B. (1993). Automatic and effortful processing of depression. *Psychological Bulletin, 113*, 247-278.

Hertel, P.T., & Milan, S. (1994). Depressive deficits in recognition: Dissociation of recollection and familiarity. *Journal of Abnormal Psychology, 103*, 736-742.

Hilgard, E.R., Atkinson, R.C., & Atkinson, R.L. (1971). *Introduction to psychology* (5th ed.). New York: Harcourt Brace Jovanovich.

Isen, A.M. (1987). Positive affect, cognitive processes and social behaviour. In L. Berkowitz (Ed.), *Advances in experimental social psychology*. (Vol. 20, pp. 203-253).

Izard, C.E. (1977). *Human emotions*. New York: Plenum.

James, W. (1890). *The principles of psychology*. New York: Holt, Rinehart & Winston.

Lacey, J.I. (1959). Psychophysiological approaches to the evaluation of psychotherapeutic process and outcome. In E.A. Rubinstein & M.B. Parloff (Eds.), *Research in psychotherapy*. (Vol. 1, pp. 160-208). Washington, DC: American Psychological Association.

Lang, P.J. (1979). A bio-informational theory of emotional imagery. *Psychophysiology, 16*, 495-512.

Lang, P.J., Bradley, M.M., & Cuthbert, B.N. (1990). Emotion, attention, and the startle reflex. *Psychological Review, 97*, 377-395.

Lazarus, R.S. (1981). A cognitivist's reply to Zajonc in emotion and cognition. *American Psychologist, 36*, 222-223.

Lazarus, R.S. (1991). Cognition and motivation in emotion. *American Psychologist, 46*, 352-367.

Le Doux, J.E. (1990). Information flow from sensation to emotion plasticity in neural computation of stimulus value. In M. Gabriel and J. Moore (Eds.), *Learning and computational neuroscience : Foundations of adaptive networks* (pp. 3-52). Cambridge, MA: Bradford Books/MIT Press.

MacLeod, C. (1990). Mood disorders and cognition. In M.W. Eysenck (Ed.), *Cognitive psychology: An International Review* (pp. 9-55). New York: Wiley.

Mandler, G. (1984). *Mind and body: Psychology of emotion and stress.* New York: Norton.

Mogg, K., Bradley, B.P., Williams, R., & Mathews, A. (1993). Subliminal processing of emotional information in anxiety and depression. *Journal of Abnormal Psychology, 102*, 304-311.

Munn, N.L., Fernald, L.D. Jr., & Fernald, P.S. (1967). *Introduction to psychology* (3rd ed.) New Delhi India: Oxford & IBH.

Oatley, K. (1988). Gaps in consciousness: Emotions and memory of psychoanalysis. *Cognition and Emotions, 2*, 3-18.

Rappaport, D. (1961). *Emotions and memory.* New York: Science Editions.

Strongman, K.T. (1973). *The psychology of emotions.* New York: Wiley.

Vrana, S.R., & Lang, P.J. (1990). Fear imagery and the startle-probe reflex. *Journal of Abnormal Psychology, 99*, 189-197.

Williams, J.M.G., Watts, F.N. MacLeod, C., & Mathews, A. (1988). *Cognitive psychology and emotional disorders.* New York : Wiley.

Worchel, S., & Wayne, S. (1986). *Psychology: Principles and applications.* NJ: Prentice-Hall.

Zajonc, R.B. (1980). Feeling and thinking: Preferences need no inferences. *American Psychologist, 35*, 151-175.

18

Impact of Emotional Adjustment on Family Adjustment and Social Adjustment

Vijayalaxmi A. Aminabhavi

Effective living depends on satisfactory adjustment of a person in the various domains of his or her life. Well adjusted people are regarded as succcessful in the art of living (Norman, 1978). Infact, among the several factors which influence adjustment of an individual in different aspects of life, emotional component of psyche seems to be an important factor. Emotions do play a significant role in shaping our behaviour across different situations.

In recent years many efforts have been made to attend to this aspect of behavioural dynamics. Denham and Burton (1996) implemented a social-emotional intervention for at-risk day care students. Students were trained to perform activities associated with relationship building and social problem solving. Children who had received intervention showed decrease in negative emotions, greater involvement and social improvement, and more initiative in positive peer activity than did controls. It supports the utility of intervention. Indoe and Pecherek (1996) have discussed about the family influences families and interactions with school effectiveness and outside agencies, mental health *vs.* social control issues, school effectiveness and the debate of whether deviants and criminals are born or made. A comparative study made by Indu and Vandana (1997) revealed that blind adolescents are better adjusted in home, health and school areas than their sighted peers. But both groups do not differ in their emotional and social adjustment. Merell

(1996) discussed new directions in psychological and educational service delivery with the early childhood/ preschool population internalizing and externalizing socio-emotional problems, as well as social competence. Guernina (1997) investigated the impact of bilingualism on the pupils' self-rated adjustment in Algeria. He found that bilingual children were less confident and socially stable than those with a single language. Aminabhavi (1997) found that post-graduate students belonging to upper middle class and coming from upper middle stratum of socio-cultural background have significantly higher level of emotional adjustment than their counterparts, while, the students of middle class and the students coming from middle stratum of socio-cultural background have significantly higher social adjustment. The present study was conducted to find out the impact of emotional adjustment on family and social adjustment.

METHOD

Sample

Ninety post-graduate students (45 males and 45 females) enrolled in various P.G. departments of Karnataka University, Dharwad participated in the study.

Measure

Mysore Personality Inventory : This measure developed by Krishnan was used to measure emotional adjustment, family adjustment and social adjustment of the selected sample. The scale measures the adjustment with various aspects like family, emotion, social, mood, reality, criminality and leadership. This scale consists of 235 items in the form of statements. The responses are given in terms of 'True' or 'False', on the separate answer sheet given to them.

Procedure

The participants were administered the Mysore Personality

Inventory and the responses were collected. The responses were scored with the help of scoring keys of three sub scales such as emotional adjustment, family adjustment and social adjustment. The obtained scores were transformed to standard scores. In this inventory, lower score shows higher adjustment and higher score shows lower adjustment. Along with the responses to the inventory some information were also collected through the biodata sheet.

Results and Discussion

The analysis of scores revealed (F 2, 87) = 11.02; ($P<.001$), that the three groups of students—emotionally adjusted, moderately adjusted and emotionally maladjusted—vary significantly in the extent of their family adjustment. Multiple comparison of mean scores with the help of Scheffe's Test revealed that emotionally adjusted and emotionally maladjusted groups differed significantly in their family adjustment ($S = -4.96$; $P<0.01$). The difference between moderately adjusted group and emotionally maladjusted group was also significant ($S=-3.28$; $P<0.01$). The emotionally adjusted group did not differ significantly from the moderately adjusted group in their family adjustment ($S=-1.39$; $P>0.05$).

The effect of emotional adjustment on social adjustment was significant [F (2,87) 12.18; $P<0.001$]. The emotionally adjusted, moderately adjusted and emotionally maladjusted differed in the degree of social adjustment.

Multiple comparison revealed that emotionally adjusted students had significantly lower level of social adjustment than the moderately adjusted students ($S=-4.69$; $P<0.01$). The moderately adjusted group had significantly higher level of social adjustment as compared with the maladjusted group ($S=-3.69$; $P<0.01$). The emotionally adjusted and moderately adjusted groups did not differ significantly in their social adjustment ($S=-1.01$; $P>0.05$). Thus it appears that emotionally adjusted and averagely adjusted students had significantly higher level of social adjustment than the emotionally maladjusted students.

It was also found that the first born, middle born and last born students differed significantly in the extent of emotional adjustment [F (2, 87) =7.03; P<0.001].

Multiple comparison of the mean scores revealed that the first born students are differing significantly from middle born (S=-3.33; P<0.01) and last born (S= -3.12; P<0.01) students in their emotional adjustment. The middle born and last born students did not differ significantly in their emotional adjustment (S=0.12 : P>0.05). It means, first born students show significantly higher level of emotional adjustment than middle born and last born people.

The finding that better the emotional adjustment higher the family and social adjustment reflects the significance of emotional adjustment to balance one's life in different spheres. It is Emotional Quotient (E.Q.) as compared to the Intelligence Quotient (I.Q.) which plays a significant role in determining adjustment in several aspects of a person's life. An individual who can very well manage his own emotions can also become capable of adjusting with anything in his life.

Another finding of the study that the first born have significantly higher level of emotional adjustment than the middle born and last born needs some comment. The first born person develops a feeling of responsibility. This feeling may enhance their emotional adjustment compared to his siblings.

It may be concluded that in the sample of young adults who are emotionally adjusted and moderately adjusted with their emotions have significantly higher family adjustment and social adjustment than the emotionally maladjusted students. Also, the first born have significantly higher level of emotional adjustment than the middle born and last born. Thus, the present findings imply the need of counselling for students with some problems in their emotional life in order to enhance their adjustment in several aspects of life.

REFERENCES

Aminabhavi V. A. (1997). A study of personality of post-graduate students in relation to their socio-economic-status and socio-cultural background. *Proceedings of 2nd Asian and 33rd Indian Academy of Applied Psychology Conference.* Hardwar, Feb. 26-28, 162-167.

Denham, S.A. & Burton, R. (1996). A social-emotional intervention for at-risk 4 year olds. *Journal of School Psychology, 34*, 225-245.

Indoe, D. & Pecherek, A. (1996). Vulnerable children : Responses from education. *Educational and Child Psychology, 13*, 43-51.

Indu, B. & Vandana (1997). Adjustment patterns of blind and sighted adolescents. *Indian Psychological Review, 48*, 75-78.

Guernina, Z. (1997). The impact of bilingualism on the pupil's self-rated adjustment in Algeria. *Psychological Abstracts, 7*, 22105.

Merrell, K.W (1996). Social emotional problems in early childhood: New directions in conceptualization, assessment and treatment. *Education and Treatment of Children, 19*, 458-473.

Norman, T. (1978). *Psychology of adjustment.* New York: D. Van Nostrand Company.

19

Arousal And Adjustment In Delinquent Children

Jayita Datta Gupta, P.K. Chattopadhyay, Pritha Mukhopadhyay, Debabrata Biswas and **Soumendra Saha**

Children who arrest the attention of mental health professionals display a wide range of problem behaviours that cause difficulty for themselves, their parents, and the society, at large. One such group of children is the delinquents, whose behaviour is primarily reflected in conflict with the environment (Kapur, 1995).

Academicians and researchers working in the field of psychopathy have been attracted by the physiological correlates in psychopathy and the nature of personality characteristics that might be prevalent, particularly, in this group. Eysenck's (Eysenck & Eysenck, 1970) proclamations that extraverted people with their poor conditioning are more likely to be poorly socialized (Nair, 1994) and that such neurotics with high score on factors of emotionality or anxiety will tend to engage more readily in antisocial acts, have been supported by many authors (Lykken, 1957; Mills, 1971; Pederson 1994; Singh, 1972). To Eysenck (1970), neuroticism is a predisposition to strong autonomic activation which produces higher cortical arousal, affecting one's behaviour (Davis & Tune, 1970).

Spence and Taylor (1953) equating anxiety with drive level have inferred that anxiety and "arousal" are synonymous. High level anxiety corresponds to low self esteem (Ford & Linney, 1995; Kahn & Fua, 1995; Nair, 1994; Singh *et al.*, 1983) and also feeling of dread, guilt, inferiority, loneliness and depression (Barnes & O'Gorman, 1995; Zeiller & Courand, 1994).

There is yet another evidence which suggests that when psychopaths or antisocial children are at rest, or presented with aversive event their average skin conductance level (SCL) is lower than normals (Lykken, 1957; Medrick & Christianson, 1977; Kossan & Newman, 1986). Findings indicating lesser effect of sensory stimulation in more psychopathic subjects also show the tendency of low cortical arousal (Hare, 1970). This is also indicated by the slower rate of cortical excitability (Freeman, 1988). The latter finding also supports theories which suggest that psychopaths are chronically underaroused and that much of their behaviour is sensation-seeking and motivated by a desire to increase arousal (Freeman, 1988).

Individuals with high anxiety and depicting a picture of the above mentioned personality are more likely to be poorly adjusted to most environmental set-up (Kahn & Fua, 1995). As has been suggested by Zeiller & Courand, (1994), delinquent children being unaware of their hatred towards their parents shift their hatred on their victims.

To sum up, it may be said that there have been few reported evidences regarding the arousal status of delinquents. If we are to help the delinquents lead a better life, we need to take a closer look at their learning potentials, which actually require adequate level of arousal. The aim of the present study was to explore the level of arousal of delinquent children and to compare the same with a group of normal controls.

METHOD

Sample

Twenty participants were taken in all. They belonged to two groups — the experimental group and the control group. The experimental group of ten boys comprised of those under arrest for various criminal offences and sent by court to the 'Observational Home For Delinquent Children'. The remaining ten boys were the normal controls. The children were all 9 and 10 years old boys (mean age being 9.5 years, and S.D. = 0.527 yrs.). They were all matched with respect to age, sex, intelligence, education and socio-economic status. They suffered from no physical, neurological and/or major psychiatric illnesses. Permission had to be taken from the juvenile court for interviewing the delinquents and undertaking physiological measures.

Measures

i) Bell's Adjustment Inventory, which measures the four areas of adjustment in children, namely, home, social, emotional and health.
ii) Junior Eysenck's Personality Questionnaire (EPQ) which measures neuroticism-psychoticism and extraversion-introversion on proper administration.
iii) children's Personality Questionnaire which measures the personality characteristics in an individual.
iv) Physiological recorder to measure the skin conductance level.

Procedure

The psychological tests which included Bell's Adjustment Inventory, CPQ and EPQ (Jr.) were first administered following standard procedures. The psychological tests were followed by the physiological measure, mentioned below. Each subject was approached separately.

In this present study the procedure used for recording SR was essentially the same as that described by Lader and Wing (1966). Double element lead electrodes were used and they were sanded bright with the inactive one filled with electrode jelly. The right thumb was wiped dry, single corn plaster was filled with electrode jelly. The 'active' electrode was positioned over the corn plaster and secured with adhesive tape. The contact medium between the electrode and the skin, used here, was the K-Y jelly. Both the electrodes were plugged in and the SR instrument was calibrated. Then the instrument (Polyrite, Inco, Ambala, India) was switched to the subject and a constant current of 14 am/cm^2 was passed through the electrodes and the voltage across the subject was balanced. The sensitivity was increased usually to 20 to 50 kilo-ohms, if necessary. The speed of the polyrite paper was 1.5 mm/sec.

Results

The results obtained from the present findings indicate the following:

1) There is no significant difference in the degree of neuroticism between the two groups.
2) The delinquents are less extraverted and had significantly lower level of skin conductance arousal compared to non-delinquents.
3) Delinquents are emotionally less adjusted although in other areas of adjustment, namely, social, health and home, they show no significant difference from the non-delinquents. The delinquents were less properly adjusted to home situations than the non-delinquents.
4) Delinquents are more assertive and dominant in their behaviour. More assertiveness and dominance also may be the reason behind their maladjustment at home.

Discussion

The results obtained in the present study support many recent findings that predict the fact that physiological correlates do prevail in psychopathy (Hare, 1968; 1970). The main results showed a significant difference existing between the two groups and that when at rest, the delinquent group of children had a lower A.N.S. arousal compared to the normals, as indicated by the lower level of skin conductance. This present finding supports many existing results contributed by several researchers (Kossan *et al.*, 1986; Lykken, 1957). Low skin conductance level not only indicates lower skin conductance reactivity, but also slow rate of ANS excitability (Freeman, 1988). It is likely that such underaroused individuals manifest behaviour patterns that are sensation-seeking and governed by a desire to increase arousal (Freeman, 1988). Moreover, underarousal means low level of anxiety. This is true as evidenced from the significantly lower state of anxiety in the delinquents measured from their self report. The results obtained in this study do not fit in well with Eysenck's theory that extraverted anxiety neurotics indulge in antisocial behaviour.

Comparison of the personality factors suggest that delinquents are less extraverted but more assertive, and dominant. Their apparent assertive behaviour may be due to the feeling of inadequacy that they are suffering from (Singh, *et al*, 1982). Although they have a tendency to be assertive and dominant, they do not seem to express themselves outwardly, even when their feelings are affected. This may add to their feelings of loneliness and depression (Barnes, 1995; Zeiller & Courand 1994). That an inverse relation exists between delinquency and extraversion has also been highlighted earlier by Crider and Lunn (1971).

A further glance at the level of adjustment in the four areas, namely, home social, health and emotional, shows no significant difference existing in the first-three areas of adjustment between the delinquents and the non-delinquents. This means that the delinquents try to maintain a cordial relationship with their family, friends and relatives, as much as practicable. Redl and Wineman (1951) assert that offenders committing crime against outsiders maintain moral values in their relationships with friends and relatives. No significant difference in home adjustment indicates that although marital disharmony may prevail, it might not be the cause of delinquent behaviour. Such disharmony may be prevalent in any family with low socio-economic status. One may, however, assume that despite their cordial relationship at home they have disliking towards their parents, as it has been suggested by Zeiller (1994) that such individuals displace their hatred and anger on their victims. Finally, due to emotional instability, their easily affected feelings lead to emotional maladjustment that might together contribute to their improper adjustment at home. In conclusion, it may be said that the delinquents with lower arousal level are also behaviourally inhibited, and hence they repress their own feelings and desires. Thus, for proper therapeutic intervention it is necessary that one gives a careful thought to their level of arousal.

REFERENCES

Barnes, J. & O'Gorman, Noel (1995). A descriptive study of juvenile delinquents. *Irish Journal of Psychological Medicine, 12*, 53-56.

Crider, A. & Lunn R. (1971). Electrodermal Lability as a personality dimension. *Journal of Experimental Research in Personality, 5*, 145-150.

Davis, D.R., & Tune, G.S. (1970). *Human vigilance performance.* London : Staples.

Eysenck, H.J. (1970). *Crime and personality.* London : Routledge & Kagan, Paul.

Eysenck, S.B.G. & Eysenck, H.J. (1970). Crime and Personality: An Empirical study of the 3-Factor Theory. *British Journal of Criminology*, 225-239.

Ford Michalle E. & Linney, Jean Ann (1995). Comparative offenders, and status offenders. *Journal of Interpersonal Violence, 10*, 56-70.

Freeman, C.P. (1988). Personality Disorder. In Comparison to Psychiatiric Studies. Edited by Kendell; R.E., Zealley; A.K. 4th ed., Churchill Livingstone (pp. 407-430).

Hare, R.D. (1968). Psychopathy, autonomic functioning and the orienting response. *Journal of Abnormal Psychology, 73*, 1-24.

Hare, R.D. (1970). *Psychopathy: Theory and Research.* New York: Wiley.

Kossan, D.S. & Newman, J.P. (1986). Psychopathy and the allocation of attentional capacity in a divided attention situation. *Journal of Abnormal Psychology, 95*, 257-263.

Kapur, M. (1995). *Mental health of Indian children.* New Delhi : Sage.

Kahn, Marvin W. & Fua, Chiff (1995). Children of South Island Immigrants to Australia : Factors associated with adjustment problem. *International Journal of Social Psychiatry*, 41 (1), 55-73.

Lader, M.H. & Wing, L. (1966). *Physiological measures, sedative drugs and morbid anxiety*. London : Oxford University Press.

Lykken, D. (1957). A study of anxiety in the sociopathic personality. *Journal of Abnormal and Social Psychology, 55*, 6-10.

Mills, M.W. (1971). Extraversion, neuroticism and the critical Flicker frequency Threshold in Antisocial personalities. *Dissertation Abstract International, 31*, 7604-7605.

Nair, Elizabeth (1994). How do prisoners and probationers explain their predicament? An Attributional analysis. *Psychologia, 37*, 66-71.

Pedersen, Willy (1994). Parental relations, mental health, and delinquency in adolescents. *Adolescence, 29*, 975-990.

Singh, J.G., Srinivas, R., & Singh, S. (1983). Deprivation and self-esteem among delinquents. *Indian Journal of Clinical Psychology*, 10, 355-360.

Singh, M., Gunthey, R.K., & Sharma, R.P. (1982). Personality Correlates of Juvenile Delinquency. *Indian Journal of Clinical Psychology. 9*, 43-45.

Zeiller, B. & Courand Barnoud, S. (1994). Criminal children and teenagers : Psychopathological Aspects. *Early Childhood Development & Care, 103*, 77-93.

20

Educational Psychology in India : Research Trends

Ashok K. Srivastava and **M.K. Raina**

Educational psychology, or the academic study of the psychology of education (Burden, 1994), is "that special branch of psychology concerned with the nature, conditions, outcomes and evaluation of school learning and retention" (Ausubel, 1968, p. 232). It establishes links between psychological inquiry, psychological knowledge and education explicit and also attempts at developing generalizable knowledge about human beings that is of interest to all social sciences. More than being a simple conduit of information it is "conceived as a complex and multidisciplinary body of knowledge and principles applied to all processes of teaching and learning" (Mohan, 1993, p. 1). What Cubberly (1920) described more than 70 years ago as a guiding science of the schools, the field of educational psychology is currently poised to regain its dominance as the guiding science of education (Mayer, 1992). It is conceived as an exciting venue for shaping and testing dominant psychological theories of the day.

What constitutes the discipline of educational psychology, is an intriguing issue. Ball (1984) failed to find any consensus among the prominent textbooks of that time. More recently, Gopal (1995), after reviewing several textbooks in the field of educational psychology (such as Cronbach, 1977; Dembo, 1990; Kaplan, 1990; Rothstein, 1990; Travers, Elliot & Kratochwill, 1993) has concluded that there is a broad consensus about the constitution of the discipline. Rothstein (1990) identified three broad areas which typically occupy practitioners :

the teaching process (such as teaching methods, styles, and management techniques), the learners and the learning process (focussing on the application of principles of cognitive and developmental psychology, individual differences, and learning styles), and the environment (dealing with the social context of classroom or home environment).

An analysis of the developments that have taken place in the field of educational psychology since G. Stanley Hall in 1860 reveals changes in its shape in the long journey : From the metaphor of learning as a response acquisition during the first-half of the twentieth century, through learning as response construction metaphor during 1950s and 1960s, to radical constructivism during 1980s and 1990s (Derry, 1992). After content analysing the *Journal of Educational Psychology* from 1910 to 1980, Ball (1984) concluded that educational psychology in early days was closely devoted to the practical issues of teachers, teaching, school learning, and school curriculum. Across the years it has become less directly related to the classroom and more interested in the academic pursuit of theory validation. There has also been an increase in the complexity of the published research. Ball (1984) referred to educational psychology as a chameleon, changing its emphasis perhaps to conform to its environment.

The teaching of psychology in India began in 1915 at Calcutta University, followed by the Universities of Mysore (1924), Aligarh (1932), and Patna (1946). After independence there has been steady increase in the number of universities offering psychology courses (Sinha, 1966). It is also regularly offered in professional institutions of agriculture, nursing, engineering, medicine, management, and education (Raina, 1989). Educational psychology does occupy an important place in India (Paliwal, 1977) and has been taught in the colleges of education or departments of psychology from the very beginning (Panda, 1991). However, as an applied branch of psychology it never attained much status in faculties of education or departments of psychology (Buch, 1972).

Studies have shown that only 3 per cent psychologists identified themselves as educational psychologists (Ganguli, 1971), and only 6 to 7 per cent of the total publications were related to educational psychology (Ganguli, 1971; Mitra, 1972). It were clinical, personality and social psychology that covered more than half of the psychology publications. Mitra (1972, p. xxii) concluded that :

> "Educational psychology has been developing at a fast rate and it can be expected that it will soon catch up with other areas. It has recorded a ten-fold increase in twenty years which is surpassed only by Developmental Psychology and Personality".

Notwithstanding the above observation, educational psychology forms an especially important ingredient in the education of teachers. The survey of teacher education in India (Singh, 1983) indicates that educational psychology is offered as a compulsory course in all the universities in India as a complete paper or combined with such courses as health education, educational measurement, educational evaluation and statistics.

In India considerable efforts have been made towards the dissemination of studies related to educational psychology. The first-three surveys of research in education contained chapters on "Personality, learning and motivation" (Rao & Mehta, 1974; Rao, Mehta & Rao, 1979; Menon & Ojha, 1987). The last two surveys are more comprehensive and cover "Research in psychology of education" (Panda, 1991; Nayar, in press). Of the three surveys sponsored by Indian Council of Social Science Research, only the first survey contained a chapter on educational psychology (Buch, 1972).

An analysis of these reviews indicates an unanimous agreement among the reviewers that the selection of problems in general bear the imprint of what interested the psychologists in the west and methods employed too were similar to those used in the west. The researchers lacked pragmatism (Menon & Ojha, 1987). The investigations were pursued for the sake of investigation without having any apparent relevance to purpose of theory in the question. Also, there has been a considerable time gap in following the Western models of researches. Panda (1991) thus observes : "While educational psychology research has thus shifted towards an understanding of information processing, information integration, congnitive processing and development of skills, Indian educational research has only very recently shown signs of moving in line with the Western trend in conceptualization" (p. 330). The reasons for all these have probably been many such as training of prominent Indian Psychologists in the West (Adair & Kagitcibasi, 1995), lack of resources (Adair, 1995) and above all lack of a supportive intellectual climate (Adair, Pandey, Begum, Puhan & Vohra, 1995).

The limitations of the surveys published so far have been that while Buch (1972) survey can now be considered as classical, the surveys of research in education primarily focussed on doctoral dissertations and institutional studies. A vast and significant aspect of the published literature in scientific journals on educational psychology remains yet to be analysed. An analysis of doctoral dissertations, in our opinion, would not be sufficient to discern the trend of research in any field of knowledge for the reason that Ph.D. provides primarily a training in pursuing, conducting a research and more serious efforts are made at later stages. These efforts get published in scientific journals since these are "the universally accepted outlet for empirical work" (Adair, Puhan, & Vohra, 1993). Doctoral theses have a limited value; however, journals provide uniform data base for assessing and delineating a trend of development in a discipline.

Against this backdrop, the Department of Educational Psychology and Foundations of Education, NCERT, New Delhi, has taken up a study (Raina & Srivastava, 1994) to analyse the published research in various Indian journals and project reports funded by the national organizations in the field of educational psychology during the last 15 years. The purpose of this analysis is two-fold: (a) to delineate the trends and identify gaps in the researches, and (b) to identify the development of indigenization in educational psychology researches. This report contains some of the results of this ongoing study. More particularly, an attempt has been made to examine the status of educational psychology research in India by analysing studies abstracted in *Indian Psychological Abstracts*.

Analysis of Studies Abstracted in Indian Psychological Abstracts

Since there is no journal devoted wholly to the research articles related to the educational psychology in India, it was considered appropriate to analyse studies abstracted in *Indian Psychological Abstracts* (1980-90) and *Indian Psychological Abstracts and Reviews* (1994-95) with a view to delineate the status of educational psychology research vis-a-vis research in other branches of psychology, topics covered, nature and size of the sample, and tools used in these studies. The *Indian Psychological Abstracts* is "a unique abstracting service for professionals, researchers, managers, and students giving them access to invaluable and uptodate literature on psychological research work in India and its application". The *Abstracts* claims to provide information that appears in about 400 journals on psychological research in India. The *Abstracts* was, however, not published during the years 1991-93. It includes studies related to different branches of psychology such as general psychology, research methods, experimental, physiological, developmental, social, clinical, educational psychology, organisational behaviour, and personality. A total of 12,374 studies were included in different issues of the journal during the periods under analysis. A summary of this analysis is outlined in the following sections.

Publications in Various Areas of Psychology

Table 20.1 shows that the maximum number of published

studies were related to the field of clinical psychology (22%) followed by social psychology (19%), personality (13%), organisational behaviour (12%), and educational psychology (9%). While there has been a decrease in the number of studies concerning other branches of psychology over the years, a high increase in the quantum of studies related to educational psychology during 1990s is observed. During the years 1994-95, educational psychology has only been surpassed by clinical psychology.

TABLE 20.1 : **Percentage of Studies Related to Different Branches of Psychology (N=12,374)**

Branch	1980-84	1985-90	1994-95	Overall
General	6	13	2	9
Research Methods	5	4	6	5
Experimental	5	5	3	6
Physiological	4	0	6	2
Developmental	4	2	5	3
Social	23	16	12	19
Organisational Behaviour	13	11	14	12
Personality	13	13	15	13
Clinical	19	29	20	22
Educational	8	7	17	9

Publications within the Discipline of Educational Psychology

Within the expanse of educational psychology (an aggregate of 1049 studies were analysed), the analysis of teaching-learning process received top priority (Table 20.2). About 12 per cent studies were related to teaching-learning process, followed by academic achievement (9%), teacher behaviour (8%), guidance/counselling (6%), educational psychology of organisation (5%), cognition/intelligence (5%), psychology of exceptional children (5%), measurement/evaluation (5%), personality (4%), and motivation/attitudes/interest (4%). It is amazing to note that a large number of studies (12%) included under 'educational psychology' in *Indian Psychological Abstracts* did not relate to the field of educational psychology. About 4 per cent studies were either not related to India or were book articles.

TABLE 20.2 : **Percentage of Studies Related to Different Areas of Educational Psychology**

S.No.	Areas	N (1090)	Percent-age
1.	Teaching-Learning Process	135	12
2.	Academic Achievement	94	9
3.	Teacher Behaviour	82	8
4.	Guidance/Counselling	64	6
5.	Educational Psychology of organisations	62	5
6.	Cognition/Intelligence	56	5
7.	Psychology of exceptional children	53	5
8.	Measurement/evaluation	54	5
9.	Personality	42	4
10.	Motivation/attitudes/interest	40	4
11.	Educational technology	33	3
12.	Creativity/Giftedness	32	3
13.	Teacher education	31	3
14.	Educational psychology of professional groups	29	3
15.	Curriculum and other study materials	29	3
16.	Psychological processes involved in skill learning	27	2
17.	Wastage and disadvantaged	25	2
18.	Study habits	15	1
19.	Youth	11	1
20.	Studies not related to educational psychology	132	12
21.	Studies not related to India/book articles	44	4

Subjects Employed in Educational Psychology Studies

About 28 per cent studies employed the adolescent respondents (secondary and senior secondary students) followed by college/university (18%), elementary (14%) and primary school (13%) students (Table 20.3). However, over the years there has been an increase in the number of studies employing pre-primary, primary and elementary school students and decrease in the participation of college/university students and adults. About 10 per cent studies were conducted on teachers.

TABLE 20.3 : **Percentage of Studies Employing Different Groups of Participants**

Groups	1980-84	1985-90	1994-95	Overall
Pre-primary	1	1	5	2
Primary	6	13	24	13
Elementary	11	13	18	14
Secondary	20	19	23	20
Senior Secondary	8	9	9	8
College/University	25	18	6	18
Adults	8	7	3	6
Teachers	12	13	7	10
Parents	1	0	0	1
Schools	1	0	0	1
Textbooks	1	0	0	1
Not specified	6	7	5	6

Table 20.4 shows that a large number of studies employed 50-100 subjects (18%), followed by less than 50 (17%), 100-150 subjects (15%), and 200-300 subjects (12%). About 13 per cent studies were conducted on more than 500 subjects. An increase in the number of studies employing less than 50 participants is observed over the years.

Measures Used in Educational Psychology Studies

A large majority of researches (43%) have used psychological tests/questionnaires/inventories/cheklists/ scales for the assessment of individual's behaviour (Table 20.5). This was followed by theoretical articles (40%), which accounted for more than half of the reported studies (66%) during the years 1985-89. The use of interview (3%) and observation (3%) and field studies (0%) methods were

TABLE 20.4 : **Percentage of Studies Employing Different Sample Sizes**

N	1980-84	1985-90	1994-95	Overall
Less than 50	14	18	20	17
50-100	18	22	13	18
100-150	16	15	15	15
150-200	8	7	9	8
200-300	10	8	18	12
300-400	6	5	2	5
400-500	5	7	4	5
More than 500	14	14	11	13
Not specified	9	4	8	7

at the lowest. However, an increase in the use of observation method and textual materials/models/films/games during the years 1994-95 was observed.

TABLE 20.5 : **Percentage of Various kinds of Measures Used in the Studies**

Measures	1980-84	1985-90	1994-95	Overall
1. Tests/Questionnaires/ Inventory/Checklist/ scale	48	24	50	43
2. Ovservation	2	1	8	3
3. Interview	4	3	3	3
4. Field Study	0	0	0	0
5. Case Study/History	0	0	2	1
6. Experimental	1	0	1	0
7. Textual material/ models/films/maps/ games	1	1	7	2
8. Teachers' Ratings	1	0	0	1
9. Examination Scores	8	5	3	5
10. Intervention	2	0	0	1
11. Theoretical Studies	31	66	24	40
12. Not specified	2	0	2	1

Discussion

The analysis shows that the field of educational psychology has not grown as expected by Mitra (1972) and it only accounts for 9 per cent (5th rank) of all the psychological studies conducted in India during the last 15 years. Clinical psychology, social psychology, personality, and organisational behaviour still have a larger share. However, there has been some changes in the recent years. A quantum jump is observed in studies related to educational psychology from 7 per cent in 1985-90 to 17 per cent in 1994-95 and decrease in studies related to clinical and social psychology. It may be due to the demand of the present day social structure of the country. More emphasis is now being placed by the funding agencies on conducting researches which have high application value.

Within the field of educational psychology a large number of studies (12%) have surprisingly nothing to do with the concerns of the discipline, particularly studies abstracted during 1980 to 1989. It is beyond understanding that why these studies have been classified in this category. It raises the question that whether the discipline of educational psychology is so general and aimless that anything can be classified under it. It may be mentioned that the field got 5th rank when these studies were included in it. If these studies are taken out of the category of educational psychology, it would probably get 6th position; a status somewhat close to what Ganguli (1971) reported 25 years ago. Further, studies concerned with the challenges faced by the present day Indian society (such as youth problems, wastage and education of the disadvantaged, and curriculum related issues) have received low priority.

Consistent with the observations of earlier researchers, the analysis revealed that majority of the studies (46%) employed secondary (10 to 12 grades) and college/ university students. It is probably due to the fact that this group is easily available to the researchers and also the researchers have direct or indirect control over these subjects. Pre-primary and primary students have received less attention of the researchers. The study also revealed that questionnaire has been a popular measure used in almost half of these studies. Since pre-primary and primary students may have difficulty in responding to the questionnaire measure, this group has received less attention of the researchers. More less attention has been paid to the parents, school as a unit, and analysis of textbooks. As the classroom instruction is organized largely by the subject matter, more attention is being paid in recent years in other countries to the analysis of the mental processes and knowledge instructions involved in learning, reading, writing, mathematics, and sciences. This area is still awaiting the attention of the Indian researchers.

Another salient feature of the studies in educational psychology is their use of sample sizes of less than 100 (in 35% studies). This is a serious problem considering the fact that questionnaire measure has been most frequently employed in these studies. The use of indepth probing strategies such as observation, interview and case study have been minimum. Another interesting feature of these studies has been that almost 40 per cent of them have been theoretical in nature. The situation has gone to the extent that 66 per cent articles reported during 1985-90 were theoretical. Though theoretical articles (such as analysing state-of-the-art, development of models, new ideas, insights, and so forth) provide an opportunity for self-analysis and reflection, they ought certainly not be dominating any field of knowledge. There has to be a major emphasis on testing these ideas than flooding the field with ideas alone. This will certainly take us nowhere. A proper balance between theoretical and empirical articles ought to be maintained.

In sum, this analysis shows that all is not well with the field of educational psychology. Considering the challenges faced by the country and potentialities of the discipline to address some of these challenges (such as achieving Universalisation of Elementary Education, low literacy, women's empowerment, and so forth), the discipline of educational psychology has not received its due share by Indian psychologists. The interest of the researchers has largely been superficial. The generalizations based on the studies employing questionnaire measures on a small sample are severely limited and do not communicate significant and meaningful messages to the policy planners. Indepth analysis of educational problems using multiple approaches and strategies would perhaps go a long way in shaping the future of the discipline of the educational psychology. Since education during the early years has significant impact on the education during later years, studies need to map the beginning years of human life in great depth. Thus, educational psychology in India will have to identify new thrusts, both theoretically as well as methodologically, to gain respectability in the Indian social/educational system.

REFERENCES

Adair, J.G. (1995). The research environment in developing countries : Contributions to the national development of the discipline. *International Journal of Psychology, 30*, 643-662.

Adair, J.G., & Kagitcibasi, C. (1995). Development of Psychology in developing countries : factors facilitating and impeding its progress. *International Journal of Psychology, 30*, 643-662.

Adair, J.G., Pandey, J., Begum, H.K., Puhan, B.N., & Vohra, N. (1995). Indigenization and development of the discipline : Perceptions and opinions of Indian and Bangladeshi Psychologists. *Journal of Cross-Cultural Psychology, 26*, 392-407.

Adair, J.G., Puhan, B.N., & Vohra, N. (1993). Indigenization of Psychology : Empirical assessment of progress in Indian research. *International Journal of Psychology, 128*, 149-169.

Ausubel, D.P. (1968). *Educational psychology : A cognitive view.* New York : Holt, Reinehart, & Winston.

Ball, S. (1984). Educational psychology as an academic chameleon : An editorial assessment after 75 years. *Journal of Educational Psychology, 76*, 993-999.

Buch, M.B. (1972). Educational psychology : A trend report. In

S.K. Mitra (Ed.), *A survey of research in psychology* (pp. 80-125). Bombay : Popular Prakashan.

Burden, R.L. (1994). Trends and developments in educational psychology : An international perspective. *School Psychology International, 15*, 293-347.

Cronbach, L.J. (1977). *Educational psychology*. New York : Harcourt Brace Jovanovich.

Cubberly, E.P. (1920). *The history of education*. Boston : Houghton Mifflin.

Dembo, M.H. (1991). *Applying educational psychology in the classroom*. New York : Longman.

Derry, S.J. (1992). Beyond symbolic processing : Expanding horizons for educational psychology. *Journal of Educational Psychology, 84*, 413-418.

Ganguli, H.C. (1971). Psychological research in India : 1920-1967. *International Journal of Psychology, 6*, 165-177.

Gopal, M. (1995). Teaching psychology in a third world setting. *Psychology and Developing societies, 7*, 22-45.

Kaplan. P.S. (1990). *Educational psychology for tomorrow's teacher*. St. Paul : West Publishing Co.

Mayer, R.E. (1992). Cognition and instruction : Their historic meeting with educational psychology. *Journal of Educational Psychology, 84*, 405-412.

Menon, S.B., & Ojha, J.M. (1987). Learning, motivation and personality : A trend report. In M.B. Buch (Ed.), *Third survey of research in education* (pp. 298-316). New Delhi : NCERT.

Mitra, S.K. (1972). Psychological research in India. In S.K. Mitra (Ed.), *A survey of research in psychology* (pp. XVII-XXXIII). Bombay : Popular Prakashan.

Mohan, J. (Ed.) (1993). *Educational psychology*. New Delhi : Wiley Eastern Limited.

Nayar, P.R. (in press). Research in psychology of education : A trend report. In NCERT (Ed.), *Fifth survey of research in education*. New Delhi : NCERT.

Paliwal, T.R. (1977). Psychology in the schools in India. In D. Catterall (Ed.), *Psychology in the schools in international perspective* (pp. 168-182). Columbus, OH : International School Psychology.

Panda, K.C. (1991). Research in psychology of education : A trend report. In M.B. Buch (Ed.), *Fourth survey of research in education* (pp. 309-466). New Delhi : NCERT.

Raina, M.K. (1989). School psychology in India. In P.A. Singh & T. Oakland (Eds.), *International perspectives on psychology in the schools* (pp. 153-164). Hillsdale, N.J. : Lawrence Erlbaum.

Raina, M.K., & Srivastava, A.K. (1994). Research trends and indigenisation of educational psychology in India : Analysis of journal articles and reports. *In Research proposals in the areas of educational psychology, guidance and counselling* (pp. 99-127). New Delhi : NCERT (DEPC&G).

Rao, T.V., & Mehta, P. (1974). Personality, learning and motivation : A trend report. In M.B. Buch (Ed.), *A survey of research in education* (pp. 135-179). Baroda : M.S. University.

Rao, T.V., Mehta, P., & Rao, M.L. (1979). Personality, learning and motivation : A trend report. In M.B. Buch (Ed.), *Second survey of research in education* (pp. 163-208). Baroda : Society for Educational Research and Development.

Rothstein, P. (1990). *Educational psychology.* New York : McGraw Hill.

Singh, L.C. (1983). *Third national survey of secondary teacher education in India.* New Delhi : NCERT.

Sinha, D. (1986). *Psychology in a third world country : The Indian experience.* New Delhi : Sage Publications.

Travers, J.F., Ellitt, S.N., & Kratochwill, T.R. (1993). *Educational Psychology.* Madison : Brown & Benchmark.

21

Reading Achievement in Relation to PASS Processes

S. Mahapatra and **U.N. Dash**

Reading is the process which enables the reader to understand the phonological, lexical and sentence structures of the written language and coordinate these featural information with the goal of extracting meaning of the text. Apparently, deficit in these skills give rise to difficulties in reading that are experienced by the disabled readers. Reading and reading disability thus appear to be the function of linguistic competence of the reader that co-exists with one's cognitive maturity. In recent years, therefore, attempts have been made to study reading behaviour in terms of proficiency in specific cognitive processes which are now assumed to underlie one's cognitive competence and determine his/her performance in an intellectual function. The process perspective followed in the present study takes into cognizance four different but interrelated cognitive processes, namely, planning, attention, simultaneous and successive (PASS) processes, which were originally suggested by Luria (1966, 1970, 1980) and later embodied within the PASS model (Das, Kirby & Jarman 1975, 1979; Naglierie & Das, 1988, 1990).

Attention refers to the waking state of the cortex and is required for optimal cortical activity. Attention, whether selective or sustained is carried out in the first block of the brain that includes the brain stem, the lower cortical area as well as the reticular activating system (RAS).

The second block which includes the occipital, temporal and parietal lobes of the cortex is responsible for carrying out the process of coding that refers to storage and processing of information. Two different modes of coding, namely, simultaneous and successive, commonly underlie all mental activities. Simultaneous processing involves organisation of information into a quasi-spatial and relational manner, whereas, successive processing involves organisation of information into a temporarily based sequential manner. These two processes of coding form the basis for the operation of the third process, that is planning.

Planning, the central concept of the PASS model, is the function of the third block of the brain that entails the frontal, especially the prefrontal areas of the cortex. It involves activities like searching, goal-setting, generation, selection and execution of plans or strategies, performance monitoring, evaluating the course of an action and decision making. Hence, it determines the nature of coding. Planning is a higher order cognitive process and is considered to be the essence of human intelligence (Das, 1984).

Though few in number, studies reveal that attention plays an important role in reading (Ackerman, Dykman, & Gardner, 1990; Copeland & Reiner, 1984; Das, 1988; Mahapatra, 1990). At the same time a good number of studies carried out in western as well as in Indian set-up suggest that both simultaneous and successive processing are essentially involved in reading (Cummins & Das, 1978; Das, Snart & Mulcahy, 1982; Dash & Dash, 1989; Kirby & Das, 1977, 1990; Leong, 1984; Mahapatra 1990; Naglieri & Das, 1988, 1990). However, the pattern of relationship between simultaneous-successive processing and reading obtained for normal readers differs from that obtained for disabled readers. Hence, proficiency in reading seems to depend upon the manner in which one processes the information obtained from written language. In other words, efficient processing of graphic, phonological, syntactic and semantic aspects of written language requires some amount of planning on the part of the reader. However, only a few studies in reading literature highlight the relationship between planning and reading achievement of children and such research attempts are still meagre in India (Das, Bisanz & Mancini, 1984; Das, Snart & Mulcahy, 1982; Ramey, 1985; Leong *et al.*, 1985; Mahapatra, 1990; Naglieri & Das, 1988, 1990). Yet, the studies are found to have their own limitations. Clearly what is needed is a careful investigation of planning behaviour of children experiencing difficulties in reading, which would help to remove such difficulties and bridge existing gap in the reading literature.

Keeping in view the above facts, an attempt was made in the present investigation to study the relationship of planning behaviour with reading achievement by examining the proficiency level of the skilled and the less-skilled readers in the four closely interrelated PASS (Planning-attention-simultaneous-successive) processes and exploring the relationship of these processes with word reading and reading comprehension. It was expected that skilled readers would be superior to the less-skilled readers in planning, attention, simultaneous and successive processes. All the processes would also show substantial relationship with reading, but planning would have the major contribution in the reading achievement of children at the Grade 5 level. Moreover, the four PASS processes would be found more differentiated for the skilled readers than for the less-skilled readers.

METHOD

Sample

A group of 50 skilled readers and a group of 50 less-skilled readers of Grade 5 were selected from a population of 340 children of the same grade covering four Oriya medium Schools in the city of Cuttack, Orissa. The mean grade level attained in terms of reading was 5.9 for the skilled readers and 2.9 for the less-skilled readers, though all were equipped with normal intelligence and had no report of any serious medical or psychiatric problem. Moreover, the children were from both the sex groups with a mean age of 10 years in each group.

Tests

The skilled and the less-skilled readers were selected on the basis of their intelligence and reading comeptence as measured by Raven's Coloured Progressive Matrices and Graded Reading Comprehension Test, respectively. Then each subject received the Oral Reading Test and a series of cognitive tests designed to measure the word decoding skill and planning, attention, simultaneous, successive (PASS) processes, repectively. The tests of planning were Visual Search, Matching Numbers, Planned Connection, Crack the Code, Planned Composition and the tests of attention were Selective Attention-Receptive and Auditory Selective Attention. Figure Memory and Tokens Test, on the other hand, were tests of simultaneous processing; whereas, successive processing tests were Digit Span, Serial Recall, Naming Time and Speech Rate. The Cognitive tests, except Digit Span, Serial Recall and Planned Composition were selected from Das's test battery known as Cognitive Assessment System (Naglieri & Das, 1987, 1988). All these tests have been used within the framework of the PASS model to study the cognitive characteristics of different groups of subjects. The tests, their administration and scoring procedures are described below.

Raven's Coloured Progressive Matrices (RCPM). This is a widely used culturally reduced test of intelligence for children aged 5 to 11 years. Consisting of 36 matrices or designs, each having a part which has been removed, the test requires the subject to choose the missing part from six possible alternatives. The 36 matrices are grouped into three series and each series is comprised of 12 matrices of increasing difficulty. Each correct identification carries a score of '1'. Hence, the maximum possible score for the test is 36.

Graded Reading Comprehension Test. Developed by Mohanty and Sahoo (1985), this test is used for children of Grades 1 through 7. The subject is given to read some passages written in Oriya, on each of which some questions are asked. A score of '1' is given for each correct answer with the maximum score for the test being 86. The obtained score is then converted into a grade score. The test is discontinued following subject's failure to answer any of the questions for a passage.

Oral Reading Test. This is an Oriya adaptation of Schonell's Word Reading Test which was used by Dash (1982). The test consists of one hundred Oriya words of varying complexity and difficulty which the subject is required to read aloud. A score of '1' is given for each correct pronunciation, with the maximum score for the test being 100. The test is discontinued with 10 consecutive errors, i.e, the incorrect pronunciations.

Visual Search. The Visual Search, a marker test of planning has been used as a test of frontal lobe dysfunction. The test consists of 20 cards. At the centre of each of the two parts of the card is a pattern inside a box called the target pattern which appears only once in a field of many distracting patterns sorrounding it. The subject is to identify the pattern in the distracting field that resembles the target pattern. The visual search cards are designed to measure two kinds of search; automatic (auto) search and controlled search. The time taken by the subject to find out the targets in each card is recorded and its mean is calculated, which serves as the score of the subject on this test.

Matching Numbers. This test is divided into three parts, each part containing eight rows of numbers. The numbers vary in length across the parts, but each row in each part consists of six numbers, two of which are identical. The subject's task is to find and underline the pair in each row, within a time limit of two minutes per part. Score on the test corresponds to the number of pairs identified correctly. The maximum possible score for the test is 24.

Planned Connection. Planned connection otherwise known as Trail Making, is a marker test of planning which has also been used for detecting frontal lobe dysfunction. The test consists of two parts, A and B. In part A, the subject is instructed to connect numbers distributed randomly over a page in correct serial order (e.g., 1-2-

3...). In part B, which consists of numbers and letters, the subject is required to draw lines alternately between numbers and letters in correct increasing sequence (e.g., 1-A-2-B-3-C...). Time taken by the subject to complete the test is recorded and its average is used as the score of the subject on the test.

Crack the Code. This marker test of planning follows the principle of '*Master Mind*'. The task consists of 6 items and 4 coloured chips. The coloured chips are placed in the first row of the circles by the investigator with the instruction to the subject that the chips are not in their proper positions. Three or four such incorrect arrangements of the chips are shown and the subject is required to decode the principle and figure out the correct order of the chips for each item in a single trial. The test is discontinued after 2 consecutive failures. The time taken by the subject to complete each item is recorded and the mean time is used as the score of the subject on the test.

Planned Composition. This is a verbal marker test of planning which requires the subject to write a story after seeing a picture card. The picture card used is Card No. 2 of the Thematic Apperception Test (TAT). The story written by the subject is rated by the investigator for expression, organisation and individuality. The maximum score for each aspect is 7. Hencc, the maximum possible score for the test is 21.

Receptive Selective Attention. This visual test of selective attention consists of two conditions, namely, physical match and name match. In each condition some picture pairs printed on a sheet are shown to the subject. Looking at these pairs, the subject is to identify the pairs which look same in physical match condition (e.g. 2 roses, 2 dogs etc.) and those which belong to same class (e.g., 2 flowers, 2 animals etc.) in name match condition. Each correct identification carries a score of '1'. The maximum possible score for the test is 20, as there are 20 such pairs in each condition of the test.

Auditory Selective Attention. This test is organised into two conditions. In condition I, the subject listens to a tape recording of some 'colour' and 'fruit' words in both male and female voices and is required to tap hand on the table by hearing the man saying the 'fruit' words. But in Condition II, the subject listens to some 'animal' and 'flower' words in both male and female voices and is to tap hand by hearing the man saying the 'animal' words, and the woman, the 'flower' words. Both correct and incorrect responses are recorded in each condition and the score is calculated by deducting one-third of the incorrect responses from the total number of correct responses in each condition.

Figure Memory. This is a marker test of simultaneous processing which consists of 20 items in the form of simple geometric patterns. The subject's task is to remember each pattern within a period of 5 seconds and subsequently locate and outline the same as embedded within a more complex pattern. A score of '1' is given for each perfect outline, with the maximum score for the test being 20. The test is discontinued after 3 consecutive failures.

Tokens. This marker test of simultaneous processing consists of 4 round and 4 square pieces from each of blue, black, yellow and white colours, 26 verbal statements and a response sheet. The subject's task is to produce the pattern as specified in the statement by using the concepts of 'Shape' and 'Colour' in various combinations. Each correct response carries a score of '1' with the maximum score for the test being 20. The test is discontinued after failure on 4 consecutive items.

Digit Span. This is a marker test of successive processing which is abstracted directly from WISC-R (Wechsler, 1974). Digits of increasing length, beginning with three digits to a maximum of nine digits are read out to the subject, who is required to recall them in correct serial order. The subject's score is the number of digits in the series of maximum length recalled correctly on either trial. Hence, the maximum possible score for this test is 9.

Serial Recall. This marker test of successive processing was selected from Dash (1982). The test consists of 12 sets of words, four from each of four-word, five-word and six-word series. After one presentation of each series, the subject is asked to recall it in correct serial order. The total number of words recalled in correct serial position constitutes the serial recall score of the subject. The maximum possible score for this test is 60.

Naming Time. This marker test of successive processing consists of numbers arranged in the form of a 2 digital matrix. The subject is required to read aloud the numbers at his/her quickest pace without committing any error. The time taken to read the numbers and the number of errors committed are recorded, from which the mean time for the numbers correctly read is calculated and is used as the score of the subject on the test.

Speech Rate. This too is a marker test of successive processing. The test requires the subject to take note of a 2 digital number triad and repeat it 10 times continuously from memory as fast as possible. The articulation time, i.e, the time taken by the subject to repeat the triad 10 times and errors committed are recorded from which the mean articulation time for correct repetitions is calculated and used as the score of the subject on the test.

Procedure

Test administration was carried out in Oriya following establishment of adequate rapport with the subjects and exposure to a few practice items. The children were tested individually in their respective schools, but in separate rooms provided by the Head-Masters of the schools. The tests were administered in four different sessions following the procedure given in the test manuals. The tests of intelligence and reading comprehension were administered in first and second sessions respectively, which were 3 to 4 days apart. The rest of the tests were administered in third and fourth sessions which were 1 day apart. The order of the tests in these two sessions was the same as described in this section and was also balanced within the sessions. The testing time for each subject was approximately 4 hours and the entire testing period ranged over 10 months.

Results

Keeping in view the objectives, the data were analysed by means of 't' test and correlational analysis. The results have been presented in separate tables.

The subjects were given the oral Reading Test following their selection on the basis of their performance on tests of RCPM and Graded Reading comprehension. The means, the standard deviations and the 't' values in respect of these tests are presented in Table 21.1.

TABLE 21.1 : **Means, Standard Deviations and *t* Values showing Group Differences on Measures of Intelligence and Reading (N=50 in each Group)**

Test		Skilled Readers	Less-Skilled Readers	*t*
RCPM.	Mean	25.34	24.98	1.15
	SD	1.51	1.62	
Graded Reading	Mean	70.00	32.52	20.18**
Comprehension	SD	4.56	12.32	
Oral Reading	Mean	69.34	55.90	4.75**
	SD	11.74	16.20	

** $p < .01$

It may be seen from Table 21.1 that the two groups who were matched for their intelligence, differed significantly from each other with respect to their competence not only in reading comprehension, but also in word decoding which is a very basic skill of reading indicating subjects' facility in lexical access. The correlation coefficients between word decoding and reading comprehension were .31, .33 and .51 for the skilled, the less-skilled and the combined group of skilled and less-skilled readers, respectively. All the correlations were found to be significant, indicating the relationship between the two skills of reading.

Both the skilled and the less-skilled readers were tested for their proficiency in planning, attention, simultaneous and successive processes. The means, the standard deviations and the 't' values for the tests of planning are presented in Table 21.2 and those for attention, simultaneous and successive processes have been presented in Table 21.3.

TABLE 21.2 : **Mean, Standard Deviations and *t* Values showing Group Differences on Measures of Planning (N=50 in each group)**

Test		Skilled Readers	Less-Skilled Readers	*t*
Visual Search	Mean	10.37	9.99	0.63
	SD	3.20	2.72	
Matching Numbers	Mean	21.74	20.22	2.71**
	SD	2.25	3.27	
Planned Connection	Mean	37.51	37.76	.11
	SD	10.23	12.61	
Crack the Code	Mean	36.50	27.39	1.95
(Time)	SD	25.40	21.20	
Crack the Code	Mean	1.24	1.34	0.59
(Score)	SD	0.84	0.86	
Planned Composition	Mean	12.26	7.26	7.43**
	SD	3.76	2.92	

** $p < .01$

It may be seen from Table 21.2 that the skilled readers were superior to their less-skilled counterparts with respect to their mean scores on two of the measures of planning, namely, Matching Numbers and Planned Composition. The remaining three tests failed to distinguish between the skilled and the less-skilled readers, probably because, they impose strict rules of task performance which might have inhibited the operation of planning process at the Grade 5 level.

Table 21.3, on the other hand, shows that the skilled readers were superior to the less-skilled readers with

TABLE 21.3 : **Mean, Standard Deviations and *t* Values showing Group Differences on Measures of Attention Simultaneous Processing and Successive Processing (N=50 in each group)**

Test		Skilled Readers	Less-Skilled Readers	*t*
Receptive Selective Attention				
Physical Match	Mean	19.58	19.08	1.77
	SD	1.06	1.70	
Name match	Mean	16.50	14.28	3.25**
	SD	3.11	3.69	
Auditory Selective Attention				
Condition I	Mean	56.80	52.85	1.47
	SD	11.37	15.23	
Condition II	Mean	40.35	34.11	2.39*
	SD	11.14	14.68	
Simultaneous				
Figure Memory	Mean	9.92	9.22	1.86
	SD	1.75	2.00	
Tokens	Mean	8.70	5.14	4.98**
	SD	3.65	3.49	
Successive				
Digit Span	Mean	5.74	5.30	2.29*
	SD	0.91	1.00	
Serial Recall	Mean	45.18	35.90	4.89**
	SD	7.31	11.25	
Naming Time	Mean	1.75	2.09	1.51
	SD	1.19	1.03	
Speech Rate	Mean	0.72	1.10	2.02*
	SD	0.40	1.26	

* $p < .05$, ** $p < .01$

respect to their mean scores on relatively complex parts of both the receptive (i.e., the name match task) and the auditory (i.e., the condition II task) measures of attention requiring the subjects to respond to the desired stimuli eliminating the distractors. Similarly, it may be seen from the same table that the skilled readers differed significantly with regard to their performance on Tokens Test, a measure of simultaneous processing and three of the measures of successive processing such as, Digit Span, Serial Recall, and Speech Rate. Figure Memory, a simultaneous measure and Naming Time a successive measure, on the other hand, could not differentiate between the two groups, possibly because of the difficulty level of these tests which was least affected by the factor of individual difference in the present study.

The results of correlational analysis employed to examine the relationship of planning, attention, simultaneous and successive processes with oral reading and reading comprehension are presented in Tables 21.4, 21.5 and 21.6 for the skilled, the less-skilled and the combined group of skilled and less-skilled readers, respectively.

It may be seen from Table 21.4 that none of the measures of planning correlated substantially with either measure of reading for the skilled readers. This however is not surprising for the fact that stable individual difference is not obtained within a homogeneous group (e.g., group of skilled or less-skilled reader of a particular age or grade level) But despite the reduced variance, planned composition showed significant relationship with both oral reading and reading comprehension for the less-skilled readers, as is evident from Table 21.5. In the combined group of skilled and less-skilled readers, on the other hand, oral reading correlated significantly with matching numbers and planned composition; and reading comprehension, with crack the code and planned composition, as is evident from Table 21.6.

Thus, oral reading appears to involve deployment of strategies pertaining to sequential memorisation of graphemes, phonemes and application of grapheme-phoneme correspondence rules which help in word decoding. Comprehension, on the other hand, seems to involve deployment of strategies relating to conceptualisation of the relationship among words and phrases through organisation and integration of ideas associated with them, which help in extracting meaning from the text.

TABLE 21.4 : **Correlation Coefficients for Measures of Reading and Cognitive Processes for Skilled Readers (N=50)**

Test	Sel. Attn. (Rec : PM)	Sel. Attn. (Rec: NM)	Aud. Sel. Attn. (C1)	Aud. Sel. Attn. (C2)	Fig. Mem.	Tok. Test	Dig. Span	Ser. Rec	Nam. Time	Speech Rate	Plan Conn.	Vis. Search	Match Numb	Crack the Code (T)	Crack the Code (S)	Plan Comp.
Oral Reading	.06	-.17	.22	.09	-.06	.40**	.13	.18	-.18	-.10	-.08	-.08	.07	.04	-.05	.16
Graded Reading Compre-hension	-.17	.00	.13	.08	.06	.33**	-.09	-.11	-.28*	-.06	-.02	-.21	-.10	.12	-.01	.23

* $p < .05$, ** $p < .01$

TABLE 21.5 : **Correlation Coefficients for Measures of Reading and Cognitive Processes for Less-Skilled Readers (N=50)**

Test	Sel. Attn. (Rec : PM)	Sel. Attn. (Rec: NM)	Aud. Sel. Attn. (C1)	Aud. Sel. Attn. (C2)	Fig. Mem.	Tok. Test	Dig. Span	Ser. Rec	Nam. Time	Speech Rate	Plan Conn.	Vis. Search	Match Numb	Crack the Code (T)	Crack the Code (S)	Plan Comp.
Oral Reading	.17	-.00	.15	.34*	.09	.28*	.30*	.39**	-.47**	-.46**	.05	.11	.17	.09	-.11	.67**
Graded Reading Compre-hension	-.21	-.25	.14	.20	.07	.46**	.29*	.26	-.47**	-.27	-.09	.09	-.18	.17	-.23	.43**

* $p < .05$, ** $p < .01$

TABLE 21.6 : **Correlation Coefficients for Measures of Reading and Cognitive Processes for Skilled and Less-Skilled Readers (N=100)**

Test	Sel. Attn. (Rec : PM)	Sel. Attn. (Rec: NM)	Aud. Sel. Attn. (C1)	Aud. Sel. Attn. (C2)	Fig. Mem.	Tok. Test	Dig. Span	Ser. Rec	Nam. Time	Speech Rate	Plan Conn.	Vis. Search	Match Numb	Crack the Code (T)	Crack the Code (S)	Plan Comp.
Oral Reading	.16	-.15	.22*	.32**	.11	.45**	.30**	.45**	.36**	-.42**	-.00	.05	.23*	.14	-.10	.55**
Graded Reading Comprehension	.04	-.27**	.19	.28**	.19	.55**	.28**	.47**	-.29**	-.29**	-.04	.06	.17	.23*	-.12	.65**

* $p < .05$, ** $p < .01$

It is also evident from Table 21.4 that neither measure of attention correlated significantly with either oral reading or reading comprehension and Tokens Test, the simultaneous measure correlated significantly with both oral reading and reading comprehension, whereas, Naming time, the successive measure correlated significantly with reading comprehension for the skilled readers. The results are again explained in terms of restriction of range and homogeneity of variance in the measured skill in these children. But in spite of this, in the group of less-skilled readers, oral reading correlated substantially with the condition II task of Auditory Selective Attention measure Tokens Test, the simultaneous measure, and Digit Span, Serial Recall, Naming Time and Speech Rate, the four successive measures. Reading comprehension, on the other hand, correlated significantly with Tokens Test, the simultaneous measure, and Digit Span and Naming Time, the two successive measures for these children as is evident from Table 21.5. However, in the combined group of skilled and less-skilled readers, oral reading correlated significantly with both parts of the auditory measure of attention and reading comprehension, with the Name Match task of the receptive measure and condition II task of the auditory measure of attention. Also for the group both oral reading and reading comprehension showed substantial relationship with Tokens Test, the measure of simultaneous processing, and Digit Span, Serial Recall, Naming Time and Speech Rate, the measures of successive processing, which are all evident from Table 21.6.

The general trend of the results suggests a definite relationship between reading and attentional process and reveals the relative contribution of the two coding processes in the reading achievement of children. Moreover, conceptual planning, as measured by planned composition appears to be the underlying skill of reading achievement of children at the grade 5 level, the basis of which is organisation and integration of knowledge. The results are in conformity to those of some earlier studies and support the hypothesis framed in this connection (Ackerman, Dykman & Gardner, 1990; Copeland & Reiner, 1984; Cummins & Das, 1978; Das 1984a, 1988; Dash &

Dash, 1989; Das, Bisanz, & Mancini, 1984; Das, Snart, & Mulcahy, 1982; Kirby & Das, 1977, 1990; Leong *et al.*, 1985; Mahapatra, 1990; Naglieri & Das, 1988, 1990; Ramey 1985).

All the three cognitive processes were assumed to contribute to the reading achievement of children, but the major contribution would be of planning. However, the results failed to confirm this expectation because the processes were not clearly differentiated for one another.

Discussion

The major purpose of the present study was to explore the relationship of planning behaviour with reading achievement. But since planning operates in close connection with the processes of attention and coding, reading behaviour was studied in the context of all the four PASS processes.

Skilled readers who were proficient in the skills of word decoding as well as comprehension were superior to their less-skilled peers in respect of their proficiency in planning, attention, simultaneous and successive (PASS) processes as suggested by the general trend of the obtained results. The results make it clear that reading proficiency depends not only on attention and coding of information but also on some amount of planning. In fact, attention and planning mediate the two modes of information coding that are essentially involved in reading.

Attention is an important aspect of human cognition. Hence, its contribution to reading achievement cannot be denied. High levels of both simultaneous and successive processing are needed for high reading achievement, since the two processes are differentially important for different aspects of reading and operate in a cyclical manner throughout the process of reading. Yet, the ultimate level of reading achievement is determined by planning, the higher order cognitive process, which enables the readers to determine and utilise an efficient way to deal with the task at hand through the application of attention, simultaneous and successive processes in conjunction with the base of knowledge. In fact, adequate vocabulary, comprehension and coding skills themselves are of little use unless one is equipped with the skill of adopting efficient strategies for utilising them optimally. However in most cases the inability to utilise appropriate strategies for information coding seems to be combined with an inadequate knowledge of vocabulary, syntactic, and semantic rules to give rise to reading deficits among poor readers (Das, Bisanz & Mancini, 1984; Mahapatra, 1990; Naglieri & Das, 1988, 1990; Ramey, 1985).

The present study makes it clear that conceptual planning determines the reading achievement of children even at the Grade 5 level. Hence, attention is to be paid to specific aspects of the written language, so that necessary information can be received and filtered into the system before an appropriate response is made. However, planning was expected to have the major contribution in the reading achievement of children, since it was a higher order cognitive process. But this could not be marked clearly as the process was not developed enough to differentiate itself from other cognitive processes and get established as an independent process in these children. In fact, normally the processes tend to differentiate from one another with increasing age and educational experiences (Dash & Mahapatra, 1989). But in children experiencing reading difficulties, initial deficits in the processes of attention and coding may restrain the development of the process of planning. Proficiency in reading, therefore, appears to be determined not only by proficiency in various cognitive processes but also by the degree of relationship among these processes.

In essence, the skilled readers, keeping in view the purpose of reading develop their own plans and strategies of mastering the content of the text and become adept in the deliberate application of that knowledge in remarkably flexible ways. The more efficient and parsimonious the plan is, the more effective is the outcome. However, planning skills come into existence only after some mastery over coding has been developed. Obviously then, some level of cognitive maturity is also needed for gaining mastery over the planning skills themselves. But this may not appear at least before age twelve, that is the period when children begin to adopt a more abstract, analytic and systematic approach to control their thinking. Hence, prior to that planning may not be found to be contributing appreciably to the reading achievement of children.

A process-oriented approach towards the study of reading behaviour of children is considered imperative because, it focusses on the underlying deficits of children and suggests ways for possible amelioration of these deficits that ultimately may promote their educational achievement. In fact, some attempt at implementing the remediation programmes have also become successful (Brailsford *et al.*, 1984; Das, 1985; Kar, Das, Das & Carlson, 1993; Krywaniut & Das, 1976; Spencer, Snart & Das, 1989).

Each of the PASS processes has its unique role to play in reading. But as deficit in one process is likely to lead to deficits in other processes, the child's confusion may go on expanding and his/her problems may proliferate further compounding the failure cycle. The existing gap between the child and his/her competent counterpart may then become wider and wider at each subsequent grade level and these years of reading failure may build up a feeling of inadequacy and dissatisfaction with the School as a result of which the Child's overall academic work may be threatened severely. Suitable programmes of remediation, therefore, should be implemented from the very beginning, following an assessment of child's competence in various cognitive processes.

Learning academic skills is, in fact, a bare necessity if success depends upon one's way through school and teaching children to plan and to evaluate the consequences of their own actions can certainly take them beyond their present level of intellectual development enabling them to meet the demands of life more successfully than ever before.

REFERENCES

Ackerman, P., Dykman, R., & Gardner, M. (1990). Counting rate, naming rate, phonological sensitivity and memory span : Major factors in dyslexia. *Journal of Learning Disabilities, 23* (5), 325-327.

Brailsford, A., Snart, F., & Das, J.P. (1984). Strategy training and reading comprehension. *Journal of Learning Disabilities, 17*, 287-290.

Copeland, A.P., & Reiner, E.M. (1984). The selective attention of learning disabled children : Three studies. *Journal of Abnormal Child Psychology, 12*, 455-470.

Cummins, J., & Das, J.P. (1978). Simultanous and successive syntheses and linguistic processes. *International Journal of Psychology, 13*, 129-138.

Das, J.P. (1984). Intelligence and information integration.. In J. Kirby (Ed.), *Cognitive strategies and educational performance.* New York : Academic Press.

Das, J.P. (1985). Global and specific remediation of reading problems. In G. d'Ydewalle (Ed.). *Cognition, information processing and motivation* (pp. 665-679). Holland : Elsevier Science.

Das, J.P. (1988) Simultaneous-successive processing and planning : Implications for school learning. In R.R. Schmeck (Ed.), *Learning styles and learning strategies* (pp. 101-129). New York : Plenum.

Das. J.P., Bisanz, G.L., & Mancini, G. (1984). Performance of good and poor readers on cognitive tasks : Changes due to development and reading competence. *Journal of Learning Disabilities, 17*, 549-555

Das, J.P., Kirby, J.R., & Jarman, R.F. (1975). Simultaneous and successive synthesis : An alternative model for cognitive abilities. *Psychological Bulletin, 82*, 87-103.

Das, J.P., Kirby, J.R., and Jarman, R.F. (1979). *Simultaneous and successive cognitive processes.* New York : Academic Press.

Das, J.P., Snart, F., & Mulcahy, R.F. (1982). Reading disability and its relation to information-integration. In J.P. Das, R.F. Mulcahy & A.E. Wall, (Eds.), *Theory and research in learning disabilities*, New York : Plenum Press.

Dash, M., & Dash, U.N. (1989). Information processing and the poor reader : Evidence for the developmental lag hypothesis. *Indian Psychologist, 6*, 85-93.

Dash, U.N. (1982). *A study of cognitive processes : Effects of schooling and literacy* Unpublished doctoral dissertation, University of Alberta, Edmonton.

Dash, U.N., & Mahapatra, S. (1989). Development and differentiation of simultaneous, successive and planning processes. *Psychological Studies, 34*, 75-83.

Kar, B.C., Dash, U.N., Das, J.P., & Carlson, J. (1993). Two experiments on the dynamic assessment of planning. *Learning and Individual Differences, 5*, 13-29.

Kirby, J.R., & Das, J.P. (1977). Reading achievement, IQ and simultaneous-successive processing. *Journal of Educational Psychology, 69*, 564-570.

Kirby, J.R., & Das J.P. (1990). A cognitive approach to intelligence : Attention, coding, and planning. *Canadian Psychology, 31*, 320-333.

Krywaniuk, L.W., & Das, J.P. (1976). Cognitive strategies in native children : Analysis and intervention. *Alberta Journal of Educational Research, 22*, 271-280.

Leong, C.K. (1984). Cognitive processing, language awareness, and reading in grade 2 and grade 4 children. *Contemporary Educational Psychology, 9*, 369-383.

Leong, C.K., Cheng, S.C., & Das, J.P. (1985). Simultaneous-successive syntheses and planning in Chinese readers. *International Journal of Psychology, 20*, 19-31.

Luria, A.R. (1966). *Human brain and psychological processes*. New York : Harper & Row.

Luria, A.R. (1970). The functional organization of the brain. *Scientific American, 222*, 66-78.

Luria, A.R. (1980). *Higher cortical functions in man* (2nd ed.). New York : Basic Books.

Mahapatra, S. (1990). Reading behaviour in children with epilepsy. *Psychological Studies, 35*(3), 170-178.

Mohanty, A.K., & Sahoo, R.N. (1985). *Graded Reading Comprehension Test*, Department of Psychology, Utkal university, Bhubaneswar, Orissa.

Naglieri, J.A., & Das, J.P. (1987). Construct and criterion related validity of planning, simultaneous, and successive cognitive processing tasks. *Journal of Psychoeducational Assessment, 4*, 353-363.

Naglieri, J.A. & Das, J.P. (1988). Planning-Arousal Simultaneous-Successive (PASS) : A model of assessment. *Journal of School Psychology, 26*, 35-48.

Naglieri, J.A., & Das, J.P. (1990). Planning, attention, simultaneous and successive (PASS) cognitive processes as a model for intelligence. *Journal of Psychoeducational Assessment, 8*, 303-337.

Ramey, G. (1985). Unpublished Doctoral Dissertation, Department of Elementary Education, University of Alberta, Edmonton, Canada.

Spencer, F., Snart, F., & Das, J.P. (1989). A process based approach to the remediation of spelling in students with reading disabilities. *Alberta Journal of Educational Research*, *35*, 269-282.

Wechsler, D. (1974). *Wechsler Intelligence Scale for Children — Revised.* New York : Psychological Corporation.

22

Information Processing Correlates of Reading

Manaswini Dash and **U.N. Dash**

Adoption of information processing approach to the study of cognitive growth has been increasing these days. Following the basic tenet of information processing approach that the internal representation of stimulus goes through several stages and undergoes considerable processing before a response in made, the PASS model integrates neuropsychological research with various cognitive concepts (Das, 1984, Das *et al.*, 1994; Luria, 1973, 1980; Naglieri & Das, 1988, 1990). (Please see Chapter 21 of this volume for a discussion of the PASS model.)

The PASS processes are dynamic in the sense that they are subject to developmental and experiential changes and they form an interrelated system. They rely on and influence each other and act in concert to perform a task, though not on an equal basis. Yet they maintain independence. For example, planning influences and is influenced by coding. At the same time, it has emerged as a separate factor from coding (Ashman & Das, 1980; Das, 1984). From a developmental viewpoint, it may be noted that planning can emerge as a separate factor only after coding is developed to a certain extent. With increasing age and grade, the two coding processes and planning become progressively differentiated, successive processing being the first to get independence (Dash & Mohapatra, 1989; Kar, Mishra, & Patnaik, 1990). Neuropsychological evidences also register the interactive and influential nature of the processes during the early years of life. But once these processes are reasonably developed, they get differentiated from each other and impairment in one may not seriously affect the functioning of the other (Luria, 1973, 1980).

The PASS model has been helpful for understanding reading ability. Simultaneous, successive as well as planning processes have correlated significantly with reading decoding and reading comprehension (Das, 1984; Kirby & Robinson, 1987: Naglieri & Das, 1987). The relationship of PASS processes and reading processes such as decoding and comprehension has been explained in terms of cyclical hierarchical involvement of simultaneous and successive processes in reading. Reading involves a hierarchy of several levels of analysis such as letter features, letters, syllables, words, phrases, ideas etc. Simultaneous and successive processes operate within and between these levels (Kirby & Das, 1990; Kirby & Williams, 1991). Skilled reading requires automatic operation of the lower levels of analysis so that attention can be devoted to the higher levels. More advanced levels of reading require planning to keep the reader's attention on the level at which the current task is focused. Thus, at different developmental levels, reading relies differently on different processes. Moreover, skilled and less-skilled readers approach the same task differently consequently yielding different patterns of relationship between different processes.

With the above considerations in mind, the present study has been designed to make an information processing analysis of reading by examining the nature of relationship between reading comprehension and decoding on the hand and the PASS processes such as attention, simultaneous, successive processes and planning on the other. It has also been attempted to examine the degree of differentiation of PASS processes as a function of age and reading competence.

METHOD

Sample

The sample consisted of 20 skilled and 20 less-skilled

readers from each of the Grades 3 and 5 selected on the basis of their performance on RCPM and the Graded Reading Comprehension Test the skilled and less-skilled readers in each grade were matched in terms of age and intelligence as measured by the RCPM. The skilled and less-skilled readers were approximately 1 grade point above and below their grade levels, respectively, thus yielding two grade-point difference in the reading level of the skilled and less-skilled readers in spite of their equality of age and intelligence. The subjects were selected from six primary schools of Puri, a town in Orissa.

Measures

All the subjects were selected on the basis of their performance on RCPM and the Graded Reading Comprehension Test. They were administered a task of decoding as well as marker tests of attention, simultaneous, successive processes and planning. Attention was measured by the test of Selective Attention-Receptive and Number Finding. While Tokens and inferencing were used as measures of simultaneous processing, succesive processing was measured by Successive Word Recall and Successive Ordering. Visual Search and Matching Numbers Measured Planning. All the tests, except the ones already mentioned in the previous Chapter, are described below.

Word Decoding Test. Developed by Dash (1992), this test measures the ability to read or decode printed words with correct pronunciation. The test consists of 100 Oriya words arranged in order of difficulty. The score on this test corresponds to the total number of words read correctly with a maximum possible score of 100. The test is discontinued after 10 consecutive failures.

Number Finding. This selective attention task consists of 2 cards each consisting of 180 numbers appearing in 18 rows and 10 columns. The child's task is to find out specific numbers within a large stimulus grid. For card 1, the target numbers are 1, 2 and 3, and for card 11, the target numbers are 4, 5, and 6. There is a time limit of 90 seconds per card. The time taken to complete each card and the number of correct responses made per card are recorded. And the time taken per correct response for each card is calculated.

Inferencing. This verbal measure of simultaneous processing was developed in Oriya by Mishra (1983). The task consists of a written paragraph followed by 13 forced-choice questions. The answers to the questions are not directly available in the paragraph, but are to be inferred from it by taking a simultaneous grasp of the meaning of the paragraph. For each correct answer, a score of '1' is given.

Successive Word Recall. This verbal measure of successive processing includes 12 lists of highly familiar words, four lists each from four-, five-, and six-word series. These lists were presented orally and the child has to repeat the series of words in the same order as presented by the examiner.

Successive Ordering. This is a nonverbal measure of successive processing requiring the child to reproduce the specific order of an event. Eight circular chips were arranged linearly on a board. The child's task was to turn the pieces on the board in the same order as demonstrated by the examiner. At first three chips were turned and with every third item one more chip is added. Thus the highest number of chips turned correctly in a trial, that is the span or ordering is recorded.

Procedure

A sample of 275 Grade 3 and 256 Grade 5 children from six primary schools of Puri town were administered the RCPM. Those children scoring within 35th to 65th percentile points on the RCPM (RCPM score between 16 to 24 in Grade 3 and between 19 to 28 in Grade 5) were further administered the Graded Reading Comprehension Test (Mohanty & Sahoo, 1985). Children who scored 1 grade point above and 1 grade point below their grade level respectively constituted the groups of skilled and less-skilled readers respectively. The skilled and less-skilled readers in each grade were administered the tests of decoding as well as attention, simultaneous, successive processing and planning individually.

Results

The means and standard deviations of the various measures of decoding, attention, simultaneous, successive and planning processes are presented in Table 22.1.

TABLE 22.1 : **Means and Standard Deviations on Various Cognitive Measures (N = 20 in each Group).**

Measures		Grade 3		Grade 5	
		Skilled	Less-skilled	Skilled	Less-skilled
Word Decoding	Mean	67.95	53.65	77.90	65.35
	SD	9.24	13.37	8.75	13.57
Selective attention	Mean	4.99	5.16	3.71	4.02
(PM)	SD	0.75	1.19	0.65	0.96
Selective Attention	Mean	8.62	10.92	6.20	7.45
(NM)	SD	2.1	4.16	0.58	2.15
Number Finding 1	Mean	4.22	3.64	2.37	2.85
	SD	0.90	0.88	0.54	0.92
Number Finding 11	Mean	4.49	4.25	3.07	3.27
	SD	1.02	1.61	0.83	1.03
Tokens	Mean	10.06	9.82	7.71	8.41
	SD	2.25	2.68	1.69	2.41
Inferencing	Mean	6.35	3.70	7.00	5.90
	SD	1.60	2.03	1.89	1.48
Successive Word	Mean	42.65	31.60	43.10	36.75
Recall	SD	7.65	7.88	6.77	8.70
Successive	Mean	4.70	4.65	5.40	4.90
Ordering	SD	0.47	0.67	0.50	0.31
Visual Search	Mean	15.79	17.65	9.49	11.03
	SD	3.74	5.40	2.26	2.43
Matching	Mean	247.15	263.80	149.40	153.08
Numbers	SD	82.05	85.15	30.68	38.23

In order to know the nature of relationship between

the individual variables, Pearson Product Moment Correlation Coefficients were calculated. The inter-correlation matrices of reading comprehension and decoding as well as attention, simultaneous, successive and planning tasks for the skilled and less-skilled readers of Grade 3 and Grade 5 subjects are persented in Tables 22.2 and 22.3 respectively. For convenience of comparison, the upper-triangular and lower-triangular matrices in each of Tables 22.2 and 22.3 respectively present the intercorrelations for the skilled and less-skilled groups of Grade 3 and Grade 5.

The results may be focused on the following aspects : (a) Relationship of reading comprehension with different measures of attention, simultaneous, successive processes and planning, (b) Relationship of reading comprehension with word decoding, and (c) Comparative analysis of intercorrelations for the skilled and less-skilled samples of Grade 3 and Grade 5 subjects.

It can be seen from Tables 22.2 and 22.3 that for the less-skilled readers of Grade 3, reading comprehension correlates significantly with inferencing and Successive Ordering tasks whereas for the skilled readers of Grade 5, reading comprehension has significant correlation with both the simultaneous processing measures and the name match condition of the Receptive Selective Attention task which require verbal mediational strategies. In Grade 5, reading comprehension, for the less-skilled readers, correlates significantly with inferencing and Visual Search, whereas for the skilled readers it correlates with Matching Numbers and the name match condition of the Receptive Selective Attention task. In younger children comprehension involves the coding processes whereas older children depend more on planning for comprehending a written passage.

So far as the relationship between reading comprehension and word decoding is concerned significant correlation between these two variables was obtained only for the younger less-skilled readers.

Comparison of inter-correlations among various information processing measures in the skilled and less-

TABLE 22.2 : **Intercorrelation Matrix of Cognitive Measures for Skilled (Upper Triangular Matrix) and Less-skilled (Lower Triangular Matrix) Readers of Grade 3 (N = 20 in each Group).**

Sl. No.	Measures	1	2	3	4	5	6	7	8	9	10	11	12
1.	Reading Comprehension	-	.29	.18	-.46	-.17	-.29	-.49	.56	.29	-.05	.05	.25
2.	Word Decoding	.54	-	-.16	-.56	.08	-.46	.30	.62	.32	.23	-.54	-.10
3.	Selective Attention (PM)	.05	-.15	-	.08	.12	.44	.26	.15	-.28	.07	.48	.30
4.	Selective Attention (NM)	-.16	-.63	.58	-	.05	.05	.65	.47	-.42	-.23	.30	.08
5.	Number Finding 1	.11	-.24	.40	.69	-	.25	-	-.31	-.15	.22	.26	.18
6.	Number Finding 11	-.33	-.09	.59	.70	.80	-	.08	-.17	.19	.29	.63	.21
7.	Tokens	.06	-.01	.33	.70	.66	.62	-	.44	.09	.08	.25	.01
8.	Inferencing	.50	.85	-.23	-.62	-.34	-.18	-.70	-	-.27	.21	-.42	.11
9.	Successive Word Recall	.39	.46	.13	.09	.13	.33	.41	-.14	-	.49	-	-.07
10.	Successive Ordering	.47	.46	-.35	-.33	.03	.06	.46	.03	.48	-	-.07	-.10
11.	Visual Search	-.04	-.16	.63	.71	.66	.69	.76	-.62	.54	.06	-	.33
12.	Matching Numbers	-.22	-.13	.28	.29	-	-.29	.03	-.16	-.17	-.10	-.09	-

Note : For $p < .05$, r critical = .44
For $p < .01$, r critical = .56

TABLE 22.3 : **Intercorrelation Matrix of Cognitive Measures for Skilled (Upper Triangular Matrix) and Less-skilled (Lower Triangular Matrix) Readers of Grade 5 (N = 20 in each Group).**

Sl. No.	Measures	1	2	3	4	5	6	7	8	9	10	11	12
1.	Reading Comprehension	-	-	-.15	-.48	-.17	.07	-.13	.16	.02	.12	.13	-.45
2.	Word Decoding	.37	-	-.25	-.21	-.16	-.31	-.13	.52	-	-.29	.02	-.33
3.	Selective Attention (PM)	-.39	-	-	.10	.07	.71	.04	-.36	.16	-.44	.70	.73
4.	Selective Attention (NM)	-.32	-.39	.52	-	.30	.27	-.12	-.12	-.04	.17	.04	.40
5.	Number Finding 1	-.18	.07	.19	.38	-	.92	-.13	-.29	.42	-.09	.79	.47
6.	Number Finding 11	-.17	.05	.12	.29	.88	-	-	-.39	.30	-.09	.85	.41
7.	Tokens	.21	-	-.17	.08	.17	.05	-	.03	-.28	-.08	-.14	.42
8.	Inferencing	.44	.56	-.38	-.68	-.25	-.22	-.11	-	-.21	.36	-.44	-.08
9.	Successive Word Recall	.28	.38	-.04	-.13	-.15	-.01	-.42	.31	-	-	-	-
10.	Successive Ordering	.23	.68	-.30	-.58	.01	.06	-.16	.35	.56	-.01	.23	.22
11.	Visual Search	-.52	.31	.21	.18	.17	.14	-.06	-.35	-.31	.12	-.30	-.29
12.	Matching Numbers	-.15	.11	-.13	-34	.42	.44	.22	.45	-.17	.17	-.06	.32

Note : For $p < .05$, r critical = .44
For $p < .01$, r critical = .56

skilled readers of Grades 3 and 5 reveals that in none of the groups of subjects simultaneous processing measures correlate significantly with successive processing measures. So far as the correlations between the two coding processes and the attention measures are concerned, out of sixteen correlations for the less-skilled and skilled readers of Grade 3, four and two correlations respectively were significant; for the less skilled and skilled readers of Grade 5, two and one correlations respectively were found to be significant.

However, out of the 8 correlations that the two simultaneous and two successive processing measures have with the two measures of planning, for the Grade 3 less-skilled children, three correlations were significant, whereas in Grade 5, the two reading status groups had one significant correlation each.

From Tables 22.2 and 22.3, it can be observed that out of eight correlations that the two planning tasks had with the four attention measures, for the less-skilled and skilled readers of Grade 3 and Grade 5, four, two, one and five correlations respectively were found to be significant. While the processes become more and more independent of each other as a function of age and reading ability, strong association between planning and attention is evident in older skilled readers.

Discussion

The study intended to examine the nature of relationship between reading comprehension, decoding and the PASS processes.

The findings of the study are in support of the results of earlier studies (Das, 1984; Dash, 1994; Dash & Dash, 1989; Kirby & Robinson, 1987; Mahapatra, 1989) in that reading involves both simultaneous and successive processing. It has been suggested that simultaneous and successive processes are cyclically hierarchically involved in the process of reading. Successive processing is required to hold a set of units of information in an arbitrary order so that the set can be recoded as a single unit at a higher level of analysis for which simultaneous processing is necessary. While both the coding processes are necessary at the beginning stage of reading, simultaneous processing becomes more and more important in advanced levels of reading comprehension by assuming its role in the adoption of an imagery based memory strategy. Skilled readers process the linguistic information at conceptual level instead of relying too much on sequential operations.

In the higher age group, as planning gradually develops as a separate factor, it assumes its increasing role in reading comprehension (Naglieri & Das, 1987). For the higher levels of comprehension, planning is required for consideration of critical informations, hypothesis making and strategy invention. It needed for the utilization of the appropriate information processing strategy according to the demand of the reading task which is characteristic of advanced levels of reading.

Significant correlation between reading comprehension and decoding obtained in none of the groups except the younger less-skilled children is suggestive of the fact that as reading competence increases, lower levels of analysis become automatic and information is processed directly at higher levels.

In the present study, with increasing age, educational experience and reading competence, more and more differentiation of the PASS processes is evident from the gradually decreasing number of significant correlations obtained among the different processing measures. Successive processing is the first and planning is the last to get their distinctiveness as separate factors. The findings are in consonance with those of other studies (Dash & Mahapatra, 1989; Mahapatra, 1989). From a developmental point of view, it can be explained that coding and planning are closely connected with each other because planning uses coded information and coding, on the other hand, also involves planning. However, independence of planning process can be inferred from the additional variance it accounts for which cannot be explained by coding processes. Coding should develop to some extent before planning can emerge as a separate intellectual function. Children facing reading difficulties might have been experiencing a lag in the development of cognitive processes. This developmental lag in their cognitive processing system can be accounted for their lesser differentiation of these processes.

It is observed that in contemporary school system, rote repetition is emphasized in the earlier grades and is gradually replaced with the ability for comprehension, conceptualization and logical organization. Thus, in school curriculum, planning gradually replaces the demand for successive processing. If this shift of demand is not realized, that is, appropriate information processing strategies are not adequately used, difficulties in reading may arise. These difficulties can be helped with remedial measures designed within the framework of PASS model. Following an assessment of the child's efficiency in various cognitive processes, instructional designs can be planned in which emphasis may be given either on remedial training or on compensatory education designed according to the concept of aptitude treatment interaction so that the child's reading skills can be improved.

REFERENCES

Ashman, A.F., & Das, J.P. (1980). Relation between planning and simultaneous successive processing. *Perceptual and Motor Skills*, 51, 371-382.

Das, J.P. (1984), Aspects of planning. In J. Kirby (Ed.), *Cognitive Strategies and Educational Performance*, New York : Academic Press.

Das, J.P., Kirby, J.R., & Jarman, R.F. (1975). Simultaneous and successive synthesis : An alternative model. *Psychological Bulletin*, 82, 87-103.

Das, J.P., Kirby J.R. & Jarman, R.F. (1979). *Simultaneous and Successive Cognitive Processes*. New York : Academic Press.

Das, J.P., Naglieri, J.A. & Kirby, J.R. (1994). *Assessment of Cognitive Processes : The PASS theory of intelligence. Boston:* Allyn & Bacon.

Dash, M. (1994). *Information Integration Models and Planning of Skilled and Less-skilled Readers*. Unpublished doctoral dissertation, Utkal University, Bhubaneswar, India.

Dash, M. & Dash, U.N. (1989). Information processing and the poor reader : Evidence for the developmental lag hypothesis. *Indian Psychologist*, 6, 85-93.

Dash, U.N. (1982). *A Study of cognitive processes : Effects of schooling and literacy.* Unpublished doctoral dissertation, University of Alberta, Edmonton,

Dash, U.N., & Mahapatra, S. (1989). Development and differentiation of simultaneous successive and planning processes. *Psychological Studies*, 34, 75-83.

Kar, B.C., Mishra, P., & Patnaik, M. (1990) *Development of Attention, Coding and Planning.* Unpublished manuscript, Department of Psychology, Utkal University.

Kirby, J.R., Das, J.P. (1990). A cognitive approach to intelligence: Attention, coding and planning. *Canadian Psychology*, 31, 320-339.

Kirby, J.R., & Robinson, G.L. (1987). Simultaneous and successive processing in reading disabled children. *Journal of Learning Disabilities*, 20, 243-252.

Kirby, J.R. & Williams, N.H. (1991), *Learning problems : A cognitive approach.* Toronto : Kagan and Woo.

Luria, A.R. (1973), *The Working Brain.* London : Penguin.

Luria, A.R. (1980). *Higher cortical functions in man.* New York: Basic Books.

Mahapatra, S. (1989). Relationship among simultaneous, successive and planning processes in skilled and unskilled readers. *Indian Psychologist*, 6, 31-39.

Mishra, H. (1983). *Simultaneous and Successive Processing in Grade Four Children.* Unpublished M. Phil. dissertation, Utkal University, India.

Mohanty, A.K., & Sahoo, R.N. (1985). *Graded reading comprehension test.* Centre of Advanced Study in Psychology, Utkal University, Bhubaneswar, Orissa.

Naglieri, J.A., & Das, J.P. (1987). Construct and criterion - related validity of planning, simultaneous, and successive cognitive processing tasks. *Journal of Psychological Assessment*, 4, 353-363.

Naglieri, J.A. & Das, J.P. (1988), Planning arousal, simultaneous, successive (PASS) : a model of assessment. *Journal of School Psychology*, 26, 35-48.

Naglieri, J.A. & Das, J.P. (1990). Planning, attention, simultaneous, successive (PASS) cognitive processes as a model of intelligence. *Journal of Psychoeducational Assessment*, 8, 303-337.

23

Role of Second Language as the Medium of Instruction

Swati Patra and **Nandita Babu**

Language can be considered the very essence of human life, performing a variety of roles in different spheres of human activity. The significance of language increases especially in a country like India where bilingualism, or multilingualism constitutes an essential part of life (Mohanty, 1994). In this multilingual scenario, the importance of a language which is the mother tongue of the child has been cited in various studies (Mohanty, 1990). It is generally accepted on sound pedagogical grounds that the Mother Tongue (MT) is best suited as the Medium of Instruction (MI) (Mohanty, 1989). Mother tongue helps promote better concept formation and cognitive development, and fosters an identity with one's environment and culture. While any language may be the language of added comprehension, only the language with which one lives and grows is best suited in achieving originality in thought and expression (Pattanayak, 1991).

However, in India we now find a mushrooming of English medium schools. Most parents, given a choice, prefer to send their children to such schools (Rout & Babu, 1996). This is because English language is considered a yardstick for aristocracy and the language of opportunity. It is regarded as an asset for upward social advancement. In the present scenario it is a fact that English is going to remain and exert a decisive influence in our life. We need English in India today for two very practical reasons : first as V.V. John puts it "we need English because we need English books" and second, because India happens to be a multilingual country (Verma, 1994). Thus different languages coexist here and each has a role to play, a contribution to make in the tapestry of Indian life.

In this context, the question arises as to the place of English in our educational system, especially the role of English as the medium/language of instruction in the schools. Considering the role and need of English in today's world, it is clear that we require to retain English and strengthen its teaching. But does this make it necessary for it to be also used as the language of instruction in our schools?

According to Cummins (1979), instruction in L_1 (first language) and consequent proficiency in L_1 will provide a sound base for the development of proficiency in L_2. Cummins points out that the ability to communicate in social situation does not necessarily testify to the ability of dealing with cognitive tasks. Thus, apart from the Basic Interpersonal Communication Skills (BICS), the school also demands Cognitive Academic Language Proficiency (CALP) which involves the ability to process linguistic information in a context reduced cognitively demanding situation. Hence, the child must continue with the development of language skills in L_1 so that he develops the CALP required for learning a second language in school. Hence minority children should be given their early education in their mother tongue or first language which will increase their motivation and will also give them the necessary social support.

Studies involving bilingual students whose L_1 was dominant and prestigious and in no danger of replacement by L_2 have produced positive effects of bilingualism — called the additive form of bilingualism. Here the bilingual adds another socially relevant language to his repertoire of skills at no cost to his L_1 competence (Cummins & Swain, 1986). However, studies which involved bilingual students from minority language groups have reported negative effects of bilingualism. This is called the subtractive bilingualism where the L_1 is gradually reduced and replaced by L_2.

One major educational implication of these findings will be to promote an additive form of bilingualism. To attain this goal, we should consider several factors such as the role and status of L_1 and L_2, the linguistic and the socio-economic characteristics of the learner and of the learning environment alongwith the importance of mother tongue medium of education.

As mentioned earlier, the minority group learning a second language gives rise to subtractive bilingualism. This is because these children come from socio-economically deprived homes and their language has a low status in the society. Hence, the minority language children should be given their initial instruction in L_1 which will give rise to additive bilingualism. Here the question arises as to whether it is also equally important for the majority language group children to have initial instruction in L_1. Considering the role and significance of L_2 in our present society, this is an important question that needs empirical investigation. It is said that since the majority language children usually come from homes where literacy is encouraged and their language is valued by the community, providing them initial instruction in L_2 will lead to additive bilingualism which will promote L_2 competence at no cost to their L_1 competence.

So, in view of the above consideration the present study is undetaken as an attempt to make a comparative analysis of the performance of children receiving instruction through different languages such as the mother tongue or first language (L_1) and second language (L_2). Thus the objective of the study is to examine the effect of language of instruction on the (a) academic achievement of children through their performance in Mathematics and General Science, and (b) language development of children including reading, writing and metalanguage skills.

METHOD

Sample

One hundred twenty children with Oriya as their mother

tongue were taken from various Oriya medium and English medium schools in Bhubaneswar. In each type of school, Grades 6 and 8 were taken, 30 students from each grade. The socio-economic status (SES) and IQ of the children were controlled.

Measures

The following tasks were given to assess children's intelligence, reading, writing, metalanguage skills and academic achievement. Of these, the tests for reading, writing and metalanguage skills were given both in Oriya (L_1) and English (L_2). The tasks are described below.

Intelligence

Raven's Progressive Matrices (RPM) Test. It consists of 60 problems, 12 each in five sets of A, B, C, D, and E. Each problem has five figures and a blank space. The S is required to judge the most appropriate answer from among the six alternatives given to fill up the blank space. A correct response is scored as 1 and a wrong response is scored zero.

Reading Skill

Decoding Test. In Oriya, Decoding test by Dash (1982) and in English, word identification test (Woodcock, 1987), each consisting of 100 words in increasing order of difficulty were given. The S is asked to read each word one after another, with correct reading being scored 1 and wrong response scored as zero.

Passage Comprehension Test. The English passage comprehension test (Woodcock, 1987) and its Oriya version developed by Das (1995) were taken. Each test consists of 68 items. The S has to read each sentence and then suggest an appropriate word in the blank space in the sentence within about 30 seconds. Correct response is scored 1 and wrong response, zero.

Writing Skill

Planned Composition Task. In this task the Ss have to write a story on a particular topic of which the opening lines were given and they have to complete it. Different but comparable topics were given both in Oriya and English. The Ss are asked to write within one page in about 20 minutes. The story is judged on a seven-point scale on the criteria of Expression, Organization, Wording, Mechanics and Individuality.

Metalanguage Skill

Definition Task. In this task the subject is required to say the meaning of 20 metarepresentational terms each in Oriya and English. The response is scored 1 if correct and zero if incorrect. The scoring is done by two persons to get valid results.

Language Task. The Oriya version of this task (Mishra & Babu, 1994) is the translation of the English task by Astington and Olson (1986). It consists of 10 stories. The S is required to choose one suitable metacognitive verb in 5 of the stories and one suitable metalinguistic verb in the other 5 stories, which best describes the story character's mental state from the four alternatives given below each story. The response is scored 1 if correct and zero, if incorrect.

Academic Achievement

Academic achievement of the subjects was measured through Mathematics achievement and Science achievement tasks. These task were prepared basing on the mathematics and science text books of the previous grade. Examining these books only those chapters common to both Oriya and English medium schools were taken. Items from these chapters were prepared in the Knowledge, Comprehension and Application category of Bloom's (Bloom, Engelhart, Furst, Hill & Krathwohl, 1956) taxonomy. The total number of items in mathematics and science is 23 and 27 for Grade 6 children in both Oriya and English medium. Similarly, for Grade 8, the total number of items is 19 and 27 respectively in mathematics and science tasks.

Results and Discussion

The purpose of the present study was to find out the effect of language of instruction or medium of instruction on children's academic achievement and language development in first language (L_1) and second language (L_2). Thirty children each from Grades 6 and 8 from Oriya medium and English medium were administered test of intelligence, reading, writing, metalanguage skills and academic achievement. Raven's Progressive Matrices (RPM) test which assessed children's intelligence, revealed no significant differences between Oriya medium and English medium children. The test for reading, writing and metalanguage were given both in Oriya and English language, the Oriya version being the translation of the English version of the tasks. The data was analyzed by 2-way Analysis of Variance (ANOVA), correlation and *t*-test. The findings are summarized as follows:

1. Comparison of the performance of Oriya medium and English medium children on tasks of reading, writing, metalanguage skills and academic achievement in their respective language of instruction reveals that Oriya medium children have performed better than English medium children.
2. Comparison of the scores of English medium children on Oriya and English version of the tasks indicates that their performance is better in Oriya version of the tasks with the exception of reading comprehension.
3. Oriya medium children's performance is better in Oriya version of the tasks when compared with English medium children. But when we compare Oriya medium and English medium children on tasks given in English, it shows the superiority of English medium children. However, it is further noted that in higher grade the difference between Oriya medium and English medium

children gradually decreases more so on Oriya version of the tasks.

4. No difference has been found between children of the two mediums in academic achievement in mathematics and Science except for Grade 6 in mathematics achievement.

5. Results indicate a developmental trend as shown in the improvement of performance by Grade 8 children over Grade 6 children.

These findings are discussed below.

Effect of Language of Instruction

A comparison of the mean scores (Table 23.1) of Oriya medium and English medium children on various tasks in their respective language of instruction shows that the performance of Oriya medium children is better both in Grades 6 and 8. The results of 2-way ANOVA also reveals that the main effect of MI is significant for reading ($F=38.7$, $df=1,116$, $p < .01$), planned composition ($F=13.99$, $df=1,116$, $p < .01$), definition task ($F=114.18$, $df=1,116$, $p < .01$) and language task ($F=4.85$, $df=1,116$, $p < .05$).

The results thus indicate that language of instruction has an important role to play in children's performance which goes in favour of Oriya medium. This can be explained by the fact that Oriya, besides being the language of instruction for these children is also their mother tongue. Even though English medium children also have Oriya as their mother tongue, their exposure to Oriya in school is limited to learning it as a subject only. On the other hand, the use of Oriya as the language/ medium of instruction has helped the Oriya medium children to acquire academic language proficiency in Oriya better. This shows that the use of mother tongue as the medium of instruction in school helps the child academically.

However, we should be careful to note that it may not be the mother tongue *per se* that is important as the medium of instruction, but the proficiency in the mother tongue that is important. Thus the child can have any

TABLE 23.1 : **Means and SDs of Grade 6 and Grade 8 Oriya and English Medium Children on all the Tasks Administered in their Respective Language of Instruction (N=30 in each case)**

Measures		Oriya Medium		English Medium	
		Grade 6	Grade 8	Grade 6	Grade 8
Decoding	Mean	92.63	90.43	81.6	88.03
	SD	6.23	6.32	6.07	4.92
Comprehension	Mean	34.9	35.53	29.67	36.47
	SD	5.86	7.39	8.52	6.67
Planned	Mean	21.1	23.2	15.3	20.77
Composition	SD	4.96	5.25	6.66	6.99
Definition	Mean	10.77	11.63	4.53	5.73
Task	SD	3.79	2.7	2.32	3.41
Language	Mean	6.0	6.3	5.37	5.67
Task	SD	1.37	1.29	1.52	2.02
Mathematics	Mean	16.13	10.73	13.13	10.97
Achievement	SD	4.07	4.76	4.23	3.24
Science	Mean	17.53	18.3	16.03	16.8
Achievement	SD	4.1	4.51	4.25	4.3

language as his MI provided he has ample opportunity to develop proficiency in that language. Of course, it is easier to develop proficiency in one's mother tongue. Since ours is an Oriya dominated society, the poor performance of English medium children may be attributed to poor proficiency in L_2 resulting from a lack of exposure to L_2 outside school. They fail to get as much support and encouragement for L_2 as for L_1, thus leading to poor competence/proficiency in L_2 when compared with L_1 performance of Oriya medium children.

So to test whether language proficiency might have influenced the children's performance, the subjects in each medium were divided into high and low proficiency groups on the basis of their oral reading score. Mean comparison of high and low proficiency groups in each medium on reading and writing tasks pointed to significant differences ($t=6.13$ and 3.11, $df=18$, $p < .01$ for Oriya MI, and $t=2.21$

and 3.26, df=13, $p < .05$ and $p < .01$ for English MI). Thus we can say that language proficiency affects children's performance. So what is important is the exposure to the language which develops proficiency in that language. Hence the issue of language of instruction should be considered in this light.

Performance of English Medium Children in L_1 and L_2

The performance of English medium children on Oriya and English version of the tasks was found to be highly correlated. With df=58, the value of the 'r' for decoding, comprehension, planned composition, definition and language task respectively are 0.74, 0.66, 0.67, 0,77 and 0.66 with $p < .01$ for all the coefficients. A look at the mean scores (Table 23.2) shows a higher score on Oriya version of the tasks compared to the English version except in Reading Comprehension.

TABLE 23.2 : **Means and SDs of Grades 6 and 8 English Medium children in. Oriya and English Version of the Tasks**

Measures	Version of Tasks	Grade 6		Grade 8	
		Mean	SD	Mean	SD
Decoding	Oriya	81.7	9.34	88.47	5.75
	English	81.6	6.07	88.03	4.92
Comprehension	Oriya	30.67	6.33	34.2	6.65
	English	29.67	8.52	36.47	6.67
Planned	Oriya	17.3	5.76	22.1	6.65
Composition	English	15.3	6.65	20.77	6.99
Definition task	Oriya	8.1	3.08	9.23	3.84
	English	4.53	2.32	5.73	3.41
Language task	Oriya	5.73	1.68	6.6	1.81
	English	5.37	1.52	5.67	2.02

The findings thus indicate that English medium children have performed equally in L_1 and L_2, though the mean is higher for tasks in L_1. Despite studying in English medium, their exposure to English (L_2) is not as much as their exposure to Oriya (L_1), thus resulting in more proficiency in L_1 compared to L_2. This again points out the importance of a language in which the child is more proficient and its implications for use as the MI in the school.

Comparison of Oriya and English Medium Children in L_1 and L_2

A comparison of Oriya medium and English medium children on Oriya version of the tasks (See Table 23.3) shows that Oriya medium children have performed better. Similarly, English medium children have performed better on the English version of the tasks compared to Oriya medium children (see Table 23.4).

TABLE 23.3 : **Means and SDs of Grade 6 and Grade 8 Oriya and English Medium Children on Oriya Version of the Tasks (N=30 in each case)**

Measures		Oriya Medium		English Medium	
		Grade 6	Grade 8	Grade 6	Grade 8
Decoding	Mean	92.63	90.43	81.7	88.47
	SD	6.23	6.32	9.34	5.75
Comprehension	Mean	34.9	35.53	30.67	34.2
	SD	5.86	7.39	6.33	6.65
Planned	Mean	21.1	23.2	17.3	22.1
Composition	SD	4.96	5.25	5.76	6.65
Definition	Mean	10.77	11.63	8.1	9.23
Task	SD	3.79	2.7	3.08	3.84
Language	Mean	6.0	6.3	5.73	6.6
Task	SD	1.37	1.29	1.68	1.81

Analysis of the mean scores indicates that the difference between Oriya medium and English medium children in Grade 6 on the Oriya version of the tasks narrows down by Grade 8. So even though Oriya medium children are expected to have better proficiency in literacy-related skills, i.e., reading and writing, in Oriya, still

TABLE 23.4 : **Means and SDs of Grade 6 and Grade 8 Oriya and English Medium Children on English Version of the Tasks (N=30 in each case)**

Measures		Oriya Medium		English Medium	
		Grade 6	Grade 8	Grade 6	Grade 8
Decoding	Mean	74.37	81.23	81.6	88.03
	SD	18.92	6.96	6.07	4.92
Comprehension	Mean	22.5	25.9	29.67	36.47
	SD	7.81	7.64	8.52	6.67
Planned Composition	Mean	-	13.4	15.3	20.77
	SD	-	4.8	6.65	6.99
Definition Task	Mean	-	5.77	4.53	5.73
	SD	-	2.61	2.32	3.41
Language Task	Mean	-	4.7	5.37	5.67
	SD	-	2.23	1.52	2.02

English medium children who are expected to have low proficiency in Oriya have performed at par with Grade 8 Oriya medium children, though the mean is slightly higher for Oriya medium children. The results of t-test shows no significant difference between Grade 8 Oriya medium and English medium on Oriya version of decoding ($t=1.26$, $df=58$, $p > .05$), comprehension ($t=0.73$, $df=58$, $p > .05$), planned composition ($t=0.71$, $df=58$, $p > .05$), and language task ($t=0.73$, $df=58$, $p > .05$) except in definition task ($t=2.79$, $df=58$, $p < .01$). On the other hand, we find significant differences as shown by t-test between grade 8 Oriya medium and English medium on the English version of the tasks except in the metalanguage task. With $df=58$, the t-values for decoding, comprehension, planned composition are 4.36, 5.71, and 4.75 with $p < .01$ and for definition task and language task, it is 0.04 and 1.76 with $p > .05$.

It is significant to note that in Grade 6, the Oriya medium children could not perform at all on the metalanguage (English) tasks, but by Grade 8, they are comparable with the English medium children (Figure 23.1). Further, on tasks of decoding and writing also the

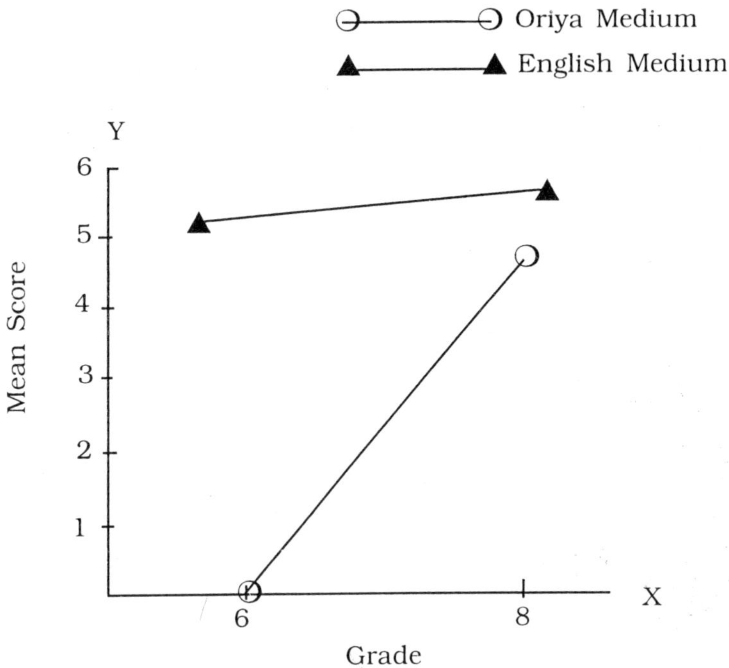

FIGURE 23.1 : **Mean Score of Grade 6 and Grade 8 Oriya and English Medium Children on Language (English) Task.**

performance of Oriya medium children has come closer to that of the English medium children by grade 8 as can be seen from the means in Table 23.4.

However, even though Oriya medium children have come closer to English medium children in English task performance by grade 8 and has also improved in their performance from grade 6 to grade 8, still in relation to English medium children, Grade 8 Oriya medium children have performed at the level of Grade 6 English medium children. On the other hand, it is seen that English medium children have done well in the English version of the tasks and are comparable to Oriya medium children in Oriya version of the tasks.

The performance of English medium children in Oriya version tasks may be explained by the fact that since

Oriya is their mother tongue, they are exposed to it outside the school. But for Oriya medium children, exposure to L_2 outside the school is very limited. Thus the improved performance of English medium children on Oriya version of the tasks can be identified as the positive effects of bilingualism. The improvement of English medium children's performance in Oriya task is remarkable compared to the performance of Oriya medium children in the English version of the tasks. So English medium children encounter an additive form of bilingualism.

Cummin's (1981) study pointed out that there was a gap of several years, on average, between the attainment of peer-appropriate fluency in L_2 and the attainment of grade norms in academic aspects of L_2. Conversational aspects of proficiency reached peer-appropriate levels usually within about two years of exposure to L_2 but a period of 5-7 years was required on average, for immigrant students to attain grade norms in academic aspects of English. It should be noted here that these studies involved immigrant students who had exposure to L_2 in their environment unlike the students taken in the present study. So it may take a longer period of time in our context to develop conversational and academic competence in L_2. However, as evident in the findings of the present study we may expect that Oriya medium children will gradually improve in their L_2 performance as they advance in grades and at a later stage they may perform at par with children coming from English medium.

Academic Achievement of Oriya and English Medium Children

Academic achievement of the children was assessed by giving them mathematics and science achievement tasks. The mean is presented in Table 23.1. Results of *t*-test show that the difference between Grade 6 Oriya and English medium in mathematics achievement is significant ($t=2.80$, $df=58$, $p <.01$) while it is not significant in Grade 8 ($t=0.23$, $df=58$, $p > .05$). In Science achievement no significant difference has been found between the two mediums although the means are slightly higher for Oriya medium children in both grades 6 and 8 (t=1.39 and 1.32 with df=58 and $p > .05$).

At an earlier age, conceptual development is facilitated by the mother tongue language because the child does not have to give emphasis both on learning the language and learning the content or subject matter. The language has become automatized. But in case of L_2, at an earlier age, the child has to learn both the language and the subject matter, so performance suffers. However, as proficiency develops in L_2, effort is directed only to learning the subject matter; so the performance improves. Further, learning subject matter requires the child to read words and comprehend it. At earlier grade, thus, comprehension is affected by decoding ability, but by later grade, decoding becomes more or less automatised and does not influence much the ability to comprehend.

Developmental Trend

There is a developmental trend in the performance of children from both MI, grade 8 children performing better than Grade 6 children. The mean scores for Grade 8 children in Oriya medium and English medium are higher than that of Grade 6 children in all the tasks. The results of 2-way ANOVA indicate that the main effect of Grade is significant only in reading comprehension and writing tasks. However, it is not significant for metalanguage tasks. Thus both Grade 6 and Grade 8 children seem to have the same degree of knowledge of the mental state words. So there is probably a particular age by which children acquire the knowledge of mental state words.

Conclusion

While deciding about the question of Medium of Instruction (MI) we should examine the role and the purpose for which a particular language is used as the MI. In school context or educational context the purpose for using a particular language is to facilitate and enhance the development of cognitive abilities. And this task can only be done through the mother tongue or the first language. According to Cummins, L_1 should be learned as the medium of instruction for the development of cognitive academic language proficiency and its subsequent generalization to L_2.

The findings of the present study support this. The Oriya medium children have performed better in L_1 compared to English medium children. Their instruction in L_1 has helped them acquire greater proficiency in L_1. The ANOVA results also report the main effect of MI to be significant which goes in favour of the Oriya medium children as indicated by their higher mean scores.

However, despite the significance of MT MI, our mother tongue education policy has failed to deliver all-round benefits for its users. So the question of medium of instruction needs careful consideration in the light of the present reality. The present study has empirically reported the superiority of Oriya medium children. However, their poor L_2 performance indicates that the present system of mother tongue education fails to meet the required conditions for generating an additive bilingualism.

According to the interdependence hypothesis of Cummins (1991), "To the extent that instruction in L_x is effective in promoting proficiency in L_x, transfer of this proficiency to L_y will occur provided there is adequate exposure to L_y (either in school or environment) and adequate motivation to learn L_y" (Cummins & Swain, 1986).

Thus what is important is not so much whether L_1 or L_2 is used for initial instruction but the potential exposure to the languages in the environment and motivation to continue developing it. Oriya medium children's proficiency in English is restricted since their experience of English is limited to a very few role-relationships and social domains. Hence they have performed poorly in English in this study, the grade 8 children performing at the level of Grade 6 English medium children. However, despite this, they have gradually improved in their L_2

performance with advance in grade. On the other hand, the English medium children have matched their counterparts in Oriya medium in L_1 performance by grade 8. So it may be that at a later stage both Oriya medium and English medium background students may perform equally in both L_1 and L_2. So future studies may investigate this. If it happens that at a later stage they perform similarly, then it is worth considering the implications of this regarding the issue of language of instruction in school.

Though the L_2 performance of Oriya medium children gradually improves, it may take a long time to develop adequate proficiency which the child, considering the increasing importance of English, can ill afford. The question of mother tongue education has always been a sentimental issue. Our mother tongue education policy has taken care of the psychological considerations by fostering our emotional and cultural interests. However, it has neglected the equally important economic and developmental interests of ours. The more tangible economic interests of the speakers of the mother tongues should also be considered. Hence the issue of MI should be decided by considering the totality of the advantages and disadvantages of having English or the regional languages as the medium of instruction.

REFERENCES

Astington, J.W. & Olson, D.R. (July 1986). Metarepresentational language in school : Thought and talk about thought and talk. *The Language of Schooling Symposium* conducted at the 21st International Congress of Applied Psychology, Jerusalem, Israel.

Bloom, B.S.; Engelhart, M.B.; Furst, E.J.; Hill, W.H., & Krathwohl, D.R. (1956). *Taxonomy of educational objectives.* The classification of educational goals. Handbook I : Cognitive domain. New York : Longmans Green.

Cummins, J. (1979). Linguistic Interdependence and educational development of bilingual children. *Review of Educational Research, 49*, 222-251.

Cummins, J. (1981). Age on arrival and immigrant second

language learning in Canada : A reassessment. *Applied Linguistics*, *2*, 132-149.

Cummins, J. (1991). Interdependence of first and second language proficiency in bilingual children. In E. Bialystok (Ed.) *Language Processing in Bilingual Children.* (pp. 70-89). Cambridge : Cambridge University Press.

Cummins, J. & Swain, M. (1986). *Bilingualism in education : Aspects of theory, research and practice.* London : Longman.

Das, J.P. (1995). *Oriya passage comprehension test.* Bhubaneswar : The Learning Clinic.

Dash, U.N. (1982). *A study of cognitive process : Effects of schooling and literacy.* Unpublished doctoral dissertation. University of Alberta, Canada.

Mishra, S. & Babu, N. (1994). *Metarepresentational language in Oriya.* CAS in Psychology, Bhubaneswar.

Mohanty, A.K. (1989), Psychological consequences of mother tongue maintenance and the language of literacy for the linguistic minorities in India. *Psychology and Developing Societies*, 2(1), 31-51.

Mohanty, A.K. (1990). Psychological consequences of mother tongue maintenance and multilingualism in India. In D.P. Pattanayak (Ed.), *Multilingualism in India.* Clevedon, England : Multilingual Matters.

Mohanty, A.K. (1994) *Bilingualism in a multilingual society.* Mysore : Central Institute of Indian Languages.

Pattanayak, D.P. (1991). *Language, education and culture.* Mysore: Central Institute of Indian Languages.

Rout, S. and Babu, N. (1996). *Parents attitude towards medium of instruction in schools : A descriptive analysis.* Unpublished Project Report, CAS in Psychology, Utkal University.

Verma, M.K. (1994). English in Indian education. In R.K. Agnihotri & A.L. Khanna (Ed.) *Second language acquisition: Sociocultural & linguistic aspects in India,* Research in Applied linguistics, Vol. 1, New Delhi : Sage Publications.

Woodcock, R.W. (1987). *Woodcock reading mastery tests — revised.* Circle Pines : Minnesota : American Guidance Service.

24

Goal Setting by Students in The Indian Cultural Context

K.N. Tripathi and **Anita Puri Singh**

Contemporary motivational theories assume some type of goal/purpose/intentionality in explaining human behaviour. According to Zukier (1986), the goals may be relatively accessible and cognitive as in current cognitive theories of motivation (Dweck & Leggett 1988; Little, 1989; Nuttin, 1984; Weiner, 1985); or less cognitive as presented by Murray (1938) in his classical need theory or unconscious as in psycho-dynamic model (Freud, 1957). The goals are assumed to provide direction for behaviour, especially in terms of choice and persistence. The present chapter attempts to provide an overview of current research in the area of goals and reports an empirical study of goals in the group of Indian students.

Psychology of Goals : An Overview

Early attempts to understand achievement did not take into account the subjective cognitive processes like goal setting. It is only recently that the students of human motivation have become interested in the study of goals and related processes. The goals are expected to provide direction for behaviour, especially in terms of liking and stability. People's cognitions are said to influence the instigation, direction and persistence of behaviour (Corno & Snow, 1986; Schunk, 1989; Weiner, 1985). Most of the human behaviours are goal oriented (Ford, 1987). The goals may not always be conscious, and they may not always be in verbalized form, but they are almost always present as a motivational force directing and organizing the stream of a person's activity. Individuals can set their own goals. Alternatively the goals may be proposed by significant others.

Goals can motivate behaviour and inform people about their capabilities (Bandura, 1988; Locke & Latham, 1990). They never affect performance automatically. They depend on the commitment of the people (Locke *et al.*, 1981). Specific goals enhance task performance through greater amount of effort required for success and self satisfaction. The goals also promote self evaluation of capabilities.

Goals may be of various types. Dweck and Leggett (1988) have proposed two types of goals, e.g. learning and performance goals. These goals generate divergent affective reactions and behaviours. Students with performance goals are assumed to be more likely to experience anxiety about their success and failure and experience lack of self esteem if they fail. On the other hand, students with learning goals are assumed to strive to improve their performance, resulting in an increase in mastery feelings and intrinsic motivation (Dweck & Leggett, 1988). These goals may influence behaviours in terms of task choice, persistence and involvement in the tasks leading to the choice of more difficult and challenging tasks and higher levels of involvement and persistence. The discrimination between performance and learning goals can be considered as a cognitive extension of intrinsic motivation theory (Deci & Ryan, 1985; Harter, 1981). Elliot and Dweck (1988) have indicated that high and low ability student's strategies for solving the task varied under different goal conditions. Nicholls and his associates (Nicholls, 1976, 1984; Nicholls & Miller, 1984; Nolen, 1988) identify two kinds of goal orientation namely, ego-orientation and task-orientation. Individuals who seek to exercise their ability via superior task performance relative to others are held to maintain an ego-orientation and people with a task-orientation to maintain self referenced conceptions of ability. Ryan (1982) has proposed that motivation for an immediate activity is partly determined by the people's perception of how immediate task success will affect their opportunity to attain the related future goals. In organizational set up Locke and Latham (1990) have reported that the strong influence of assigned goals on personal goals and subsequent performance stems from various features of the goal setting context. They further suggest that assignment of performance goal enhances employee's confidence in goal attainment. Locke and Lotham (1990) also report that goal assignments promote self confidence.

Recently Pintrich and Garcia (1991) have examined the role of motivational and cognitive strategies in different types of goal settings. Findings suggest that an intrinsic orientation to learning is clearly linked to the use of cognitive strategies. Extrinsic goal orientation does not have a strong and direct link to student's motivational beliefs nor did higher levels of extrinsic orientation have a positive multiplicative effect on student's cognitive engagement when combined with high level of intrinsic orientation.

De Vos (1968) has reported that in the Japanese culture, effort for success is more motivated by a concern for the reaction of significant others, loyalty to one's group than by satisfaction of internal personal needs. He has shown that in Japan achievement is a less individualistic phenomenon than it is perceived to be in western culture. Minoura (1975) has presented the view that the Japanese values focus on the family, the community and the meeting of other's expectations. Bronfenbrenner (1970) reported that teachers reward the achievement of student groups rather than individuals. Remirez and Price-Williams (1976) have reported that Mexican-American children have a stronger tendency to attain something for other. These studies indicate that achievement goals and means held by people are primarily shaped by culture in which they live and grow.

Sex differences also play an important role in shaping the achievement goals. McClelland's (1961) initial work did not focus on sex differences. The researches, however, failed to produce similar pattern of achievement goals and efforts among males and females (Lesser, Karawitz &

Packard, 1963; Veroff, Wileox & Athkinson, 1953). Attributional studies further suggest that males tend to attribute their success to internal and stable causes and show high estimation of their ability and future expectation. On the other hand, the females experience a different pattern of attribution characterized by presonal responsibility of failure, external attribution for success and lower estimation of their abilities and performance (Bar-Tal, 1978; Weiner 1974). Age-related changes are also found to determine achievement cognitions. Veroff (1977) has noted that achievement motivation may be shaped differently at different ages. Child may show a desire for competence during early childhood, and in the course of development he may opt socially competitive patterns. During adolescence a child may develop on integrative achievement pattern which may include self and other competitiveness. In the Indian context, Tiwari and Misra (1977) have reported that the strength of need for achievement increases with age. Stipek (1984) has evidenced that five kinds of changes may be observed in the course of development of achievement motivation, namely behavioural, cognitive, value related, affective and goal related. In the Indian setting Agrawal and Misra (1986) and Singhal and Misra (1989) have examined the role of contextual variables in conceptualizing achievement. They have pointed out that the individualistic notion of achievement is not sufficient to account for the achievement concern among Indians. They found that social concern was a dominant goal of achievement.

The Present Study

The present research tries to understand the structure of achievement goals in relation to age, sex and school background. In the contemporary Indian context developmental tasks are relatively more gendered as compared to the western world. However, this differential is moderated by the kind of schooling experience of children. At present two major streams of schooling are present. One is schooling in government run schools where traditional values prevail and nominal fee is charged. While the other is related to public schools which are modern, individualistic in orientation and charge heavy fee. These two streams posit contrast in terms of values and ideals preached and practiced.

METHOD

Participants

Equal number of male (N=80) and female (N=80) students studying in convent and government schools of Bhopal city in central India, enrolled in grades tenth and twelth participated in the study. Thus a total of 160 students participated in the study. Participation in the study was voluntary. The students belonged to science, arts and commerce streams of study. The average age of all the participants was 16.1 years, whereas mean age for the tenth grade students was 15.08 years and twelfth grade students was 17.03 years respectively.

Measures

An open ended questionnaire comprising of 10 items related to goals and personal account of the way the goals are set was constructed. The questionnaire dealt with the type of goals, sources of goals, determination of goals, causes for selecting these goals, perceived certainty in relation to goal completion, importance of goals in life, the strategies for attaining the goals and expectancy of success related to goals. The participants were free to narrate their goals and provide a personal account of the way the goals are set and achieved.

The responses obtained from participants were content analysed and following broad categories of goals were identified i.e. educational achievement, career/job orientation, social recognition, social welfare work, family orientation, economical and personal. Item 2 deals with the development of goals. Participants were asked to indicate the sources which contribute to the formation of these goals. The responses were content analysed and following broad categories were obtained, i.e. home, family, self and inspired by other significant sources. Item 3 dealt with the time period when goal was formed. Responses were analysed in terms of following categories : during studying in primary grades, recently, undecided. Item 4 was related to reasons for attraction of goals. The responses were content analysed and arranged in the following categories : personal, family, social, economic, attractiveness of goal. Item 5 dealt with participant's judgement about confidence in attaining the goals. Responses were analysed in terms of following categories: high, moderate, partial and uncertain. Item 6 dealt with the significance of goals in life. The responses were content analysed and categorized as follows i.e., very high, moderate and little. Item 7 dealt with the efforts made to achieve goals. The participants were asked to indicate the ways/means which contribute to the attainment of these goals. The open ended responses were categorized in the following broad categories i.e. study, guidance, training, knowledge acquisition and effort. Item 18 dealt with the expectation of attaining the goal. The open ended responses were categorized in the following categories i.e. high, average and low.

Procedure

After seeking the permission from school authorities the participants were individually administered the questionnaire measure. The use of open ended questionnaire facilitated access to insider's view of achievement goals. The participants were free to respond in Hindi or English language.

Results

The main purpose of data analysis was to know the structure of goals across different groups so that variations in achievement cognition and related aspects can be determined as a function of school, grade and gender of the participants. The data consisted of frequencies of responses. The taxonomies of achievement goals is given in Table 24.1.

Achievement Goals Across Groups

Table 24.2 presents the frequencies of goals by gender, school culture and age. Chi-Square analysis revealed that sex differences were significant for goal choice (χ^2=21.38, $p<.01$). The girls reported larger frequencies (114) of goals related to academic achievement as compared to boys (89). In contrast, boys reported larger frequencies of goals related to job/career, social recognition, social welfare, family orientation and financial than girls.

TABLE 24.1 : **A Taxonomy of Goals**

Personal	Family Related	Societal
- Professional Education	- Happy respectable family life	- Social status
- Excellence in subject	- Good daughter/son	- Becoming Famous
- Higher Marks	- Support to family	- To become a good citizen
- Success in examination		
- Higher Education		
Career Or Job Related		
- Business		
- Professional occupation (Engineering/Doctor/Teacher)		
- Army/Government job		
- Bank Services/Private sector		
- Civil services/Administrative		
- Commercial profession (Fashion Designing/Taxtile designing/Interior/Decorator/ Commercial painter/Singer/ Dancer/Stenographer		

School culture also influenced the goal choice made by the students, (χ^2=14.54, $p<.05$). The students of convent schools showed larger frequencies of goals related to educational achievement, career/job orientation, social recognition and personal nature. On the other hand, Government school students reported larger number of goals related to social welfare.

TABLE 24.2 : **Frequency of Achievement Goals for Different Groups**

Goals	Gender (a)		Type of School (b)		Grade (c)	
	Girls	Boys	Convent	Govt.	10th	12th
Educational achievement	114	89	129	74	95	108
Career/Job orientation	109	123	123	109	123	109
Social recognition	29	29	32	26	25	33
Social work/Welfare	12	25	14	23	25	12
Family orientaion	16	34	26	24	29	21
Financial	3	15	9	9	9	9
Personal	26	31	39	18	25	32

(a) χ^2=21.38, $p<0.01$; (b) χ^2=14.54, $p<0.05$; (c) χ^2=9.41, $p>.05$

TABLE 24.3 : **Time Perspective of Goals**

Goals	Gender (a)		Type of School (b)		Grade (c)	
	Girls	Boys	Convent	Govt.	10th	12th
Immediate	8	13	3	18	12	9
Long Range	40	42	36	46	42	40
Mid Range	19	18	23	14	14	23
Mixed	13	07	18	02	12	08

(a) χ^2=3.07, $p>.05$; (b) χ^2=26.92, $p<0.01$; (c) χ^2=3.47, $p>.05$

Developmental changes were not statistically significant for the goals (χ^2=9.41, $p>0.05$). However, the trend of responses indicated that older students reported larger frequencies of goals in the area of educational and personal achievement whereas younger participants reported larger frequencies in favour of career/job oriented goals.

The goals reported by the participants were also analyzed in terms of its range in future life. Table 24.3 presents the frequencies and percentages of responses of male and female participants regarding the time period of goals set. It can be observed that 51.25% participants set long term goals followed by 23.13% as medium range and 13.13% as short-term goals. However, 12.5% participants had described mixed type of goals.

Although, gender difference in the preference of goals of different ranges was not statistically significant, χ^2=3.07, p>.05, a suggestive superiority of females for the setting of short and long-term goals was observed. While relatively greater percentage of male participants have set their goals as medium range or of mixed types in comparison to female participants.

School culture played an important role in the preference of goals of different ranges (χ^2=26.92, p<.05). Students of government schools reported larger number of short-term and long-term goals. In contrast, relatively greater percentage of convent school students have set their goals as medium range or of mixed type in comparison to government school students.

Grade related difference in the preference of goals of different ranges was not significant (χ^2=3.46, p>.05). However, the trend indicated that 10th grade students showed superiority for setting short-term and mixed type of goals as compared to 12th grade students. Similarly more students of 12th grade narrated their goals of long-term and mid-term range as compared to the students of 10th grade.

Description of goals by the participants was analysed in terms of their nature. It was found that 53.13% participants set their goals of general nature and 46.88% participants reported goals of specific nature. Gender difference was not significant for the nature of goals (χ^2=2.03, p>.05). However, larger number of male participants set general goals as compared to female participants. On the other hand, more females set specific goals as compared to male students. Role of school also was not significant (χ^2=.62, p>.05). However, results evince that larger number of students of convent school set general kinds of goals as compared to government school students. The government school students reported specific kinds of goals. Grade related difference was not significant. However, relatively larger number of students of tenth grade reported goals of general nature as compared to the students of twelfth grade. The specific goals were set more by the twelfth grade students as compared to tenth grade students.

Sources for setting the Goals

The sources for setting goals appear in Table 24.4. It is

TABLE 24.4 : **Sources for Setting Goals**

	Gender (a)		Type of School (b)		Grade (c)	
Sources	Girls	Boys	Convent	Govt.	10th	12th
Home/Family	81	84	91	74	87	78
Self	48	75	59	64	65	58
Inspired by other significant source	62	29	54	37	44	47

(a) χ^2=17.92, p<0.01; (b) χ^2=2.92, p>0.05 ; (c) χ^2=0.54, p>0.05

TABLE 24.5 : **Reasons for Setting Goals**

	Gender (a)		Type of School (b)		Grade (c)	
Reasons	Girls	Boys	Convent	Govt.	10th	12th
Personal	107	107	114	100	104	110
Family/Social	48	53	51	50	56	45
Economic	29	29	28	30	28	30
Attractiveness of goal	52	42	44	50	48	46
Others	15	14	15	14	15	14

(a) χ^2=1.27, p>0.05; (b) χ^2=1.28, p>0.05; (c) χ^2=1.44, p>0.05

evident that the sources for setting goals varied considerably. Data indicated that external or exogenous factors played an important role in setting the goals for girls as compared to their male counterparts. School and grade related changes did not indicate any significant trend.

Reasons for Goal Selection

Content analysis was performed on the responses given by the subjects to understand the reasons for selecting the goals. Table 24.5 shows that gender, school culture or developmental change did not show any significant difference related to reasons for selecting the goals. Almost all participants invariably shared attribution to personal, family/social, financial, goal attractiveness and other factors as main reasons for selecting these goals.

Certainty of Goal Completion

The participants were also asked to indicate the perceived certainty of goal completion. The obtained responses indicated that all the students irrespective of their school, gender and grade were sure to complete their goals. Table 24.6 shows that majority of the participants were of the opinion that they will complete and attain their goals.

TABLE 24.6 : **Perceived Certainty for attaining Goals**

Level of	Gender (a)		Type of School (b)		Grade (c)	
Certainty	Girls	Boys	Convent	Govt.	10th	12th
High	39	33	41	71	40	32
Moderate	25	32	27	30	23	34
Partial	15	13	10	18	16	12
Uncertain	1	2	2	1	1	2

(a) $\chi^2=1.83$, $p>0.05$; (b) $\chi^2=4.16$, $p>0.05$; (c) $\chi^2=3.91$, $p>0.05$

Perceived Expectancy of Success

The responses shown in Table 24.7 indicate the perceived expectancy of success in achieving the goals. The male and female students were equally optimistic about their goals. Majority of them showed optimism in relation to the chances of their success. School culture showed significant difference about the expectancy of success. The convent school students were more optimist as compared to government school students on the measure of perceived expectancy of success. Grade differences were not significant. A similar trend was reported by the students of 10th and 12th grades regarding the degree of expectancy of success.

TABLE 24.7 : **Perceived Expectancy of Success**

Expectancy of	Gender (a)		Type of School (b)		Grade (c)	
Success	Girls	Boys	Convent	Govt.	10th	12th
High	47	43	57	33	43	47
Average	20	25	18	27	27	18
Low	13	12	5	20	10	15

(a) χ^2=0.77, p>0.05; (b) χ^2=17.22, p<0.01; (c) χ^2=2.97, p>0.05

Discussion

The aim of the study was to examine the nature of goals which pupils construe and to see how these goals are determined by certain background variables, namely school culture, sex and grade. Findings of the study evince that achievement is a multifaceted phenomenon. The present results also indicate that the goals and means of achievement are construed in a number of ways. It was found that goals are related to three levels of existence of a person, namely individual, family and society. The maximum variation was found under the first category. These goals represent the end states or outcomes as well as specific behaviours or processes.

The present results suggest that the social and ecological context plays important role in shaping the choice of goals. This study has explored the role of gender, developmental level (grade) and type of school in determining the goal setting behaviour. The analysis of data brings out certain interesting trends. In general, the boys assigned importance to the goals which involve obligation, relationship and social responsibility. The girls, however, mentioned educational achievement goals more frequently than boys. The responses of girls are reflective of reactions to their backward conditions and a desire to go upward. Girl students also view education as the only means for uplift of their standard of life. As expected the convent school students reported larger number of goals reflecting personal and individual accomplishment in contrast to the government school students. Convent school being reflective of individualistic ethos emphasizes more on the personal strivings. Perhaps the family atmosphere prevailing in the case of these children emphasizes the values of modernity and individualism which in turn directly or indirectly shape their goal preferences. The results did not show much variation in relation to the developmental age. A mixed trend with more or less similar emphasis on individualistic and collectivistic goals was evident.

The female students' goals were of global nature whereas male students reported target oriented goals. Surprisingly school and developmental age, did not show much variation in relation to the location of goals across the life span. In terms of location in life span it was found that boys prefer more goals of immediate nature as compared to girls. As far as, long term goals are concerned, they were preferred equally by the boys and girls. In regard to the type of school the government school students reported larger number of goals of immediate and long term concern as compared to convent school students. This pattern of findings implies socialisation of western kind as a factor shaping the motivational dynamics of convent school students.

The reasons for goal selection emerged from the present study were almost same in all the groups. Thus personal, family concern, attractiveness of the goal and economic reason formed the priority order. It seems that being in contact with media, all the groups have structured their concerns and engagement in a somewhat overlapping fashion.

On the whole the present findings suggest that the subjective experience of goals has certain characteristics which differentiate it from the traditional model of achievement motivation. The results also indicated that certain goals involved long-term or prolonged activities, persistent effort and location in the distant future while others were short range goals and involved merely segments of behaviour.

REFERENCES

Agarwal, R. & Misra, G (1986). A factor analytic study of achievement goals and means : An Indian view. *International Journal of Psychology, 21*, 717-731.

Bandura, A. (1988). Self regulation of motivation and action through goal system. In V. Hamilton, G.H. Bower & N.H. Frigda (Eds.) *Cognitive perspective on emotion and motivation.* Dordreht, the Netherlands : Kluwar Academic Publishers.

Bar Tal, D. (1978). Attributional analysis of achievement related behaviour. *Review of Educational Research, 48*, 259-271.

Bronfenbrenner, U. (1970). *Two worlds of childhood : U.S. and U.S.S.R.* New York : Russell Sage.

Corno, L. & Snow, P.E. (1986). Adopting teaching to individual differences among learners. In M.C. Wittrock (Ed.) *Handbook of research on teaching.* New York : Mac Millan.

Deci, E.L. & Ryan, R.M. (1985). *Intrinsic motivation and self determination in human behaviour.* New York : Plenum.

Devos, G.A. (1968). Achievement and innovation in culture and personality. In E. Norbeck, D. Price Williams & W.M. McCord (Eds.) *The study of personality : An inter-disciplinary approach.* New York : Holt.

Dweck, C.S. & Leggett. E.L. (1988). A social cognitive approach to motivation and personality. *Psychological Review, 95*, 256-273.

Elliot, E.S. & Dweck, C.S. (1988). Goals : An approach to motivation and achievement. *Journal of Personality and Social Psychology, 540*, 5-12.

Ford, D.H. (1987). *Humans as self constructing living systems. A developmental perspective on behaviour and personality.* Hills dale, N.J : Erlbaum.

Freud, S. (1957). Instincts and their vicissitudes. In J. Rickman (Ed.) *A general selection from the works of Sigmund Freud.* Garden city, NY : Doubleday.

Harter, S. (1981). A model of mastery motivation in children. Individual differences and developmental change. In W.A. Collins (Ed.) *Aspects of development of competence. The Minnesota symposium on child psychology,* Hillsdale, N.J. : Erlbaum.

Lesser, G.S.; Karawitz, R.N. & Packard, R.C. (1963). Experimental arousal of achievement in adolescent girls. *Journal of Abnormal and Social Psychology, 66,* 59-66.

Little, B.R. (1989). Personal projects analysis : Trivial persuits, magnificent obsessions and the search for coherence. In D.M. Buss and N. Cantor (Eds.) *Personality Psychology : Recent trends and emerging directions.* New York : Springer Verlag.

Locke, E.A. & Latham, G.P.(1990). *A theory of goal setting and task performance.* Englewood Cliff, NJ : Prentice Hall.

Locke, E.A.; Shaw, K.N.; Saari, L.M. & Latham, G.P. (1981). Goal setting and task performance, *Psychological Bulletin, 90,* 125-152.

McClelland, D.C. (1961). *The achieving society.* New Jersey : Von Nostrand.

Maehr, M.L., & Nicholls, J.G. (1980). Culture and achievement motivation : A second look. In N. Warren (Ed.) *Studies in cross cultural psychology (Vol. 3).* New York : Academic Press.

Minoura, Y. (1975). Value orientations found in British Columbian and Japanese school books. The 1920s-1970's. *Unpublished Master's thesis, University of Victoria.*

Micholls, J.G. (1976). Efforts is virtuous, but is better to have ability : Evaluative responses to perceptions of ability, and effort. *Journal of Research in Personality, 10,* 306-315.

Murray, H.A. (1938). *Explorations in personality.* New York : Oxford University Press.

Nicholls, J.G. (1984). Achievement motivation, conception of ability, subjective experience, task choice and performance. *Psychological Review, 91,* 328-346.

Nicholls, J.G., & Miller, A.T.C. (1984). Development and its discontent : The differentiation of the concept of ability in J.G. Nicholls (Eds.). *Advances in motivation and achievement (Vol. 7)* Greenwich : Jai Press.

Nolen, S.B. (1988). Reasons for studying : Motivational

orientations and study strategies. *Cognition and Instruction, 5*, 269-287.

Nuttin, J. (1984). *Motivation, planning and action : A relational theory of behavioural dynamics*, Hillsdale, N.J. Erlbaum.

Pintrich, P.R., & Garcia, T. (1991). Students goal orientation and self regulation in the college classroom. In M. Maehr & P.R. Pintrich (Eds.) *Advances in motivation and achievement* (Vol. 7) Greewich : Jai Press.

Ryan, R.M. (1982). Control and information in the interpersonal sphere : An extension of cognitive evaluation theory, *Journal of Personality and Social Psychology, 43*, 450-461.

Ramirez, M. & Price-Williams, D.R. (1976). Achievement motivation in children of three ethnic groups in the United States. *Journal of Cross-Cultural Psychology, 7*, 49-60.

Schunk, D.H. (1989). Self efficacy and cognitive skill learning. In C. Ames and R. Ames (Eds.) *Research on motivation in education (Vol. 3); Goals and cognitions*. Ban Diego : Academic Press.

Singhal, R. & Misra, G. (1989). Variation in achievement cognitions : Role of ecology, age and gender. *International Journal of Intercultural Relations, 13*, 93-107.

Stipek, D.J. (1984). The development of achievement motivation. In R. Ames & C. Ames (Eds.) *Research in motivation in Education (Vol. 1)* Student motivation. New York : Academic Press.

Tiwari, A.N. & Misra, G. (1977). A study of achievement motive in relation to prolonged deprivation. *Psychologia, 20*, 172-179.

Veroff, J. (1977). Process Vs. impact in men's and women's achievement motivation. *Psychology of Women Quarterly, 1*, 283-293.

Veroff, J.; Wilcox, S. & Atkinson, J.W. (1953). The achievement motive in high school and college women. *Journal of Abnormal and Social Psychology, 48*, 108-119.

Weiner, B. (1974). *Achievement motivation and attribution theory*. Morristown; General Learning Press.

Weiner, B. (1985). An attributional theory of achievement motivation and emotion. *Psychological Review, 92*, 548-573.

Zukier, H. (1986). The paradigmatic and narrative modes in goal-guided inference. In R.M. Sorrentino & E.T. Higgins (Eds.) *Handbook of motivation and cognition*. New York : Guilford Press.

25

Environmental Indicators of Child Development

Fakir M. Sahoo; Bhakta B. Dash and
Pradeep Mohapatra

The issue of the development of tribal children in India constitutes a formidable challenge. The environmental constraints faced by the tribals, the economic hardship, staggering rate of drop-outs from the school, multiplicity of tribal languages, and other socio-cultural factors complicate the problem. Despite several attempts to integrate tribal population into the mainstream, this objective is far from being realized.

There are 350 main tribes in India with 100 spoken languages. Although tribals constitute 12% of the total Indian population, the proportion of their distribution varies across States. In some of the States, tribal population constitutes 70 to 80% of the State's population. The tribals represent differences in the area of life styles, child-rearing, food habits, rituals, occupations, and amusement forms.

The remedial development programmes for tribal children derive force from the thesis that development for all children needs to be even. In India, children in urban and affluent homes develop at a faster rate. The initial deficits shown by tribal children become cumulative with passage of time. These cumulative deficits need to be arrested not only by remedial education given at school but also by appropriate remedial child-rearing training given to mothers. Since it is difficult to encompass all the tribal groups within the scope of a single study, the present investigation is planned for a specific tribal group in Orissa.

Orissa, an eastern State of the Indian Union, is a museum of tribal cultures. It is the home of 62 Scheduled Tribes. Kondas, Juangas, Sauras and Santals are the predominant tribes that inhabit in Orissa. About one-fourth (24%) of the total population (approximately 33 million) of the State consists of tribals; the disadvantaged groups (Scheduled Castes and Scheduled Tribes) constitute 40 per cent of the State's population.

Orissa is economically backward; 41.1% of its population live below the poverty line. It happens to be one of the three bottom States in the rank of per capita incomes. The average per capita income in Orissa is estimated to be Rs. 1,455 whereas it is Rs. 2,142 for a person in India. Amongst Scheduled Castes (SC) and Scheduled Tribes (ST) population of Orissa, the percentages of people living below the poverty line are reported to be 63% in rural areas and 33% in urban locations.

In terms of literacy, Orissa is ranked 23rd in the list of 25 States. The percentages of literate people in Orissa and India are respectively 48 and 52. With respect to the health indicators, it is shown that life expectancy at birth is 59 years at the national level whereas it is 57 years for Orissa. Infant mortality rate (IMR) for India is 80 for every 1000 whereas it is 126 in Orissa. In addition, number of hospitals and dispensaries for one thousand square kilometre area is 11.7 in the country and it is 8.3 in Orissa. Thus, Orissa represents a depressive scene in terms of economic, education and health indicators.

Plurality is an important feature of Indian society. The kind of cultural mosaic in Indian system is not a horizontal one, but a vertical one. Orissa represents an area of economic depression; it lags behind other States in terms of economic, educational and health indicators. With a view to alleviating problems of rural mass in Orissa, there is both urgency and saliency.

Further, a high proportion of SC/ST population in Orissa demands research attention. Although some non-government agencies are working in the tribal pockets of

Orissa, most of their activities are geared for improving agricultural practices. A significant aspect of these activities involves the training of lady workers (called Anganbadi workers); these Anganbadi workers train pre-schoolers in a group-context. Children below six years of age from two or three villages meet at the Anganbadi and the lady workers teach them healthful habits and other aspects of good living.

However, these attempts have not yielded satisfactory outcomes. While Anganbadi workers are supposed to enlist the cooperation of the mother of the child, the active involvement of the mother has seldom been possible. This problem is manifest in tribal areas to a great extent.

It is asserted that an active involvement of the mother in the developmental process of the child during early years is very crucial. The developmental stimulation received from outside agency such as "Anganbadi" would be effective only when supported by mothers at home. Consequently the training of mothers forms an integral aspect of child's development.

The central role of mother does not preclude the contribution of other environmental factors. Yet, mother is viewed as a provider of all these environmental factors. The interaction of the child and its care-taker in the midst of environmental factors provides a meaningful context for examining child's development. In this sense, the development emphasized here denotes "total interactional context".

The Setting and the Sample

The study is anchored to the district of Mayurbhanj in Orissa. The district lies between 20^0 17' and 22^0 34' North Latitude and between 85^0 40' and 87^0 10' East Longitude. The district covers an area of 40,218 sq km. with a population of 18,84,580 persons.

Mayurbhanj is basically a tribal district harbouring several types of castes and tribes. There are 18 types of castes and tribes which include Ahir, Gaura, Amata, Begal, Bahuti, Baise, Baisnab, Baxahi, Barna-Sankar, Bauri,

Bhandari, Brahman, Chasa, Dhobi, Gaura, and Chasi. In the tribes category there are 40 types of which Santals, Kolhas, Bhumija, Bathudi, and Bhuyans are predominant. The Santal is the largest tribe and it constitutes 29% of the population of the district. The total population is 397,854.

Santals are normally dark or very brown in skin colour. Hairs are coarse, black and occasionally curly. The zygomatic arches are pronounced. The root of the nose is depressed. The average cephallic index is 76.1. The average stature is 161.4 cm. The Santals are subdivided into 12 patrilineal exagamous sibs such as Hansda, Murmu, Kisku, Hembram, Marandi, Soren, Tudu, Bashe, Besra, Paunria, Conren, and Bedea.

Originally Santals were forest-dwellers. But in course of time many of them preferred to live in semi-forest areas. The main occupations of Santals include agriculture, household industry (handicrafts) and collection of forest products. Some of them take up manual labour and some people engage themselves in business and mechanical trades.

The Santals speak their own language "Santali". It is a fine expressive language to denote natural objects. However, they have to depend on other languages such as Oriya to represent abstract and modern ideas. They transcribe their language in a script called "Olchuki".

With respect to literacy, it is shown that 31 per cent people of Mayurbhanj district are literate. It may be pointed out that 48 per cent people in Orissa are literate. Amongst Santals' literacy rate is 12 per cent for men and 3 per cent for women. Two important features are marked with respect to education of Santals. There is a marked difference between urban and rural Santals, also between men and women. For example, there are no post-graduate degree holder in engineering, medicine and agriculture amongst women.

Research Questions

At the theoretical level, there is no integrative attempt to assess development. Each theorist has emphasized factors close to his or her theoretical stance. Although intervention studies have been attempted, it has been difficult to assess the impact of intervention owing to the lack of comprehensive measurement.

The present investigation is directed to assess the child's development as perceived by the tribal and non-tribal mothers. Instead of some isolated indicators, four specific classes of environmental indicators have been conceptualized: sensory input, child and care-takers' interaction dimension, care-takers' dimension, and intra-family dimension. The sensory input variables include exposure to physical objects, nutrition, health care, play materials, adult verbalization, and extensiveness of peer networks. The child and care-takers' dimensions include parental contact, maternal interaction, mother's emphasis on reasoning and autonomy, interest in child's activities, and satisfaction with the child. Care-takers' dimensions include mothers' well-being and her life satisfaction. Finally, intra-family factors include presence of generation and daily routines.

It may be pointed out that measurement involves indigenous elements. For instance, care is taken to measure the exposure to play materials in terms of the play things a child is likely to find in its own natural habitat. This method avoids the problem of "imposed etic" as far as practicable. In other words, emically derived dimensions were used.

The primary objective of the study was to compare Santal mothers with non-Santal mothers on several developmental indicators. In addition, child rearing directed towards boys vis-a-vis girls was also examined.

Method

The study adopts a 2 (tribal versus non-tribal setting) × 2 (mothers of boys versus mothers of girls) factorial design. The tribal mothers of boys and girls are compared with non-tribal mothers of boys and girls. The dependent variables include factors of sensory inputs, care-takers and child interaction, care-takers characteristics, and intra-family category.

As indicated earlier, 493 (286 tribal and 207 non-tribal) mothers participated in the study. Of 286 tribal mothers, 145 participants were mothers of boys and 141 participants were mothers of girls. Of 207 non-tribal mothers, 107 participants were mothers of boys and 100 participants were mothers of girls. Participants were randomly sampled from places around the city of Baripada, Mayurbhanj district of Orissa. Their age ranged 20 years to 45 years and the average number of their children was four. Mothers had only four years of schooling. In contrast, the non-tribal mother's age ranged from 22 to 42 years. The average number of children was two. They had only ten years of schooling experience.

The Survey Instrument

The Child's Developmental Inventory (CDI) developed by Sahoo (1994) was used. It consists of child's developmental indicators. It includes four categories of indicators : (a) sensory inputs, (b) child and care-taker interactional factors, (c) care-takers' dimensions, and (d) intra-family factors.

The sensory input measures child's exposure to physical objects, provision of nutrition, health care, play materials, adult verbalization, and extensiveness of child's peer networks.

The child and care-taker's interactional factors include parental contact, mothers' interaction, mothers' emphasis on reasoning, mothers' emphasis on autonomy, interest in child's activities, and satisfaction with the child.

The care-takers dimensions constitute mothers' wellbeing and her life satisfaction.

The intrafamily factors include stress, existence of generation and daily routine and schedules.

In addition, CDI is used to collect particulars regarding socio-demographic features of mothers. These features include age, education, and number of child of mothers. It also includes age and education of child's father.

Procedure

The mothers were contacted in their own habitat. They were interviewed with the help of the Child Developmental Inventory (CDI). They were asked to answer all questions about a particular child in the age range of 2 to 6 years. The responses of mothers were scored. Besides the measures of developmental indicators, socio-demographic features were also scored.

Results

The scores of tribal mothers were compared with those of non-tribal mothers on each of the developmental indicators. Analyses of Variance (ANOVA) were carried out to examine the role of setting as well as the sex of the child.

Sensory Inputs

The analysis of data with respect to exposure to physical objects shows significant sex effect, F (1, 489) = 11.07, $p < .01$ (see Table 25.1). As shown by Table 25.2, mothers of girls provide greater exposure to physical objects than do mothers of boys (M =2.25 and 1.97, respectively). There is significant culture effect, F (1, 489) = 435.58, $p < .01$. The examination of mean scores as shown by Table 25.2 reveals that mothers of tribal children provide less exposure to physical objects than do mothers of non-tribal children (M =1.15 and 3.56, respectively). The result shows significant Culture × Sex effect, F (1, 489) = 5.41, $p < .05$. As shown by Figure 25.1, with change of setting from non-tribal to tribal location, the gap between mothers of boys and mothers of girls widens with respect to their attempts to expose children to physical objects. Mothers of tribal children provide less nutrition to their children compared with non-tribal mothers and do differ significantly in this respect, F (1, 489) = 321.18, $p < .01$. The non-tribal mother provide greater nutrition to their children than do tribal mothers (M = 3.82 and 1.94,

TABLE 25.1 : **Analysis of Variance Performed on Sensory Input Variables**

Variables	Source	df	MS	F
Physical objects	Culture	1	701.54	435.58**
	Sex	1	17.83	11.07**
	Culture × Sex	1	8.72	5.41*
	Error	489	1.61	
Nutritional Level	Culture	1	421.59	321.18**
	Sex	1	.51	.39
	Culture × Sex	1	.22	.17
	Error	489	1.31	
Health Care	Culture	1	.80	2.03
	Sex	1	4.47	11.34**
	Culture × Sex	1	.73	1.85
	Error	489	.39	
Play Materials	Culture	1	1889.36	894.29**
	Sex	1	58.76	27.81**
	Culture × Sex	1	301.05	142.49**
	Error	489	2.11	
Adult Verbalization	Culture	1	343.54	184.44**
	Sex	1	5.30	2.84
	Culture × Sex	1	3.02	1.62
	Error	489	1.86	
Extensiveness of peer Network.	Culture	1	248.13	62.89**
	Sex	1	67.44	17.09**
	Culture × Sex	1	4.35	1.10
	Error	489	3.94	

* $p < .05$
** $p < .01$

respectively). However, tribal and non-tribal mothers do not differ significantly with respect to the provision of health care. The examination of mean score shows that tribal mothers provide as much health care as do non-tribal mothers (M =1.88 and 1.96, respectively). With respect to health care, mothers of boys differ significantly

TABLE 25.2 : **Means and Standard Deviations of Scores on Sensory Input Indicators of Reported by Mother**

Indicators	Source	Boys		Girls		Combined	
		M	SD	M	SD	M	SD
Physical Objects	Tribal	0.85	1.11	1.45	1.17	1.15	1.18
	Non-Tribal	3.49	1.36	3.63	1.81	3.56	2.55
	Combined	1.97	1.79	2.35	1.82		
Nutrition	Tribal	1.94	0.98	1.95	1.08	1.94	1.03
	Non-Tribal	3.88	1.31	3.76	1.24	3.82	1.28
	Combined	2.91	1.49	2.86	1.46		
Health Care	Tribal	1.94	0.73	1.82	0.70	1.88	0.72
	Non-Tribal	2.10	0.49	1.82	0.46	1.96	0.50
	Combined	2.02	0.64	1.82	0.61		
Play Materials	Tribal	2.36	0.72	1.78	0.73	2.07	0.78
	Non-Tribal	4.81	1.24	3.07	0.84	3.94	1.38
	Combined	3.59	1.57	2.43	1.01		
Adult Verbalization	Tribal	2.43	1.10	2.54	1.38	2.49	1.25
	Non-Tribal	3.99	1.36	4.37	1.63	4.18	1.51
	Combined	3.21	1.45	3.46	1.75		
Extensiveness of peer Network	Tribal	4.40	1.89	3.60	1.80	4.00	1.89
	Non-Tribal	5.75	1.83	5.12	2.24	5.44	2.06
	Combined	5.08	1.98	4.36	2.13		

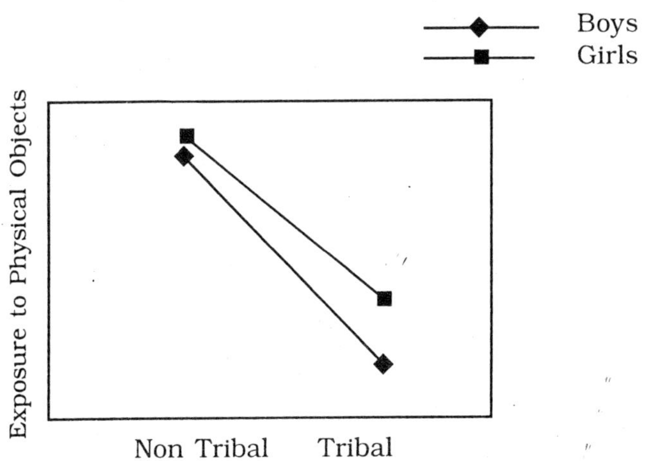

FIGURE 25.1: **The Culture × Sex Effect for Exposure to Physical Objects**

from mothers of girls, F (1,489) = 11.34, p<.01. Mothers of boys provide greater health care than mothers of girls (see Table 25.2). With respect to play materials, significant culture effect as well as sex effect are indicated, F (1,489) = 894.29, p<.01, F (1,489) = 27.81, p<.01. It is shown that tribal mothers provide less play materials than non-tribal mothers (M=2.07, 3.94, respectively). It is also indicated that mothers of boys provide more play materials than girls' mothers. The result shows significant Culture × Sex effect, F (1,489) = 142.49, p<.01. As depicted by Figure 25.2, with change of setting from non-tribal to tribal location, the gap between mothers of boys and mothers of girls narrows with respect to their attempts to expose their children to play materials. The significant effect of culture is also shown on adult verbalization, F (1,489) =184.44, p<.01. The non-tribal mothers report greater verbalization than do tribal mothers (M=4.18 and 2.49, respectively). The analysis on peer network suggests significant effect of culture, F (1, 489) = 169.89, p < .01. Non-tribal mothers report greater extensiveness of peer network than tribal mothers (M=5.44 and 4.00, respectively). The sex effect is also significant. It is shown that mothers of boys report greater peer network for their

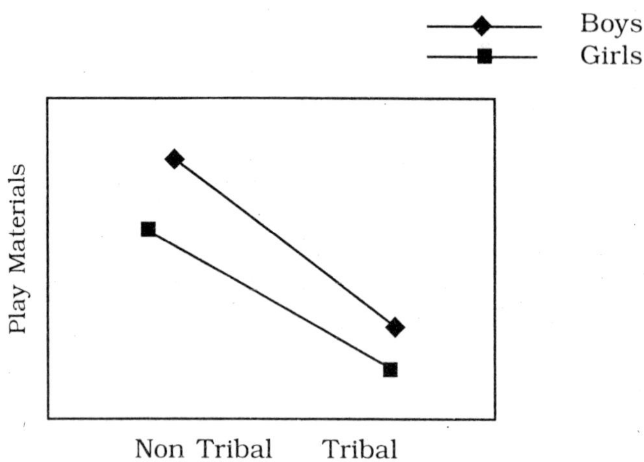

FIGURE 25.2 : **The Culture × Sex Effect for Play Materials**

sons than do they report for their girls.

Taken together, non-tribal mothers report greater amount of children's exposure to physical objects, nutrition, play materials, adult verbalization, and extensiveness of peer network. In addition, mother of boys report greater health care, peer network and exposure to play materials for their sons. Mothers of girls, however, report greater exposure to physical objects for their daughters than for her sons.

Care-taker and Child Interaction Dimension

The Analyses of Variance performed on parental contact shows significant culture effect, F (1, 489) = 139.97, p<.01 (see Table 25.3). As shown by Table 25.4, non-tribal mothers indicate greater parental contact than do tribal mothers (M=5.68 and 4.14, respectively). The result also shows significant sex effect, F (1, 489)=6.12, p<.05. Mothers of boys report greater contact with their sons than do mothers of girls for their daughters (M =5.43 and 4.39, respectively). Moreover, significant culture effect on maternal interaction is indicated, F (1, 489) =183.73, p<.01. As shown by Table 25.4, non-tribal mothers report greater maternal interaction than do tribal mothers (M=4.94 and 3.31, respectively). The sex effect is also significant, F (1, 489) = 50.64, p<.01. The examination of mean scores reveals that mothers interact more with their sons than with their daughters (M = 4.54 and 3.72, respectively). Furthermore, the result shows significant culture effect with respect to emphasis on reasoning, F (1, 489) = 600.86, p<.01. It is shown that non-tribal mothers use reasoning to a greater extent than do mothers of tribal children (M =7.37 and 30.00, respectively). The significant effect of sex is also shown, F (1, 489) = 100.88, p<.01. As shown by Table 25.4, mothers of boys use greater reasoning than mothers of girls (M=6.15 and 4.21, respectively). The results show significant Culture × Sex effect for reasoning. As shown by Figure 25.3, with change of setting from non-tribal to tribal location the gap between mothers of boys and mothers of girls narrows with respect to their emphasis on reasoning. With respect to autonomy,

TABLE 25.3 : **Analysis of Variance Performed on Care-Taker and Child Interaction Dimensions**

Dimensions	Source	df	MS	F
Parental Contact	Culture	1	290.67	139.97**
	Sex	1	127.12	6.12*
	Culture × Sex	1	2.65	1.27
	Error	489	2.08	
Maternal Interaction	Culture	1	325.61	183.73**
	Sex	1	89.75	50.64**
	Culture × Sex	1	0.77	0.43
	Error	489	1.77	
Reasoning	Culture	1	2346.34	600.86**
	Sex	1	393.94	100.88**
	Culture × Sex	1	162.95	41.73**
	Error	489	3.90	
Autonomy	Culture	1	233.58	110.39**
	Sex	1	.80	.38
	Culture × Sex	1	4.84	2.29
	Error	489	2.12	
Interest in Child's Activities	Culture	1	443.99	197.32**
	Sex	1	.41	.18
	Culture × Sex	1	8.17	3.63
	Error	489	2.25	
Satisfaction with child	Culture	1	399.74	110.87**
	Sex	1	558.96	155.04**
	Culture × Sex	1	180.09	49.95
	Error	489	3.60	

* $p<.05$
** $p<.01$

the result shows significant culture effect. F (1, 489) = 110.39, $p<.01$. Non-tribal mothers extend greater autonomy for their children than do tribal mothers (M=3.82 and 2.42, respectively).

Furthermore, the result shows significant culture effect with respect to mothers' interest in child's activities, F(1, 489) = 197.32, $p<.01$. The examination of mean scores shows that non-tribal mothers demonstrate greater interest in their children's activities compared with tribal mothers (M=5.24 and 3.30, respectively). With respect to

TABLE 25.4 : **Means and Standard Deviations of Scores obtained from Measures of Care-Taker and Child Interaction Factors**

Indicators	Source	Boys		Girls		Combined	
		M	SD	M	SD	M	SD
Parental Contact	Tribal	4.54	1.49	3.73	1.56	4.14	1.58
	Non-Tribal	6.31	0.92	5.04	1.57	5.68	1.43
	Combined	5.43	1.56	4.39	1.70		
Maternal Interaction	Tribal	3.76	0.93	2.86	1.33	3.31	1.23
	Non-Tribal	5.31	1.38	4.57	1.73	4.94	1.60
	Combined	4.54	1.38	3.72	1.73		
Reasoning	Tribal	3.35	1.96	2.64	1.51	3.00	1.79
	Non-Tribal	8.95	2.31	5.78	2.14	7.37	2.74
	Combined	6.15	3.51	4.21	2.39		
Autonomy	Tribal	2.54	1.55	2.30	1.58	2.42	1.57
	Non-Tribal	3.74	1.21	3.91	1.32	3.83	1.27
	Combined	3.14	1.54	3.11	1.68		
Interest in Child's Activities	Tribal	3.37	1.19	3.23	1.50	3.30	1.35
	Non-Tribal	5.05	1.39	5.42	1.93	5.24	1.68
	Combined	4.21	1.53	4.33	2.02		
Satisfaction with Child	Tribal	2.92	0.98	4.07	2.24	3.49	1.81
	Non-Tribal	3.61	0.64	7.14	2.96	5.38	2.75
	Combined	3.27	0.92	5.61	2.98		

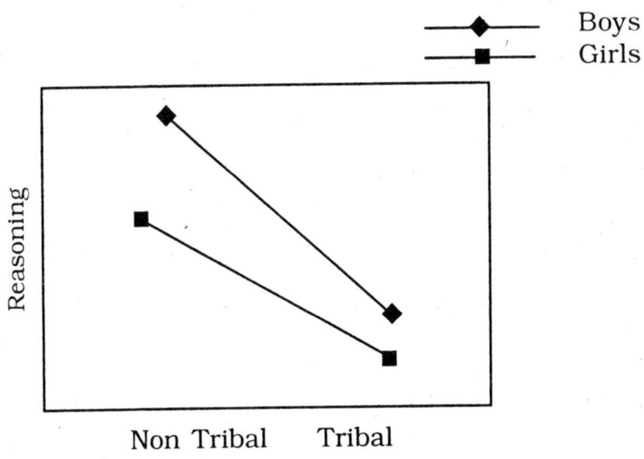

FIGURE 25.3 : **The Culture × Sex Effect for Reasoning**

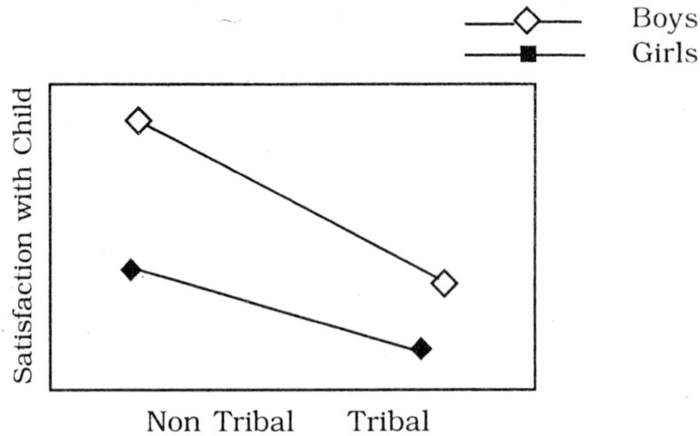

FIGURE 25.4 : **The Culture × Sex Effect for Satisfaction with Child**

the extent of satisfaction with the child, results show significant effect of culture, F (1, 489) = 110.87, p<.01. Non-tribal mothers show greater satisfaction than to tribal mothers (M=5.38 and 3.49, respectively). Similarly the result shows significant sex effect, F (1, 489) = 155.04, p<.01. Mothers express greater satisfaction with girls than with boys. The result also shows significant Culture × Sex effect, F (1, 489) = 49.95, p<.01. As shown by Figure 25.4, with change of setting from non-tribal to tribal location, the gap between mothers of boys and mothers of girls narrows with respect to mothers' satisfaction with their children.

In sum, non-tribal mothers report greater parental contact, maternal interaction, reasoning, autonomy, interest in children's activities, and satisfaction with their children than do Santal Mothers. Mothers of boys report greater parental contact, maternal interaction, and reasoning than do mothers of girls. However, mothers of girls report greater satisfaction with their daughters compared to mothers of boys.

Care-takers' Dimension

The analysis with respect to this dimension reveals significant effect of culture for well-being, F (1, 489) =

TABLE 25.5 : **Analysis of Variance Performed on Care-Takers' Dimensions**

Dimensions	Source	df	MS	F
Well-Being	Culture	1	230.35	132.98**
	Sex	1	3.76	2.17
	Culture × sex	1	2.31	1.33
	Error	489	1.73	
Life Satisfaction	Culture	1	125.31	75.40**
	Sex	1	23.35	14.05**
	Culture × Sex	1	9.61	5.78*
	Error	489	1.66	

* P < .05
** P < .01

TABLE 25.6 : **Means and Standard Deviations Scores obtained from Care-Takers Indicators**

Indicators	Source	Boys		Girls		Combined	
		M	SD	M	SD	M	SD
Well-Being	Tribal	2.92	1.15	3.21	1.23	3.07	1.20
	Non-Tribal	4.42	1.09	4.47	1.77	4.45	1.46
	Combined	3.67	1.35	3.84	1.61		
Life Satisfaction	Tribal	2.81	1.26	2.64	1.20	2.73	1.23
	Non-Tribal	4.12	1.36	3.35	1.34	3.74	1.40
	Combined	3.47	1.46	3.00	1.31		

132.98, p<.01; and for life satisfaction, F (1, 489) = 75.40, p<.01. As shown by Table 25.6, non-tribal mothers report greater well-being compared with tribal mothers (M = 4.45 and 3.07, respectively). Similarly, non-tribal mothers report greater life satisfaction than do tribal mothers (M=3.74 and 2.73, respectively). Moreover, with respect to the role of child's sex, there is no significant effect for well-being, F (1, 489) = 2.17, n.s. But there is significant effect for life satisfaction, F (1, 489) = 14.05, p<.01 (see Table 25.5). The mean score on this dimension reveals that mothers of boys report greater life satisfaction than do mothers of

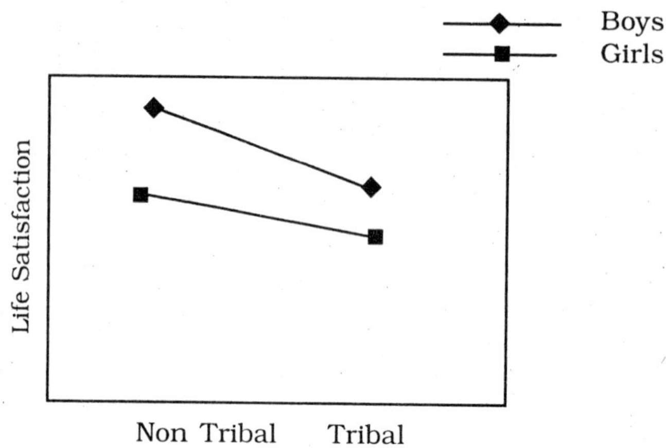

FIGURE 25.5 : **The Culture × Sex Effect for Life Satisfaction**

girls. The result shows significant Culture × Sex effect, F (1, 489) = 5.78, p<.05. As shown by Figure 25.5, with change of setting from non-tribal to tribal location, the gap between mothers of boys and girls narrows with respect to their life satisfaction.

In general, non-tribal mothers report greater well-being and life satisfaction than do tribal mothers. In addition, mothers of boys manifest higher life satisfaction than do mothers of girls.

Intra-Family Dimension

On this dimension, the ANOVA reveals that there is significant effect of culture for stress experience, F (1, 489) = 9.61, p<.01 (see Table 25.7). As shown by Table 25.7, non-tribal mothers experience greater stress than do tribal mothers (M=1.74 and 1.51, respectively). The result also shows significant sex effect, F (1, 489) = 32.82, p<.01. The examination of mean scores indicates that mothers of girls express greater stress than do mothers of boys (M = 1.86 and 1.39, respectively). The result shows significant Culture × Sex effect, F (1, 489) = 14.80, p<.01. As shown by Figure 25.6, with the change of setting from non-tribal to tribal location, the gap between mothers of boys and

TABLE 25.7 : **Analysis of Variance Performed on Intra-Family Dimensions**

Dimensions	Source	df	MS	F
Stress	Culture	1	6.13	9.61**
	Sex	1	20.94	32.82**
	Culture × Sex	1	9.44	14.80**
	Error	489	0.64	
Existence of Generation	Culture	1	285.31	134.76**
	Sex	1	40.35	19.06**
	Culture × Sex	1	2.88	1.36
	Error	489	2.12	
Daily Schedule	Culture	1	637.72	211.90**
	Sex	1	24.15	8.02**
	Culture × Sex	1	3.02	1.00
	Error	489	3.01	

* P < .05
* P < .01

TABLE 25.8 : **Means and Standard Deviations of Scorcs Obtained from Intra-Family Indicators**

Indicators	Source	Boys		Girls		Combined	
		M	SD	M	SD	M	SD
Stress	Tribal	1.41	0.80	1.60	0.69	1.51	0.78
	Non-Tribal	1.37	0.88	2.11	0.83	1.74	0.93
	Combined	1.39	0.83	1.86	0.79		
Existence of Generation	Tribal	3.21	1.44	2.74	1.45	2.98	1.46
	Non-Tribal	4.87	1.28	4.14	1.62	4.51	1.50
	Combined	4.04	1.61	3.44	1.68		
Daily Schedule Routine	Tribal	2.69	1.94	2.45	1.87	2.57	1.91
	Non-Tribal	5.20	1.20	4.53	1.68	4.87	1.49
	Combined	3.95	2.10	3.49	2.10		

mothers of girls narrows with respect to stress experience. The result shows significant culture effect for existence of generation, F (1, 489) = 134.76, p<.01. Non-tribal mothers report greater existence of generation than do

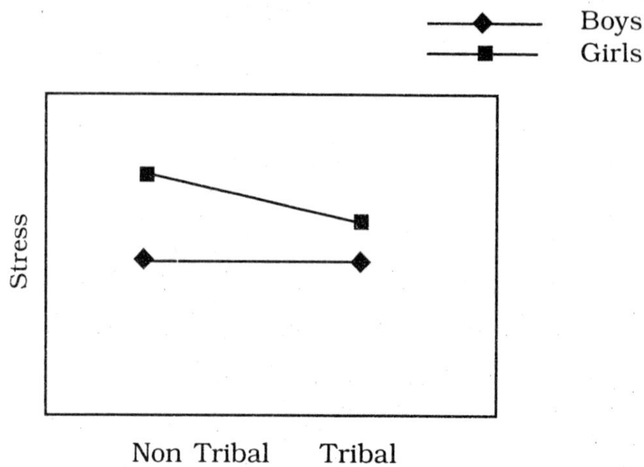

FIGURE 25.6 : **The Culture × Sex Effect for Stress**

tribal mothers (*M*=4.51 and 2.98, respectively). The result also shows significant sex effect, *F* (1, 489) = 19.06, p<.01. Mothers of boys report greater presence of generation than do mothers of girls (*M*=4.04, 3.44, respectively). Finally, the result shows significant culture effect, *F* (1, 489) =211.90, p<.01. The examination of mean scores shows that non-tribal mothers report greater daily schedules of routine than do tribal mothers (*M*=4.87 and 2.57, respectively). The result also shows significant sex effect, *F* (1, 489) = 802 p<.01. As shown by Table 25.8, mothers of boys report greater daily schedules of routine compared with mothers of girls (*M*=3.95 and 3.49, respectively).

Taken together, non-tribal mothers report greater existence of generation and daily schedules of routine than do tribal mothers. However, non-tribal mothers also experience greater stress compared with tribal mothers. Mothers of girls report greater stress compared with mothers of boys. But mothers of boys report greater existence of generation and daily schedules than do mothers of girls.

Discussion

The assessment of the social environment of the Santal child presents the handicaps which characterize such children. The responses of Santal mothers vis-a-vis non-Santal mothers show clear and visible lags in development indicators associated with the Santal child.

In the context of sensory inputs, it is shown that the amount of physical stimulation is lower for Santal child in comparison with the non-Santal child. The Santal child not only experiences less physical objects and play materials compared with non-Santal child, the Santal child receives less nutrition. Similarly, Santal children come across less adult verbalization than do non-Santal children. Moreover, non-Santal mothers report more extensive peer network for their children than do Santal mothers. These indices constitute important elements of child's social environment and their role in accelerating infant and early childhood development has been stressed by a number of studies (Yarrow, Rubenstein & Pederson, 1975).

Similar pattern is revealed with respect to the child and care-takers' dimension. Non-Santal mothers report greater parental contact, maternal interaction, emphasis on reasoning and autonomy than do mothers of tribal children. Santal mothers also lag behind non-Santal mothers with respect to their interest in child's activities and satisfaction with the child. It may be pointed out here that these indicators represent the quality of interaction. Previous studies have shown that these indicators are positively related to child's growth and competence (Saraswati & Dutta, 1990).

The role of mothers' well-being and life satisfaction has been identified as significant indicators of child's development. The present study has shown that Santal mothers have lower well-being and life satisfaction compared with non-Santal mothers. It may be postulated that the deficiency of these factors is likely to adversely affect the quality of interaction between the child and the care-taker. The poor quality of interaction, in turn, is likely to affect child's growth and competence.

In the context of intra-family factors, it is found that non-Santal mothers report a greater degree of presence of generation than do Santal mothers. Although this factor does not usually feature in western-based developmental inventories, it is considered indigenous and significant in Indian socio-cultural system. The validation study has also documented its importance (Sahoo, Kar, Mohapatra & Sethi, 1996). In addition, non-Santal mothers have reported greater degree of daily routine and schedule than do Santal mothers. This factor is indicative of time perspective. The linkage between time orientation (in terms of having fixed and scheduled hours for bathing, eating, working and other activities) and development has also been evinced.

The comparison of mothers of boys and mothers of girls offers some interesting features. It is shown that mothers provide greater exposure of play materials to their sons than do they provide for their daughters. Boys also receive greater health care than do girls. Furthermore, boys are more exposed to extensive peer network than are girls, though girls have greater exposure to physical objects.

Similar sex difference is revealed in other areas. Mothers report greater degree of parental contact and maternal interaction with their sons than do they report for their daughters. As expected, mothers report greater emphasis on reasoning while dealing with their sons compared with their daughters. However, mothers of girls indicate greater satisfaction with their daughters compared with the level of satisfaction with sons.

The pattern of difference in socializing boys vis-a-vis girls reflects cultural practice in our social system. Boys get certain advantages in terms of additional play materials, health care, parental contact and maternal interaction. Mothers of boys also derive greater life satisfaction compared with mothers of girls. It appears that having a male child is quite comforting to parents. Of course, girls, more often than boys, are given additional physical objects. It is also interesting to note that mothers of girls have greater satisfaction with their daughters than are mothers of boys with their sons, but mothers of girls also experience greater stress compared with mothers of boys. This paradox is possible in view of the fact that mothers of girls are happy with their daughter for the present but mothers are apprehensive of girls' future.

The overall pattern of Culture × Sex effect offers some salient features. It is shown that the gap between mothers of boys and mothers of girls widens only with respect to exposure to physical objects. At non-Santal setting, there is little difference between mothers of boys and mothers of girls. At Santal setting, mothers of girls provide greater exposure of physical objects to their daughters. With respect to all other indicators, the difference between mothers of boys and mothers of girls narrows to a point of negligible difference when setting changes from non-tribal to tribal location. More specifically, when the setting is non-tribal, mothers of boys report greater exposure of play materials, greater emphasis on reasoning and greater experience of life satisfaction than do mothers of girls. However, such differences do not exist in Santal setting. On the contrary non-Santal mothers of girls demonstrate greater satisfaction with their daughters and greater stress than do non-Santal mothers of boys. Such differences are non-existent amongst Santal mothers. This pattern explicates the sex-linked socialization practice in different cultural systems.

Major Implications

The study has both theoretical as well as practical implications. Theoretically the study offers a comprehensive framework of identifying possible indicators of child's development. Instead of confining to a specific parameter, it attempts to represent environmental stimulation in its total context.

From application point of view, the need for intervention is highlighted. Mothers of Santal children are found to lag behind their non-tribal counterparts in many respects. Multi-level, multi-strategy intervention in needed to bridge the gap between these two sub-populations. The restrictiveness of the social environment in which tribal children find themselves impairs their development.

It is important to recognize that the use of intervention requires assessment prior to intervention as well as following intervention. A culturally indigenous and comprehensive assessment tool of this nature is very useful for this purpose.

REFERENCES

Sahoo, F.M. (1994). *The Child's Developmental Inventory*. Unpublished report. Psychology Department. Utkal University, Bhubaneswar, India.

Sahoo, F.M.; Kar, A.; Mohapatra, P. & Sethi, M. (1996). Assessment of the role of social environment in tribal and non-tribal children as perceived by their mothers. *Journal of Community Guidance and Research, 13*, 113-127.

Saraswathi, T.S. & Dutta, R. (1990). Poverty and human development; socialization of girls among the urban and rural poor. In G. Misra (Ed.) *Applied social psychology in India*. New Delhi : Sage Publication.

Yarraw, L.J.; Rubenstein, J.L. & Pederson, F.A. (1976). *Infant and environment : Early cognitive and motivation development*. London : John Wiley & Sons.

AUTHORS' NOTE

The study is based on a project awarded (by the Bernord van Leer Foundation of the Netherlands) to the first author. The authors wish to express their indebtedness to the Bernord Foundation for such financial support. Request for reprints may be sent to F.M. Sahoo, Psychology Department. Utkal University, Bhubaneswar-751 004 (India).

26

Pragmatic Dimension in The Speech of Mothers and Their Children

Babban Mishra

The studies of pragmatics and acquisition of communicative competence suggest that children possess a varied linguistic repertoire and are capable of using appropriate forms in different speech events (Goldstein, 1994). This shift towards pragmatics has also led to the realization of the importance of parent-child interaction in shaping the course of language acquisition. The specific way parents talk to their children seems to be an effective factor in developing communicative skills during mother-child discourse. Since face-to-face conversation is the cradle of language use (Clark, 1996), children learn language almost solely in conversational settings. In this connection, mothers are considered to be the prime agents of socialization and their communicative styles with their children serve to determine the type of language mastered by them and to perpetuate certain information processing strategies that affect later learning. Studies have examined the characteristic ways of mother's verbal interactions with children and how these interactions influence their later language development. Anglin (1995) asserts that language learning is accomplished through a process of cultural transmission in which parents and other members of the society enable their children by interacting and conversing with them in learning how to talk and to understand speech. Hardey Brown *et. al.*, (1981) have found that the adoptive mother imitated the infant vocalizations and the amount of her contingent vocal responses to the child was related to infant's language development at one year's of age. Cunningham and others (1980) have found that the mothers of normal children initiated more frequent interaction than mothers of retarded children. Normal children also, in turn, proved more responsive to their mother's interactions than retarded children. Thus, it is evident that mother does have her impact on children's language development. Some features of child language appear to depend mostly on their frequency of occurrence in mother's language. Klein (1974) found that a child's adoption of the subject, verb and object ordering was clearly determined by the mother's language. Thus, the characteristics of the mother's speech significantly predict the later speech of the child.

Since, the nature of language in case of children is elusive, adults always use more directives, imperatives and questions in comparison to young children. They use short, grammatically simple and well formed sentences while talking to very young children. What a child produces in imitation reflects only what is available in her spontaneous speech. The role of motherese in this connection can hardly be denied. What mothers actually speak are closely related to the above mentioned qualities. And, there has been a lot of controversy as to how sensitive children are in using communicative categories while interacting with their mothers in the early stages of language acquisition. Corte *et al.*, (1983) have reported thirteen dimensions reflected in mother's speech directed to children as being instrumental in their language comprehension.

It has been shown by Miller (1975) that children's real linguistic responses can be better elicited in game playing situations. Games appear to be the best promoters of interactive competence and prove to be facilitative in eliciting the utterances in its full grown form (Bruner, 1983). For useful functions in children's development, play is necessary to fulfil the need to be stimulated and diverted, to express natural exuberance, to experience change for its own sake, to satisfy curiosity, to explore and experiment within risk free conditions. Farver and Wimbarti (1995) have examined the distinctive role of mothers as play-partners and how socio-cultural context shapes play with different partners with thirty Indonesian children aged 18 to 36 months. It was found that level of object play and mutual involvement in co-operative social pretend play increased with age. Youngblade and Dunn's (1995) children were also observed at home with their siblings and mothers and measures of pretend play and child's behaviours and family discourse about feelings were collected. Results suggest individual differences in the amount and sophistication and social pretend play of the children are related to experiences in the relationships which they had with their mothers. Pellegrini and Perlmutter (1989) have observed that children tend to exhibit high levels of competence when they interact with valued toys and with peers/adults. But, the only limitation of game playing situation was that the responses of the children were restricted towards a particular activity and, thus, they were not independent to talk to anybody else. Olszwersky and Fuson (1986) have emphasized the idea that children expressed themselves fully when they were free to move anywhere at their homes with their family members. In Indian context, studies done by Mishra and Jaiswal (1997) and Mishra and Pandey (1996) have also showed that pragmatic dimensions have greater impact in developing children's linguistic preferences which are enhanced in the spoken languages of their mothers. Thus, the impact of motherese hypothesis is evident. Thus, keeping above in mind, the children in the present investigation were tested in a constructed situation as well as in natural condition. The frequencies with which the mothers use certain communicative categories are also expected to be reflected in their children's language. The goals of the present study were as follows :

1. To test the developmental trends in the use of communicative categories by children of different age groups and to see the similarity in their mothers' speech in game playing as well as in free speech condition.
2. To find out the changes across different age levels

by examining the similarity in the use of communicative categories by mothers and children.

3. To study the shift variation, if any, in the use of communicative categories by the mothers and their children in game playing and free speech conditions.

METHOD

Sample

Twenty-four mother-child pairs participated in the study. The children were in the age range of 24 to 48 months and they were again tested after the passage of five years. The age of their mothers was not taken into consideration. Children (equal number of males and females) were from Gorakhpur city, Uttar Pradesh. They spoke Hindi as their native language.

Procedure

The verbal responses of children were taken up for observation and recording either in playing a game or in free speech condition. In game playing situation, the mothers were requested to teach the game of carrom board by inviting the children as '*Aavo Aqj Ek Khel Khelana Sikhayen*'. After arranging the stimulus materials properly, whenever they started to play the game a tape recorder was run and their utterances were tape recorded for a period of 45 minutes. The children were given chocolates after finishing the game.

The same mother-child pairs were again approached after the time gap of 60 months and their verbatim utterances were tape recorded for 45 minutes. The purpose of this part of the study was to note the developmental changes in using communicative categories after the passage of time. The patterns of the study remained same and the tape recorded speeches were then transcribed for analysis.

The next part of the study was related to the free verbal responses of mother-child pairs at their residences while interacting with their family members and they were free to move anywhere and to talk to anybody else at any time. First of all, the target children were located and whenever they started to talk with any of their family members the same was recorded verbatim. Since, children were allowed to move through the entire house, it was necessary for the experimenter to follow them maintaining a steady distance so that the speech samples could be easily tape recorded. When the time was over, the subjects were provided few pieces of chocolates as reinforcement for their participation in the study. All mother-child pairs were retested after a gap of 60 months, like game playing condition, with a view to know the developmental changes in the use of communicative categories.

RESULTS

As has been discussed in the review of literature, the impact of mothers' language on their children has been highly emphasized (Hardey Brown, 1981; Cunningham *et al.*, 1980). Thus, the goal of the present analysis was to see the similarity in use of communicative categories by mothers and their children. It was thought that the similar communicative categories used by children, as their mothers, will indicate the impact of their prime agent of language socialization i.e. the mothers. For this purpose the mean scores for all the dimensions were computed following Corte *et al.*, (1983). Keeping the magnitude of mean scores, the hierarchy of pragmatic dimensions used by mothers as well as their respective children was determined. The number of times a particular dimension was reflected in subject's verbal manifestation was the criterion of the calculation of mean scores which appear in Tables 26.1 and 26.2. The predominantly used communicative system can easily be observed from the tables. At the same time the relation between the category used by the mothers and their respective children in their speeches can also be observed from the results summarized in Tables 26.1 and 26.2.

It is clear that the children of younger age groups

TABLE 26.1 : **Mean Scores of Pragmatic Dimensions during Game Playing Situation**

Pragmatic Dimensions	Child's Speech				Mother's Speech			
	Time-1		Time-2*		Time-1		Time-2*	
	Younger	Older	Younger	Older	Younger	Older	Younger	Older
Labelling	6.15	5.40	30.00	6.42	4.47	2.50	20.00	12.85
Request for information	2.50	2.25	2.14	0.57	4.05	5.47	4.28	3.14
Suggestion	2.10	3.65	0.42	0.00	8.45	5.42	1.42	0.14
Prescriptives	0.65	0.80	9.28	0.14	0.57	0.72	15.71	1.00
Proscriptives	0.60	0.16	1.42	0.57	0.37	0.50	2.57	0.57
Phono Corrections	3.50	0.50	0.00	0.00	1.17	0.70	0.00	0.00
Ref. Corrections	0.50	0.33	0.00	0.00	1.20	0.80	0.28	0.00
Description	2.50	0.91	7.14	1.42	0.97	4.30	5.28	2.14
Displaced Speech	2.90	6.12	0.28	0.28	1.10	0.85	0.00	0.14
Con. Soc. Expressions	0.10	0.11	0.00	0.14	0.10	0.90	0.14	0.28
Social Play	4.30	6.35	0.00	0.00	5.65	5.82	0.00	0.00
Fillers	1.75	1.67	2.14	0.57	1.17	0.72	0.57	0.14
Others	0.00	0.00	0.71	0.00	0.00	0.00	0.57	0.00

* After 60 months.

TABLE 26.2 : **Mean Scores of Pragmatic Dimensions during Free Speech Condition**

Pragmatic Dimensions	Child's Speech				Mother's Speech			
	Time-1		Time-2*		Time-1		Time-2*	
	Younger	Older	Younger	Older	Younger	Older	Younger	Older
Labelling	8.95	11.55	58.55	165.00	2.20	0.57	42.14	77.50
Request for information	1.80	2.32	2.85	5.00	4.75	2.92	17.14	37.50
Suggestion	2.50	1.75	0.00	0.00	1.63	0.90	0.28	0.00
Prescriptives	0.60	0.92	1.14	0.00	3.33	1.27	7.43	6.00
Proscriptives	0.96	0.55	0.71	0.00	1.16	0.60	7.43	0.00
Phono Corrections	0.00	0.00	0.00	0.00	0.30	0.00	0.00	0.00
Ref. Corrections	0.16	0.25	0.14	0.00	0.50	0.00	0.14	1.50
Description	3.40	0.92	2.42	4.00	2.10	0.40	3.43	1.50
Displaced Speech	1.20	1.20	2.14	5.00	0.96	0.20	1.72	2.50
Con. Soc. Expressions	0.00	0.00	0.00	0.00	0.10	0.00	0.00	0.00
Social Play	5.80	8.02	0.14	0.00	0.60	2.52	1.00	0.00
Fillers	4.30	2.80	0.00	0.50	0.20	0.00	0.00	1.00
Others	4.90	2.02	0.00	0.00	0.50	0.10	0.00	0.00

* After 60 months.

used predominantly the communicative category of "Labelling" (M=6.15) in game playing situation as compared to children of older age groups. When the children were reappproached after the time gap of 60 months, similar use of communicative categories was found in the case of younger children (M=30.0) for the category of "Labelling". It was also suggested by Anglin (1995) that children learn early to name objects that are functionally relevant and experimentally salient for them. That is why they have learnt to label the objects earlier than other forms of pragmatic systems. The second frequently used communicative category was 'social play' for the children of both the age groups. It was consonant with the liking of playful situations for their exploratory value. Retested after the time gap of five years, it was noted that the second frequently used communicative category was 'prescriptive' in the case of younger children (M=9.28) 'Description' (M=1.24) in the older children.

With regard to mother's speech, the most frequently used categories were 'suggestion' (M=8.45) and 'social play' (M=5.65) in the case of younger children. In the case of older children, this communicative category was shifted to 'Social Play' (M=5.82) and 'Request for information' (M=5.47). This suggests that mothers were either engaged in instructing their children or checking their knowledge. But, when the same mother-child pairs were again tested after the time gap of five years, drastic changes in using communicative categories by their mothers were noted. They used most frequently 'Labelling' (M=20.0), 'Prescriptive' (M=15.71) and 'Description' in the case of younger children while 'Labelling' (M=12.85), 'Request for information' (M=3.14) and 'Description' (M=2.14) in the case of older children.

Thus, results show that the dimensions of pragmatic system emphasized by mothers and children are not uniform and the roles of mothers as well as their children are entirely different. Since labelling reflects the curiosity of children to know more and more about their surrounding, mothers select the intent of communication on the basis of the age of their children and their need at the time. Nelson (1981) has also found that labelling is related to concept learning in children. The relationship between labelling and concept learning should not be confused. It should be clear that labelling does not lead necessarily to the concept learning in children. It is believed that when a child starts having the knowledge of the world i.e. the surrounding in which she/he resides, she/he starts naming the things around him/her which is labelling and by this the child starts learning the concept.

The results obtained in free speech condition are summarized in Table 26.2. Contrary to game playing situation, the results of free speech situation are most interesting because children in this situation were more free in using language. The most frequently used communicative category was Labelling (M=8.95) and 'Social Play (M = 5.80) in the case of younger children as well as in the case of older children. As children progressed with age, they continued to use labelling as a predominant communicative category and the second communicative category was 'Request for information' in the case of younger children. But as far as older children were concerned, the 'Conventional social expression' was found to be an effective communicative category in the verbal manifestations of those children. As expressed earlier, the mothers of these children have predominantly used 'the request for information', 'Prescriptives' and 'Social Play' in the case of younger children as well as in the case of older children. But, after the passage of time, they have used 'Labelling' as the most dominant communicative category in the case of younger as well as older children. And, the next frequently used communicative categories are 'Request for information', 'Prescriptives' and 'Description' in the same order.

Discussion

Since, the purpose of the present investigation was to find out the influence of mother's speech characteristics on their children's verbal expressions, the thirteen types of dimensions of pragmatic systems reflected in mother's as well as their children's verbal expressions were taken into consideration. As suggested by Corte *et al.*, (1983), parents who have extended language facility to their children by talking them more and more can pass on prerequisites of language development. It was hypothesized that children's roles would be shifted in the light of communicative expressions imposed on them by their mothers. But, on the basis of results, children maintained their identity in using different types of dimensions of pragmatic systems. The reason may be that when the mother expected from her child the use of a particular linguistic expression, the child did not favour the use that type of linguistic expression and tried to negate her. The children used the pragmatic dimensions to communicate their information according to their own preferences. Hence, children's freedom and self initiative in using communicative categories seem to dominate.

Although psychologists have reported that several characteristics of mother's speech predict significantly the later speech of the child (Dubber & de Blauw, 1978) yet, such cases were not seen in the present investigation. Only 'Social Play' provided partial demonstration of this phenomenon. The pragmatic categories used in free speech condition by children as well as their mothers were entirely different. It seems that children felt more independent in using communicative categories when they were on their own and beyond any restriction being imposed by anybody else. Thus, the proper linguistic enhancement in children can be seen in free speech samples as compared to the samples of restricted situation. The reason may be that children appear to practice what they have heard from others in the free speech condition. Thus, the findings of the present investigation are in consonance with the principles of 'motherese hypothesis'. Cross (1977) suggests that mothers are sensitive to their child's underlying receptive, cognitive abilities and have the ability to monitor the child's psycholinguistic abilities rather than the characteristic level of his/her spontaneous speech.

It is suggested that semantic interpretability and relevance are the crucial features in facilitating language acquisition through motherese. Newport *et al.*, (1977) have remarked that mother makes syntax conspicuous for the child, underlining constructions by placing them in salient positions in surface structure or by providing exemplars. Thus, the mother's linguistic input in children's specific dimensions of pragmatic system is evident.

REFERENCES

Anglin, J.M. (1995) Classifying the World Through Language : Functional Relevance, Cultural Significance and Category name learning, Special Issue; Language Culture and World View, *International Journal of Intercultural Relations, 19*, 161-81.

Bruner, J.S. (1983) *Child's Talk*, New York : Norton.

Clark, H.H. (1996) *Using Language*, Cambridge University Press.

Corte, M.D.; Benedict, H. & Klein, D. (1983) The Relationship of Pragmatic dimensions of mother's speech to the referential expressive distinction, *Journal of Child Language*. 10, 35-43.

Cunningham, C.E.; Reuler, E.; Blackell, J. & Deck, J. (1981) Behavioural and Linguistic Developments in the interactions of normal and retarded children with their mothers, *Child Development*, 52, 62-70.

Farver, J.A. & Wimbarti, S. (1995) Indonesian Children's Play with Their Mothers and older siblings, *Child Development*, 66, 1493-1503.

Goldstein, J.H. (1994) *Toys Play and Child Development*, Cambridge University Press.

Hardey Brown, K.; Plomin, R & De Fries, J.C. (1981) Genetic and Environmental influences on the rate of communicative development in the first year of life, *Developmental Psychology*, 17, 704-717.

Klein, D. (1974) *World Order : Dutch Children and Their Mothers, Publication No. 9*, Institute for general linguistics, University of Amsterdam.

Miller, M. (1975) *Pragmatic Constraints on the linguistic realization of 'semantic intentions' in early Child Language* (telegraphic speech). Paper presented at 3rd International Child Language Symposium, London.

Mishra, B. & Jaiswal, S. (1997) *Motherese Hypothesis*, Unpublished Master's Dissertation, D.D.U. Gorakhpur

University, Gorakhpur.

Mishra, B & Pandey, R. (1996) *Motherese Hypothesis and Deprivation*, Unpublished Master's Dissertation, D.D.U. Gorakhpur University, Gorakhpur.

Nelson, K. (1981) Individual Difference in Language Development: Implications for Development and Language, *Developmental Psychology*, 17, 170-187.

Newport, E.; Gleitman, H. & Gleitman L. (1977) Mother I'd rather do it myself : Some effects and noneffects of maternal speech style. In C. Snow & C. Ferguson (eds.). *Talking to Children: Language Input and acquisition*, Cambridge. C.U.P.

Olszerwersky, P. & Fuson, K.C. (1986) Pre-schooler's dyadic speech about nonpresent during joint play, *Discourse Processes*, 9, 221-235.

Pellegrini, A.D. & Perlmutter, J. (1989) Classroom Contextual effects on children's Play. *Developmental Psychology*, 25, 289-96.

Youngblade, L.M. & Dunn, J. (1995) Individual Differences in young children's pretend play with mother and sibling : Links to relationships and understanding of other people's feelings and beliefs, *Child Development*, 66, 1472-92.

Effects of Mal-Nutrition and Environment on Intellectual Ability

Santa Misra and **Banamali Mohanty**

In recent years there has been a reawakening of interest in the behavioural and physiological consequences of early malnutrition/undernourishment and perceptually impoverished rearing environment. The effects of differential early nutritional status on intellectual ability of animals are quite equivocal. In some instances, early undernutrition was found to retard the growth of intellectual abilities of animals (Pachon, McGuire, & Rasmussen, 1995; Ricciuti, 1993; Rogan & Gladen, 1993). In some other instances, early undernutrition was not found to have adverse effect on the intellectual capacities of the animals (Byrne, Whiten, Henzi, & McCulloch, 1993; Santucci, Daud, Almedia, and de Olive-iva, 1994).

In addition to the early nutritional status, the quality of physical rearing environment is found to have differential effects on the intellectual abilities of animals. The quality of physical environment refers to both enriched (sensory stimulation) and impoverished (sensory deprivation) environment. Results of the studies manipulating the quality of the early rearing environment to show its effect on intelligence of animals are often contradictory. Some studies revealed that animals reared in an impoverished environment were found to be inferior in intellectual ability to their enriched counterparts (Benton, 1990; Chattopadhyay, De, & Biswas, 1993; Lawrence, Pethrick, McLean & Deans, 1994; Mohanty & Behera, 1997; Mohanty & Pramanick, 1996). However, contradictory results have been reported in some other studies (Bugajski, Borycz, Glod, & Bugajski, 1995; Evans, 1984; Tees, Buhrmann, & Hanley, 1990).

Recent studies using rats as subjects indicate that housing in an enriched environment can partially ameliorate the deleterious effects of undernutrition, although the details of these benefits remain subject to disagreement (Bhide & Bedi, 1984; Katz & Davies, 1983; Levitsky & Barnes, 1972; Mohanty & Mohapatra, 1990; Mohanty & Patra, 1997; Sara, King, & Lazarus, 1976). However, some other studies employing mice as subjects reported no ameliorative effect of enrichment on behaviour of mice (Crnic, 1983). Whether this is a meaningful species difference or one due to some methodological difference is at present unclear, and could only be resolved by parallel experiments using identical methodologies. Further, work along these lines could provide useful information about how behavioural impairments caused by undernourishment or malnutrition in animals might be offset by enriched experience.

Unfortunately, no attempt has been made so far to show the joint effect of nutrition and environment on the intellectual ability of rats. The purpose of the present study was, therefore, to determine the interaction effect of early nutritional status and early rearing environment on the intellectual or reasoning ability of albino rats. Moreover, the study aims at finding out whether rearing in an enriched environment would ameliorate the deleterious effects of undernutrition on intelligence of rats.

METHOD

The objective of the present study was to show the effects of early nutritional status (ENS), early rearing environment (ERE), and the interaction effect of ENS and ERE on the intellectual ability of rats. The study involved a 2×2 factorial randomized group design having 10 rats per cell. Both the factors were between—group factors, with two levels of ENS (undernutrition/nonmalnutrition), and two levels of ERE (impoverished/enriched). The dependent measure was the intellectual abilities of rats measured by Hebb-Williams maze test.

Subjects

Rattus norvegicus var. *albinus* (*Wistar* strain) male (n =40), bred and raised in our laboratory, served as subjects. All these rats were the offsprings of 10 mothers. All litters were reared in the laboratory wiremesh cages (30 × 30 × 24 cm) with their mothers until an average age of 25 days (range= 23-28 days) under same light regimen (12 : 12 hour light-dark cycle), with water and food available *ad lib* to all mother-rats.

Apparatus

Hebb-Williams maze supplied by Techno Electronics, Lucknow (Serial No. 470071) was used. It consisted of a box with an entrance alley and a food compartment at opposite corners of an open field. The box was mounted on four stands permitting the observer to sit and observe by the side of the apparatus at the time of testing.

The entrance alley (start box) and the food compartment (goal box) were both of 15.24 × 30.48 cm with a height of 13.0 cm. The open field was of 76.20 × 76.20 cm with a height of 13.0 cm. The floor and all the sides were painted bluish white. The floor of the open field was divided into 36 squares. The size of each square was 12.70 × 12.70 cm with a thin black outlining. These served as markers for placing the barriers in each test, and also served to define error zones.

The barriers, used to construct the problems, were painted bluish white and were made from dressed lumber of 1.27 cm thickness of different sizes. They were constructed in such a way that set on edge, they reached exactly from the floor of the box to the screen top. They were made to the following specifications : 2 barriers, each of 12.70 cm in length; 4 barriers, each of 25.40 cm in length; 2 barriers, each of 38.10 cm in length; 2 barriers, each of 50.80 cm in length; and 1 barrier of 63.50 cm in length. A small piece of sheet metal, 5.08 × 1.27 cm was nailed to the bottom of each barrier as a support to keep it standing on edge. A transparent thin glass sheet covered the apparatus.

Procedure

Each rat was weighed before it was assigned to differential treatment conditions. On the day of weaning at an average age of 25 days after birth all rats were divided randomly into two equal groups, 20 in each. Each group was randomly assigned to one of the two nutritional conditions—undernourished and normally nourished. The group of rats assigned to the undernourished condition had free access at all times to a poor quality diet which was a laboratory prepared diet, containing only flour and salt. On the contrary, the group of animals assigned to the normally nourished condition had free access to a good quality diet at all times. This diet was also a laboratory prepared diet containing flour, salt, grams, milk powder, eggs, groundnut oil, and vitamins; green cabbages were also supplied to this group of animals regularly. Water was always available *ad lib* to all animals of both the groups. The split-litter technique was used whenever possible in assigning rats to the two nutritional conditions.

Half of both undernourished and normally nourished groups of rats were reared in one of the two perceptually stimulating environments—impoverished and enriched conditions. The subjects which were placed into a perceptually impoverished environment were housed singly in individual cages (30 × 30 × 24 cm) that were kept in a standard rack in darkness. The housing cages were devoid of any inanimate stimulus objects. The rack containing the cages was sorrounded by sound attenuating material with white masking noise that was constantly delivered through speakers, which were placed in the opposite ends of the cage rack. The rack containing the cages was oriented so that a rat could not see any other rat. The darkness in which these rats lived was complete except a few minutes of dim light everyday or two, for filling water bottles and putting food in the food plates, and for a period of about 20 minutes every week or so when lights were turned on for cage cleaning.

The other half of both the groups of rats were placed into a perceptually enriched environment in which they were housed singly in individual cages (same size as the impoverished rats), containing a single plaything, was changed every alternate days, such as a plastic spoon, a jingling bell, a teething toy, a wooden block, a plastic ball, a mirror, a jigger, a bell or a sandbox. Flashing Christmas tree lights was placed in front of the rack containing these cages, and the rack was oriented so that each rat could not see the other. In this condition, the rats were maintained in a room with 12 hours light-dark cycle, and received intermittent auditory stimulation in the form of radio music.

Thus, there were four treatment combinations of rats undernutrition—impoverished environment (UN-IE), undernutrition-enriched environment (UN-EE), normal nutrition-impoverished environment (NN-IE), and normal nutrition-enriched environment (NN-EE).

All the groups of rats were kept under their respective treatment conditions for 60 days, immediately after weaning, with water and food available *ad lib.* None of the animals was handled during rearing.

From the 54th days of differential treatment all the rats were subjected to a 23 hours food deprivation schedule till the completion of the test.

The entire procedure of Hebb-Williams maze test was mainly divided into two sessions : (a) preliminary training, and (b) Testing. From the 61st day of differential treatment each rat was given preliminary training in the Hebb-Williams maze. The preliminary training was divided into three phases.

First Phase. From the 61st day of differential training, the rats, two at a time, were put into the entrance box of the Hebb-Willams Maze for 5 minutes. Later, they were exposed to the maze field and were allowed to find their way to the food compartment (goal box). They were allowed to eat food in the goal box for a brief period of time after which they were given food outside the goal box on a table. In total, each rat was given 1 hour time for eating the food either inside or outside the goal box. However, it was never fed in its home cage. The rats were handled sufficiently before and after each session. This phase continued for 3 days.

Second Phase. From the 64th treatment day the rats of different treatment groups were given the practice problems A, B, C, D, E and F. The problems were created by putting barriers of different sizes at different places in the open field. The length and number of barriers used for the practical problems are as follows:

A – 38.10 cm – one, 50.80 cm – one
B – 25.40 cm – one, 38.10 cm – one
C – 12.70 cm – one, 50.80 cm – one
D – 25.40 cm – two
E – 12.70 cm – one, 25.40 cm – two, 38.10 cm – one
F – 12.70 cm – two, 25.40 cm – one, 38.10 cm – one

Problem A was given in first adaptation session, problem B in the second adaptive session, and so on until series A to F was completed. The problems were changed serially from session to session. The series was repeated until the rats ran to the food compartment immediately upon being placed in the box. At no time was the same training problem used on succeeding occasions.

Third Phase. From the 69th day of differential treatment the rats were put into the maze individually with as much handling as possible. The same practice problem series (A to F) was again presented, one problem a day. Time was recorded from the moment the animal was placed in the entrance alley until it took its first bite of food in the goal box. When it reached the food, it was allowed to take a few bites and was then replaced in the entrance alley (starting box). Again it was allowed to go to the food being timed as previously.

The above process was repeated nine times a day until the animals reached the criterion of making 9 runs to food in a total of 60 seconds on two consecutive occasions. When an animal did not run as fast it should, it was given less amount of food and extra handling.

The rats were given 10 to 15 minutes to eat in the goal box and then were allowed to eat outside, but not in the home cage/room. Those rats, completing criterion earlier than the rest of the group, were still given training, for 4 trials instead of 9 trials to keep up the habit. All the rats reached the criterion (i.e., 9 runs in 60 seconds on two consecutive days) within 8 days.

The purpose of the preliminary training was to train the rat to find food in the goal box, to adopt to the apparatus and to handling, and to establish a habit of eating in the food box. After much training, the animal would go to the food without fear and with a minimum of exploratory behaviour, in spite of change in the position of the barriers.

The second session was the testing session. The thin continuous crossed lines correspond to the lines painted on the floor of the apparatus. The dotted or broken lines mark the boundaries of error zones. The solid lines show the position of barriers.

From the 77th day of differential treatment, the testing session was started. In the testing session, the rats were given seven runs in the 1st problem situation and then were allowed to eat outside their living cages. Twenty-three hours later, the same procedure was repeated with the second problem, and so on until all the 12 test problems were completed. No day was missed and all conditions were kept as constant as possible. The problems were created by placing different barriers of different sizes at different places of the open field.

The dependent measure for each test problem was the total number of error zones entered by each rat. Time did not count. An error was scored each time when an animal's two forefeet crossed into an error zone. Each error zone was indicated by the dotted lines. Where a blind alley contained two error zones (two dotted lines), two errors were scored if the animal crossed the second error line. However, no error was counted when it retraced from the blind alley through the first error zone. When an animal, having retraced from an error zone turned about and went back, a further error was scored. The total number of error zones entered by an animal in all the 12 test items was the final score for that animal which was taken account for analysis.

A ceiling fan was switched on to give a masking sound. The lighting condition and movement in the room were controlled as far as possible. The maze was cleaned and dried up before the next animal was tested. All testing was done between 7.30 a.m. to 5.30 p.m.

RESULTS

The analysis of variance (ANOVA) of the body weights of rats of four differential treatment groups recorded just before they were subjected to different treatment conditions revealed that the groups did not differ significantly, $F(3, 36) < 1$. In other words, the body weights vis-a-vis age of animals of four differential treatment groups were kept under experimental control.

The Means (M) and Standard Deviations (SDs) of both number of trials taken by the subjects to reach the criterion of learning (making 9 runs to food in a total of 60 seconds on two consecutive days) and number of errors committed by the subjects of four differential treatment groups in the Hebb-Williams maze test are presented in Table 27.1.

A bivariate ANOVA was performed on the number of trials taken by the subjects of four differential treatment groups to reach the criterion of learning in Hebb-Williams maze test. The results revealed significant effects of early nutritional status (ENS), early rearing environment (ERE), and ENS × ERE interaction (see Table 27.2). Further analysis of group means of trials by Scheffe method revealed that all possible group comparisons were statistically significant except the comparison between UN-EE and NN-IE groups.

Another bivariate ANOVA was performed on the number of errors committed by the subjects of four differential treatment groups in the Hebb-Williams maze test. The results revealed that the main effects of both ENS and ERE, and ENS × ERE interaction effect were

TABLE 27.1 : **Means and Standard Deviations of Trials Taken and Errors Committed by Four Differential Treatment Groups in the Hebb-Williams Maze Test**

	Test Trials		Number of Errors	
Treatment Groups	M	SD	M	SD
UN-IE	70.20	5.06	254.50	13.12
UN-EE	45.30	4.15	162.30	5.53
NN-IE	46.80	6.05	166.00	7.80
NN-EE	36.80	3.68	136.60	4.57

TABLE 27.2 : **Bivariate ANOVAs Performed on the Number of Trials Taken to Reach Criterion of Learning and Number of Errors Committed by Four Differential Treatment Groups in the Hebb-Williams Maze Test**

Source of	df	Test Trials		Number of Errors	
variation		MS	F	MS	F
A (Early Nutritional Status)	1	2544.03	70.67*	32604.10	412.55*
B (Early Rearing Environment)	1	3045.03	118.01*	36966.40	467.75*
A × B	1	555.03	21.51*	9859.60	124.76*
Subject w. groups	36	25.80	-	79.03	-

* $p < .01$

found to be statistically significant (see Table 27.2). Further analysis of group means of errors by Scheffé method revealed that all possible group comparisons were statistically significant except the comparison between UN-EE and NN-IE groups.

Discussion

It is evident from Table 27.2 that varying levels of ENS had differential effects on learning to criterion. The early undernourished rats (M = 57.75, SD = 4.62) took more trials to reach the criterion of learning in the Hebb-Williams maze than their normally nourished counterparts (M = 41.80, SD = 5.01). The significant differential effects of varying levels of ERE indicated that the rats reared in a perceptually impoverished environment (M = 58.50, SD = 5.57) took more trials to reach the criterion of learning in the Hebb-Willams maze than the rats reared in a perceptually enriched environment (M = 41.05, SD = 3.92). The significant ENS × ERE interaction effect showed that criterion of learning was quickest for normally nourished rats reared in a perceptually enriched environment, whereas learning was slowest for undernourished rats housed in an impoverished environment. The significance of group comparisons by Scheffe method indicated that the detrimental effects of early undernutrition on the criterion of learning of animals in the Hebb-Williams maze were ameliorated by their early enriched experiences.

Increase of the number of trials signifies retardation of learning in Hebb-Williams maze. The results, therefore, revealed that both early undernutrition and early impoverished rearing environment had adverse effects on the rate of learning of animals. Moreover, the detrimental or retarding effects of early undernourishment on the learning ability of rats became even greater in conjunction with early perceptual impoverishment as seen by the more number of trials taken by the UN-IE group of rats to reach the criterion of learning (see Table 27.1).

Table 27.2 also indicates that the varying levels of ENS had differential effects on the number of errors committed by rats in the Hebb-Williams maze test. The early undernourished rats (M = 208.40, SD = 10.07) committed more errors than their normally nourished counterparts (M = 151.30, SD = 6.39). Similarly, the significant differential effects of varying levels of ERE indicated that the perceptually impoverished rats (M = 210.25, SD = 10.79) committed more errors in the Hebb-William maze test than the perceptually enriched rats (M = 149.15, SD = 5.07). Moreover, the significant ENS × ERE interaction effect indicated that the amount of error was lowest in the normally nourished rats housed in a perceptually enriched environment, whereas the amount of error was highest in the undernourished rats reared in a perceptually impoverished environment. The significance of group comparisons by Scheffe method showed that the deleterious effects of early undernutrition on the Hebb-Williams maze performance of animals were ameliorated by their early enriched experiences.

Increase of errors in Hebb-Williams maze test signifies poor intelligence or lack of reasoning capacity. The results of the present study, therefore, revealed that both early undernutrition and early impoverished rearing environment had deleterious effects on the intellectual abilities or reasoning capacities of animals. Moreover, the detrimental or retarding effects of early undernutrition on the intellectual functioning or reasoning capacities of rats became even greater in conjunction with early perceptually impoverished rearing environment as evidenced by the greater number of errors committed by the UN-IE group of rats in the Hebb-Williams maze test. The adverse effect of undernutrition on intellectual ability of animals is in consonance with some earlier findings (Pachon *et al.*, 1995; Ricciuti, 1993; Rogan & Gladen, 1993), and is in contradiction to some other findings (Byrne *et al.*, 1993; Santucci *et al.*, 1994). Similarly, the adverse effect of early impoverished experience or early sensory deprivation on Hebb-Williams maze performance is in support of some earlier findings (Benton, 1990; Chattopadhyay *et al.*, 1993; Lawrence *et al.*, 1994; Mohanty & Behera, 1997; Mohanty & Pramanick, 1996) and is in contradiction to some other findings (Bugajski *et al.*, 1995; Evans, 1984; Tees *et al.*, 1990). The interaction effect of nutrition and environment, or the amelioration of the deleterious effects of early undernutrition on the intellectual abilities and reasoning capacities of animals by their enriched experiences is in consonance with some earlier findings (Bhide & Bedi, 1984; Katz & Davies, 1983; Levitsky & Barnes, 1972; Mohanty & Mohapatra, 1990; Mohanty & Patra, 1997; Sara *et al.*, 1976) and is in contradiction to some other findings (Crnic, 1983).

It may be concluded that early undernutrition/ undernourishment and early sensory deprivation/ impoverished experience have similar behavioural effects; both have retarding or detrimental effects on the intellectual abilities and reasoning capacities of animals; and the deleterious effects of early undernutrition on intellectual functioning of rats are ameliorated by their early enriched perceptual experiences.

REFERENCES

Benton, D. (1990). The impact of increasing blood glucose on psychological functioning. *Biological Psychology, 30*, 13-19.

Bhide, P.G., & Bedi, K.S. (1984). The effects of a lengthy period of environmental diversity on well-fed and previously undernourished rats. I. Neurons and glial cells. *Journal of Comparative Neurology, 227*, 296-304.

Bugajski, J., Borycz, J., Glod, R., & Bugajski, A. (1995). Crowding stress impairs the pituitary adrenocortical responsiveness to vacopressin but not corticotropin-releasing hormone stimulation. *Brain Research, 681*, 223-228.

Byrne, R.W., Whiten, A., Henzi, S.P., & McCulloch, F.M. (1993). Nutritional constraints on mountain baboons (Papio Ursinus): Implications for baboon socioecology. *Behaviour Ecology and Sociobiology, 33*, 233-246.

Chattopadhyay, P.K., De, S., & Biswas, D. (1993). Impact of parental deprivation on cognitive functioning : An exploratory study. *Indian Journal of Clinical Psychology, 20*, 63-68.

Crnic, L. (1983). Effects of nutrition and environment on brain biochemistry and behaviour. *Developmental Psychobiology, 16*, 129-145.

Evans, G.W. (1984). The effects of pathway configuration, landmarks, and stress on environmental cognition. *Journal of Environmental Psychology, 4*, 323-335.

Katz, H.B., & Davies, C.A. (1983). The separate and combined effects of early undernutrition and environmental complexity at different ages on cerebral measures in rats. *Developmental Psychobiology, 16*, 47-58.

Lawrence, A.B., Petherick, J.C., McLean, K.A., & Deans, L.A. (1994). The effect of environment on behaviour, plasma cortisol and prolactin in parturient sows. Special issue : Advances in pig behaviour science. *Applied Animal Behaviour Science, 39*, 313-330.

Levitsky, D.A., & Barnes, R.H. (1972). Nutritional and environmental interactions in the behavioural development of the rat : Long-term effects. *Science, 176,* 68-71.

Mohanty, B., & Behera, D.R. (1997). Direct versus indirect contact with enriched environment : Effects on learning and memory of albino rats. *Psychological Studies* (In Press).

Mohanty, B., & Mohapatra, M. (1990). *Maternal housing condition and nutritional status : Effects on discrimination learning and its reversal learning of adult offspring.* Unpublished M.Phil. Dissertation, Utkal University.

Mohanty, B., & Patra, R. (1997). *The influence of early nutrition and rearing environment on exploration, learning, and memory of rats.* Unpublished M.Phil. Dissertation, Utkal University.

Mohanty, B., & Pramanick, S. (1996). Variations in perceptual experiences : Effects on exploratory behaviour and depth perception of albino rats. *Indian Psychologist, 8,* 47-52.

Pachon, H., McGuire, M., & Rasmussen, K.M. (1995). Nutritional status and behaviour during lactation. *Physiology and Behaviour, 58,* 393-400.

Ricciuti, H.N. (1993). Nutrition and mental development. *Current Directions in Psychological Science, 12,* 43-46.

Rogan, W.J., & Gladen, B.C. (1993). Breast feeding and Cognitive development. *Early Human Development, 31,* 181-193.

Santucci, L.B., Daud, M.M., Almedia, S.S., & de Olive-iva, L.M. (1994). Effects of early protein malnutrition and environmental stimulation upon the reactivity to diazepam in two animal models of anxiety. *Pharmacology, Biochemistry, and Behaviour, 49,* 393-398.

Sara, V.R., King, T.L., & Lazarus, L. (1976). The influence of early nutrition and environmental rearing on brain growth and behaviour. *Experientia, 32,* 1538-1540.

Tees, R.C., Buhrmann, K., & Hanley, J. (1990). The effect of early experience in water-maze spatial learning and memory in rats. *Developmental Psychobiology, 23,* 427-439.

28

Environmental Enrichment to Overcome the Effect of Undernutrition

Banamali Mohanty

The effects of differential early nutritional status upon the behavioural correlates of emotionality, activity, learning, and memory of animals are quite equivocal. In some studies undernourished rats were found to be more emotional or more neophobic (Mohanty & Samal, 1997; Mohanty & Tarannum, 1989; Salas, Pulido, & Torreros, 1991), more active or restless (Levine, 1991; Smart, 1974), poorer in learning (Castro & Ruddy, 1989; Davidson, Flynn & Jarrard, 1992; Mohanty & Mohapatra, 1990) and retarded in memory capacity (Cratt, Murphy, & Wemstron, 1994; Mohanty & Patra, 1997; Nagy & Porada, 1991; Pachon, McGuire, & Rasmussen, 1995; Ricciuti, 1993) in comparison to their wellnourished counterparts. In some others, wellnourished rats were found to be more emotional (Badishtov, Overstreet, Kashevskaya, & Viglinskaya, 1995), more active (Barnett, Smart, & Widdowson, 1971), deficients in learning ability (Sharma & Kulkarni, 1992; Yehuda, Mei-Tal, & Youdim, 1991), and impaired in memory capacity (Santucci, Daud, Almedia, & deOlive-iva, 1994) than the undernourished ones.

Similarly, results of the studies on the effects of the quality of early physical rearing environment on emotionality, activity, learning, and memory of animals are also contradictory. Some studies revealed that animals reared in a perceptually impoverished (sensory deprivation) environment were more emotional (Pisula, Ostaszewksi, & Matysiak, 1992; Schapiro, Bloomsmith, Porter, & Suarez, 1996), more active (Beattie, Walker, & Sneddon,

1996; Keeling & Duncan, 1991; Mohanty & Pramanick, 1996), slow learners (Mohanty & Behera, 1997; Reed, Skiera, Adams, & Heyes, 1996), and poorer in memory capacity (Anderson & Schooler, 1991; Arnold & Spear, 1995; Buhrmann & Hanley, 1990), than the animals reared in a perceptually enriched (sensory stimulation) environment. However, contradictory results have been reported in some other studies (Haemisch, Voss & Gartner, 1994; Lavenex & Schenk, 1995; Nunez, Ferri, Gurcia, & Escorihuela, 1995; Peterson, Simonsen, & Lawson, 1995; Tees, Buhrmann, & Hanley, 1990).

Some recent studies (Bhide & Bedi, 1984; Katz & Davies, 1983) indicate that enriched experience of animals acquired through housing/rearing in an enriched environment can partially ameliorate the deleterious or detrimental effects of malnutrition/undernourishment, although the details of these benefits remain subject to disagreement (Crnic, 1983). Whether this is a meaningful species difference or due to some methodological difference is at present unclear, and could only be resolved by parallel experiments using identical methodologies. Unfortunately, no attempt has been made so far to show the joint effect of early nutritional status and early rearing environment on emotionality, acitivity, learning, and memory. The purpose of the present study was to determine the joint effect of early nutritional status and early rearing environment on selected behavioural correlates of emotionality, spontaneous motor activity, acquisition of a discrimination task, and retention of a passive-avoidance learning task.

EXPERIMENT 1

The objective of this experiment was to show the individual effect of early nutritional status (ENS), early rearing environment (ERE), and the joint effect of ENS and ERE on emotionality. The various measures of emotionality observed were ambulation, thigmotaxis, rearing, grooming, defecation, and urination. The experiment involved a 2×2 factorial design having 10 rats per cell. Both the factors were between-group factors, which were two level of ENS (undernourished/well-nourished) and two levels of ERE (perceptually impoverished/enriched), respectively. The dependent variable consisted of various indices of emotionality.

METHOD

Subjects

Rattus norvegicus var. *albinus* (*Wistar* strain) male (n = 40), bred and raised in our laboratory, served as subjects. All these rats were the offsprings of 10 mothers. All litters were reared in laboratory wire mesh cages (30×30×24 cm) with their mothers until an average age of 25 days (range = 23-27 days) under same light regimen (12 : 12 hour light-dark cycle). On the day of weaning at an average age of 25 days after birth all the rats were divided randomly into two equal groups, 20 subjects in each. Each group was randomly assigned to one of the two nutritional conditions—undernourished and wellnourished. The group of rats assigned to the undernourished condition had free access at all times to a poor quality laboratory prepared diet containing only flour and salt. On the contrary, the group of rats assigned to the wellnourished condition had free access at all times to a good quality laboratory prepared standard diet containing flour, salt, grams, milk powder, eggs, groundnut oil and vitamins; and green cabbages were also supplied to this group regularly. Water was always available *ad lib* to all animals of both the groups. The split-litter technique was used whenever possible in assigning rats to the two nutritional conditions.

Half of both undernourished and wellnourished groups of rats were reared in one of the two perceptually stimulating environments—impoverished and enriched. The subjects which were placed into a perceptually impoverished environment were housed singly in individual cages that were kept in a standard rack in darkness. The cages were devoid of any inanimate stimulus object. The rack containing the cages was surrounded by sound attenuating material with white masking noise that was constantly delivered through speakers which were placed in the opposite ends of the cage rack. The rack containing the cages was oriented so that a rat could not see any other rat. The darkness in which these rats lived was complete except a few minutes of dim light every day or two, for filling water bottles and putting food pellets on the floors of the cages, and for a period of about 20 minutes every week or so when lights were turned on for cage cleaning.

The other half of rats of both the nutritional groups were placed into a perceptually enriched environment in which they were housed singly in individual cages containing a single plaything, was changed every alternate days, such as a plastic spoon, a jingling bell, a teething toy, a wooden block, a jingler, a mirror, a ball, or a sandbox. Flashing Christmas tree lights was placed in front of the rack containing these cages, and the rack was oriented so that each rat could not see the other. In this condition, the rats were maintained in a room with 12 hour light-dark cycle, and received intermittent auditory stimulation in the form of radio music. Thus, there were four treatment combinations of rats : undernourished - perceptually impoverished (UN-PI), undernourished-perceptually enriched (UN-PE), wellnourished-perceptually impoverished (WN-PI), and wellnourished-perceptually enriched (WN-PE).

Apparatus. For the measurement of various indices of emotionality, an open field was used. The open field was a 88.9 × 88.9 cm wooden box with 47.5 cm high walls. The floor and the walls were covered with black enamel painted rexins. The floor was marked off into 25 (16 peripheral and 9 central) 17.7 × 17.7 cm squares by thin and faint white lines. The box was covered with a conical frame draped with mosquito net. A 15-watt frosted bulb was mounted in the centre of the frame, 68.96 cm above the floor of the open field.

Procedure. All the groups of rats were kept under their respective treatment conditions (dietary and housing), as described under subjects, for 60 days immediately after weaning. On the 61st day of differential treatment, all subjects were given a habituation trial in the open field for 5 minutes each.

On the 62nd treatment day, each rat was carried to the testing room in a carrying cage. Each subject was dark adapted for 5 minutes and then was gently placed in the centre of the open field. Each animal was observed in the open field for 10 minutes. The behaviour of the rats observed in the open field were : ambulation-side (number of peripheral squares entered), ambulation-centre (number of central squares entered), rearing (frequency of standing on hind limbs), grooming bouts (frequency of body and face washing), defecation (number of facal boluses deposited), and urination (number of drops of urine left). When an animal placed at least both forepaws into a square, it was counted as one square entry.

The open field was cleaned and dried up before the next animal was tested. During testing the room was made completely dark. There was no other source of light except the light as provided in the test apparatus. A ceiling fan was switched on to continually mask external noise. All testing was done between 8.00 a.m. and 5.30 p.m.

Results and Discussion

The analysis of variance of the body weights of animals of four treatment groups recorded just before they were subjected to different treatment conditions revealed a non-significant grouping effect, F (3, 36) <1. In other words, the body weights vis-a-vis age of the animals of different treatment groups were kept under experimental control.

Means (M) and Standard Deviations (SDs) of the various indices of emotionality of four differentially treated groups of rats are presented in Table 28.1.

The total ambulation scores for each rat was found out by adding the ambulation-side and ambulation-centre scores. The analysis of variance (ANOVA) performed on the ambulation scores (see Table 28.2) revealed that ENS, ERE, and ENS × ERE effects were found to be statistically significant.

TABLE 28.1 : **Means and Standard Deviations of Various Indices of Emotionality of Four Differential Treatment Groups of Rats Observed in the Open Field**

Indices of Emotionality	Differential Treatment Groups							
	UN-PI		UN-PE		WN-PI		WN-PE	
	M	SD	M	SD	M	SD	M	SD
1. Total ambulation	38.20	3.29	62.50	6.40	64.70	3.53	148.80	9.96
2. Thigmotactic Ratios	0.21	0.04	0.26	0.04	0.30	0.06	0.44	0.02
3. Rearing ups	9.10	2.60	13.00	2.58	13.70	2.21	22.30	2.75
4. Grooming bouts	11.40	2.50	8.40	2.37	7.30	2.21	5.60	2.88
5. Defecation	12.30	2.54	10.30	1.89	6.70	1.42	3.20	1.55
6. Urination	12.60	2.76	10.70	2.21	4.80	2.10	3.20	1.99

The thigmotactic ratio is a measure of the wall-hugging tendencies of the animals. A thigmotactic ratio is derived by dividing the number of central squares entered by the total number of squares entered in a unit time by an animal. The ANOVA performed on the thigmotactic ratios (see Table 28.2) revealed significant main effects of both ENS and ERE, and ENS × ERE interaction effect was also significant.

A bivariate ANOVA performed on the number of rears made by the subjects of four differential treatment groups (see Table 28.2) revealed that ENS and ERE main effects, and ENS × ERE interaction effect were statistically significant.

In the experimental literature face washing and body washing of animals are termed as preening and grooming, respectively. However, Archer (1973) regarded both face washing and body washing as grooming. In the present experiment grooming included both face washing and body washing bouts. A two-factorial ANOVA performed on the grooming scores (see Table 28.2) revealed significant main effects of both ENS and ERE. No other effect was found to be significant.

In the experimental literature defecation and urination have been recognized as two major correlates of emotionality (Archer, 1973). The ANOVA performed on the number of bolies defecated by the subjects of four differential treatment groups during a 10 minute observation period in the open field (see Table 28.2) revealed the significant main effects of both ENS and ERE. However, the ENS × ERE interaction effect could not reach the level of significance.

A bivariate ANOVA performed on the number of urine drops left by the subjects of four differentially treated groups during a 10 minute open field observation period (see Table 28.2) showed significant ENS and ERE effects. No other effect was significant.

From Table 28.2 it is quite evident that early nutritional status has differential effects on all behavioural measures of emotionality. Animals undernourished during their early days of life, beginning from their weaning, were

TABLE 28.2 : ***F* ratios of Six Separate Analyses of Variance Performed on Six Indices of Emotionality**

Source of Variation	df	Indices of Emotionality					
		Ambulation	Thigmotactic Ratio	Rearing	Grooming	Defecation	Urination
A (Early Nutritional Status)	1	778.12**	91.00**	74.60**	19.01**	111.70**	112.33**
B (Early Rearing Environment)	1	718.95**	50.00**	60.33**	8.82**	20.95**	5.88*
A × B	1	218.69**	10.00**	8.53**	<1	1.56	<1
Subject w. groups	36	—	—				

* $p < .05$
** $p < .01$

found to be more emotional than their wellnourished counterparts.

Early rearing environment was also found to have differential effects on all behavioural measures of emotionality. Animals having perceptually impoverished experiences during their early days of life were found to be more emotional in comparison to the animals having enriched experiences.

Early nutritional status was found to interact significantly with the early rearing environment on the measures of ambulation, thigmotactic ratios, and rearing. The amount of ambulation, thigmotactic ratio, and rearing ups was lowest when the animals received undernourishment and reared in a perceptually impoverished environment. On the contrary, the amount of ambulation, thigmotactic ratios, and rearing ups was highest when the animals were provided with wellnourishment and reared in a perceptually enriched environment. Analysis of means of ambulation scores, thigmotactic ratio, and rearing scores of four differential treatment groups by Scheffe method revealed that all group comparisons were found to be statistically significant except the difference between UN-PE and WN-PI groups. This finding indicated that the deleterious effects of undernutrition on ambulatory behaviour, thigmotaxis, and rearing ups of rats were ameliorated by their early enriched perceptual experiences.

EXPERIMENT 2

The objective of this experiment was to show the effect of early nutritional status (ENS) and early rearing environment (ERE) and the joint effect of ENS and ERE on spontaneous motor activities of rats. The experiment involved a 2×2 factorial randomized group design having 10 rats per cell. The factors were same as described in Experiment 1.

Method

Subjects. Forty male *Wistar* strain albino rats, bred and raised in our laboratory, served as subjects. The dietary condition, housing condition, and division of subjects into four randomized groups after weaning at an average age of 25 days (range = 23-27 days) were the same as described in Experiment 1.

Apparatus. For the measurement of spontaneous motor activity a photoactometer, supplied by M/s Techno Electronics, Lucknow (Model No. PA-3, Serial No. 5100022), was used. The size of the activity chamber of the photoactometer was 29.5 × 29.5 cm with 14.5 cm high walls. The floor of the activity chamber was a detachable wire-netted plate and the top of the activity chamber had a detachable metal lid. There were three photocells in each of two adjacent walls at a height of 1 cm above the floor of the activity chamber. The photocells were located equidistant from one another. The photocells could be activated by red beams of light projected from opposite walls just pointing to the photocells. An automated impulse counter recorded the number of interceptions of the beam of light.

Procedure. The design and procedure of the present experiment in respect of dietary conditions, rearing environments, assignment of animals into various treatment combinations, duration of rearing, age of weaning, and period of habituation, were the same as described in Experiment 1. Other details of the present experiment are given below :

During the habituation period on the 61st day of differential treatment, each subject was hibituated to the photoactometer without the focus of beams of red light inside the activity chamber. On the 62nd day of differential treatment, the test day, each subject was carried to the testing room in a carrying cage, dark adapted for 5 minutes, and then was gently placed in the middle of the activity chamber of the photoactometer. Each rat was observed in the photoactometer for 10 minutes. Number of interceptions of the light beam, due to whole or part body movement of the subject, was recorded by an automated digital counter.

Observation of each animal in the photoactometer was

done only for one day. Other conditions were same as described in Experiment 1.

Results and Discussion

The analysis of variance of the body weights of rats of the four treatment groups recorded just before they were subjected to different treatment conditions revealed that the groups did not differ significantly, $F(3, 36) < 1$. In other words, the body weights vis-a-vis age of animals of different treatment groups were kept under experimental control.

An analysis of variance was performed on the spontaneous motor activity scores of four treatment groups of subjects. The results revealed that varying nutritional status had differential effects on spontaneous motor activity scores, $F(1, 36) = 534.11$, $p < .01$. Undernourished animals ($M = 177.40$, $SD = 28.24$) were found to be more active, more aroused, or more restless than the wellnourished rats ($M = 130.85$, $SD = 12.71$).

Varying levels of early rearing environment had also differential effects on the activity or arousability of the subjects, $F(1, 36) = 351.26$, $p < .01$. Perceptually impoverished rats ($M = 173.0$, $SD=32.86$) were found to be more active or more aroused than their perceptually enriched counterparts ($M = 135.25$, $SD = 16.42$).

ENS × ERE interaction effect was also found to be significant, $F(1, 36) = 61.92$, $p < .01$. The amount of activity was highest for undernourished rats reared in an impoverished environment. On the contrary, the amount of activity or degree of arousability was lowest for wellnourished rats housed in an enriched environment. The average spontaneous motor activity scores of UN-PI, UN-PE, WN-PI, and WN-PE groups of subjects were 204.20 ($SD=7.70$), 150.60 ($SD=5.32$), 141.80 ($SD=7.58$), and 119.90 ($SD=4.15$), respectively. Further analysis of these group means by Scheffe test indicated that all possible group comparisons were found to be statistically significant. In other words, the facilitatory effect of undernurition on the spontaneous motor activities of rats was inhibited by their early enriched perceptual experiences.

EXPERIMENT 3

This experiment tried to determine the individual as well as the joint effects of early nutritional status (ENS) and early rearing environment (ERE) on the discrimination learning ability of rats. The experiment involved a 2×2 factorial randomized group design having 10 rats per cell. The factors were same as described in Experiment 1.

Method

Subjects. Forty male *Wistar* strain albino rats, bred and raised in our laboratory, served as subjects. All other conditions were the same as described in Experiment 1.

Apparatus. For the acquisition of a discrimination task, a discrimination box was used. The discrimination box consisted of two identical choice compartments of 30 × 30 cm with 14 cm high walls. Each compartment had an entrance door of 7.5 × 14.0 cm. The waiting compartment from which an animal could enter into any one of the choice compartments was 25 × 15 cm with 14 cm high walls. The two discriminanda of equal area were a black triangular disc and a black circular disc which could be attached on the back walls of any of the choice compartments.

Procedure. The design and procedure of the present experiment in respect of dietary conditions, rearing environments, assignment of animals into various treatment combinations, duration of treatment, age of weaning, and period of habituation, were the same as described in Experiment 1. Other details of the present experiment are given below :

From the 55th treatment day, all the animals were subjected to 22½ hour food deprivation schedule. On the 61st day of differential treatment, each subject was given a habituation trial in the discrimination box without the discriminanda although food was available in both choice compartments. For the discrimination learning task, the black triangular disc was the positive stimulus (S^+), and the black circular disc was the negative stimulus (S^-). The visual patterns to be discriminated were presented in the choice compartments in a prearranged random manner. The learning involved a simultaneous discrimination task without opportunities for correction. From the 62nd treatment day, each rat was tested for the acquisition of a discrimination task. Each rat was placed in the waiting compartment of the discrimination box. Entering into the choice compartment containing a black triangular disc, the subject was rewarded with 100 milligrams of food. No subject was given any food when it entered into the compartment containing the black circular disc. Each subject was removed from the compartment 30 seconds after it has taken food in case of a correct choice or 30 seconds after it reached the wrong side. Each rat was given 10 trials daily with 1 minute inter-trial interval till criterion learning. The criterion learning was at least 9 correct responses out of 10 on two consecutive days.

Results and Discussion

The analysis of variance of the body weights of rats of the four treatment groups recorded just before they were subjected to different treatment conditions revealed a nonsignificant grouping effect, $F(3, 36) < 1$. In other words, the body weights vis-a-vis age of rats of different treatment groups were kept under experimental control.

A bivariate ANOVA was performed on the number of days taken by the subjects of different treatment groups to reach the criterion of discrimination learning. The results revealed that varying nutritional status had differential effects on acquisition of discrimination task, $F(1, 36) = 166.81$, $p < .01$. Undernourished rats ($M=7.55$, $SD = 1.28$) were found to be slow learners than their wellnourished counterparts ($M = 4.75$, $SD = 0.85$).

Varying levels of early rearing environment had also differential effects on acquisition of discrimination task,

F (1, 36) = 54.47, p <.01. Learning was found to be slower in animals reared in a perceptually impoverished environment (M = 6.95, SD = 1.85) in comparison to that in animals reared in a perceptually enriched environment (M = 5.35, SD = 1.31).

ENS × ERE interaction was also found to be significant, F (1, 36) = 5.32, p <.05. Learning was quickest for wellnourished rats housed in an enriched environment. On the contrary, learning was slowest for undernourished rats reared in an impoverished environment. The average number of days taken by the subjects of UN-PI, UN-PE, WN-PI and WN-PE groups to reach the criterion of learning were 8.60 (SD = 0.84), 6.50 (SD = 0.53), 5.30 (SD = 0.67), and 4.20 (SD = 0.63), respectively. Analysis of these group means by Scheffe test revealed that all possible group comparisons were statistically significant. In other words, the detrimental effects of early undernutrition on the discrimination learning abilities of the subjects were ameliorated by their early perceptually enriched experiences.

EXPERIMENT 4

The objective of the present experiment was to assess the separate and combined effects of early nutritional status (ENS) and early rearing environment (ERE) on the rats' retention of a step-down passive avoidance learning task. The experiment involved a 2×2 factorial randomized group design having 10 rats per cell. The factors were same as described in Experiment 1.

Method

Subjects. Forty male *Wistar* strain albino rats, bred and raised in our laboratory, served as subjects. All other conditions were same as described in Experiment 1.

Apparatus. For the measurement of passive avoidance learning, a step-down passive avoidance apparatus was used. The inside dimensions of the apparatus were 40 cm square, with composition board walls of 60 cm high.

The central raised platform was 13 cm square, and its top was 5.5 cm above the surrounding grid floor. The top of the platform was hinged so as to activate a timer while the animal remained on the platform.

Procedure. The design and procedure of the present experiment in respect of dietary conditions, rearing environments, assignment of animals into various treatment combinations, duration of treatment, age of weaning, and period of habituation, were the same as described in Experiment 1. Other details of the present experiment are given below :

On the 61st day of differential treatment, each subject was given a habituation trial in the step-down passive avoidance apparatus without shock. From the 62nd treatment day, training procedure was started. Each subject was given a single daily pretraining trial for 5 days on the step-down passive avoidance apparatus. Each pretraining trial consisted of placing the animal on the elevated platform and allowing it to step-down onto the grid floor and remain there for 10 seconds before being removed to its housing room. No shock was given during these pretraining trials. On the 67th day, the training day, as each rat stepped down from the island it received a single footshock (1.75 mA, scrambled for 2 seconds) through a shock generator attached to the grid floor of the aparatus. Twenty-four hours after training, all subjects were given retention trials, one trial each, in the apparatus. An arbitrary time limit of 180 seconds was imposed on all retention trials. The training day step-down latencies and the retention day step-down latencies of each subject were recorded by the help of the timer attached to the top of the platform of the step-down passive avoidance apparatus.

Results and Discussion

The analysis of variance of the body weights of rats of the four treatment groups recorded just before they were subjected to different treatment conditions revealed that the groups did not differ significantly, $F (3, 36) < 1$. In other words, the body weights vis-a-vis age of rats of different treatment groups were kept under experimental control.

Means (M) and Standard deviations (SDs) of both training day and retention day step-down latencies (in seconds) of four differential treatment groups of subjects are presented in Table 28.3.

TABLE 28.3 : **Means and Standard Deviations of Both Training Day and Retention Day Step-Down Latencies (in seconds) of Four Differential Treatment Groups**

Treatment Groups	Training Day		Retention Day	
	M	SD	M	SD
UN-PI	2.5	0.74	8.2	1.14
UN-PE	2.8	0.92	124.5	4.38
WN-PI	2.7	0.95	83.5	5.30
WN-PE	3.0	0.67	150.0	10.54

An analysis of variance performed on the training day step-down latencies of four different treatment groups of subjects revealed that neither the ENS [$F(1, 36) < 1$] nor the ERE [$F(1, 36) = 1.34$, $p > .05$] had differential effects on their training day step-down latencies. Similarly, the ENS × ERE interaction effect was also not found to be significant, $F(1, 36) < 1$. In other words, subjects of four different treatment groups were more or less equal with regard to their training day step-down latencies.

Another bivariate ANOVA was performed on the retention day step-down latencies of the subjects of four differential treatment groups. The results revealed that varying nutritional status had differential effects on the retention day step-down latencies of animals, $F(1, 36) = 640.97$, $p < .01$. Undernourished rats (M = 66.35, SD = 59.86) descended from the platform faster than their wellnourished counterparts (M = 116.75, SD = 35.07). Low retention step-down latencies signifies low retention or poor memory of the learnt materials.

Varying levels of early rearing environment had also differential effects on the retention day step-down latencies of rats, F (1, 36) = 2107.99, p <.01. Animals reared in a perceptually impoverished environment (M = 45.85, SD = 38.81) descended from the platform faster than the animals reared in a perceptually enriched environment (M = 137.25, SD = 15.26).

ENS × ERE interaction was also found to be significant, F (1, 36) = 156.45, p <.01. The retention day step-down latencies were highest for wellnourished rats reared in an enriched environment. On the contrary, it was lowest for undernourished rats reared in an impoverished environment. Anlaysis of group means by Scheffe method revealed that all possible group comparisons were statistically significant. In other words, the deleterious effects of early malnutrition/undernourishment on the memory capacities of animals are ameliorated by their early perceptually enriched experiences.

GENERAL DISCUSSION

The present study reveals some interesting results of great theoretical and practical relevance. Low scores on ambulation, thigmotaxis, and rearing ups, and high scores on grooming bouts, defecation, and urination would indicate high emotionality, and the reverse would indicate low emotionality (Archer, 1973). Thus, the undernourished rats were found to be more emotional or neophobic than the wellnourished rats. The adverse effect of undernutrition on emotionality is in consonance with some earlier findings (Mohanty & Samal, 1997; Mohanty & Tarannum, 1989; Salas *et al.*, 1991) and is in contradiction to some other findings (Badishtov *et al.*, 1995). Similarly, the undernourished rats were found to be more active, more aroused or more restless in comparison to the wellnourished rats. The adverse effect of undernourishment on activity or arousability is in support of some previous findings (Levine, 1991; Smart, 1974) and is in contradiction to some other findings

(Barnett *et al.*, 1971). Moreover, early malnourished subjects were found to be retarded in discriminatory abilities and poorer in memory capacities in comparison to the wellnourished subjects. The adverse effects of early undernutrition on discrimination learning abilities and memory capacities of rats are in consonance with some earlier findings (Castro & Ruddy, 1989; Cratt *et al.*, 1994; Davidson *et al.*, 1992; Mohanty & Mohapatra, 1990; Mohanty & Patra, 1997; Nagy & Porada, 1991; Pachon *et al.*, 1995; Ricciuti, 1993) and are in contradiction to some other findings (Santucci *et al.*, 1994; Sharma & Kulkarni, 1992; Yehuda *et al.*, 1991). In short, undernutrition/ undernourishment during the early postweaning days of life of rats causes more emotionality, more activity or arousability, deficiency in discrimination learning ability, and retardation in memory capacity.

Perceptually impoverished environment signifies deprivation of sensory stimulation. Animals reared in such an environment early in life are said to be deprived of varieties of sensory stimulations, and thus, have acquired impoverished perceptual experiences. On the contrary, perceptually enriched environment provides a varieties of sensory stimulation to the subjects, and thus, the subjects have aquired enriched perceptual experiences early in life. The results of the present study revealed that perceptually impoverished rats were found to be more emotional or more neophobic, and more active or more aroused than the enriched rats. The adverse effects of early sensory deprivation on emotionality and activity of rats are in support of some earlier findings (Beattie *et al.*, 1996; Keeling & Duncan, 1991; Mohanty & Pramanick, 1996; Pisula *et al.*, 1992; Schapiro *et al.*, 1996) and are in contradiction to some other findings (Haemisch *et al.*, 1994; Lavenex & Schenk, 1995). Similarly, the impoverished subjects were found to be poorer in both discrimination learning abilities and memory capacities than their enriched counterparts. The adverse effects of early impoverished perceptual experience on learning and memory are in consonance with some earlier findings (Anderson & Schooler, 1991; Arnold & Spear, 1995;

Buhrmann & Hanley, 1990; Mohanty & Behera, 1997; Reed *et al.*, 1996) and are in contradiction to some other findings (Nunez *et al.*, 1995; Peterson *et al.*, 1995; Tees *et al.*, 1990). In short, impoverished perceptual experience early in life of animals causes more emotionality, more activity or arousability, retardation in learning, and retardation in retention or memory.

Early nutritional status was found to interact significantly with the early rearing environment on all the dependent measures observed in the present study except three indices of emotionality (i.e, grooming, defecation, and urination). Animals undernourished and reared in an impoverished environment during their early ages of life were found to be most emotional, most restless, slowest in learning, and most retarded in memory. Animals wellnourished and reared in a perceptually enriched environment early in life were found to be least emotional, least aroused or least restless, quickest in learning and best in memory capacity.

It may be concluded that early undernourishment and early impoverished perceptual experience have similar behavioural effects; the deleterious or detrimental effects of early undernutrition on behaviour of animals are ameliorated by their enriched experiences acquired through rearing in a perceptually enriched environment, particularly, during their early ages of life.

REFERENCES

Anderson, J.R., & Schooler, L.J. (1991). Relationship of the environment in memory. *Psychological Science, 2*, 396-408.

Archer, J. (1973). Tests of emotionality in rats and mice : A review. *Animal Behaviour, 21*, 205-235.

Arnold, H.M., & Spear, N.E. (1995). Isolation disrupts retention in preweaning rat pups. *Behavioural Neuroscience, 109*, 744-758.

Badishtov, B.A., Overstreet, D.H., Kashevskaya, O.P., & Viglinskaya, I.V. (1995). To drink or not to drink : Open field behaviour in alcohol-preferring and non-preferring rat strains. *Physiology and Behaviour, 57*, 585-589.

Barnett, S.A., Smart, J.L., & Widdowson, E.M. (1971). Early nutrition and the activity and feeding of rats in an artificial environment. *Developmental Psychobiology, 4,* 1-15.

Beattie, V.E., Walker, N., & Sneddon, I.A. (1996). An investigation of the effect of environmental enrichment and space allowance on the behaviour and production of growing pigs. *Applied Animal Behaviour Science, 48,* 151-158.

Bhide, P.G., & Bedi, K.S. (1984). The effects of a lengthy period of environmental diversity on well-fed and previously undernourished rats. I. Neurons and glial cells. *Journal of Comparative Neurology, 227,* 296-304.

Buhrmann, K., & Hanley, J. (1990). The effect of early experience on water maze spatial learning and memory in rats. *Developmental Psychobiology,23,* 427-439.

Castro, C.A., & Ruddy, J.W. (1989). Early life malnutrition impairs the performance of both young and adult rats on visual discrimination learning tasks. *Developmental Psychobiology, 22,* 15-28.

Cratt, S., Murphy, C.G., & Wemstron, J. (1994). Glucose effects on complex memory and nonmemory task : The influence of age, sex, and glucoregulatory response. *Psychobiology, 22,* 92-105.

Crnic, L. (1983). Effects of nutrition and environment on brain biochemistry and behaviour. *Developmental Psychobiology. 16,* 129-145.

Davidson, T.L., Flynn, F.W., & Jarrard, L.F. (1992). Potency of food deprivation intensity cues as discriminative stimuli. *Journal of Experimental Psychology, 18,* 174-181.

Haemisch, A., Voss, T., & Gartner, K. (1994). Effects of environmental enrichment on aggressive behaviour, dominance hierarchies, and endocrine states in male DBA 2J mice. *Physiology and Behaviour, 56,* 1041-1048.

Katz, H.B., & Davies, C.A. (1983). The separate and combined effects of early undernutrition and environmental complexity at different ages on cerebral measures in rats. *Developmental Psychobiology, 16,* 47-58.

Keeling, L.J., & Duncan, I.J. (1991). Social spacing in domestic fowl under semi-natural conditions : The effect of behavioural activity and activity transitions. *Applied Animal Behaviour Science, 32,* 205-217.

Lavenex, P., & Schenk, F. (1995). Influence of local environmental olfactory cues on place learning in rats. *Physiology and Behaviour, 58,* 1059-1066.

Levine, B.F. (1991). Spontaneous motor activity during the development and maintenance of diet induced obesity in rats. *Physiology and Behaviour, 50,* 573-581.

Mohanty, B., & Bhera, D.R. (1997). Direct versus indirect contact with enriched environment : Effects on learning and memory of albino rats. *Psychological Studies* (In Press).

Mohanty, B., & Mohapatra, M. (1990). *Maternal housing condition and nutritional status : Effects on discrimination learning and its reversal learning of adult offspring.* Unpublished M.Phil. Dissertation, Utkal University.

Mohanty, B., & Patra, R. (1997). *The influence of early nutrition and rearing environment on exploration, learning and memory of rats.* Unpublished M.Phil. Dissertation, Utkal University.

Mohanty, B., & Pramanick, S. (1996). Variations in perceptual experiences : Effects on exploratory behaviour and depth perception of albino rats. *Indian Psychologist, 8,* 47-52.

Mohanty, B., & Samal, S. (1997). *Nutritional and environmental interactions in emotionality and activity of albino rats.* Unpublished M.A. Dissertation, Utkal University.

Mohanty, B., & Tarannum, S. (1989). *Effects of maternal undernourishment and impoverished housing on body weight and emotionality of adult offspring.* Unpublished M.A. Dissertation, Utkal University.

Nagy, Z.M., & Porada, K.J. (1991). Effects of undernutrition by rearing in large litters on acquisition and memory of active-avoidance learning in mice. *Bulletin of the Psychonomic Society, 29,* 351-354.

Nunez, J.F., Ferri, P., Gurcia, E., & Escorihuela, R. (1995). Postnatal handling reduces emotionality ratings and accelerates two-way active avoidance in female rats. *Physiology and Behaviour, 57,* 831-835.

Pachon, H., McGuire, M., & Rasmussen, K.M. (1995). Nutritional status and behaviour during lactation. *Physiology and Behaviour, 58,* 393-400.

Peterson, V., Simonsen, H.B., & Lawson, L.G. (1995). The effect of environmental stimulation on the development of behaviour in pigs. *Applied Animal Behaviour Science, 45,* 215-224.

Pisula, W., Ostaszewksi, P.M., & Matysiak, J. (1992). Effects of physical environment and social experience on stimulus seeking behaviour and emotionality in rats. *International Journal of Comparative Psychology. 5,* 124-137.

Reed, P., Skiera, F., Adams, L., & Heyes, C.M. (1996). Effects of isolation rearing and mirror exposure on social and asocial discrimination performance. *Learning and Motivation, 27,* 113-129.

Ricciuti, H.N. (1993). Nutrition and mental development. *Current Directions in Psychological Science, 12,* 43-46.

Salas, M., Pulido, S., & Torreros, E.C. (1991). Neonatal

undernutrition and self-grooming development in the rat : Long-term effects. *Physiology and Behaviour. 50*, 567-572.

Santucci, L.B., Daud, M.M., Almedia, S.S., & DeOlive-iva, L.M. (1994). Effects of early protein malnutrition and environmental stimulation upon the reactivity to diazepam in two animal models of anxiety. *Pharmacology, Biochemistry, and Behaviour, 49*, 393-398.

Schapiro, S.J., Bloomsmith, M.A., Porter, L.M., & Suarez, S.A. (1996). Enrichment effects on rhesus monkeys successively housed singly, in pairs, and in groups. *Applied Animal Behaviour Science, 48*, 159-171.

Sharma, A.C., & Kulkarni, S.K. (1992). Evaluation of learning and memory mechanisms employing elevated plus-maze in rats and mice. *Progress in Neuropsychopharmacology and Biological Psychiatry, 16*, 117-125.

Smart, J.L. (1974). Activity and exploratory behaviour of adult offspring of undernourished mother-rats. *Developmental Psychobiology, 7*, 315-321.

Tees, R.C., Buhrmann, K., & Hanley, J. (1990). The effect of early experience in water-maze spatial learning and memory in rats. *Developmental Psychobiology, 23*, 427-439.

Yehuda, S., Mei-Tal, R., & Youdim, M. (1991). The effect of iron-deficiency and electric shock on learning in rats. *International Journal of Neuroscience, 57*, 81-94.

29

Epilogue: The Challenge of Relating Psychology to Social Development

Girishwar Misra and **Uday Jain**

In the preceding chapters the contributors have shared their views and findings from psychological research pertaining directly or less directly, to the different domains of social development. Taking a lead from there, an effort is made in this chapter to reflect on certain broad issues related to social development and the possible role of psychological research in understanding and facilitating social development.

The Notion of Development

The concept of development in the modern world has assumed a singular universal status. It stands for linear progress, particularly in material terms. The notion of development as practiced in the contemporary world is rooted in a peculiarly individualistic model of human functioning centered on economic considerations. The same has become a normative category. The experience of economic prosperity in the Western countries has supplied a model of development rooted in the modernist perspective. It was often legitimized through claims for objectivity, rationality and progress. As a result, universalism, homogeneity and globalization in terms of aspirations, values and commitments came to occcupy key positions on the agenda for development.

The ideology underlying the above mentioned model of development constitutes an integral part of modernity and has only limited value outside this world view. The emphasis on economic development unambiguously led to many negative effects on the society and environment and, therefore, has become suspect in many corners. A close relationship between developmental activities and unmindful exploitation of natural resources and increase in environmental pollution and ecological imbalance is intensely experienced. This notion of development attributes certain characteristics to human beings and empowers them to exploit the natural resources to the benefit of human society. Psychological research usually follows this model of development and explores the determinants of behaviour in order to enhance the capabilities of human beings to exploit physical resources in their interest. This has been exemplified in psychological research on achievement motivation, attitude towards modernization, development of values, organizational behaviour, intelligence, quality of life, and the processes of social influence.

The blind following of growth model ignored certain important dimensions of social development. For example, study of spiritual dimensions and development of religious values were considered as unworthy of investigation as they appeared detrimental to modern development. Such as argument cannnot be considered as essentially true or false. Such conceptions are the results of a particular type of ideology, namely, modernization. This model is ethnocentric and came into existence in the socio-historical circumstances of the western industrialized world. The non-western countries simply followed this model which served the purpose of subjugating them by the power centres in the western world. While accepting an alien model, the non-western nations were declared as developing or underdeveloped and fell in the web of a power-dependence relationship. These poor nations emulated western culture in the hope of becoming 'modern' and rich. Any thing, including traditional knowledge, was treated as a matter to be discarded not fitting in the model of development. This was in tune with the agenda of globalization.

Later, and perhaps too late, the realization of an

appreciation of cultural variety, diverse societal circumstances, life styles and differential availability of resources made it clear that a uniform model of development in any universal sense is not viable. It appears that development with justice will have to respect the indigenous values and needs of a particular society (J.B.P. Sinha, 1990). This argument leads to the concept of endogenous development.

Endogenous Development

As an alternative, the concept of endogenous development, which respects the traditional values practiced in one's native culture and sustain society, has been proposed. In this sense, the concept of development goes beyond any monolithic view and situates the dialogue on development within the historico-cultural experiences of particular societies. The design of development has to be made available from within as development's pre-requisites are available within the developing entity. The remedy for problems need to be identified within the domains of specific cultures.

The concept of endogenous development, however, has yielded diverse responses. It seems that there is need to integrate social, human, cultural and spiritual values in the process of development. Development has to ensure the advancement of the individual as a participant in the spiritual, moral and material orders. It is argued that cultural and social sustainability should form the basis of such an endeavour (Misra. 1998). However, with increasing interdependence and sharing among the countries across the globe isolated development has become inconceivable. It seems that neither isolated culture-specific development nor imposition of a western model of development can be treated as the answer to the present challenges faced by the Indian society. The pursuit of indigenous development should, therefore, be coupled with preparations for possible linkages with global trends. These twin goals should be treated with equal emphasis.

Challenges to Traditional Psychology

The role of psychology in the context of exploring alternative models of development necessitates a change in the disciplinary perspective. This change is from its focus on 'self-contained' individualism to the notion of a socially embedded person; from a reductionistic analysis to holistic description; from quantitative statistical treatment of data to more qualitative understanding; from universal principles to cultural specificity; from cognitivist orientation to constructionist approach; from scientistic objectivity to understanding through subjectivity. In brief, the psychological concepts are in flux. They are increasingly shifting in the direction of social relevance and cultural appropriateness.

The purpose here is not to provide the details of any of the shifts as space does not permit us to do so, but to reflect briefly on the failure of dominant psychology which should have paved the way for this shift. One can take the example of social psychology which is supposed to deal with social behaviour and thereby social development. Elsewhere, (Jain & Misra, 1995, Flick, 1998), it has been argued that social psychology lacks 'social' in its content as only the individual is in focus and studied in the so called investigations of social behaviour. The dominant trend is to psychologize whatever phenomenon is studied. Artificiality of the experimental situation and unwanted objectivity have reduced the social to individual level. The goal of scientific research about social behaviour remains similar to the study of psychological processes of de-contextualised individuals with the sole aim of finding the general laws of social behaviour. This seems to be a paradox. The study of social behaviour which by definition, involves social situation of which the individual constitutes an integral part misses the very process it seeks to understand by its failure to situate the individual in the context of society. Logically, the individual cannot be isolated from situation on account of the demands of objectivist methodology. The individual is an inseparable constituent of the social situation under study. The other parts of the situation such as social institutions, and cultural forces that shape people's outlook and actions and in turn, are affected by them, cannot be ignored if we want to have a meaningful analysis. In this context social development essentially includes a matrix of social situations and not only the individual as envisaged in the traditional social psychology.

Another set of arguments comes from the social constructionists which at time appears as solipsistic but contains questions that cannot be ignored. For example, that socio-historical conditions make a specific social 'reality' possible and hence, prediction and control the cherished goals of science — do not seem probable or logical. The existing social processes such as negotiation, communication and linguistic usage help construct the 'reality' which does not have any fundamental grounding within individual's personal cognitive schema or the central processing unit in its own right. Knowledge is a social product and involves sharing and relating between the members of a community. Because of this sharing certain forms of knowledge are sustained and others are discarded by the community.

This formulation explains why diverse cultures provide differing world-views embedded in their practices which sustain them. For the same reason western psychological concepts, theories and methods of knowing cannot be treated as universal. A single culture can lead us to culture specific knowledge which may be useful and meaningful to that society but may not be so in case of others. The social psychologists who accept the social context as a prime candidate for scrutiny to understand social phenomena also go beyond any causal analysis of social phenomena. The main argument is that if one measures all the objective conditions surrounding the lives of several individuals one cannot know the level of social development or for that matter, any social phenomenon because agreements and the relationships made among members cannot be subjected to causal analysis. They are embodied within the laws, customs, folkways and languages shared by the people living in the community.

This context is more important than the objective conditions. However, social psychology for long has ignored this reality. It is believed that the scientific methods are more relevant to objective conditions and scientists are prone to be dominated by the scientific methods than the phenomenon under study. However, we live in an intentional world filled by intentional objects. The index of social development must include the quality of social relationships and intentions as reflected in every day cultural practices.

Interest in alternate paradigms in social psychology is increasing. At the same time, growth of social psychology in the traditional mode is continuing, probably with the hope that some day psychological science may acquire similar accuracy in prediction and control as achieved by the advanced physical sciences. This issue seems like a spiders' web—the more one tries to find the ends the more knots one creates. Therefore, a fresh, and critical look is warranted.

Towards Reconstruction

At present the role of psychological knowledge in the process of social development has not been adequately articulated. However, it seems clear that whatever findings are available through research may enter in the social processes for constructing specific knowledge pool shared by the different groups. This does not mean that every thing goes in the knowledge pool. It depends on how much is shared by the members of a particular society. As this sharing goes on, the common consciousness regarding the direction of social development expands.

The hegemony of the positivist view is being questioned and alternative thinking has already been initiated. This provides an opportunity to articulate cultural insights and their relevance in the present context. Such an effort may help in framing new forms of theory and metatheory to shape our life and world of experience. For example, in the Indian view all knowledge is considered as sacred and moral. The question of morality is so pervasive that if one fails in one's 'duty' to the family members it is considered unethical. One can explore this idea and see how it can be applied to construct the concept of social development. One would like to address questions such as, What structural changes will be needed at different levels? How can the available technology be directed to the service of a moral order in society? What sort of communication is helpful in establishing morality in public life ?

Research on moral behaviour and moral judgement provides examples of socio-cultural influences. For instance Jain (1991) used the famous Heinz dilemma and prepared different versions showing the beneficiaries as self, family, relation, friend and stranger. It was assumed that in the Indian context people observe morality in the context of relationship with the individual. The young adults used different criteria in their judgment while offering justification. Similarly, Misra (1991) reported that, in thinking about moral issues, judgements favoring immanent justice showed a clear developmental trend from childhood to young adulthood. The most interesting finding of this study was that generosity and helping both were determined more on the basis of empathy than the level of cognitive maturity of moral reasoning. These studies demonstrate the significance of social context in determining our behaviour. Social duties and customs monitoring social relationships are of prime concern. D. Sinha's suggestions in regard to the study of Indian personality (see his contribution to this volume) are useful in understanding people in a particular socio-cultural context. Many social issues in Indian context are being explored by psychologists. The concepts of detachment (Pandey & Naidu, 1992), embedded self (Dhwan *et al.*, 1995; Misra & Giri, 1994; D. Sinha & Tripathi, 1994; Tripathi, 1988), nurturant task leader (J.B.P. Sinha, 1980, 1993a), management by values (Chakraborty, 1991), social manipulation (Pandey, 1980), extension motivation (Pareek, 1970), dependency orientation (J.B.P. Sinha, 1974), achievement cognition (Agarwal & Misra, 1986) are some examples of such socially relevant concepts. The study of emotions (Jain, 1994; Paranjpe & Bhatt, 1997) has further shown the relevance of a famous Indian theory on Rasa which has incorporated Indian concepts holistically and provides a more intensive and comprehensive analysis than that provided by western psychological theories. Misra and Gergen (1993) have delineated the different meaning systems in Indian and western cultural contexts. These efforts show the possibility of alternate psychological concepts (see D. Sinha, 1996) and pave the way towards a more comprehensive understanding of the problems of Indian society.

Assessments of the progress of psychology in India (Dalal, 1998; Gergen *et al.*, 1996; Mohanty, 1988; 1990; Pandey, 1988; J.B.P. Sinha, 1993b) indicate that all is not well with the discipline. Cultural sensitivity and call towards indigenization (Misra *et al.*, 1995; D. Sinha, 1994, 1997) have yielded a range of moves including serious explorations of concepts of Indian origin (Paranjpe, 1984, 1998). Concepts and theories available in our traditional texts reflect wisdom gleaned through thousands of years of scholarly study of our own developing culture. Their utility in understanding the Indian psyche is undeniable. But, they must fit in with if not conform to the landscape of the modern scientific discourse. Happily, attempts at invoking traditional notions in seeking to understand psychological and social processes are no longer made simply because they appear to be exotic and fashionable like the 'ethnic' appeal in dress designing and food preferences. At present, psychologists throughout the world seem to display some degree of disenchantment with the typical Euro-American model of psychology and its limitations in explaining the complex socio-cultural realities of a different world. This disenchantment is reflected in growing willingness to allow the immediate social context to dominate research concerns, methodology and the conceptual framework. Theoretical models different from the ones borrowed from the West are more freely utilized and traditional constructs are unapologetically used as scaffoldings for different levels of theoretical integration. One could brand this new shift as reactionary particularly since the western models are still taken as anchor points and the new approaches are always pitted against the imaginary vision of a universal psychology which would continue to elude us unless we are able to contextualise our scientific discourse. Therefore, disenchantments and reactions are not enough; they may cause some symptoms of restlessness and movement but a direction would still be lacking. The studies reported in this volume show definite signs of outgrowing the borrowed paradigm and consciousness of the limitations of the western psychology. There is an eagerness to make psychology different, relevant and meaningful for the society.

On the whole, the preceding chapters are forceful in exemplifying above eagerness. But still there is a long way to go because a majority of our research endeavours favour *status quo* and report or document the life conditions. They confine to normal science and feel contented if the results approximate the findings of other researchers. Their academic linkages with other disciplines are often very weak. Their interventional efforts often meet less than expected success (Tripathi, 1988) because of ahistoricity and decontextualization. Since social problems are located in the socio-historical context it is necessary that they are defined and solved anew in every generation (Misra & Verma, 1994). Culturally relevant and scientifically adequate psychology can offer a dynamic analysis of the people and help in implementing the policies. We need alternative psychological strategy to bring about structural and behavioural changes (Mehta, 1998).

It is hoped that Indian psychologists will confront the issues constructively and respond proactively by assessing the societal conditions and undertaking culturally appropriate research and action.

REFERENCES

Agarwal, R. & Misra, G. (1986). A factor analytic study of achievement goals and means. *International Journal of Psychology, 21*, 717-731.

Chakroborty, S. (1993). *Managereal transformation by values : corporate pilgrimage*. New Delhi : Sage.

Dalal, A.K. (1996). A science in search of its identity : Twentieth century psychology in India. *Indian Psychological Abstracts and Reviews, 3*, 201-244.

Flick, U. (1998). *The psychology of the social*. Cambridge : Cambridge University Press.

Jain, U. (1994). Socio-cultural construction of emotions. *Psychology and Developing Societies, 6*, 151-168.

Jain, U. (1991). The subjective construction of morality: The Indian experience. *Indian Journal of Social Work, 42*, 379-388.

Gergen, K.J.; Glurece, A.; Lock, A.; & Misra, G. (1996). Psychological sceince in cultural context. *American Psychologist, 51*, 496-503.

Jain. U. & Misra, G. (1994). The social concerns of social psychology. *Indian Journal of Psychology, 69*, 125-132.

Mehta, P. (1998). *A psychological strategy for alternative human development*. New Delhi : Sage.

Misra, G. (1998). Contemporary human condition : Challenges and possibilities. In Anima Sen & A.K. Sen (Eds). *Challenges of contemporary realities : A psychological perspective on future of human society* (pp. 273-280). New Delhi : *New Age* International.

Misra, G. (1991). Socio-cultural influences on moral behaviour. *Indian Journal of Social Work, 42*, 179-194.

Misra, G. & Giri, R. (1993). Is Indian self predominantly interdependent? *Journal of Indian Psychology, 11*, 15-19.

Misra, G., Jain, U. & Singh, T. (1995). On the cultural frame of social cognition. *Indian Psychological Abstracts and Reviews, 2*, 1-36.

Misra, G. & Gergen, K.J. (1993). On the place of culture in psychological science. *International Journal of Psychology, 28*, 225-253.

Misra, G. & Verma, S. (1995). Social problems, psychology and social policy. *Journal of the Indian Academy of Applied Psychology, 20*, 97-105.

Mohanty, A.k. (1988). Beyond the horizon of Indian psychology: The Yankee Doodler. In F.M. Sahoo (Ed.), *Contemporary psychology in the Indian context*. (pp. 1-8), Agra: National

Psychological Coroporation.

Mohanty, A.K. (1990). Psychology in India: Still at the crossroads? *Psychology and the Developing Societies*, *2*, 117-136.

Pandey, N. & Naidu, R.K. (1992). Anasakti and health: A study of non-attachment. *Psychology and Developing Societies*, *4*, 89-104.

Dhawan, N., Roseman, I.J., Naidu, R.K. & Rettek, S.I. (1995). Self concepts across two cultures: India and the United States. *Journal of Cross-Cultural Psychology*, *26*, 606-621.

Pandey, J. (1988). Psychology in India: The emerging trends in eighties. In J. Pandey (Ed.) *Psychology in India: The state of the art (Vol. 3)*. (pp. 339-359). New Delhi : Sage.

Pareek, U. (1968). A motivational paradigm of development. *Journal of Social Issues*, *24*, 115-122.

Paranjpe, A. (1984). *Theoretical psychology: Meeting of the east and west*. New York: Plenum Press.

Paranjpe, A. (1998). *Self and identity in modern psychology and Indian thought*. New York: Plenum Press.

Paranjpe, A.C. & Bhatt, G.S. (1997). Emotion: A perspective from the Indian tradition. In H.S.R. Kao & D. Sinha (Eds.). *Asian perspectives on Psychology* (pp. 127-143). New Delhi: Sage.

Sinha, D. (1997). Indigenizing psychology: In J.W. Berry, Y.H. Poortinga & J. Pandey (Eds.). *Handbook of cross-cultural psychology, Second Edition*. (pp. 129-170). Boston MA: Allyn and Bacon.

Sinha, D. (1996). Culture as the target and culture as the source: A review of cross-cultural psychology in Asia. *Psychology and Developing Societies*, *8*, 83-105.

Sinha, D. (1994). Indigenisation of psychology in India. *Indian Psychological Abstracts and Reviews*, *1*, 179-215.

Sinha, D. & Tripathi, R.C. (1994). Individualism in a collective culture: A case of coexistence of opposites. In U. Kim, H.C. Triandis, C. Kagitcibase, S. Chot & G. Yoon (Eds.) *Individualism and collectivism: Theory, method and applications*.(pp 123-136). New Delhi : Sage.

Sinha, J.B.P. (1970). *Development through behaviour modification*. Bombay : Allied.

Sinha, J.B.P. (1980). *The nurturant task master*. New Delhi : Concept.

Sinha, J.B.P. (1990). Role of psychology in national development. In G. Misra (Ed.) *Applied social psychology in India*. (pp. 171-200). New Delhi : Sage.

Sinha, J.B.P. (1993a). A model of effective leadership style in India. In A.M. Jaeger & R.N. Kanungo (Eds.). *Management in developing countries* (pp. 252-263). London: Routledge.

Sinha, J.B.P. (1993b). The bulk and the front of psychology in India. *Psychology and Developing Societies*, *5*, 135-150.

Tripathi, R.C. (1988a). Aligning development to values in India. In D. Sinha & H. Kao (Eds.). *Social values and development in Asian perspectives* (pp 12-28). New Delhi : Sage.

Tripathi, R.C. (1988b). Applied social psychology. In J. Pandey (Ed.). *Psychology in India: The State-of-the-Art : Basic and Applied Social Psychology, Vol. (2)*, (pp. 95-157). New Delhi: Sage.

List of Contributors

Dr. Vijayalaxmi A. Aminabhavi, Reader in Psychology, Karnataka University, Dharwad-580003.

Prof. Anand Prakash, Department of Psychology, University of Delhi, South Campus, Delhi-110021.

Dr. Nandita Babu, Reader, CAS in Psychology, Utkal University, Bhubaneswar-751004.

Mr. D. Biswas, Department of Psychology, University of Calcutta, 92, APC Road, Calcutta-700009.

Prof. P.K. Chattopadhyay, Department of Psychology, University of Calcutta, 92, APC Road, Calcutta-700009.

Prof. A.K. Dalal, Psychology Department, Allahabad University, Allahabad-211002.

Mr. Bhakta B. Dash, Lecturer in Psychology, Puri Women's College, Puri-752001.

Dr. Manaswini Dash, Demonstrator, CAS in Psychology, Utkal University, Bhubaneswar-751004.

Dr. U.N. Dash, Reader & Head, CAS in Psychology, Utkal University, Bhubaneswar-751004.

Ms. Jayita Datta Gupta, Department of Psychology, 92 APC Road, Calcutta-700009.

Prof. Meenakshi Gupta, Department of Humanities & Social Sciences, Indian Institute of Technology, Powai, Mumbai-400076.

Prof. Kasturi Jachuck, CAS in Psychology, Utkal University, Bhubaneswar-751004.

Prof. Uday Jain, Head, Psychology Department, Barkatullah University, Bhopal-462026.

Mrs. Rachna Johri, Lecturer in Psychology, Lady Sri Ram College, Lajpat Nagar, New Delhi-110024.

Mr. K. Krishnamohan, Research Fellow, Department of Psychology & Parapsychology, Andhra University, Vishakhapatnam-530003.

Prof. B. Krishnamurthy, Department of Psychology, Gulbarga University, Gulbarga-585106.

Dr. S. Mahapatra, CAS in Psycholoy, Utkal University, Bhubaneswar-751004.

Prof. Girishwar Misra, Head, Psychology Department, Delhi University, Delhi-110007.

Dr. Babban Mishra, Reader in Psychology, Gorakhpur University, Gorakhpur-273009.

Ms. Santa Mishra, Lecturer in Psychology, Banki College, Banki, Cuttack (Orissa).

Dr. Banamali Mohanty, Reader, CAS in Psychology, Utkal University, Bhubaneswar-751004.

Mr. Pradeep Mohapatra, CAS in Psychology, Utkal University, Bhubaneswar-751004.

Dr. P. Mukhopadhyay, Department of Psychology, University of Calcutta, 92, APC Road, Calcutta-700009.

Ms. Swati Patra, CAS in Psychology, Utkal University, Bhubaneswar-751004.

Ms. Sumita Rai, Department of Humanities & Social Sciences, Indian Institute of Technology, Kanpur-208016.

Prof. M.K. Raina, Head, Department of Educational, Psychology & Foundations of Education, NCERT, Aurobindo Marg, New Delhi-110016.

Mr. S. Saha, Department of Psychology, University of Calcutta, 92, APC Road, Calcutta-700009.

Dr. Fakir M. Sahoo, Reader, CAS in Psychology, Utkal University, Bhubaneswar-751004.

Mrs. Aneeta Puri Singh, Lecturer in Psychology, M.L.B. Girls' P.G. College, Bhopal.

Dr. Shailendra Singh, Associate Professor, OB Area, Indian Institute of Management, Prabandh Nagar off Sitapur Road, Lucknow-226013.

Dr. Sunita Singh-Sengupta, Behavioural Sciences Group, Indian Institute of Management, Joka, Diamond Harbour Rd., P.B. No. 16757, Alipore Post Office, Calcutta-700027

Prof. Arvind K. Sinha, Department of Humanities & Social Sciences, Indian Institute of Technology, Kanpur-208016.

Prof. Durganand Sinha, 8, Malviya Road, Allahabad-211002.

Ms. Abhilasha Srivastava, Department of Humanities & Social Sciences, Indian Institute of Technology, Powai, Mumbai-400076.

Dr. Ashok K. Srivastava, Reader, Department of Educational Research & Policy Perspectives, NCERT, Aurobindo Marg, New Delhi-110016.

Ms. K. Suneetha, Department of Psychology & Parapsychology, Andhra University, Vishakhapatnam-530003.

Dr. A.K. Tewari, Reader in Psychology, K.S. Saket P.G. College, Faizabad-224001.

Dr. K.N. Tripathi, Reader in Psychology, Barkatullah University, Bhopal-462026.

Prof. Jyoti Verma, Institute of Psychological Research & Service, Patna University, Patna-800016.

Dr. U. Vindhya, Reader in Psychology, Andhra University, Vishakhapatnam-530003.

Index